Impact of AI Technologies on Teaching, Learning, and Research in Higher Education

Shivani Verma
Km. Mayawati Government Girls P.G. College, India

Pradeep Tomar
Gautam Buddha University, India

A volume in the Advances in Educational Technologies and Instructional Design (AETID) Book Series

IGI Global
PUBLISHER of TIMELY KNOWLEDGE

Published in the United States of America by
IGI Global
Information Science Reference (an imprint of IGI Global)
701 E. Chocolate Avenue
Hershey PA, USA 17033
Tel: 717-533-8845
Fax: 717-533-8661
E-mail: cust@igi-global.com
Web site: http://www.igi-global.com

Library of Congress Cataloging-in-Publication Data

Names: Verma, Shivani, editor. | Tomar, Pradeep, 1976- editor.
Title: Impact of AI technologies on teaching, learning, and research in higher education / Shivani Verma and Pradeep Tomar, editors.
Other titles: Impact of artificial intelligence technologies on teaching, learning, and research in higher education
Description: Hershey, PA : Information Science Reference, [2021] | Includes bibliographical references and index. | Summary: "This book explores the phenomena of the emergence of the use of artificial intelligence and other emerging technologies in teaching and learning in higher education. Recent technological advancements and the increasing speed of adopting new technologies in higher education are explored in order to predict the future nature of higher education in a world where artificial intelligence is part of the fabric of our universities"-- Provided by publisher.
Identifiers: LCCN 2020021498 (print) | LCCN 2020021499 (ebook) | ISBN 9781799847632 (hardcover) | ISBN 9781799864448 (paperback) | ISBN 9781799847649 (ebook)
Subjects: LCSH: Education, Higher--Effect of technological innovations on. | Educational technology. | Artificial intelligence.
Classification: LCC LB2395.7 .I47 2021 (print) | LCC LB2395.7 (ebook) | DDC 371.33--dc23
LC record available at https://lccn.loc.gov/2020021498
LC ebook record available at https://lccn.loc.gov/2020021499

This book is published in the IGI Global book series Advances in Educational Technologies and Instructional Design (AETID) (ISSN: 2326-8905; eISSN: 2326-8913)

British Cataloguing in Publication Data
A Cataloguing in Publication record for this book is available from the British Library.

All work contributed to this book is new, previously-unpublished material.
The views expressed in this book are those of the authors, but not necessarily of the publisher.

For electronic access to this publication, please contact: eresources@igi-global.com.

Advances in Educational Technologies and Instructional Design (AETID) Book Series

ISSN:2326-8905
EISSN:2326-8913

Editor-in-Chief: Lawrence A. Tomei, Robert Morris University, USA

MISSION

Education has undergone, and continues to undergo, immense changes in the way it is enacted and distributed to both child and adult learners. In modern education, the traditional classroom learning experience has evolved to include technological resources and to provide online classroom opportunities to students of all ages regardless of their geographical locations. From distance education, Massive-Open-Online-Courses (MOOCs), and electronic tablets in the classroom, technology is now an integral part of learning and is also affecting the way educators communicate information to students.

The **Advances in Educational Technologies & Instructional Design (AETID) Book Series** explores new research and theories for facilitating learning and improving educational performance utilizing technological processes and resources. The series examines technologies that can be integrated into K-12 classrooms to improve skills and learning abilities in all subjects including STEM education and language learning. Additionally, it studies the emergence of fully online classrooms for young and adult learners alike, and the communication and accountability challenges that can arise. Trending topics that are covered include adaptive learning, game-based learning, virtual school environments, and social media effects. School administrators, educators, academicians, researchers, and students will find this series to be an excellent resource for the effective design and implementation of learning technologies in their classes.

COVERAGE

- Instructional Design Models
- Collaboration Tools
- Social Media Effects on Education
- Virtual School Environments
- Classroom Response Systems
- Hybrid Learning
- Higher Education Technologies
- K-12 Educational Technologies
- Online Media in Classrooms
- E-Learning

The Advances in Educational Technologies and Instructional Design (AETID) Book Series (ISSN 2326-8905) is published by IGI Global, 701 E. Chocolate Avenue, Hershey, PA 17033-1240, USA, www.igi-global.com. This series is composed of titles available for purchase individually; each title is edited to be contextually exclusive from any other title within the series. For pricing and ordering information please visit http://www.igi-global.com/book-series/advances-educational-technologies-instructional-design/73678. Postmaster: Send all address changes to above address.

Titles in this Series

For a list of additional titles in this series, please visit:
http://www.igi-global.com/book-series/advances-educational-technologies-instructional-design/73678

Digital Learning Architectures of Participation
Nigel Ecclesfield (FRSA, UK) and Fred Garnett (FRSA, UK)
Information Science Reference • © 2021 • 289pp • H/C (ISBN: 9781799843337) • US $165.00

Participatory Pedagogy Emerging Research and Opportunities
Martha Ann Davis McGaw (McGaw Davis Foundation, USA) and Simone McGaw-Evans (Georgia State University, USA)
Information Science Reference • © 2021 • 150pp • H/C (ISBN: 9781522589648) • US $155.00

Visual Approaches to Instructional Design, Development, and Deployment
Shalin Hai-Jew (Kansas State University, USA)
Information Science Reference • © 2021 • 228pp • H/C (ISBN: 9781799839460) • US $185.00

Teaching Language and Literature On and Off-Canon
José Manuel Correoso-Rodenas (Universidad Complutense de Madrid, Spain)
Information Science Reference • © 2020 • 370pp • H/C (ISBN: 9781799833796) • US $195.00

Handbook of Research on Advancing Language Equity Practices With Immigrant Communities
Lourdes Cardozo-Gaibisso (Universidad ORT Uruguay, Uruguay) and Max Vazquez Dominguez (University of North Georgia, USA)
Information Science Reference • © 2020 • 433pp • H/C (ISBN: 9781799834489) • US $245.00

For an entire list of titles in this series, please visit:
http://www.igi-global.com/book-series/advances-educational-technologies-instructional-design/73678

IGI Global
PUBLISHER of TIMELY KNOWLEDGE

701 East Chocolate Avenue, Hershey, PA 17033, USA
Tel: 717-533-8845 x100 • Fax: 717-533-8661
E-Mail: cust@igi-global.com • www.igi-global.com

Editorial Advisory Board

Table of Contents

Detailed Table of Contents

Education is significant in our lives. Learning is the main feature that is connected to education. Education increases the power of visualization and differentiation between right and the wrong. The future of education is directly related to innovative tools and computing abilities of the intelligent machines, opening to new potentials and tasks for teaching and learning in education with the prospective to primarily changing the governance and the inner architecture of institutions of higher education. Education in these days has become very expensive for the poor guardians (with meager income) of the capable students to get admission in the reputed institutes of their choice. Education indeed helps to know the real values in relation to social and cultural behavior so that one can become a decent person in nature in society. It also shows the limitations and risks in the life of a modern student. This chapter explores using artificial intelligence in higher education.

Virtually everyone has to make hundreds of decisions every day in his day-to-day life. "Good decision making" means we are informed and have relevant and appropriate information on which to base our choices among alternatives. Decision support systems are emerging as a very powerful tool for making rational decision based on various sources of information. In this chapter, the authors attempt to understand how the intelligent decisions are required for any successful endeavour. In this complex world where information explosion has good and bad news, both finding analysing

Artificial intelligence (AI) is developing at a fast speed and has incessantly impacted the modern world for decades. AI technologies are beneficial for all kinds of industries, including businesses, economics, transportation, hospitals, schools, universities, and so forth. Many researchers have investigated the development of artificial intelligence in education (AIEd), specifically on how AI assists teaching, learning, assessment, references, and collaboration. Several questions arise. What impact do AI technologies have on education? How do AI technologies assist teaching (e.g., curriculum, assessment, student learning, and teaching practices)? How do teachers cope with AI Technologies in education? What are the ethical concerns of AI technologies? What are the barriers of AI-based learning in education? The purpose of this chapter is to explore the evolution and the challenges of AI technologies in education. Major research on AI from 1999 to 2019 will be reviewed. Problems with AI in education will be raised and solutions for solving the issues will be recommended.

Computers are being utilized in field in education for many years. In last few decades, research within the field of artificial intelligence (AI) is positively affecting educational application. Advanced machine learning and deep learning techniques could be used for extracting knowledgeable information from crude information. In this chapter, the authors have analysed the impact of artificial intelligence in the education domain. The authors will discuss how with the development of machine learning techniques in last few decades, machine learning models can anticipate student performance. By learning about every student, models can identify the shortcomings. Then the authors will propose different approaches to improve student performance. Teachers can also use this model to understand student perception levels in a better way so that they can modulate their lectures according to student perception levels.

Education and learning are the most important aspects of the evolution of societies. They have been a favorite subject for philosophers and psychologists to work upon. Same questions are now being re-dealt by computer scientists in current scenarios. Although evolution is a continuous process, the pace of evolution is not a linear graph. Children acquire a huge amount of knowledge with very little input from teachers, friends, parents, and surroundings. Understanding how human brain works and more precisely, how the child brain actually functions is opening the path of researches in artificial intelligence (AI).

The quality of higher education can be enhanced only by upgrading the content and skills towards knowledge. Hence, knowledge representation and reasoning play a chief role to represent the facts, beliefs, and information, and inferring the logical interpretation of represented knowledge stored in the knowledge bases. This chapter provide a broad overview of knowledge, representation, and reasoning along with the related art of study in the field of higher education. Various artificial intelligent-based knowledge representation and reasoning techniques and schemes are provided for better representation of facts, beliefs, and information. Various reasoning types are discussed in order to infer the right meaning of the knowledge followed by various issues of knowledge representation and reasoning. .

AI is a branch of computer science that gives the ability to a computer to think and make decisions like humans. It stimulates the human brain in the computer and makes appropriate decisions when required. AI-enabled education impacts the designing of curriculum, mode of instruction, and many more. The use of these tools revolutionizing the education sector with the progression of ICT tools have now become AI-enabled. The main feature of an AI-enabled tool is personalization. These AI-enabled tools work like intelligent assistants for the students. The intelligent system having features like answer the queries of the students, give assistance, support learning, provide

30 students in each class. With AI many possibilities can be seen in the teaching and learning system considering interest and understanding of an individual, which will increase efficiency of the education system.

The future of higher education is intrinsically linked with developments on new technologies and computing capacities of the new intelligent machines. In this field, advances in artificial intelligence open to new possibilities and challenges for teaching and learning in higher education with the potential to fundamentally change governance and the internal architecture of institutions of higher education. The role of technology in higher learning is to enhance human thinking and to augment the educational process, not to reduce it to a set of procedures for content delivery, control, and assessment. With the rise of AI solutions, it is increasingly important for educational institutions to stay alert and see if the power of control over hidden algorithms that run them is not monopolized by tech-lords. This chapter will cover all the positive and negative aspects of AI technologies on teaching, learning, and research in higher education.

This chapter has presented the idea and use of artificial and natural intelligence technologies. A system of professional education, on the one hand, is one of the main institutions of human socialization, and the formation of a harmoniously developed, active, creative personality, on the other hand, ensures the reproduction and development of the personnel potential of the society. Realization of the goals of education is carried out in interaction with the socioeconomic environment, the dynamic change of which predetermines the conditions for the activity of educational institutions. An acceleration of scientific and technological progress in all areas of knowledge raises the task for ensuring the continuous growth of professional skills throughout the whole life. Structural and institutional replacing in professional education is reflected in various models of higher professional education. These alternative technology-mediated environments reflect the increasing need to serve a generation of learners who prefer to learn through experience or by interacting with learning tools.

Preface

Artificial Intelligence (AI) technology evolves and joins various industries; it could allow colleges and universities to pursue an adaptive, rigorous and individualized experience for higher education students. Potentially, AI could result in a less expensive and more responsive approach to higher education by improving student outcomes and helping institutions scale quality education for students. Members of the technology, curriculum and research teams should be collaborated to evaluate how AI impacts higher education and what opportunities the technology could offer in the future. Through this book we have described how AI technology can contribute to richer experiences for higher education learners who will then be able to reflect on their own learning. This book also described how personalized learning can be supported by tools that enhance student and group experience, reflection, analysis and theory development. This book discusses how learning with AI tools will have new opportunities to analyze vast data sets of instructional behavior collected from rich databases, containing elements of learning, affect, motivation, and social interaction. How intelligent tutors may provide many of the benefits of a human tutor and also provide real-time data to instructors and developers looking to refine teaching methods are also described in this book. We have also explored how AI is vital in higher education and also identified how it can solve the various challenges e.g. personalized teaching and learning. Apart from that some challenges concerning the implementation of various AI applications in higher education are addressed. A rigorous analysis is done in this book regarding AI resources, human-computer interfaces, dialogue systems, inquiry-based collaborative learning.

The future of higher education is intrinsically linked with developments on new technologies and computing capacities of the new intelligent machines. In this field, advances in AI open to new possibilities and challenges for teaching and learning in higher education, with the potential to fundamentally change governance and the internal architecture of institutions of higher education. Students are placed now at the forefront of a vast array of possibilities and challenges for learning and teaching in higher education. Solutions for human-AI interaction and collaboration are already available to help people with disabilities. Within higher education, there are enormous untapped opportunities for product/services companies, administrators, educators, start-ups and technology professionals to begin embracing AI across the student-ecosystem and infuse innovation to traditional academic processes by leveraging disruptive technologies. A great opportunity exists in disrupting the traditional call-center model of support to students by implementing bots that are designed to provide quick and efficient answers 7x24x365 to students on basic issues and challenges. As the bots learn from the new questions and answers over periods of times, these can be leveraged across campuses, programs, on-line and other student segments. They can inspire educators to apply them in education to augment learners and teachers for a more engaging process. This type of human-machine interface presents the immediate potential to change the way we learn, memorize, access, and create information. These solutions present new openings for education for all, while fostering lifelong learning in a strengthened model that can preserve the integrity of core values and the purpose of higher education. We consider that there is a need for research on both positive and negative impact of AI on higher education. There is a need to even explore about the ethical implications of the current control on developments of AI and the possibility to wither the richness of human knowledge and perspectives with the monopoly of few entities. We also believe that it is important to focus further research on the new roles of teachers on new learning pathways for higher degree students, with a new set of graduate attributes, with a focus on imagination, creativity, and innovation; the set of abilities and skills that can hardly be ever replicated by machines. The role of technology in higher learning is to enhance human thinking and to augment the educational process, not to reduce it to a set of procedures for content delivery, control, and assessment. With the rise of AI solutions, it is increasingly important for educational institutions to stay alert and see if the power of control over hidden algorithms that run them is not monopolized by tech-lords. The question of how long it will take to use this type of interface to enhance human memory and cognition is one which we are currently unable to answer. This wave of interest and investments in AI will soon impact on universities. This book covers all the positive and negative aspects of AI in higher education.

The aim of this book is to explore various application, techniques & use of AI in smart teaching and learning by exploring the new technical, functional, non-functional future smart technologies for smart education system. This book also aims to identify and discuss the AI capabilities, demonstrating critical technological solutions to make the teaching smart and efficient. The chapters of this book are written by experienced researchers and specialists from all over world, providing a unique gathering of information relating to the role. The significance and impact of AI technologies are also discussed very effectively. This book will provide valuable knowledge and insights to vast spectrum of readers at different hierarchical levels, from graduates to research scholars and also beneficial to incorporate all the discussed systems into practical use. This book is divided into fifteen chapters where each chapter has a distinct focus.

1 Artificial Intelligence in Higher Education: First Attempt

Education is significant in our life. As learning is the main feature which is connected to education. Education increases the power of visualization and to differentiate between right and the wrong. The future of education is directly related to Innovative tools and computing abilities of the intelligent machines, opening to new potentials and tasks for teaching and learning in education with the prospective to primarily changing the governance and the inner architecture of institutions of higher education. Education in these days has become very expensive for the poor guardians (with meager income) of the capable students to get admission in the reputed institutes of their choice. Education indeed helps to know the real values in relation to social and cultural behavior so that one can become a decent person in nature in society. It also shows the limitations and risks in the life of a modern student. The role of the technology in modern education helps to lookout the current trends and to resolve the problems using Artificial Intelligence in higher education.

2 Artificial Intelligence: New Pathways and Challenges in Higher Education

Virtually everyone has to make hundreds of Decisions every day in his day to day life. "Good Decision Making" means we are informed and have relevant and appropriate information on which to base our choices among alternatives. Decision Support Systems are emerging as a very powerful tool for making rational decision based on various sources of Information. In this chapter we will try to understand that how the intelligent decisions are required for any successful endeavour. In this complex world where Information Explosion has Good and Bad news both finding analysing the adequate information is a tedious task which always requires an expert advice. In today's Digitalised World various programs are designed especially for the education sector which helps both the learner and tutor for learning environment. Technology can reduce time to make decisions for the fussy or confused learner thereby providing assistance.

3 Technology-Enabled Education: Paradigm Shift in Higher Education

The Government of India has especially focused on the Artificial Intelligence and machine learning- based courses in the higher education system as they have realized that the strength of India lies in higher education. Keeping in view the importance of technology in bringing a paradigm shift in the education sector, the Ministry of Human Resource Development (MHRD) is putting continuous efforts to give a push to digitalize higher education. In this chapter, authors have studied various initiatives taken by the Indian government to bring changes in Higher Education by imparting Artificial Intelligence. By developing techniques and algorithms using AI one can impart basic cognitive skills of teachers to computers; by this, one can delegate some teaching to machines and thus improve educational outcomes.

4 Artificial Intelligence in Higher Education and Learning

Artificial Intelligence is very emerging technology which is much popular in education technology. AI plays vital role to e-teaching and e-learning in higher education. In this chapter major focus is on to explores the wonders of the development of AI in higher education for teaching and learning process. It analyses educational ramifications of rising innovations in transit students learn and how organizations instruct and develop. Late inventive degrees of progress and the accelerating getting new headways in cutting edge training are researched to predict the future thought of cutting-edge instruction in all actuality as we probably are aware it where man-made reasoning is a bit of the surface of our universities. The role of AI in higher education is presented in detail by systematic review.

5 Teaching and Learning With Artificial Intelligence

Artificial Intelligence (AI) is developing at a fast speed and has incessantly impacted the modern world for decades. AI technologies are beneficial for all kinds of industries, including businesses, economics, transportation, hospitals, schools, universities, and so forth. Many researchers have investigated the development of Artificial Intelligence in education (AIEd), specifically on how AI assists teaching, learning, assessment, references, and collaboration. Several questions arise. What impact do AI technologies have on education? How do AI technologies assist teaching (e.g., curriculum, assessment, student learning, and teaching practices)? How do teachers cope with AI Technologies in education? What are the ethical concerns of AI technologies? What are the barriers of AI-based learning in education? The purpose of this chapter is to explore the evolution and the challenges of AI technologies in education. Major research on AI from 1999 to 2019 will be reviewed. Problems with AI in education will be raised and solutions for solving the issues will be recommended.

6 Role of Machine Learning in Modern Education and Teaching

Computers are being utilized in field in Education for many years. In last few decades research within the field of Artificial Intelligence (AI) is positively affecting educational application. Advanced machine learning and deep learning techniques could be used for extracting knowledgeable information from crude information. In this chapter, authors have analysed the impact of Artificial Intelligence in the education domain. Authors will discuss how with the development of Machine learning techniques in last few decades, machines learning models can anticipate student performance. By learning about every student, models can identify the shortcomings and then authors will propose different approaches to improve student performance. Teachers can also use this model to understand students perception level in a better way so that they can modulate their lectures according to student's perception level.

7 Self-Learning System for Child Development Using Conversational AI and Natural Language Processing (NLP)

Education and learning are the most important aspect of the evolution of the societies and the world in today's shape. It has been a favorite subject for philosophers and psychologists to work upon. Same questions are now being re-dealt by computer scientists in current scenarios. Although evolution is a continuous process, yet the pace of evolution is not a linear graph. This evolution started from the Stone Age, when civilizations and human race were not existing. The pace of evolution has got irrational acceleration with root inventions and innovations e.g. fire and wheel. Later the invention of diesel engines, industrial machines, electricity, electric bulb and invention of electric motors were amazing. These also gave faster acceleration to the growth of society and human race. Children acquire a huge amount of knowledge with very little input from teachers, friends, parents and surroundings. Understanding how human brain works? And more precisely, how child brain actually functions, is opening the path of researches in AI.

8 Artificial Intelligence-Based Knowledge Representation and Reasoning

Nowadays, researchers have made a lot of efforts with technology and innovation to upfront the education and bring it "out of the box" using various artificial intelligent-based educational systems. The quality of higher education can be enhanced only by upgrading the content and skills towards knowledge. Hence, knowledge representation and reasoning plays a chief role to represent the facts, beliefs & information and inferring the logical interpretation of represented knowledge stored in the knowledge bases. This chapter provides a broad overview of knowledge, representation and reasoning along with the related art of study in the field of Higher education. Various artificial intelligent-based knowledge representation and reasoning techniques and schemes are provided for better representation of facts, beliefs and information. Various reasoning types discussed in order to infer the right meaning of the knowledge followed by various issues of knowledge representation and reasoning. Finally, conclude the chapter.

9 Simulation of Human Brain: Artificial Intelligence-Based Learning

Artificial Intelligence (AI) is a branch of computer science that gives the ability to computer to think and make a decision like humans. It stimulates the human brain in the computer and makes appropriate decisions when required. AI-enabled education impacts the designing of curriculum, mode of instruction, and many more. The use of these tools revolutionizing the education sector with the progression of ICT tools and now become AI-enabled. The main feature of AI-enabled tool is personalization. These AI-enabled tools work like the intelligent assistant for the students. The Intelligent system having features like, answer the queries of the students, give assistance, support learning, provide or take assignments, and provide reinforcement material according to their opted courses. A teacher has a minimum intervention with this process and has the role of a facilitator only. This chapter concludes that the AI-enabled teaching-learning process can't replace classroom teaching; instead, it is handy. In the future, AI could replace the need of a teacher in class to some extent.

10 Influence of Artificial Intelligent-Based Vocational Courses on Self-Concept of Students

Artificial Intelligence (AI) these days is becoming more popular choice among students because of its large scope in different fields of life and career. The present chapter is based on how the vocational courses of AI have its effect on the students' Self Concept. The two groups of students have been taken for the study one group having vocational trade as AI and basics (150 students) and another group having non vocational subjects (150). The chapter has two goals: To compare level of Self-Concept of students with AI based Vocational trade subject and students without any vocational courses, and; to analyze gender difference among students in relation to Self- Concept. The samples were selected by simple random sampling. T-test analysis showed that the two groups had significant difference between their levels of Self-Concept. The students with AI based vocational subject are having higher Self-Concept than that of students of Non Vocational subjects.

11 Impact and Latest Trends of Intelligent Learning With Artificial Intelligence

Artificial Intelligence (AI) has been used mainly on education in some methods that contribute to the development of competencies and test systems. With the continued development of educational AI solutions, it is hoped that AI will help address the need for learning, education, and teaching. AI can enhance performance, personalization and streamline administrative tasks in order to give teachers time and freedom to learn and adapt — uniquely human skills that would battle on machines. The AI dream of education is one where the best results for students are obtained, based on the best qualities of machinery and teachers. The development of curriculum based on the specific needs of individual students has been a concern for educators for many years, but the AI presents teachers with an unprecedented degree of distinction to handle 30 students in each class. With AI many possibilities can be seen in the teaching and learning system considering interest and understanding of an individual, which will increase efficiency of the education system.

12 Impact and Role of AI Technologies on Teaching, Learning, and Research in Higher Education

The future of higher education is intrinsically linked with developments on new technologies and computing capacities of the new intelligent machines. In this field, advances in artificial intelligence open to new possibilities and challenges for teaching and learning in higher education, with the potential to fundamentally change governance and the internal architecture of institutions of higher education. The role of technology in higher learning is to enhance human thinking and to augment the educational process, not to reduce it to a set of procedures for content delivery, control, and assessment. With the rise of AI solutions, it is increasingly important for educational institutions to stay alert and see if the power of control over hidden algorithms that run them is not monopolized by tech-lords. This chapter will cover all the positive and negative aspects of AI technologies on teaching, learning, and research in higher education.

13 Impact of Artificial and Natural Intelligence Technologies With Avatar-Based Teaching, Learning, and Research in Russian Modern Universities

This chapter has presented the idea & use of Artificial and Natural Intelligence Technologies. A system of professional education, on the one hand, is one of the main institutions of human socialization, and the formation of a harmoniously developed, active, creative personality, on the other hand, it ensures the reproduction and development of the personnel potential of the society. Realization of the goals of education is carried out in interaction with the socioeconomic environment, the dynamic change of which predetermines the conditions for the activity of educational institutions. An acceleration of scientific and technological progress in all areas of knowledge raises the task for ensuring the continuous growth of professional skills throughout the whole life. Structural and institutional replacing in professional education is reflected in various models of higher professional education. These alternative technology mediated environments reflect the increasing need to serve a generation of learners who prefer to learn through experience or by interacting with learning tools.

14 Artificial Intelligence and Its Implications in Education

Computer equipment, software, and online service have succeeded in introducing improvements and enhancements to the classrooms and teaching methods in recent years. Yet, using Artificial Intelligence (AI), the real disruption of education has to come. Artificial Intelligence has proven its position as a game-changing force in various fields, in the past causing unprecedented transformations. Using AI, expert systems can be programmed to communicate with the environment through technologies such as visual perception, speech recognition and intellectual behavior, which we can find to be inherently human. This chapter aims to discuss the role of artificial intelligence in the education sector including its market size, the effect of AI in education, case studies of current AI presence in education (smart content, smart tutoring systems, virtual facilitators and learning environments, etc.) to improve learning and life outcomes for all. Finally chapter concludes with the issues and problems.

15 Learning With Artificial Intelligence Systems: Application, Challenges, and Opportunities

Nowadays, Artificial Intelligence (AI) is a part of our lives. Everything that we do on the internet is influenced to a various extent by AI. It can automate multiple tasks in education as well as in other domains. The education domain is mainly benefited by AI, especially for learning purposes. There may be the software to perform all activities which need automation. This software can point out that the course needs improvement. AI software can give students and educators helpful feedback. Data that is powered by AI also helps schools, teachers, and support students. There are lots of benefits of AI in education, which improves the learning experience of the students, for example, personalization, teaching, grading, feedback on course quality, creating a global classroom, monitoring performance, and a lot more. At the point when another promising innovation develops, and when the constraint of innovation and the difficulties of applying are regularly not accurately seen, at that point the innovation may appear to open fundamentally additional opportunities for taking care of old issues.

This book will explore the phenomena of the emergence of the use of AI in teaching and learning in higher education. Recent technological advancements and the increasing speed of adopting new technologies in higher education will be explored in order to predict the future nature of higher education in a world where artificial intelligence is part of the fabric of our universities. In this book we also investigate educational implications of emerging technologies on the way students learn and how institutions teach and evolve. We will also try to pinpoint some challenges for institutions of higher education and student learning in the adoption of these technologies for teaching, learning, student support, and administration and explore further directions for research.

Shivani Verma
Km. Mayawati Government Girls P. G. College, India

Pradeep Tomar
Gautam Buddha University, India

Chapter 1
Artificial Intelligence in Higher Education:
First Attempt

Kapil Sethi
https://orcid.org/0000-0002-3728-716X
Shoolini University, India

Shweta Chauhan
Puffins International School, India

Varun Jaiswal
https://orcid.org/0000-0001-8068-0672
National Centre for Disease Control, India

ABSTRACT

Education is significant in our lives. Learning is the main feature that is connected to education. Education increases the power of visualization and differentiation between right and the wrong. The future of education is directly related to innovative tools and computing abilities of the intelligent machines, opening to new potentials and tasks for teaching and learning in education with the prospective to primarily changing the governance and the inner architecture of institutions of higher education. Education in these days has become very expensive for the poor guardians (with meager income) of the capable students to get admission in the reputed institutes of their choice. Education indeed helps to know the real values in relation to social and cultural behavior so that one can become a decent person in nature in society. It also shows the limitations and risks in the life of a modern student. This chapter explores using artificial intelligence in higher education.

DOI: 10.4018/978-1-7998-4763-2.ch001

1. INTRODUCTION

Education is a vital instrument for the improvement of the country. Most by far of the populace on the planet would accept that achievement and to procure cash is a basic factor, be that as it may, it isn't directly considering the way that without training, nobody can get accomplishment for which learning the social and social qualities (Owens, 1995). Learning is the primary component just as a device which is associated with instruction to learn and know various things which constantly assists with teaching an ever increasing number of understudies/people in the zone around. Practically all the time one inquiry consistently emerges in the brain of understudies that "Why instruction is so significant?" and the appropriate response is on the grounds that it is progressively significant piece of our life (Morreale and Pearson, 2008). Training is such a lot of basic for achievement all through in our regular day to day existence. Without instruction, one can't investigate the new musings which demonstrate that they are not prepared to develop the world in the light of the way that without contemplations there is no imagination and without innovativeness, there is no turn of events. Over the world, a few countries might be progressively evolved and some are unquestionably not (Wals and Jickling, 2002). The country which is creating, the more taught person's proportion analyzes to the country which isn't as quite a bit of created. Instruction is the component which gives the people the necessary learning, data, aptitude, procedure, and permits them to know their privileges and obligations toward their family, society, and the nation (Gartner and Lipsky, 1987). Training builds the intensity of representation, so one can viewpoint to see the world without any problem. Instruction develops the limits and the abilities to battle the shamefulness, brutality, abuse and different components (Dewey, 2007). Essentially, as the face is the impression of the heart, the degree of instruction fabricates the status of the state or the nation. In a wide range of countries, the structure takes after that rich understudies get bit by bit more training and poor won't (Delpit, 2006). Instruction in nowadays has gotten costly and the helpless gatekeepers the very pinnacle of fit understudies can't consider getting their wards conceded into such establishments (Sallis, 2014). We require a system that will give an equivalent measure of opportunities to both rich and helpless understudies who thusly can contribute in the improvement and advancement of the country. By giving instruction, we wipe out the dejection and every person in the country will get mainstream and contributes their association in building up their country (Hofstede, 1986).

As indicated by Nelson Mandela, the most acclaimed individual tells about instruction "Training is the most compelling weapon which you can use to change the world" (Mandela, 2014). Training ends up being incredible watchmen, understudies, representatives, experts, family members and genuine individuals

(B. U. Levinson, 2001). Being in contact with an informed individual and having a brilliant conversation with him expands learning and presents a particular creativity and fulfillment in the psyche (Cole and Shastry, 2009). Training makes the national improvement process brisk (Fägerlind and Saha, 2016). The lifestyle of its kin can be dependent up generally, the Nationals can make sure about. The significance of training and its vitality can be fathomed from the way that when we are imagined, our social orders start instructing us around a major thing for the duration of regular day to day existence (Fägerlind and Saha, 2016). An infant fires adjusting new words and develops a jargon dependent on what his people educate him. They show him who is his father, mother, sister, sibling, and so on and how to continue with each individual giving them due respect (Von Glasersfeld, 1998). They additionally pass on him valuable information about ethics and morals fitting from the soonest beginning stage when he has a sensitive nature so these qualities stay inside him for whatever length of time that he can think back as molding (Noddings, 2013). How we act with our blood connection and how much regard we have for our seniors is a prompt consequence of our fundamental training in our youth times (Lickona, 1996). So it is all in all correct to express that individual's fundamental training begins at his home. Gatekeepers deal with their youth not that basically into the underlying advances when he starts making sense of how to walk; they additionally control them on the means to be taken with conduct, moral quality and respect (Eisner, 2017). They instruct him about the law and estimations of mankind and why they ought to be checked to turn into an average individual. As the youngster grows progressively settled, his desires and needs to get more prominent and watchmen endeavor their best to give him the best instructive circumstance to make his fantasies work out as expected (Zipes, 2013). Today, the current instructive structure has been diminished to a trade of bearings and data and that's it. While in earlier cases the perspective of training was to fill extraordinary characteristics and morals in an individual's mindfulness (Best and Kahn, 2016). Today we have glided away from this belief system because of the fast commercialization in the preparation part.

In right now, it is basic to consider the vitality of a not too bad training. A better than average instruction doesn't simply contain going to class or school to get a degree. It goes past that. If someone can peruse or form, has gone to the classes and accomplished a degree, it doesn't mean he is completely instructed (Bourdieu and Nice, 1977). This is just an area of the instruction that makes one mindful to what exactly is critical on the planet and since by far most of the world needs a degree. In this method, he gets the capacity to perceive what is basic for him, what is correct or wrong. In figure 1, it shows their training based issues and its answer with AI.

Artificial intelligence (AI) has officially entered the higher education realm, both hypothetically and in early practice. According to the report *Artificial Intelligence Market in the US Education Sector,* AI will grow by 47.7 percent from 2018 to 2022,

Figure 1. Common problems and their solution using AI

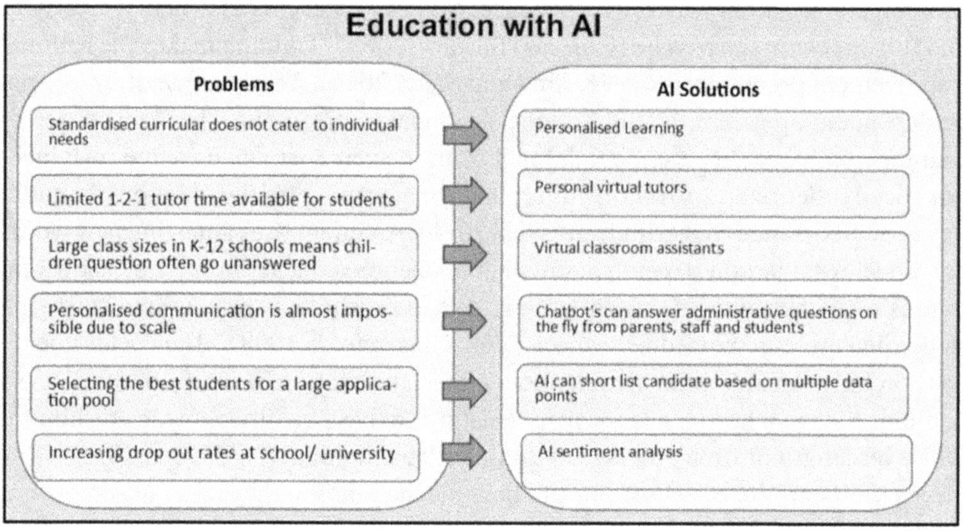

and several technological and educational powerhouses are committing substantial resources and personnel to develop digital platforms that use AI.

2. BACKGROUND

2.1 Some Important Factors That Show "Why Higher Education Is So Important in Our Life".

- Moral training causes a person to develop socially just as financially. Instruction makes us steadfast and urges us to play out our day by day life practices in most perfect manners (Doran, 1981), get new capacities, secure new abilities and mindfulness that improves life consistently (Seligman, Ernst, Gillham, Reivich, and Linkins, 2009).
- Higher instruction gives an individual all the fundamental devices and mindfulness about how he can acquire his day by day dinners (Eisenberg, 2010). He generally gets information about how he can raise the status of life while fulfilling his family's regular necessities.
- Education makes an individual mindful of his privileges and obligations. He/she understands his obligation to rehearse his ability to cast a ballot and pick an average delegate among decisions (Apple, 2013).

- A honorable training illuminates the specialty of living to a person without limits. It enlightens him to best use the nation's benefits for advancement.
- An individual improves as an appointed authority to perceive the valid from bogus and great from terrible (Stocker, 1979).
- Education gives singular finding out about incredible characteristics, good and great obligations all through life.
- Being taught, a man can battle with the diverse social shades and feels empowered to dispose of such issues (Sharp, Green, and Lewis, 2017).
- An taught government official realizes how to carry on publically and how to talk with the media properly. He likewise perceives the necessities and yearnings of the overall population and does as well as can possibly be expected to satisfy them.
- An taught proficient treats individuals with compassion, unobtrusiveness and really thinks about their government assistance through each and every available methodology.
- A skilled instructor shows his understudies effectively and realizes how to utilize ideal information and training for the general improvement of society (Glaser, 1984).
- An instructed society can help everyone with singular development and improvement in their different fields.

2.2 Higher Education in this Modern Era

- Today the basic reason for driving the child into a pre-school at the youthful age of three is that the gatekeepers are stressed over the likelihood that their child will be "left-behind" who are truly encountering the identical thoughtless practice each day (Asis, 2006). It is a commonplace sight to see little youngsters conveying extremely substantial packs to class, which truly stunts their physical turn of events.
- Today, the significant reasonableness among understudies is to challenge extraordinary difficulties for a particular degree to get a particular position. Thusly, instruction has ended up being surprisingly marketed and moderately like a business today, with foundations charging high costs for degrees that guarantee great situations since they have "tie-ups" with the associations (Marginson, 2006). However simultaneously, they are leaving their occupations following 3-4 months or the larger pieces of them are not satisfied.
- Currently, a greater part of understudies are going into such establishments which have extraordinary showcasing and advancing arrangement and which make terrific assurances to welcome people in the midst of affirmation times

(Smith and Piele, 2006). So people are not affected by the educators and the greatness of instructing yet the notification and exceptional developments being constrained by the establishment.

- It is seen that each informed individual realizes how to speak pleasantly with individuals from wherever in this world, however they have neglected to review how to talk deferentially to older folks in their own families, for example, guardians and others. Today the main objective of getting preparing has been decreased to procuring cash and that's it.
- A individual's improvement and the way wherein instruction is spread among people are influenced by society's duty to an immense degree (Lasswell, 1948; Trow, 2007). Our overall population should attempt to make a space that is valuable for all zones of society in getting a not too bad instruction.

It is the training which makes us great person and recognizes us from further alive animals on earth. It is our instruction that gives us the learning and capacities to use our inventive endowments to their most noteworthy potential (Scott, Mcguire, and Shaw, 2003). To have a decent life and to get the insightful and physical fulfillment that continues for a long time, it is noteworthy to get educated. Nobody however training can help our overall population with advancing further and instruction is the principle part that is comparably critical for all associations, ethnicity and parties since it can motivate everyone (Seidman, 2013).

Training is a method of refreshing our aptitudes and achieving all the more learning and champion among different methods credible (Tuckman and Harper, 2012). Training starts at home so we should figure out how to ensure that the earth in our homes is valuable for our children to adapt anyway much as could sensibly be normal (Delpit, 1988). Other than our homes, we should in like manner attempt to contribute from our side as much as possible for the progression of our general public and our nation.

Computational help has changed the world in almost every space. The multifaceted troublesome procedure has been profited by the computational techniques through observing, dynamic and assessment. AI procedures have conveyed high yield regarding productivity, decrease in cost and time prerequisite in about all fields, for example, electrical, clinical, bioinformatics, science, data innovation and so forth. There are a few difficulties in the instruction framework which are mind boggling and can be profited by the utilization of AI.

Machine learning is a part of Artificial intelligence that provides frameworks with the ability to automatically learn and enhance the experience without being explicitly programmed. Machine learning focuses on the innovation of advanced computer programs that can get access and use it to learn for themselves. The way towards learning starts with perception or data (for example, direct instances or instruction) in order to find the patterns in data and settle for better decisions in the future, based on the examples that are provided. The essential point is to allow the computer to learn automatically without human interaction or help.

In most cases now machine learning is used for prediction on the bases of previous experiences and finds a new solution. Most of the organization uses this technique for different purpose like prediction; automatically take decisions, comparisons, design new model, etc. Now machine learning technique is growing day by day and the outcome of the same is much faster, depending upon the technique we are using for data mining. Machine learning comes under the broad umbrella of data mining. Data mining have various techniques that are used in machine learning like classification, clustering, regression, association rules, outer detection, sequential patterns, and prediction. Data mining is the computational process of discovering patterns in large data sets, in order to extract information from it and transform it into an understandable structure for future use. Since Machine learning process is more accurate and less error-prone when compared to data mining and it is much more capable to take its own decision and resolve the issues. Machine learning and data mining explore different area as well as the education sector. It is beneficial for educators to access students data, predict student achievements level and find students performances for example which student needs extra attention (figure 2).

Figure 2. AI in higher education

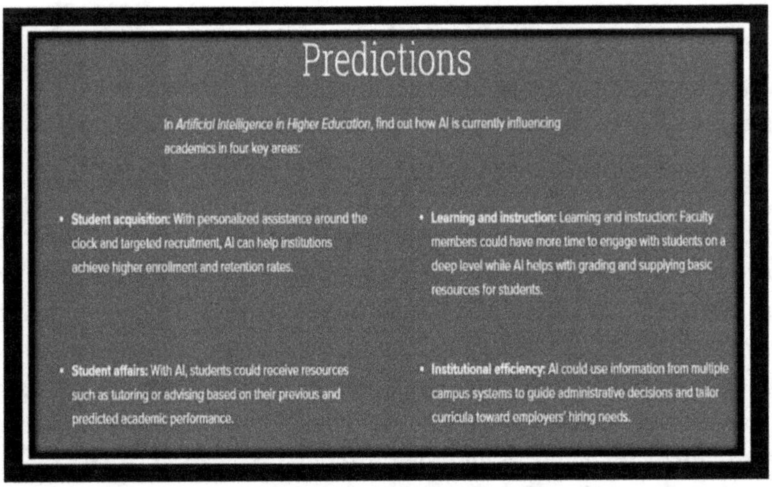

Higher education is very important when the student choose the right stream in secondary school education. Higher education creates the life of the student, so it is important to choose the subject or stream accurately. Selecting a career in a definite stream describes the future of a student (Alexander et al., 2011). However, it is challenging for a student to choose a stream (subjects) at an initial age and go for higher education. Selection of inappropriate subjects by the students due to peer and parental stress (Edwards & Quinter, 2011; Olamide & Olawaiye, 2013) or lack of proper information may outcome failure or dropout in a future career. Hence, it is essential for the students to choose the appropriate stream carefully which is best suited to them for better and successful direction.

In-stream/subject selection in higher education, a large number of factors play their influencing role (Alias & Bakar, 2010; McEvoy, 2003). Stream selection under influence of celebrities, famous personalities like role models, actors, actresses and politicians (Edwards & Quinter, 2011) often fail to discover their internal potential, capabilities, and attitude which may result in the selection of inappropriate stream (Aslam & Khan, 2011). In some conditions, providing support through online career guidance (Lodders & Meijers, 2017), teachers, tuition centers and coaching institutes (Sharma & Sidhu, 2011; Shumba & Naong, 2012) proves to be of limited help to the students because of their suggestions are mostly based on current trends and market demands, which may end ups in selecting a wrong stream irrespective of their (student) interest and their early performances (Aslam & Khan, 2011). Overall available systems which help the students to choose the stream /subject do not use data mining (DM) and machine learning (ML) methods based on data of successful scholar of their different stream/subject. It was also observed the present career counseling methods are not based on practical observation or technical formulas to provide an accurate selection of the stream/subject (Borchert, 2002). Instead, they are expensive with prolonged deciding time and away from the reach of many potential students (Johnstone & Marcucci, 2007).

Generally, students select medical, non-medical, commerce, arts, and social science stream for a bright future (Cheney, Ruzzi, & Muralidharan, 2005). When the student secure good marks they are expected to opt science stream. In many countries like India, secondary education is a more important phase (Agarwal, 2006; Li & Bray, 2007) for students as they have to select a major stream of their careers. The Indian education system is not flexible in terms of changing subjects once students have opted. For example, a commerce student cannot opt for medical and non-medical stream. Generally, stream selection for career happens in three ways (Figure 3); the first one is selecting stream influenced by parents and relatives, the second one is selecting stream by own choice and the third one is selecting stream by the help of career guidance/counselors (McEvoy, 2003).

Figure 3. Students select their higher education stream in three ways.

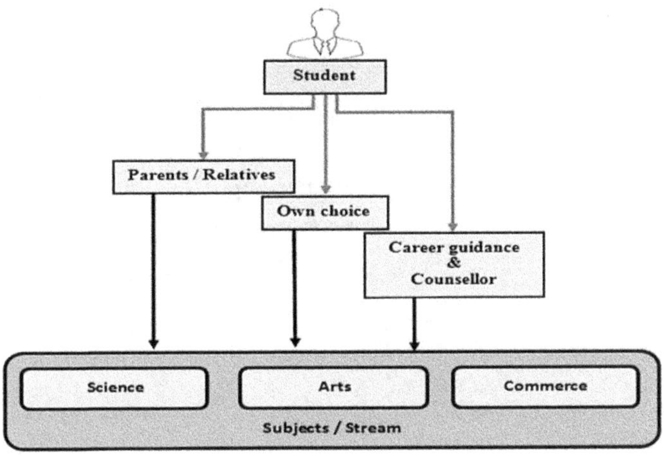

3. ROLE OF TECHNOLOGY IN THE HIGHER EDUCATION

3.1. The Role of Technology in the Higher Education for Better Future

As we set out on the Fourth Industrial Revolution, clearly development will accept a central activity in practically all pieces of our lives (Cortese, 2003). Exploration by the World Economic Forum assesses that 65% of children entering grade school will end up in occupations that today don't exist (Elder, 2018).

By 2020 its assessed there will be 1.5 million new digitized vocations over the globe. Meanwhile, 90% of affiliations right currently have IT aptitudes lack, while 75% of educators and studies mirror a gap in their ability to address the issues of the IT workforce. To set up the capacity required for the propelled economy, directions must be balanced as snappy as the enthusiasm for IT aptitudes is developing with time (Csorny, 2013). Encounters from the effect of mental, social and natural elements are ascending out of "the new craft of learning" (Becker and Luthar, 2002). Along these lines to oversee comprehension and direction conflicts in our complex and quickly impelling present reality, instructive models considering interdisciplinary examination which are fundamental to make extraordinary educating and learning conditions figure 4.

Figure 4. AI and machine learning improve the education.

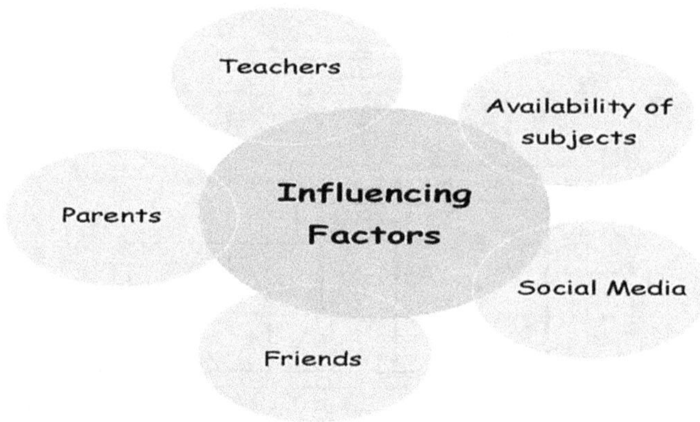

3.2 Collaborative and Deep Learning

Today the science's all-encompassing viewpoint is uncovering better approaches to manage training. A fundamental consistent master on imagination and learning, accentuates the power of development to impact and improve the scholarly network by giving experiences that expeditious profound learning (Blumenfeld, Kempler, and Krajcik, 2006). These empower the understudies to adapt helpfully, try out, reshape models and handle information both outwardly and verbally.

Envision a homeroom containing remote innovation, remotely accessible switches, switches and a synchronized instrument to make "canny" condition for the advancement of genuine Internet of Things (IoT) things, the board and experiences by understudies (Sivakumar, Robertson, Artimy, and Aslam, 2005; Watson, McKeown, and Casado, 2006). Creation occurs in different scenes for example, in the study hall in the midst of assignment based learning or close by lively development peers by methods for hackathons (Nandi and Mandernach, 2016). Understudies show the frameworks they make in a test framework and model with cloud-based development at home. Educators are engaged with an adaptable learning association while helping out companion instructors over the world. Learning science's interdisciplinary bits of information are advancing better approaches to manage instruction.

By applying learning science bits of data to IT guidance [56], we can make a dynamic, automated and hands-on learning establishment that is extraordinarily created, flexible, related and building up the limit foreseen that would control the pushed economy.

3.3 Understanding Learning Science's Impact on Education

Through its Education strength model, the U.S. Maritime power developed an electronic thinking based instructing structure to emulate the acts of remarkable aides (Burton and Brown, 1979). Advancement and hands-on labs drive this structure with understudy results indistinguishable from or beating those using the human guide. The stage is in like manner versatile in a way not oversaw by up close and personal aides. Counting propelled gadgets expands the other options and reach of modified instruction system. For example, enhancing the force of eye to eye and online teachers, learning and assessment improved with sorted out cutting edge gadgets can be astoundingly incredible.

4. ISSUES, CONTROVERSIES AND PROBLEMS

4.1. Various Individual Roles Influencing for Higher Education

1. **Role of teachers while choosing a stream:** Deficient and wrong information prompts catastrophes. Here and there understudies likewise take wrong decisions because of absence of information. The main key to keeping away from such catastrophes is direction from specialists like educators and experienced people. In a few conditions, understudies disregard their energy, interests and follow their parent's choice or social capital instead of to satisfy their own fantasies appeared in figure 5.

Figure 5. Various influence factors.

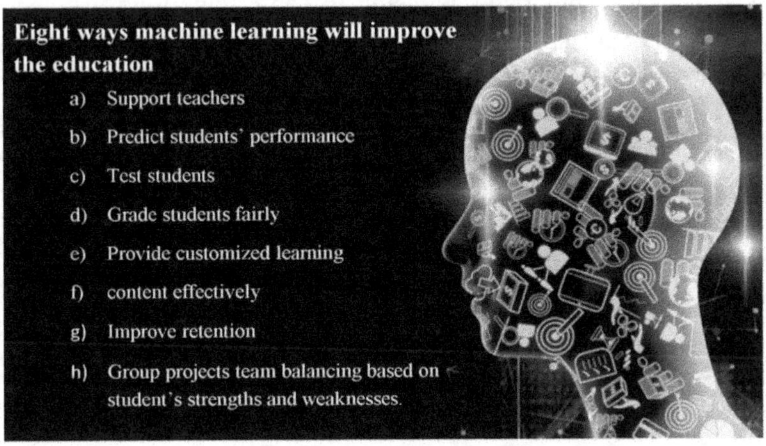

2. **Role of parents:** Guardians are the essential establishment of building a prosperous and shimmer profession for their kids. Guardians must have legitimate examination accomplished for the correct profession alternative for their youngsters. Disregarding, they ought not demand or power and life their kids to pursue a profession of their decision or dream which they themselves had longed for (Ali, 2015). In the steady conversation, they can clarify the instances of effective and energy followed individuals from different divisions. Be that as it may, they ought to be reasonable for permit their relatives to hold fast to their own fantasies. The outcome may be once in a while repulsive if guardians attempt to force their children on their picked way. Students ought to consistently offer need to their decision and simultaneously, it ought to be appropriately checked and amplified by guardians to discover if it's a right way for their youngsters for an effective vocation. Important direction parent's help causes the kids to certainly shape their future. In country India, the instructive sex hole is a direct result of the assorted parent's demeanor toward teaching the young lady in the public eye. Right now, everybody comprehends the point that young lady's training has significant externalities for remodeling general social government assistance.
3. **Role of friends:** It is frequently observed that closest companions are a significant impact in picking the subject/stream voluntarily. A companion builds an inspirational and serious condition between them to perform best to accomplish enormous and become higher throughout everyday life. So it's clear that on the off chance that the companions are good, at that point they will persuade towards greatness however in the event that they are not, at that point life can be a calamity and can ruin what's to come.
4. **Influenced by social media:** Web based life is a device of updates and change in cutting edge life. Understudies are exceptionally empowered by internet based life through celebrated characters like entertainers, government officials, agent, models, sportsperson, and so forth and overlook their point in the dream of resembling them or tailing them.
5. **Availability of subjects:** The accessibility of subjects is one of the significant components, particularly in provincial and urban spots. Here and there subject determination depends on the accessibility of subjects and the understudy needs to settle regarding those matters reluctantly influencing a misguided course of things to come and advanced education.

5. HIGHER EDUCATION EFFECTS IN STUDENT'S GROWTH

5.1 Supporting the Growth of the Nation

Especially taught people advantage the nations to develop (Faure, 1972). System makers and officials persistently endeavor to make a predominant condition in the public eye. A nation won't be considered as an overarching nation in the occasion on the off chance that it doesn't have incredible quality HR. Taught business are creating administration and paying assignments to fabricate better establishment in the country (Jongbloed, Enders, and Salerno, 2008). Specialists are working constantly to make an unrivaled world. There are unmistakable social points of interest of training and the nations are its spectators.

5.2 Moral Values

An informed individual will most likely develop better for good and good characteristics appeared differently in relation to an uneducated person. The nonattendance of instruction makes issues like notion, forceful conduct at home, shortcoming and helpless desires for ordinary solaces (Hunter, 2008). An informed individual knows the importance of tidiness and neatness. Instruction will ascend to open the entryway for both man and ladies and taught people will have the ability to make a sound society.

5.3 Back Bone of a Society

Taught people are the establishment of society. The nonattendance of training delivers different social issues like shortcoming, deepest clash, helpless desires for ordinary solaces and some more. Simply taught people can comprehend the estimation of the affiliation, structure and social protection (Russell and Norvig, 2016). Just trained people will have the ability to outline an unblemished and sound society. The correct training will help the normal people with finding a fitting answer for their issues.

5.4 Education Can Create Better Human Beings

It isn't feasible for an uneducated individual to take the right choice. An uneducated individual will likely develop unfortunate propensities, bring low certainty and disappointment. Directly through the correct instruction, an individual can create incredible quality, great characteristics and good characteristics (Roco and Bainbridge, 2003). Just well training individual will know the estimation of guidance and they will presumably have an increasingly broad vision. In addition, without incredible quality training, a sound society can't be formed (Ary, Jacobs, Irvine, and Walker, 2018).

5.5 Personal Growth

we should get an average nature of guidance with a particular ultimate objective to get the greatest limit (Friese, Pittman, and Hendee, 1995). If we are making arrangements for the future, an individual should complete the conventional training from the apparent schools in India and personal growth (Umashankar and Dutta, 2007). Incredible quality schools realize the right strategy to set up a not too bad local. All the enormous affiliations are looking for people, who are significantly arranged and have special aptitudes. Without fitting guidance, the individual won't have the ability to serve an affiliation or accomplish most extreme limit.

5.6 Understanding the Responsibilities

It isn't feasible for an uneducated individual to be totally mindful of his obligations. Just an educated individual thinks about his own and social obligations. An uneducated individual will most likely transform into a significant weight or a hazard to overall population, who don't have anything to offer back to the overall population (Lantos, 2001). Appropriate instruction prepares an individual to think verifiably their own preferred position and besides enables him to give something back to society. As a social being, it is a commitment to give something back to society and improve something for the people to come.

6. CHALLENGES IN EDUCATION

The way of life of an instructive association is the aftereffect of the feelings, perceptions, associations, airs, created and unwritten rules that shape and effect each piece of school limits (Bruner, 1996). School culture in like manner fuses increasingly strong issue, for example, the physical and eager security of understudies, the relationship of study halls and open spaces, or how much a school handles and praises ethnic, etymological, or social arranged assortment. Effects that change or alter any piece of this mix will most likely influence the general culture of a school or association (Skrtic, 1991).

Challenges in Education:

1. Diversity – One of the difficulties in instruction is perceiving the expanded assorted variety of students in our homerooms and the teaching methods that

take into account various students and gatherings of students. Understudies having a place with various locales, places, religions should be instructed similarly (Brown, 2000).

2. Digital familiarity – Education is driven by moral obligation, fitness to adequately and morally explain data, online personality, computerized skill levels, citizenship, cybersecurity, access, and value of chance to every single understudy (Wang, Wiesemes, and Gibbons, 2012).
3. Digital citizenship – Understanding to live deferentially and constantly in reality with the computerized progresses are changing the habits where we interface, convey, grant and relate to one another (Ohler, 2011).
4. Identity and security – In the automated world, understanding our personality and to shield the things we have to keep a person's character hidden and comparative with the others as well (B. A. Levinson, 1996).
5. Cyberbullying – Understanding the effect of this sort of direct as for schools and society, the long stretch and suffering impact of such practices (Meredith, 2010).
6. Global connectedness – understanding the impact and Implications of living in the all around related world including comprehension and respect for the dialects, culture and character of others (Lehtomäki, Moate, and Posti-Ahokas, 2016).
7. De-privatized practice – understanding the rise of training, in school's establishments where educators and understudies are cooperating in progressively open conditions, where the sharing of solidarity and learning is regarded and enabled (Kruse and Louis, 1993). This remembers the change for seeing educators as the sole authority inside their own study hall, seeing them fill in as a piece of a group where their work with students is consistently 'in perspective on' their partners.

7. SOLUTIONS AND RECOMMENDATIONS

7.1. Artificial Intelligence Tools Used Worldwide in Higher Education

Thinking about man-made brainpower, it's sensible that scenes from a sci-fi spine chiller come in the psyche. Robots are battling with people, men are beginning to look all starry eyed at a PC who is figuring out how to feel and comprehend the feelings. iPhones defeating their customers. Be that as it may, shouldn't something be said about a homeroom?

Shouldn't something be said about a study hall?

For a broad time, educators have endeavored to energize each and every understudy (school understudy) with their individualized informative necessities.

That gets unfathomably extraordinary in a homeroom of twenty, thirty, forty, or fifty understudies all required to float through the comparable government endorsed test, paying little brain to mindfulness. The use of man-caused thinking to can agitate the traditional and possibly hurting one-gauge fits all model of present-day directions (Bergmann and Sams, 2012).

AI calculation has recently begun helping instructors fill the unfilled holes while demonstrating which subjects' understudies are experiencing the most (Kotsiantis, 2012; Michalski, Carbonell, and Mitchell, 2013). Computer based intelligence and writing slate go hand - in - hand will change the method of instruction, here are a portion of the Artificial Intelligence apparatuses utilized worldwide in training (Martin, 2012; Ann I Morey, 2004) figure 6.

Figure 6. Progress report of students while using AI.

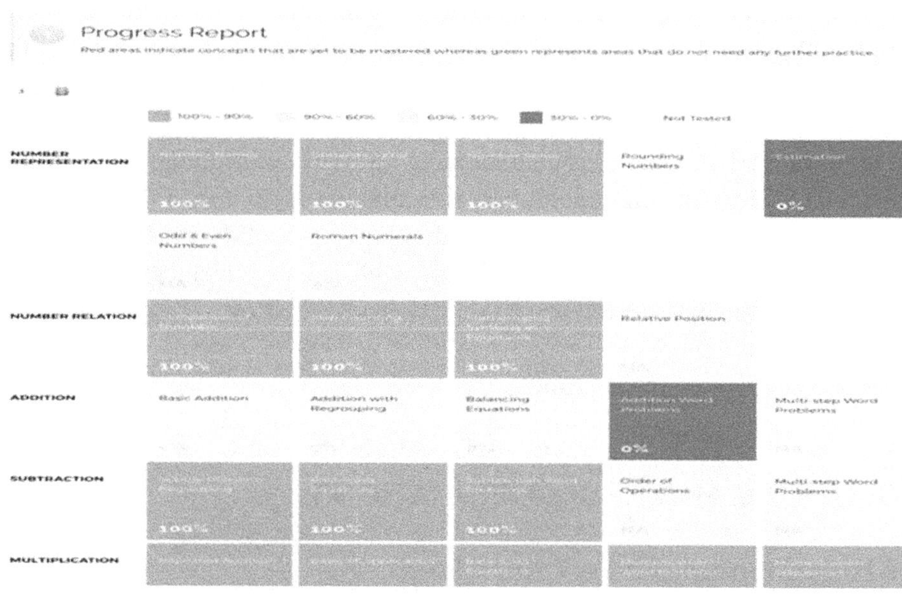

- Thinkster Math: A web interface "the math application that offers a surprising human touch," by The New York Times, Thinkster Math is a coaching application that blends real math instructive modules with an altered showing style (Wadhwa). The application allocated each understudy a foundation manage who watches their mental technique unfurl very much arranged on a screen. To begin with, Thinkster Math gives the customer assorted issues fitting to their scope of capacities, ranges of abilities. As understudies turn out to be the manner by which they've accomplished an answer, the application separates their created work to make sense of where they've turned out gravely or confused a fundamental basic reasoning advance. Thinkster Math upgrades each understudy's reason method by giving video help to stuck understudies and quick, customized input.

- Brainly: Brainly (https://brainly.in/) is the online networking learning site for study hall questions. Brainly utilizes a Machine Learning calculation for sifting the spams. It permits the understudy to ask homework practices from various subject and get programmed, checked answers from individual understudies across various areas around the world (Choi et al., 2015; Choi et al., 2016). Brainly causes understudies to think of their own right answer. If you have an understudy who bearings the study hall, the person in question can offer answers on responses and work towards transforming into a Brainly society judge. Brainly has experts on a grouping of school subjects and endeavors to make a study hall like system for that altered chalkboard contact.
- Content Technologies, Inc.: Worldwide textbooks are helpful for cardboard removed types of understudies who look, think, issue unwind and process information the equal. Content Technologies, Inc. CTI is an AI association using profound Learning to make changed perusing material that fits the necessities of specific courses and understudies (Chen, Mashhadi, Ang, and Harkrider, 1999). Teachers import schedule into a CTI motor. CTI equipment by then pros the information text information and utilizations a computerized reasoning calculation that executes calculations to make modified understanding material and coursework subject to focus thoughts (Brusilovsky and Peylo, 2003). Right when was the last time, your study hall read a course perusing spread to cover, utilized each page of preparing questions or truly watched connections between in-class work and named examining. CTI plans to fill that gap and assist wholesalers with making amazing course books proper for each individual understudy.
- Mika: Mika offers AI-based preparing apparatuses for students after the school hours, Mika give customized regard for every understudy. In addition, if you think adjusted thought is just for grade school understudies battling with scientific issues like long division, duplication. Mika has some skill in advanced education instructing to fill the holes in college study halls notorious for address based homerooms (Mahon, Bryant, Brown, and Kim, 2010). The application is guided by every understudy through unique learning process, keeping clients aware of their step by step advance and changing activities to each understudy specific battle.

- Netex Learning: Netex Learning give the educators to structure a program over an assortment of computerized stages and gadgets for the understudies. The most actually incompetent understudies unite join intelligent parts like sound, video, and self-assessments to their propelled practice structures, all inside redid learning with a cloud-based stage (Ercan, 2010; Wadhwa). With Netex, educators can make altered understudy materials to be dispersed on any automated computerized stage while giving instruments to video conferencing, conversation on the point, customized assignments and investigation discovering that show a visual portrayal of every single individual understudy and their self-improvement. It will upgrade mindfulness among the understudies over the worldwide on the significance of instruction.

7.2 Current Trend to Solve the Problem Using Artificial Intelligence in Higher Education

1. Alternative Assessment: Broadly elective appraisal is viewed as a choice to uniform, standard referenced, different choice testing and commonly asserts the accompanying highlights (Brusilovsky, 1999). Simulated intelligence in elective evaluation helps in a few different ways in instruction not many as features:
    a. Student investment in defining objectives and models for appraisal.
    b. Performing a task, making a curio/item.
    c. Use of more elevated level reasoning or potentially critical thinking abilities.
    d. Estimating metacognitive, joined and intrapersonal aptitudes just as scholarly items.
    e. Evaluating critical instructional occasions.
    f. Contextualization in a certifiable application.
    g. Utilization of decided models, known early, which describe gauges for good execution.
2. Constructivism: Artificial insight assumes a significant job in the constructivism. Improving the cerebrum and pondering the intensity of the kids. Man-made intelligence assists with drawing graphs and different sorts of fun exercises dependent on their conduct (Pan, Cheok, Yang, Zhu, and Shi, 2006).
3. Critical Thinking: AI sifts through the article examination and assessment issues over and judgment. In Universities and Colleges, AI assists with discovering the best fit answer for a specific issue. Among various answers for an issue, AI can help to discover the best fit arrangement.

4. Foreign Language Learning: AI Natural Language Processing assists with making an interpretation of one language into another dialect. This could be conceivable because of man-made reasoning (Barson, Frommer, and Schwartz, 1993).
5. Inquiry-Based Learning: Due to headways in web innovation all the schools and establishments begin taking their inquiries on the web. One can find out about the specific subject by means of the request based and learning-based framework. Man-made brainpower empowers chatbots and gives assistance to various understudies to learn (Tan, Yeo, and Lim, 2005).
6. Multicultural Education: Humans are multicultural; there is assorted variety in culture and training. Man-made reasoning assists with understanding diverse religion dialects. Understudies over the globe can comprehend and get familiar with an alternate sort of dialects (Ann Intili Morey, 2000).
7. Teacher as Researcher: In the college, Institutes and school, the educators are going about as an analyst. A considerable lot of the understudies are working under the task coaches to present their undertakings and theory. Man-made brainpower encourages specialists to keep the record of their examination, AI can help in customized exploration, proposal or exploration paper, news stories dependent on their zone of premiums (Learner, 2006; Santa and Santa, 1995).
8. Technology in Teaching: Artificial Intelligence helps in the robotized Grading of understudy's denotes, a portion of the normal assignments are overseen by the PC chatbots to help understudy instruction actually (Lawless and Pellegrino, 2007; Roblyer and Doering, 2006).
9. Tools for Accessing Literature: AI gives the apparatuses to the composed writing around the world. The prelude of AI advancement is its unprecedented ability to continually pick up from the accumulated data. Along these lines, the better the calculation, the more data about the subject got and progressively expansive the far reaching investigation, the more accurate the ensuing forecast of result happens (Novak, Razzouk, and Johnson, 2012). Outside writing, man-made reasoning modified robots are starting at now equipped for composing contents (Murphy, Murphy, and Arkin, 2000). Really, Bloomberg, diverse news associations and money related firms have been using robot columnists to compose information driven substance with man-made reasoning customized author that transforms information into some important stories, like Wordsmith (Van Dalen, 2012). It gives the advancement to customers to automate their sythesis using rules-based organizations with various circumstances (Sugisaka and Hazry, 2007)

8. RISKS AND LIMITATIONS

There are barely any limitations with the execution of AI advancement:

- Poor educator selection: A couple of teachers are impenetrable to this and ought to be managed through the change in like manner.
- Fear Factor: As with a few organizations teachers may feel that AI information could at last supplant them and will, along these lines, be hesitant to push forward activities devouring the advancement (Winston and Prendergast, 1984).
- Adoption at scale: AI joining requires empowering from various partners like – watchmen, understudies, teachers, chiefs, and policymakers. This can be difficult to achieve quickly.
- Subject constraints: AI won't be appropriate to all subjects. For example, modified learning and electronic looking into are presumably not going to work in sensible subjects with a strong enthusiastic segment to assessment, for instance, performance, craftsmanship, sustenance advancement and physical guidance (Groffen et al., 2013).
- Investment: With schools under more monetary load than whenever in late memory, an association of AI development at scale is exorbitant and not all schools will have straightforward access to such resources (Luehrmann, 1972).
- Privacy, information and cybersecurity: This is presumably the main most serious danger of AI sending guidance so near unattractive data that is required for progress. In the training circumstance, this test is persuaded more by the technique that will deal with minors' near unattractive data and information. At the end of the day, there will be increasingly solid portrayal. Healthy cybersecurity and data insurance technique will be fundamental to advance.

CONCLUSION

Computer based intelligence turns into a developing piece of our day by day carries on with, it's no big surprise that instructive establishments are hustling to find the need to grow more ability to keep the motor of AI advancement running. Be that as it may, not exclusively is instruction being changed similar to science, innovation, building, and math (STEM) educational programs, yet the training business all in all is being changed by AI. Progressively, instructive organizations from rudimentary to advanced education just as grown-up and proficient learning are being changed by astute frameworks that are helping people learn better and accomplish their learning destinations. Utilizing smart AI-controlled frameworks can extraordinarily improve the effectiveness of numerous instructive establishments, bring down their working costs, give them more prominent perceivability into pay and costs, and improve the general responsiveness of the instructive foundations. Computer based intelligence change the training scene in up and coming years.

REFERENCES

Agarwal, P. (2006). *Higher education in India: The need for change*. Working paper.

Alexander, P. M., Holmner, M., Lotriet, H. H., Matthee, M. C., Pieterse, H., Naidoo, S., & Jordaan, D. (2011). Factors affecting career choice: Comparison between students from computer and other disciplines. *Journal of Science Education and Technology*, *20*(3), 300–315. doi:10.100710956-010-9254-3

Alias, M., & Bakar, M. N. F. B. A. (2010). Factors Contributing to Programme Choice and Subsequent Career Selection among Engineering Students. *People*, *7*, 9.

Apple, M. W. (2013). *Educating the right way: Markets, standards, God, and inequality*. Routledge.

Ary, D., Jacobs, L. C., Irvine, C. K. S., & Walker, D. (2018). *Introduction to research in education*. Cengage Learning.

Asis, M. M. (2006). Living with migration: Experiences of left-behind children in the Philippines. *Asian Population Studies*, *2*(1), 45–67. doi:10.1080/17441730600700556

Aslam, M. Z., & Khan, A. R. (2011). *A proposed decision support system/expert system for guiding fresh students in selecting a faculty in Gomal university, Pakistan*. arXiv preprint arXiv:1104.1678

Barson, J., Frommer, J., & Schwartz, M. (1993). Foreign language learning using e-mail in a task-oriented perspective: Interuniversity experiments in communication and collaboration. *Journal of Science Education and Technology*, *2*(4), 565–584. doi:10.1007/BF00695325

Becker, B. E., & Luthar, S. S. (2002). Social-emotional factors affecting achievement outcomes among disadvantaged students: Closing the achievement gap. *Educational Psychologist*, *37*(4), 197–214. doi:10.1207/S15326985EP3704_1 PMID:23255834

Bergmann, J., & Sams, A. (2012). *Flip your classroom: Reach every student in every class every day*. International Society for Technology in Education.

Best, J. W., & Kahn, J. V. (2016). *Research in education*. Pearson Education India.

Blumenfeld, P. C., Kempler, T. M., & Krajcik, J. S. (2006). *Motivation and cognitive engagement in learning environments*. Academic Press.

Borchert, M. (2002). *Career choice factors of high school students* (Unpublished Master of Science thesis). University of Wisconsin-Stout.

Bourdieu, P., & Nice, R. (1977). *Outline of a Theory of Practice* (Vol. 16). Cambridge University Press.

Brown, R. (2000). Social identity theory: Past achievements, current problems and future challenges. *European Journal of Social Psychology*, *30*(6), 745–778. doi:10.1002/1099-0992(200011/12)30:6<745::AID-EJSP24>3.0.CO;2-O

Bruner, J. S. (1996). *The culture of education*. Harvard University Press.

Brusilovsky, P. (1999). Adaptive and intelligent technologies for web-based eduction. *Ki, 13*(4), 19-25.

Brusilovsky, P., & Peylo, C. (2003). Adaptive and intelligent web-based educational systems. *International Journal of Artificial Intelligence in Education*, *13*, 159–172.

Burton, R. R., & Brown, J. S. (1979). An investigation of computer coaching for informal learning activities. *International Journal of Man-Machine Studies*, *11*(1), 5–24. doi:10.1016/S0020-7373(79)80003-6

Chen, A. Y., Mashhadi, A., Ang, D., & Harkrider, N. (1999). Cultural issues in the design of technology-enhanced learning systems. *British Journal of Educational Technology*, *30*(3), 217–230. doi:10.1111/1467-8535.00111

Cheney, G. R., Ruzzi, B. B., & Muralidharan, K. (2005). *A profile of the Indian education system*. Prepared for the New Commission on the Skills of the American Workforce.

Choi, E., Borkowski, M., Zakoian, J., Sagan, K., Scholla, K., Ponti, C., & Bielski, M. (2015). Utilizing content moderators to investigate critical factors for assessing the quality of answers on brainly, social learning Q&A platform for students: a pilot study. *Proceedings of the 78th ASIS&T Annual Meeting: Information Science with Impact: Research in and for the Community*. 10.1002/pra2.2015.145052010069

Choi, E., Munoz, R., Mukhlas, D., Balak, M., Farias, L., Jara, D., & Burkov, O. (2016). Understanding user motivations for asking and answering a question on brainly, online social learning network. *IConference 2016 Proceedings*.

Cole, S. A., & Shastry, G. K. (2009). *Smart money: The effect of education, cognitive ability, and financial literacy on financial market participation.* Harvard Business School Boston.

Cortese, A. D. (2003). The critical role of higher education in creating a sustainable future. *Planning for Higher Education, 31*(3), 15–22.

Csorny, L. (2013). *Careers in the growing field of information technology services.* Academic Press.

Delpit, L. (1988). The silenced dialogue: Power and pedagogy in educating other people's children. *Harvard Educational Review, 58*(3), 280–299. doi:10.17763/haer.58.3.c43481778r528qw4

Delpit, L. (2006). *Other people's children: Cultural conflict in the classroom.* The New Press.

Dewey, J. (2007). *Experience and education.* Simon and Schuster.

Doran, G. T. (1981). There'sa SMART way to write management's goals and objectives. *Management Review, 70*(11), 35–36.

Edwards, K., & Quinter, M. (2011). Factors influencing students career choices among secondary school students in Kisumu municipality, Kenya. *Journal of Emerging Trends in Educational Research and Policy Studies,* 2(2), 81–87.

Eisenberg, M. B. (2010). Information literacy: Essential skills for the information age. *DESIDOC Journal of Library and Information Technology, 28*(2), 39–47. doi:10.14429/djlit.28.2.166

Eisner, E. W. (2017). *The enlightened eye: Qualitative inquiry and the enhancement of educational practice.* Teachers College Press.

Elder, G. H. (2018). *Children of the great depression.* Routledge. doi:10.4324/9780429501739

Ercan, T. (2010). Effective use of cloud computing in educational institutions. *Procedia: Social and Behavioral Sciences,* 2(2), 938–942. doi:10.1016/j.sbspro.2010.03.130

Fägerlind, I., & Saha, L. J. (2016). *Education and national development: A comparative perspective.* Elsevier.

Faure, E. (1972). *Learning to be: The world of education today and tomorrow.* Unesco.

Friese, G. T., Pittman, J. T., & Hendee, J. C. (1995). *Studies of the use of wilderness for personal growth, therapy, education and leadership development: An annotation and evaluation*. University of Idaho, Wilderness Research Center.

Gartner, A., & Lipsky, D. K. (1987). Beyond special education: Toward a quality system for all students. *Harvard Educational Review*, *57*(4), 367–396. doi:10.17763/haer.57.4.kj517305m7761218

Glaser, R. (1984). Education and thinking: The role of knowledge. *The American Psychologist*, *39*(2), 93–104. doi:10.1037/0003-066X.39.2.93

Groffen, D. A., Koster, A., Bosma, H., van den Akker, M., Aspelund, T., Siggeirsdóttir, K., & Jónsson, P. V. (2013). Socioeconomic factors from midlife predict mobility limitation and depressed mood three decades later; Findings from the AGES-Reykjavik Study. *BMC Public Health*, *13*(1), 101. doi:10.1186/1471-2458-13-101 PMID:23379351

Hofstede, G. (1986). Cultural differences in teaching and learning. *International Journal of Intercultural Relations*, *10*(3), 301–320. doi:10.1016/0147-1767(86)90015-5

Hunter, J. D. (2008). *The death of character: Moral education in an age without good or evil*. Basic Books.

Johnstone, D. B., & Marcucci, P. N. (2007). *Worldwide trends in higher education finance: Cost-sharing, student loans, and the support of academic research*. Commissioned paper V. Lynn Meek and Dianne Davies, 81.

Jongbloed, B., Enders, J., & Salerno, C. (2008). Higher education and its communities: Interconnections, interdependencies and a research agenda. *Higher Education*, *56*(3), 303–324. doi:10.100710734-008-9128-2

Kotsiantis, S. B. (2012). Use of machine learning techniques for educational proposes: A decision support system for forecasting students' grades. *Artificial Intelligence Review*, *37*(4), 331–344. doi:10.100710462-011-9234-x

Kruse, S. D., & Louis, K. S. (1993). *Developing Professional Community in New and Restructuring Urban Schools*. Academic Press.

Lantos, G. P. (2001). The boundaries of strategic corporate social responsibility. *Journal of Consumer Marketing*, *18*(7), 595–632. doi:10.1108/07363760110410281

Lasswell, H. D. (1948). The structure and function of communication in society. *The Communication of Ideas, 37*, 215-228.

Lawless, K. A., & Pellegrino, J. W. (2007). Professional development in integrating technology into teaching and learning: Knowns, unknowns, and ways to pursue better questions and answers. *Review of Educational Research, 77*(4), 575–614. doi:10.3102/0034654307309921

Learner, R. A. (2006). teacher as researcher. *Teachers Engaged in Research: Inquiry Into Mathematics Classrooms. Grades, 3-5*, 129.

Lehtomäki, E., Moate, J., & Posti-Ahokas, H. (2016). Global connectedness in higher education: Student voices on the value of cross-cultural learning dialogue. *Studies in Higher Education, 41*(11), 2011–2027. doi:10.1080/03075079.2015.1007943

Levinson, B. A. (1996). *The Cultural Production of the Educated Person. Critical Ethnographies of Schooling and Local Practice. SUNY Series, Power, Social Identity, and Education*. ERIC.

Levinson, B. U. (2001). *We are all equal: Student culture and identity at a Mexican secondary school, 1988–1998*. Duke University Press. doi:10.1215/9780822381075

Li, M., & Bray, M. (2007). Cross-border flows of students for higher education: Push–pull factors and motivations of mainland Chinese students in Hong Kong and Macau. *Higher Education, 53*(6), 791–818. doi:10.100710734-005-5423-3

Lickona, T. (1996). Eleven principles of effective character education. *Journal of Moral Education, 25*(1), 93–100. doi:10.1080/0305724960250110

Lodders, N., & Meijers, F. (2017). Collective learning, transformational leadership and new forms of careers guidance in universities. *British Journal of Guidance & Counselling, 45*(5), 532–546. doi:10.1080/03069885.2016.1271864

Luehrmann, A. W. (1972). Should the computer teach the student, or vice versa? *Proceedings of the Spring Joint Computer Conference*.

Mahon, J., Bryant, B., Brown, B., & Kim, M. (2010). Using second life to enhance classroom management practice in teacher education. *Educational Media International, 47*(2), 121–134. doi:10.1080/09523987.2010.492677

Mandela, N. (2014). Education is the most powerful weapon which you can use to change the world. *Computer, 8*.

Marginson, S. (2006). Dynamics of national and global competition in higher education. *Higher Education, 52*(1), 1–39. doi:10.100710734-004-7649-x

Martin, F. G. (2012). Will massive open online courses change how we teach? *Communications of the ACM, 55*(8), 26–28. doi:10.1145/2240236.2240246

McEvoy, C. (2003). *Factors that Influence Parental Choice of School and Experiences in a Rural Education Market*. National University of Ireland Maynooth.

Meredith, J. P. (2010). Combating cyberbullying: Emphasizing education over criminalization. *Fed. Comm. LJ*, *63*, 311.

Michalski, R. S., Carbonell, J. G., & Mitchell, T. M. (2013). *Machine learning: An artificial intelligence approach*. Springer Science & Business Media.

Morey, A. I. (2000). Changing higher education curricula for a global and multicultural world. *Higher Education in Europe*, *25*(1), 25–39. doi:10.1080/03797720050002170

Morey, A. I. (2004). Globalization and the emergence of for-profit higher education. *Higher Education*, *48*(1), 131–150. doi:10.1023/B:HIGH.0000033768.76084.a0

Morreale, S. P., & Pearson, J. C. (2008). Why communication education is important: The centrality of the discipline in the 21st century. *Communication Education*, *57*(2), 224–240. doi:10.1080/03634520701861713

Murphy, R., Murphy, R. R., & Arkin, R. C. (2000). *Introduction to AI robotics*. MIT Press.

Nandi, A., & Mandernach, M. (2016). Hackathons as an informal learning platform. *Proceedings of the 47th ACM Technical Symposium on Computing Science Education*.

Noddings, N. (2013). *Caring: A relational approach to ethics and moral education*. Univ of California Press.

Novak, E., Razzouk, R., & Johnson, T. E. (2012). The educational use of social annotation tools in higher education: A literature review. *The Internet and Higher Education*, *15*(1), 39–49. doi:10.1016/j.iheduc.2011.09.002

Ohler, J. (2011). Digital citizenship means character education for the digital age. *Kappa Delta Pi Record, 47*(sup1), 25-27.

Olamide, S. O., & Olawaiye, S. O. (2013). The factors determining the choice of career among secondary school students. *International Journal of Engineering Science*, *2*(6), 33–44.

Owens, R. G. (1995). *Organizational behavior in education*. Academic Press.

Pan, Z., Cheok, A. D., Yang, H., Zhu, J., & Shi, J. (2006). Virtual reality and mixed reality for virtual learning environments. *Computers & Graphics*, *30*(1), 20–28. doi:10.1016/j.cag.2005.10.004

Roblyer, M. D., & Doering, A. H. (2006). Integrating educational technology into teaching (Vol. 2). Pearson/Merrill Prentice Hall.

Roco, M. C., & Bainbridge, W. S. (2003). *Overview converging technologies for improving human performance Converging technologies for improving human performance*. Springer. doi:10.1007/978-94-017-0359-8

Russell, S. J., & Norvig, P. (2016). *Artificial intelligence: a modern approach.* Pearson Education Limited.

Sallis, E. (2014). *Total quality management in education.* Routledge. doi:10.4324/9780203417010

Santa, C. M., & Santa, J. L. (1995). Teacher as researcher. *Journal of Reading Behavior, 27*(3), 439–451. doi:10.1080/10862969509547891

Scott, S. S., Mcguire, J. M., & Shaw, S. F. (2003). Universal design for instruction: A new paradigm for adult instruction in postsecondary education. *Remedial and Special Education, 24*(6), 369–379. doi:10.1177/07419325030240060801

Seidman, I. (2013). *Interviewing as qualitative research: A guide for researchers in education and the social sciences.* Teachers College Press.

Seligman, M. E., Ernst, R. M., Gillham, J., Reivich, K., & Linkins, M. (2009). Positive education: Positive psychology and classroom interventions. *Oxford Review of Education, 35*(3), 293–311. doi:10.1080/03054980902934563

Sharma, J., & Sidhu, R. (2011). Sources of stress among students preparing in coaching institutes for admission to professional courses. *The Journal of Psychology, 2*(1), 21–24. doi:10.1080/09764224.2011.11885458

Sharp, R., Green, A., & Lewis, J. (2017). *Education and social control: A study in progressive primary education.* Routledge. doi:10.4324/9781315210179

Shumba, A., & Naong, M. (2012). Factors influencing students' career choice and aspirations in South Africa. *J Soc Sci, 33*(2), 169–178. doi:10.1080/09718923.2012.11893096

Sivakumar, S. C., Robertson, W., Artimy, M., & Aslam, N. (2005). A web-based remote interactive laboratory for Internetworking education. *IEEE Transactions on Education, 48*(4), 586–598. doi:10.1109/TE.2005.858393

Skrtic, T. M. (1991). *Behind special education: A critical analysis of professional culture and school organization.* Love Publishing Company.

Smith, S. C., & Piele, P. K. (2006). *School leadership: Handbook for excellence in student learning*. Corwin Press.

Stocker, M. (1979). Desiring the bad: An essay in moral psychology. *The Journal of Philosophy*, *76*(12), 738–753. doi:10.2307/2025856

Sugisaka, M., & Hazry, D. (2007). Development of a proportional control method for a mobile robot. *Applied Mathematics and Computation*, *186*(1), 74–82. doi:10.1016/j.amc.2006.05.214

Tan, S. C., Yeo, A. C. J., & Lim, W. Y. (2005). Changing epistemology of science learning through inquiry with computer-supported collaborative learning. *Journal of Computers in Mathematics and Science Teaching*, *24*(4), 367–386.

Trow, M. (2007). *Reflections on the transition from elite to mass to universal access: Forms and phases of higher education in modern societies since WWII. In International handbook of higher education*. Springer.

Tuckman, B. W., & Harper, B. E. (2012). *Conducting educational research*. Rowman & Littlefield Publishers.

Umashankar, V., & Dutta, K. (2007). Balanced scorecards in managing higher education institutions: An Indian perspective. *International Journal of Educational Management*, *21*(1), 54–67. doi:10.1108/09513540710716821

Van Dalen, A. (2012). The algorithms behind the headlines: How machine-written news redefines the core skills of human journalists. *Journalism Practice*, *6*(5-6), 648–658. doi:10.1080/17512786.2012.667268

Von Glasersfeld, E. (1998). Cognition, construction of knowledge, and teaching. In *Constructivism in science education*. Springer.

Wadhwa, D. (n.d.). *Using Artificial Intelligence Technologies For Personalized Learning And Responsive Teaching: A Survey*. Academic Press.

Wals, A. E., & Jickling, B. (2002). "Sustainability" in higher education: From doublethink and newspeak to critical thinking and meaningful learning. *International Journal of Sustainability in Higher Education*, *3*(3), 221–232. doi:10.1108/14676370210434688

Wang, R., Wiesemes, R., & Gibbons, C. (2012). Developing digital fluency through ubiquitous mobile devices: Findings from a small-scale study. *Computers & Education*, *58*(1), 570–578. doi:10.1016/j.compedu.2011.04.013

Watson, G., McKeown, N., & Casado, M. (2006). *NetFPGA: A tool for network research and education.* Paper presented at the 2nd workshop on Architectural Research using FPGA Platforms (WARFP).

Winston, P. H., & Prendergast, K. A. (1984). *The AI business: commercial uses of artificial intelligence*. Massachusetts Institute of Technology.

Zipes, J. (2013). *When dreams came true: classical fairy tales and their tradition.* Routledge. doi:10.4324/9780203949672

Chapter 2
Artificial Intelligence:
New Pathways and Challenges in Higher Education

Mani Arora
Mayawati Government Girls Post Graduate College, India

ABSTRACT

Virtually everyone has to make hundreds of decisions every day in his day-to-day life. "Good decision making" means we are informed and have relevant and appropriate information on which to base our choices among alternatives. Decision support systems are emerging as a very powerful tool for making rational decision based on various sources of information. In this chapter, the authors attempt to understand how the intelligent decisions are required for any successful endeavour. In this complex world where information explosion has good and bad news, both finding analysing the adequate information is a tedious task that always requires expert advice. In today's digitalised world, various programs are designed especially for the education sector, which helps both the learner and tutor. Technology can reduce time to make decisions for the fussy or confused learner, thereby providing assistance.

INTRODUCTION

Education is a ongoing process from birth which starts as early as a child comes in the phase of understanding and continues till the last breath of his life. Virtually everybody has got to create hundreds of Choices every day in his day to day life. "Good Decision Making applying the knowledge and wisdom gained during the process of learning into the practical situation. Decision Support Systems are rising

DOI: 10.4018/978-1-7998-4763-2.ch002

as a awfully powerful tool for making rational decision based on numerous sources of Information. During this chapter we will try to perceive that how the intelligent decisions are required for any successful endeavour? In this complicated world where Information Explosion has good and worst news both, finding and analysing the adequate information could be a tedious task which always requires a professional recommendation. This chapter will also describe the use of various options and features which are available for the learning of educational scholars and guiding them in line with to their various abilities. In today's Digitalised World various programs are designed particularly for the education sector which helps both the learner and tutor for learning environment. Technology will cut back time to create choices for the fussy or confused learner thereby providing assistance.

What Is Intelligence?

The ability to accumulate knowledge or skills and then applying into the assorted means for solving problems is generally termed as intelligence. The basic human behaviour for e.g. to take decision at the time of risk of fire or any emergency is delineated as intelligence. Whereas even the most sophisticated work of an insect or an animal is rarely termed as intelligence. Human beings are termed as born intelligent however machines are created to resolve only what is outlined in their programming, and once any machinery created capable enough to show intelligence just like any other human being it is termed as Artificial Intelligence. The main stages in the process of decision making can be classified into the four categories: learning, understanding, applying learning with the help of perception, and using language to take the decision.

And when all these components are programmed even through a human being into the machinery it's termed as artificial intelligence.

Artificial Intelligence is outlined as

"Everything we love about civilization is a product of intelligence, so amplifying our human intelligence with artificial intelligence has the potential of helping civilization flourish like never before – as long as we manage to keep the technology beneficial." As stated by Max Tegmark, President of the Future of Life Institute

"AI is a computer system able to perform tasks that ordinarily require human intelligence... Many of these artificial intelligence systems are powered by machine learning, some of them are powered by deep learning and some of them are powered by very boring things like rules." by DataRobot CEO Jeremy Achin.

NEED FOR ARTIFICIAL INTELLIGENCE

AI is required to create a computer programming system which has an intelligent behavior with the capacity to explain and advice its end users.

Artificial Intelligence is an algorithm which Helps machines to find solutions to complex problems.

Artificial intelligence can be categorised as:

- **Narrow AI:** It is also referred to as "Weak AI,". This type of artificial intelligence needs the help of humans along with their programming. Weak AI is often usually centred on performing only one task at a time in a very well context. Whereas this Artificial Intelligence may seem intelligent, but they are working only on the basic guidance of human intelligence.
- **Artificial General Intelligence (AGI)**: AGI, sometimes referred to as "Strong AI,". This artificial intelligence is mow seem everywhere in todays world. For e.g. the robots seem in the movie" Robot" or the movie 2.0m Ra.One(2011), Krish3 (2013)m Tarzan (2004) Phuntroo(2016) etc.... AGI could be a computer with general programming and, much like a individual, it can use the programming to resolve any equation.

ARTIFICIAL INTELLIGENCE EXAMPLES

1. Google Maps on the way to commuting
2. Price estimation by Uber or Ola or any Cab
3. Email-Spam Filters
4. Plagiarism Checker
5. Face recognition by Facebook or Google drive
6. Online shopping search and advice.
7. Google voice to text searching
8. Japnese robot standing outside the malls
9. Personal Assistant like Siri and Alexa
10. Spotify and Netflix T.V. reommendations

IMPORTANCE OF ARTIFICIAL INTELLIGENCE

- **AI helps in repetitive tasks and finding the odd one.** However Artificial Intelligences is totally different from hardware-driven, routine daily tasks. Besides the automating manual tasks, AI is helpful in performing, high-volume, computerized tasks accurately and without fatigue. But For this type of work, human also has to remains essential with the computer system and generate the proper data to be inputted to the computer for finding out the correct information.

- **Intelligence is increased by Artificial Intelligence:® Artificial Intelligence** helps in increasing the learning to existing products. AI does not work as an individual application. Rather, it work on the products we are already using and the product will be improved with the help of Artificial Intelligence. Automation, conversational platforms, sensible machines are all the products added with artificial intelligence within or outside the geographical area, from providing data or information and doing in any kind of analysis.
- **A progressive learning algorithm (PLA) is a feature of Artificial Intelligence. PLA is** a technique in which information in helpful to do the programming. AI finds same repetitive blocks and regularities in data and programming so that the algorithm acquires a skill: The Progressive learning algorithm not only expertise itself by simply repeating the task again but also predicts and give estimates what should be the next best possible step which a human can also think likewise. Foe e.g. in case of ludo which goti is to move forward by coming any number on the dice. These all suggestions are the part of PLA(s) and work as a feature of Artificial Intelligence.
- **Deeper data analysis is also possible through AI** There are certain data which requires more data to analyse and earned knowledge. Where layers are hidden one over the other to go for the deep learning and analysis. The more we provide the more the deeper it will cover. For e.g. for any kind of detective and problem solving situation deeper and deeper data is required to do the proper analysis.
- **Accuracy is the term for AI:-**Take the example of Google Photos it will ask again and again for the similar face to group one person photo under one umbrella and gives a message to improve searching this all is based on deep learning and it keep giving more accurate results the more we use them. Similarly in the other fields also, AI techniques derived from deep learning, image identification and object recognitions helps in the result of better accuracy every time.
- **Data is most important in AI.** In terms of AI data can also be denoted as an intellectual property because every time algorithm is teaching itself. There is a sort of competitiveness amongst data itself as every algorithm and every data is very useful to take the analysis and if the data is best the result will also be the best which shows the intelligence.

DECISION SUPPORT SYSTEM AND INTELLIGENCE

Artificial Intelligence is the technique that makes computer thinks more intelligently than Humans. Intelligent Decision Support System or an IDSS is required to help in decision making by setting all the alternatives, evaluating them by finding out the possible course of action and predicting the result of action with the help of taught learning algorithm. Ideally, an intelligent decision support system or IDSS is made like a human consultant: it supports in decision making by collecting and analysing data, identifying and recognising problems, proposing possible alternatives and evaluating each of the possible alternatives. The main objective of the AI techniques present in any intelligent decision support system is to make possible these tasks to be performed by machinery rather than a human, while involving human capacities as nearby as possible. It is also sometimes called as machine Intelligence because it shows the intelligence showed by the machine rather than the natural intelligence shown by the humans generally. Artificial intelligence (AI) is branch of computer science related to creating smart machines or computers capable of performing all those tasks that typically require human intelligence to be conducted. AI is a multidisciplinary part of computer science with many approaches, but with the high-tech in machine learning and deep data analysis that creates a paradigm shift in every industry of each and every sector.

In the world of understanding present is the key to the past, then perhaps in longer turn the future is the key to the present. Except for understanding present and the past are the keys for the future Information comes through various sources like pictures, graphics, images, sounds numbers and impressions. The method of organising and examining the data and then converting it into information first and then knowledge about the various available options is termed as Modelling. Models are made to assist the Decision Makers in understanding the possible outcomes of choosing an alternative. The models can from information representation to complex Mathematical relationships or of any kind. The Decision Support System can be classified into various categories supported the necessity and the sort of work they are providing to the end consumer. Some major of them are as follows:

1. **Data Driven DSS**: This is a kind of support system which helps in the retrieval of data from various sources and identifying in the work of data selection and data validation. Data is the key element in any Artificial Intelligence based application
2. **Communications Driven DSS**: This decision support system uses modern communication techniques which helps in facilitating communication and its programming identifies the similarities and differences between these communication devices to interact with each other.

3. **Group Driven DSS**: This Decision Support System helps in finding out the unstructured problem by the group of individuals which are literally performing on its behind and which can't be communicated as human. The set of decision makers' work as a one group to figure out and sort the problem because all their work is dependent on single decision besides they all are working in a group.
4. **Document Driven DSS**: Documentation is extremely essential in every field as to record each and every thing. It may be in type of text number or images. This sort of DSS combines the various types of speeded storage and processed technologies that help in total retrieval and analysis of Data.
5. **Model Driven DSS:** Researches are based on data whether of any kind financial statistical or mechanical. But Raw data cannot be processed directly it needs models to process validate and interpret with the help of MDSS
6. Knowl**edge Driven DSS: These** type of the DSS are the actual system which creates any IDSS because these are aware about the specification of a particular domain problem that may be arose in that domain and ways to solve these problems. This KDSS work as the base line of IDSS
7. **WEB Based DSS: Web** is the main source of searching and exploring data. This DSS helps in finding new data, validation of data, finding errors and duplicity in data. Web based DSS is very helpful in working with secondary data for any kind of model.

Decision Support Systems or DSS helps in bringing the specified information together to take the decision for IDSS. Decision Support Systems (DSS) are actually computer based system that collects data and information from various sources, assist within and outside the organization and then analysing it. It also facilitates the evaluation of various assumptions and then the utilization of specific models in the form of IDSS. Management Information System(MIS) a kind of DSS has a long history back from early 1980's where programs are designed in such a how that quantitative data are often revealed easily, without much effort, accurately without involving any human biasness. These are also referred as Knowledge based System (KBS). When all these systems are designed intelligently in order to support analysis in every well-defined situation supported information. Therefore Decision support system (DSS) provides the opportunity to enhance the quality and result of decision and hence the chance to enhance the management of corporations.

The simplest definition for Intelligent Decision Support system is

IDSS=DSS +AI

There must be three characteristics which must be reflected in any Intelligent Decision Support System:

1. It must access data from varied available sources.
2. It must facilitate the development of a new model of the across selection process.
3. It provides a GUI (Good User Interface) through which end users can easily search and find out across the web.

ARTIFICIAL INTELLIGENCE AND EDUCATION SYSTEM

Education is one of the one amongst the foremost important issues all over the world. Education plays a critical role in preparing the students and new generation future ready which can use artificial intelligence for the new development. Bridging the gap between AI skills and the education goes beyond the adoption of technologies to facilitate ease out and helpful in learning. It also means redesigning, rethinking the content and methods delivered across all level of educational institution. The objective of any higher education institution is to provide knowledge at that particular point of time. This context can be taken as comprehensive scenario involving to get higher number of students as enrolment one over the other. Now a day's, IDSS is adopted gradually by almost all kind of institutions as the most efficient tool to deal with any kind of situation, where efficiency is the prerequisite to take any decision. Decision support systems (DSS) uses artificial intelligence (AI) methods to efficiently solve problems that are cannot be normally solved by using any formal techniques. In this context, technologies such as the Semantic Web, linked data, big data, and machine learning are such examples which provide collective support for institutions and organizations to make decisions more rationally.

The current need to rapid developments in all fields of education and AI exerts itself. Nowadays Government is trying to adopt new means and measures to fill the gap between what is taught through books and what is the requirement of industry. Artificial Intelligence (Ai) is mow becoming a tool for every country to grow in the field of research and development and practice with the new upcoming technologies. Decisions are required at every stage from seeking admission searching college or university knowing the procedure and getting into it. But it all comes later on. First and foremost is "what is the best decision according to the ability of the student presently in the current Environment for the future prospects" Children are more prone to screen time which is very harmful for their personal growth and this a topic of worry among educators, psychologists, and parents, but on the other hand artificial Intelligence is now becoming hands on tools for the new learning even in the disasters situations online learning is the only method which does not hinder the path of knowledge and is helpful for the children.

Artificial Intelligence (AI) can easily automate various necessary activities of Education like grading, finding out areas of Improvement; Tutors which are artificially created can help students even at distance places in real time anywhere and at any place. AI has a great scope in the feedback system both for the students and the educators. Feedback works only when it is given in constructive manner and on time. With the Help of Artificial Intelligence Feedback collection and analysis time can reduced to the minimum in order that it becomes more useful.

Communication with a computer, instead of a physical speaker, can make students feel motivated about asking questions. "When students practice speaking with native speakers, nobody tells them how they did," said Zhou. With this new communication technology, learners get immediate feedback where they have committed the mistakes which can easily be rectified without any shame and embarrassment they what other will think about their mistakes.

Whatever we have taught about Education Medium Artificial Intelligence (AI) has totally changed the way it seems to be. The Human Computer Interaction in term of teaching learning process cannot totally replace the need of the teacher but can surely assist the teacher in much desired way of research and development. Use of AI in Education (for better or worse) is a matter of research and how it is used in the Education Industry. Student can learn from anywhere and anytime with his own ease to get the knowledge and thus declining the proper structure of school or college or even the higher Education. But the value added things like personality development, behavioural change, co-curricular activities, discipline and living a well life which comes automatically along with the education will be missed through this platform of teaching. But in the near future AI has the power to replace almost everything which we have taken as granted. We are already on the way to future of education. Not only the education but many administrative routine tasks can also be very easily handled by this technology as varying from filling the forms to admission, taking tests, giving virtual tours, evaluating answer sheets making reports and suggestions for the betterment.

ARTIFICIAL INTELLIGENCE IN INDIA

According to the statistics given by the Human Resource & Development (HRD) Ministry of India in 2016, there is a shortage of 1 million teachers across the country. India is a country which is wide spread over leaps and bounds and distributed across the small villages and streets. India with the population of 133 crores need access to each and every part of country everywhere its not possible to reach the students

Figure 1.

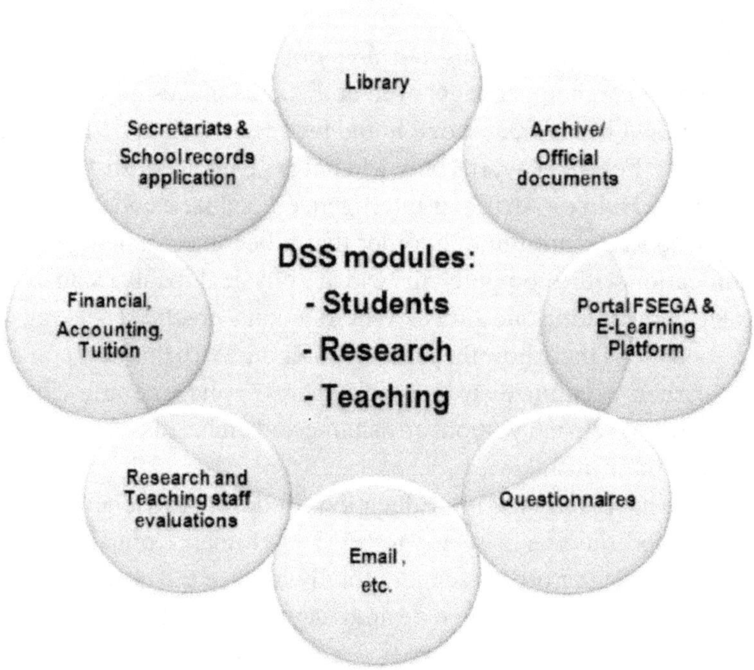

with such a shortage of teachers. The only solution of this problem is an education which is inclusive and brings even the most distant student under one umbrella. The student sitting in far village of Andaman and Nicobar can easily access the lectures going on the National Capital Region. AI has given the solution of less number of teachers along with the inclusive education to all. In the country like India where even after education making a fundamental right everyone is not inclined towards education but is more interested in learning livelihood. AI gives the solution for all by providing the education to all those who need it but can't afford it to have to travel distance and the physical structure is not available nearby to their area. Human Computer Interaction can bring boom the Education Industry serving mankind to all.

Artificial Intelligence Helps Education Industry in Many Different Ways

1. **Personalise Learning**: All the scholars have different aptitude, learning skill and orientation. With the assistance of AI only that content is delivered which is required and suited to the scholar. It totally denies the common content availability for all the students as in the traditional learning process. In a

classroom of 60 or 50 students where a teacher teaches it is on a particular pace and speed. But the need of each and every student is different and here comes the importance of AI technologies. Each and every student has different learning and grasping abilities. A single teacher can only teach guide and motivate the students but not capable enough to full fill needs of each and every student It can also determine any student strengths and weaknesses. This kind of blended education system helps students at different levels along with the teaching in one classroom, with AI facilitating the learning, education and offering support to any kind of student wherever required during the existing process of teaching and learning. Generally students have the tendency not to speak up in front of the teachers as they feel shy or insulted for not knowing the simple and straightforward contents. AI helps to get rid of their personal doubts without knowing others which build up their confidence as well. Nowadays student spend their most of time on the screen. They prefer sitting and continuously using their own/ parents' Smartphone or tablets. Besides only playing games if that screen time can utilise in the teaching learning solution it will be beneficial as a two way sword making learning interesting and reducing time wastage.

2. **Smart Classrooms**: Smart classrooms are the big examples of AI technology where face to face and online interactions are both present in a more hybrid manner. Smart Classrooms shows an enormous development in the recent era. When education isn't possible for the students who are into the remote area smart classrooms helps in teaching which is extremely similar like actual teaching within the classroom. It promotes face to face interaction as same of traditional learning teaching pedagogies. Even it is not interrupted by any of the physical hindrance like disaster, epidemic, distance, non-availability of teachers in remote areas, and the specialized knowledge of a particular subject. Smart classrooms doesn't means that all the students are called together a teacher teaches as per the prescribed syllabus and students are ready for the exams, rather than smart classroom helps in developing the personalised plan as per the requirement of each and every students' need so that he can cope up with everybody.
3. **Smart Campus**: Monitoring Attendance, automatically monitor and control over every facility, parking area, building alarms, room utilization, lighting and heating facility etc are easily monitored and controlled through the smart AI. Each and every instruction is to tend to students, teachers, members and therefore the workers in any university or college for the management. Biometric attendance may be a quite Narrow AI where automatically it calculates the stay time of any employee or student within the campus without giving misleading results. Attendance now can easily be managed by the AI without any pressure

either by the management or the students over any faculty and also it shows the transparency by giving the actual results what they have and removing biasness of any human for the favouritism. Many management things required within the campus like either lighting switch off or cut, parking at their own respective places in order to avoid jam or any other type of cruise, which class is to be taken at which allotted class-rooms or any other facility which is to be provided all across the Campus. Artificial Intelligence here plays a crucial role by helping and providing assistance to all or any of these works by reducing work burden and saving time as well. Initially Technology seems costlier than using humans to work but in later stages its cost becomes negligible and even recover its cost as well. Any technology takes a cost of installation and training but once its done its provide much more benefit. Schools can utilize this AI technology it its own need based way like giving direction to the students within the campus itself where to go in a much complicated corridor, even its helpful in allocating the seats in any of the crowded event. The expenditure so occurred will be much lesser than actually paying for the people and the task will be done even in much easier way without any cumbersome situation making it easier to perform.

4. **Great Customer Service**: Customers are treated as God. In any Educational institution nowadays even students are taken as Customers along with the parents who are coming to the college with a dream that his child will become a big picture one day. But there are certain points which are needed to be clear at one time or the other but most of time there queries are undone or even the teachers and working staff are unable and also not available to answer the question of each and every student/parent. AI comes into the scenario which work as personal assistant and can easily help all the customers even sitting at home. Queries like admission time, admission list, time table, questions on the topic and final expenditure, upcoming events, extracurricular activities going on it college, various committees which are made to help the student are easily made available with the help of AI.
5. **Up gradation of Course curriculum**: Course curriculum is designed by the university which is followed by the teachers to deliver the lectures to the students. Every student is different from one another and so its understanding level. Teacher and the students have to build the gap in between the structure so designed and to the understanding. University also needs suggestion to improve and enhance the curriculum as per the requirement of the industry and the students. This AI technique reviews the adaptive technique as per the requirements of the students and suggests time to time changes required for the up gradation of the curriculum. Feedback is the process which is very crucial in the process of learning. In a face to face teaching process once the lecture

is delivered student has to wait for the feedback and queries and University has to wait for the suggestion to improve its curriculum. Sometimes students remain confused even after explaining are the concepts and unable to get the concepts which is easily cleared out by the help of Artificial Intelligence. AI(Artificial Intelligence) serves the AI should be a critical element of any STEM (Science Technology Engineering and Mathematics) curriculum. Human Computer Interaction is the need of the hour and is already present in the way of supplemental model way of teaching and learning process.

6. **Monitoring Performance of latest researches**: Patents and copyrights are the intellectual property of any University and the country as a whole. Researchers are done by the young mind which can think out of the box but they also need the help of technology for practical implementing the researches. How the researches are done, what is the quality of the research and keeping record of the previous research for the help of future students with the help of block chain technology helps in monitoring the Performance.
7. **Virtual Counsellors**: Virtual Counsellors are available in various of interaction styles, various voice wearable, humanoid robotics etc. They all help in various segments starting with the various course selection, course engagement and course completion. All the queries every time cannot be handled by the counsellors so appointed. Virtual Counsellors created with the help of technology can serve the purpose 24X7 without any human intervention.
8. **Boon for the Teachers:** Teachers are the community which enlighten the path of others by showing them the correct way. Many people live with the fear that with the development of Technology which can easily do the work of teachers and can easily replace the teachers. This fear leads them to the non acceptability of the new technology. Besides only teaching teachers have to do various monotonous jobs like paper setting, creating mark sheets, evaluation, assessment, grading, examination duties, making records, admissions which curbs their most of time and efficiency and they are unable to focus fully on their research activities. . AI can help the teachers in a very easy way in performing these routine tasks intelligently. Whereas when we talk about Technology it can perform all the functions logically or algorithmically but cannot connect to any other human emotionally or psychologically which is also a need of education. Thus a flipped way of both the teachers and the technology helps in further research and guidance to the students. In his blended or supplemental model teachers will always remain in the frontline of teaching process and the technology will assist the through the backend thereby giving them more time for the work like research and development. Knowledge transmission does not only involve whatever is set or written is to be given to the students rather it is a connection between the teachers and the students in a cognitive, social

psychological and emotional aspect where the teacher does not remain only teacher but becomes a mentor or a guide which is responsible for the overall development of the their mentees or learners as a whole.

Even in the case of Distance Education where demand of teachers are high but their physical movement is not possible every time from one place to another AI gives them hand on experience and a quality learning to the students who are keen to learn better. Mode of learning is also changing from delivering lectures than self studying first with the help of given material understanding and then asking questions from the teachers which is helpful to clear their doubts. This method of technology assistant teaching not only helps the teacher but also the students to think and require something new which is helpful in further research.

9. **Education for all:** India has always promoted the policy of Education for all. Education is the fundamental right lies in the constitution of India. This gives the right to study the basic education for every child. But education should be all accessible and inclusive for each and every child. When there is a shortage of Teachers in country Like India technology serves the purpose of providing accessible and inclusive education to even the rural students who otherwise don't have the access and facilities available unlike urban region students who have the availability of both physical and artificial teachers along with them. The main ones include
    a. Hardware-Desktop/laptop/mobile phone
    b. Proper Connection of Internet and its speed
    c. Cost which is to bear for getting Internet Connection.
    d. Students should have a basic knowledge of using Hardware and Software
    e. Means of Communication like language
    f. Availability of Content on the topics to be taught.
10. **Online Invigilation over Remote Areas**: After teaching next comes the time of knowledge testing earned by the students. Examination is a tedious process where Invigilation or Proctoring is an Integral part. On above that Remote Proctoring is again a tough task . Physical teaching and examination is normal process but Technology play important role where examinations are to be evaluated at a distance place using Web cam, computer system and obviously with the help of artificial Intelligence.
11. **Answer Sheet Evaluation**: Evaluation of Answer sheets is again painful for the Teachers eternity. Collecting them at one particular place, evaluating them confidentially and without any discrimination is must for any Higher Education University. Artificial Intelligence here plays a crucial role by taking the exam and evaluating the answer sheet of objective type questions. Although research

is also going on for the evaluation of subjective type answer sheets which will help students not to migrate from their native places even for the sake of giving examination to the nearby nodal centers.

12. **Adaptive Teaching:** This is also known as an educational method where a set of computer algorithm is prepared to deliver the contents and satisfy unique need of each learner. It changes to transform the learner from a passive mode of just receiving what is taught to them to be an active member in the educational process. In this learning method a program is designed first along with its ambition level it will achieve which is adaptable to the environment rather than finding out its scope after coming out with degree and then finding out its adaption in the market. In the traditional method where plan and budgets are made first, in any adaptive programming value for money and all other technical support have adaptive approach to be integrated to the environment and providing facilities to get the work done.
13. **Analysis of Feedback:** Feedback is process of knowing the outcome from the audience for which the teachers are delivering he lecture. Feedback can be both Positive or negative. Positive Feedback gives Simulation to maintain the working and Negative Feedback gives motivation to improve. But this Process can only be helpful if its analysis is done honestly which is not biased and it can only be done honestly by the machine and not by the humans. Humans psychologically take the things about themselves through the glasses of their own perception. Thus an honest analysis of Feedback not only helps students and the teachers to improve but also to the entire curriculum to meet the demands of current scenario and the industry as a whole. This is very helpful in the teaching learning process which not only tells the truth but also user doesn't feel embarrassed anything hard about himself in front of the computer . Thus analysis of Feedback is quite beneficial advantage of technology in the whole process.

Bill Gates has quoted "*The idea that you could talk to an [virtual] advisor that would understand different misconceptions and arbitrary linguistics around it, that'll certainly come in the next decade. And they'll be a very nice supplement and the beauty of this is it could be completely free.*"

EXAMPLES OF ARTIFICIAL INTELLIGENCE IN EDUCATION

With the development of Artificial Intelligence Education Industry is also growing into technology equipped world where everything can be done online. It has totally disseminated the need of physical presence for any kind of training and the geographical distance to learn something. Following are the some examples of various platforms given on the web which are helpful in the Education Sector. These are just few examples many more are available as per the need of the user.

- **Cram101** (Content Technologies INC.) This platform is helpful in breaking the text of the text books into smaller sections which can be read easily and for practice various fill in the blanks true false and short questions are also available.
- **Facts101:** This platform provides the summary of each and every chapter into a digital form and is easily available to the end users.
- **Netex Learning**: This platform provides online teaching assistance in the form of Audio or Video lectures. It also provides to develop their own learning management system which can train the employees of any organisation through lectures conferences learning modules etc.
- **Carneige Learning 's Mika Software**: This software is best suited for the feedback analysis. It provides the feedback to the new coming generation about the activities, their drawbacks and any remedial courses if they require in any point of time
- **Solutions such as the Presentation Translator**: This is helpful in remote teaching and learning process. If for any reason a student is unable to attend the physical classes this software provides the instructions as well as all the lectures at their own place to provide education.
- **Thinker Math:** Mathematics is a subject from which many students are scared off. This software is boon for them; it relates the maths curriculum with the real life situation so that the concepts are easily understood even by the kids of young age. During solving the problem if any student is stuck off at any particular place it gives immediately the real time feedback and much suggestion to improve and overcome the problem. This is a very popular platform among students which combines professional teaching with the AI technology to make Mathematics much simpler and easier to use.
- **Brainly:** As the name signifies this software works as collaborative software between the students. They can communicate ask questions solve problems work together many activities and can verify answers from the fellow students.

OUR FUTURE TALENT

Life is a practical teacher which takes the exam first and then teaches the lesson. Whatever is taught during school and college education unless and until not applied into actual practice is no use. Many researches show that by the end of 2030 industries are prone to AI technology and it will become their part of it. So in order to make our future generation ready to be a smart workforce there are two basic characteristics one has to learn

Well aware with the use of AI technology and using it in a manner it is required.

Work as a tea, where they altogether can solve the problems by combining together and helping each other in a team.

Now kids are well aware about the digital world with their birth only. Smart phones and tablets are no longer havoc for them, they can easily play games, videos and even can create their own even before going to the school. AI syllabus in a well integrated form with the school and college curriculum not only help students to make new experiments and make new developments which will make out future generation ready for the work in well needed manner for the industry.

CHALLENGES OF USING ARTIFICIAL INTELLIGENCE

With every opportunity there comes a challenge with a free gift to fight with it and learn something new

The first and foremost need and challenge of Artificial Intelligence is Data. There is a basic principle GIGO "Garbage In and Garbage out" that simply means whatever data is provided to the system analysis is done the basis of that data only. So selecting, verifying and validating data is the most tedious challenge to use AI properly.

The second challenge is that any algorithm which is designed can be used only for a pre determined and defined task. Beyond the so set well defined algorithm a computer cannot do any other task. A health care system cannot calculate tax. An algorithm defined to drive car cannot play chess because it is not defined to do so.

The third challenge is difference of technological development in various parts of the world. Most developed countries have very easy access to the new technology whereas the developing countries will face the basic need of non availability of Infrastructure which helps in the AI technology. So the difference of learning will always be there.

The fourth challenge is to prepare teachers. Teaching learning process will be incomplete unless and until the teacher is not well trained into the AI technology. A teacher who knows how to use the technology well can only develop the real time solutions for the environment and for the learners as a whole. A well equipped teacher can only prepare the future workforce.

The fifth challenge is of Research. Research is an integral and very important aspect of any education. Research not only shows the path of new experiments and developments but also leads to the growth of overall country. Creating a think tank and research repository is a must in this field if proper research is conducted with the help of artificial Intelligence knowledge system. Future generation will only be ready if he it is trained in the future technology. Where research is not done, doors to new development are closed, mind is burdened only with the history and unable to try something new which not only minimize the cost but also moves the country as the front leader of the world.

The sixth challenge deals with ethics, accountability, transparency and security of data collection and the knowledge system. Data taken from any source is concerned with copyright and patents issue. From where data is taken need the permission to be accessed and used by some other person as a whole. Data privacy and ownership of data feeding algorithms makes security of data a big challenge in front of the users who are developing and using the data for application and any platform. There are various situations one has to take decisions regarding data ownership and ethically using the data for common purpose. Using and implementing data without validating make create legal issues causing and attracting for the penalty and thereby abiding the rules and making the new developments.

In other words thorns are there to protect the flowers. Similarly Challenges are there to face and finding the new solutions. A single learning module system cannot help to do any variation in the situation which is always possible in real life time. Whatever is planned and designed in a particular situation with the help of given set of algorithms will not change automatically or adjust according to the variations. An algorithm designed to drive a car with auto pilot will not change if suddenly the GPS system fails and a sudden road block if it is not reported by the technology. In the Education process there is a huge gap between the present and future generation. This teaching generation is learning this AI technology as early as from 2001 where the future generation is well equipped with this technology from the birth only. In the technology world previously the generation was changing in the 50 years than comes to 20 and now the technology will change only in 6 years equivalent to 50 years of change. It simply signifies than one has to learn adapt and improve oneself as fast as the technology is changing in order to move the fast changing world.

WHAT WOULD YOU CHOOSE?

If you had the option of choosing between a pre-set menu that's generic or enjoying a meal that's been customized just for your particular taste buds, what would you prefer?

Traditional learning method is somewhere failing to serve its purpose to teach the students as per their need of the future generation. Holding Students back at the places where teaching is going on but students are not aware about the learning is a tedious task. Especially where there is no modification in the teaching procedure. It leads to children dropping out. Elementary School education is must for all the students but when they fail to learn they are declared as Failure in a very early stage and are detained from learning and going to school for exploring the world. A student-driven approach toward education boosts retention and encourages each individual to learn how to apply concepts to trouble-shoot real issues happening in the world. Teaching only by lecture and chalk duster method is no longer acceptable to the students anymore. They are fast changing generation. If any lecture is to be completed into one hour they want to finish it as fast as within 20 minutes of span time. Artificial Intelligence satisfies and gives challenges to the intelligence of the new tech learners thereby exploring and experimenting the new world.

CONCLUSION

Learning with the help of Artificial Intelligence helps student personally by showing their progress bar and giving individualized feedback thereby creating interest in their personal studies. The ethical development of such innovations will require both teachers and students to have a robust understanding of how to work with data and AI to support their participation in society and across the professions. Taken into consideration that there are often multiple answers to a problem and several paths to arrive there - we call this non-linear learning. Such a form of learning helps a student develop knowledge along with the ability to think at both an individual and group-level, while fine-tuning skills and touching upon academic, social and emotional facets. In short, it is much more wholesome. A simplistic, traditional, archaic learning model that lacks vision cannot enable today's generation of students to be thought leaders who solve the complex problems of the world. Learning must change to serve an actual purpose that is societal relevant. Learning not only enables the actual purpose of only feeding the pre determine set of instructions but it leads to exploring the new world where curiosity and experiments makes the learning fun and easy to learn rather than a boredom process. Physical teaching learning process cannot be replaced by any Artificial Intelligence nut a blend of both with the help of Supplemental model can bring the whole change for this generation which gives Education System a new Boon to the Education Industry which will ready the new generation workforce.

REFERENCES

Haugeland. (1985). *Artificial Intelligence: The Very Idea*. MIT Press.

Laanpere, M., Pata, K., Normak, P., & Põldoja, H. (2014). Pedagogy-driven Design of Digital Learning Ecosystems. *Computer Science and Information Systems*, *11*(1), 419–442. doi:10.2298/CSIS121204015L

Yadav, A. (2016). Computational Thinking as an Emerging Competence Domain. In M. Mulder (Ed.), *Competence-Based Vocational and Professional Education: Bridging the Worlds of Work and Education* (pp. 1051–1067). Springer International Publishing AG.

Zhong, Y. (2006). A Cognitive Approach to Artificial Intelligence Research. *International Conference on Cognitive Informatics*. 10.1109/COGINF.2006.365682

Chapter 3
Technology-Enabled Education:
Paradigm Shift in Higher Education

Poonam jatwani
Government College for Women, Faridabad, India

Pradeep Tomar
Gautam Buddha University, India

Vandana Dhingra
Department of Technology, Savitribai Phule Pune University, Maharashtra, India

ABSTRACT

The Government of India has especially focused on artificial intelligence and machine learning-based courses in the higher education system as they have realized that the strength of India lies in higher education. Keeping in view the importance of technology in bringing a paradigm shift in the education sector, the Ministry of Human Resource Development (MHRD) is putting continuous efforts to give a push to digitize higher education. In this chapter, the authors have studied various initiatives taken by the Indian government to promote digital education in higher education by imparting artificial intelligence. By developing techniques and algorithms using AI, one can impart basic cognitive skills of teachers to computers; by this, one can delegate some teaching to machines and thus improve educational outcomes. Online digital learning will play an important role in transforming Ancient India into Digital India.

DOI: 10.4018/978-1-7998-4763-2.ch003

INTRODUCTION

The society is moving fast from the industrial age towards the information age. The impact of technology can be seen in many fields like industry, hospitals, banks, agriculture, weather forecasting, politics, commerce and education etc. One must agree that technology has grabbed the whole world in its fists and has affected every person in our society.

Way back in the 20th Century, an educated person was he who could read and write. But now, the up-gradation of technology particularly Machine-learning and Artificial Intelligence is conquering the whole world, so the definition has changed to those who can read, write and at the same time are computer literate and the complexity of acquiring education is no longer achievable within the closed boundaries of a classroom. Education (Nayor, 1982) is a social process that is deemed to develop desirable qualities and traits in people. The need and capability to acquire these qualities vary with time, place, and technology. Education is thus a process which apart from acquiring certain skills, also helps in using them efficiently in a relevant context and with understanding. During the last 20 years, the importance of education has increased in all the most every walk of life. With the support of AI and ICT as in the current environment-conscious world importance of education and acceptability of AI have emerged as a social necessity.

Although the use of AI in the education sector in India is not very old, it has picked up very fast. Today using this new platform of digital learning, meticulously planned virtual classes are being conducted throughout the country by the ever sincere teachers that have enabled the young learners to connect with their teachers and classmates from the comfort of their homes. Through these technologies- enabled classes all possible efforts are being made to reach out to the students with academic input. Parents have the opportunity not only to monitor and supervise but also to get a direct insight into the teaching-learning process is carried out on this virtual platform. It is a new experience and a new way of learning. To make learning easy PPT with text can be shared on a specific app from where it can be downloaded easily. App can be accessed by laptop, mobile phone, or desktop.

Higher education can better inculcate knowledge among the students through the e-Learning process and virtual classes. Keeping all this in view, today's Government, as well as institutions, have started formulating the policies for the better use of digital learning so that education does not take a backseat. This new environment will enable teachers and learners to continue to interact with each other and will also ensure that children are actively and meaningfully engaged. Higher education has a social responsibility to be proactive in the efforts towards incorporating digital age skills as education must be relevant in changing local, national, and global contexts.

The introduction of new technologies in learning and teaching, especially AI and machine learning, can be seen as offering teachers powerful tools for the design and implementation of learning. The convergence of technologies has made learning more lucrative, and information provided as the computer is now linked with many more media like sound, 3-dimensional graphics, animation, live video clips, and the Web. AI algorithms have the potential to solve many educational problems. For its successful implementation, there is always a need to experience new tools, devising strategies, redesigning their pedagogies, and even revamping their schedules. As an educationist, I ardently believe that we are in the most dynamic space with rapid changes, altering our views and perspectives.

HISTORY OF EDUCATIONAL USES OF COMPUTERS

The first use of computers in the educational sector was seen in 1950 with a computer-driven flight simulator used to train pilots of MIT, USA.

The first attempt to use computers with school children was made in 1959 when the IBM team reported a program to teach binary arithmetic to New York Elementary School students via a "typewriter inquiry station" connected to an IBM 650 computer.

In 1960 the University of Illinois and Control Data Corporation started a project PLATO (Programmed Logic for Automatic Teacher Operations) having several adult education applications. PLATO project makes CBI available at many schools.

Another educational use of computers as evidenced by the development of LOGO language during the 1970s by Papert and his colleagues at the Massachusetts Institute of Technology (MIT) in the USA. LOGO helps in developing computer programs and also trains persons to think analytically and logically.

In the 1970s portable computers having time-sharing operating system was designed that need less power, were very cheap and were of small size. Such types of computers were made available by the government in schools of France, the U.K. and in the US.

With time, more user-friendly software's were developed. Due to distributed data processing and development in data communication, Computers were adopted in schools on a large scale (Lockard, 1987).

The period from 1960 to 1980 was identified by time-sharing activities offered by universities and instructional computing projects, which were developed on large scale mainframe systems. Many microcomputers were purchased by educational institutions for research and administrative functions such as accounting, payroll, and inventory control (Ratho, 1995).

In the meanwhile, television was invented. In 1975, the Satellite Instructional Television Experiment (SITE) started to telecast educational programs with the help of television in India. Television made learning very entertaining and was easily available for mass education.

The 90's seen the proliferation of personal computers (Bitter, 1989). Many application softwares were designed which further added impetus to this proliferation. With this computer were introduced at all levels of the education system.

The concept of intelligence machine was given by Sidney Pressey of Ohio State University in 1924 (Fry,1960) and a mechanical teaching machine was created to instruct students without a human teacher.

ROLE OF HIGHER EDUCATION IN SHAPING INDIA GROWTH

Today India is capable to help the institutions in their journey to achieve their vision and become better by aligning their best practices with national and international standards. Knowledge, coupled with creativity and innovation is the most powerful currency that Universities and higher education institutes create and contribute to society and nation. Today it is important to follow the emerging Technological Trends that are shaping the future educational landscape. Enough latest interactive teaching is changing the role of education with the introduction of multimedia, and an innovative effort of an institution helps in its academic excellence.

At the university stage, students can pursue their further studies-general or professional education. It gives students the facility to engage vigorously and fearlessly in the pursuit of truth, interpret old knowledge and beliefs in the light of new needs and discoveries, and promote leadership qualities to lead their life. Universities also have the function of supplying society with competent men and women, well-versed and fully expert and well-skilled professional in every domain. Apart from teaching and training, universities also do several tasks related to research and dissemination (Gore, 1994).

The role of higher education is significant in human resource development and capacity building of individuals, to cater to the needs of the economy, society, and the country as a whole, thereby, contributing to the development of the nation. Higher educational institutes have the capacity as well as capability to adapt to changes. Online digital learning will play an important role in transforming ancient India into Digital India. It will change the ways of teaching and learning. With a change in time, the field of education is also undergoing a transformation.

Online digital learning and virtual classes are very effective to enhance the higher education scenario in the coming generation. It would also help in rising Gross Enrolment Ratio (GER) in higher education along with employment benefits. It is a new experience and a new way of learning which saves time for learner. Distant students can easily avail education. There is no age limit of learners. Students can take help and use resources anytime. Online learning is more effective because it is accompanied by various teaching aids. e-learning is free from boring lecture methods, it includes other methods like demonstration project methods and audio-visual effects.

DEVELOPMENT OF COMPUTER AND ARTIFICIAL INTELLIGENCE-BASED EDUCATION

To improve learning outcomes, computers were introduced in the education system but many educators having a fear of replacement of teachers with computers oppose its usage. But their answer was criticised and teachers were given an assurance that upcoming software would improve the teaching-learning process by deallocating the routine instructional presentation, drill, and practice duties from teachers to machines. By doing so, the teacher would be free and have more time to interact with students. Keeping this in mind, various instructional programs were designed. Some of which are given below:

Computer Aided Instruction (CAI)

The objective of Computer-aided instruction is to improve academic performance (Criswell, 1989). CAI programs provide study material, well-presented notes, and tutorials on the internet to enhance learning outcomes. Tutorial in the form of text, graphics, sound, video to facilitate instruction. CAI promotes self-directed learning among students. A lot of data and tutorial is available on the web but what to learn and when to learn is the choice of individual learner. Various worksheets, test, multiple choice questions, games and feedback form are based on CAI. There is no need to have a good command of programming languages. With a little knowledge about computer handling one can use CAI package easily. Suppose after reading a particular tutorial if a student wants to check his performance, this can be easily done using CAI. First of all, the computer ask a question based on that tutorial one at a time. The student submits his answer, if the answer is correct then only student is given the next question. But if the answer is incorrect in that scenario software will skip complicated questions until students show mastery in a particular topic. In this way, CAI programs are helpful to summarize student performance.

Advantages of CAI:

- Students at CAI terminals can proceed through lessons at their own rate.
- Student has to learn alone.

- Individualised instruction is good for the slow learner as well as for bright students.
- Promote self-learning habit and one can use it as per his convenience.
- Helpful to reduce the extra workload of teachers where there is a shortage of staff.
- Experiments of biology and chemistry subjects can be effectively conducted using CAI.
- Evaluation of specific lessons is independently handled.

Computer Managed Instruction (CMI)

CMI is used to enhance learning by providing automated management of elements of the student's learning environment. CMI systems help teachers in their task of controlling and managing the content, pace, sequence, and method of learning of the students in their charge. The developed software is used to gather data of students and generate objective tests. The result is provided by calculating marks that is used for diagnostic or assessment purposes. It also accepts the results of tests marked subjectively by teachers and analyses the performance of tests. The computer provides feedback to an individual student on test performance. As there is no relationship of pupil-teacher so the concept cannot be understood without the help of instruction easily.

Advantages of CMI:

- Teaching remains incomplete in the absence of evaluation. Keeping this in mind CMI provides a mechanism for the evaluation and assessment of the students.
- Saves time of learner.
- Online learning is not too expensive.

Intelligent Tutoring System (ITS)

There are many problems that can be solved by skills that are exhibited by humans only. To solve such problems skills like creativity, common sense, insight, self-awareness, and imagination are required. Artificial Intelligence (Siau,2018) is the intelligence exhibited by a machine or software, and the learning systems based on AI techniques is known as Intelligent Tutoring Systems. It is a software program in which human intelligence and knowledge have been incorporated into machines. With this rising requirements, ITS has been designed. The central goal of ITS is to impart the learning capabilities of a human being to machines. Therefore, ITS (Bill,

2017) are programs designed to teach as a good teacher would. Internet packages are nowadays so costly. Slow internet speed is the biggest failure of online learning.

Advantages of ITS:

- It gives instructions to the learners without involving a human teacher.
- ITS can impart artificial intelligence concepts, knowledge representation and communication strategies to monitor response, to analyse answers of the question submitted either it is right or wrong, to check student progress, to find why a student is making an error and to evaluate in which areas the student is lagging behind.
- The amalgamation of intelligence in the teaching process converts learning more responsive and interactive.

WHERE ARE WE TODAY?

In the traditional model of education, a special building is dedicated to teaching and learning. Children from far and wide reach the school every morning. On their way, they laugh, play, and have so much fun. Children also enjoy while going together, laughing, joking, playing, and teasing each other. The students of the same age group study together in their respective classrooms. Their teacher is a real person who makes them sit together and teaches them the same topic. For creating interest and capturing concentration, teachers give them homework, and questions are asked in the class from the study books of common curriculum. They play together and help each other in their home assignments too. It makes learning easy and interesting. The building of educational premises provides such a healthy environment where the students grow by sharing and informally interacting with each other. They get an opportunity to share their experiences and help each other. The time table is well organized and provides exposure to learn other skills in a fun way. There are numerous activities and competitions in the school. Children participate and there is clear physical and mental development among them. Students participate with full enthusiasm in extra-curricular activities and learn a lot of skills like tolerance, cooperation, and adjustment in an enjoyable way.

Digital education is completely different from traditional education. For digital education, no special building is required. Students study online by sitting inside the comfort of one's houses. Each student has to sit on a computer in a room in their respective houses and study alone using the internet. A computer has millions of books. Reading is done on a screen that displays movable text. PPT, e-content, notes, tutorial, audio, and video lectures, e-books are available on the web that can be accessed freely by many students. It is an age of automation, mechanization, digitalization, and computerization.

But with the passage of time, creative and innovative application of machine learning and AI has improved both access to education and the quality of that education. Nowadays the internet plays a very vital role in the process of empowering technology in educational activities. According to recent studies, it has been observed that innovations like Twitter to communicate messages and YouTube in sharing video information have proved helpful in the dissemination of education. Social networking sites like Facebook are emerging as a compelling platform to encourage language development, interpersonal communication (interpersonal skills development in digital format), group collaboration (By engaging with "friends" in which one can collaborate with others in groups), and of course, ICT skills improvement (students gain ICT skills without the need for boring step-by-step instruction but learn by their own).

Usage of multimedia tools in education has resulted in increased productivity and retention rates because people remember 20% of what they see, 40% of what they see and hear, but about 75% of what they see, hear and do simultaneously. The concept of online learning called the virtual classroom, which contains all the course material, has made it possible for the learner to create meaningful and constructivist learning environments. Students can enroll online and participate in any country in the world with internet access. Machine learning and AI-based applications are promoting open and distance learning (ODL) courses to fulfill the requirements of learners. With the help of AI technology, smart education has been developed which is a more effective, efficient, flexible, and comfortable way of learning (Ziu, 2016).

Education is not mere accumulation of information. Educational institutes take the responsibility to not only educate the children but also to take care that the children develop their social skills and feel confident in the classroom. Computerization can certainly help gain information in a better way but schooling is much more than acquiring facts. It is life experience where children interact with others, have fun, and learn the values of sharing and caring. Students move out from their houses to reach school and study together the same curriculum in the same room by the same teacher. Students sit together in the classroom, go home together, learn the same things, help one another with the homework, and talk about it. Thus give them a chance to grow together. But in today's time technology has brought a lot of advancement through this new platform of online classes. Digital teaching is done through online pre-recorded lectures, online submission, and doubt solving sessions. There are lots of online courses available for students. Online learning is required because of geographical location, hectic working style, medical and financial condition, and can help to upgrade one's existing qualification. However, internet bandwidth is an essential pre-requisite for online education. To provide quality internet at an affordable price to all the students wherever they are being a big challenge. It is less capable than human tutors in areas of dialogue and feedback. It is expensive both to develop and implement e-content. Due to budget and time constraints, it is not commercially feasible for real-world application. Evolution is time-consuming and difficult. Classroom interaction is missing. Human teachers encourage and motivate the children in many ways which are lacking in digital learning.

Blended online learning is a balanced mix of traditional face to face instructional activities with an appropriately designed online experience. In effective delivery of content approximately 25% credit goes through online mode. Technology cannot replace great teachers. But, technology in the hands of great teachers can bring digital transformation.

TEACHING WITH TECHNOLOGY

The major benefits of incorporating technologies in teaching are:

- **Growth:** e-Learning is through computer software using the internet in a virtual classroom. Teachers prepare PPT and develop e-content using a lot of ICT tools for teaching. Although it takes a long preparation time to deliver quality content but in this way, teachers are becoming more technology savvy. They can share their ideas, problems with others and are aware of new upcoming tools and innovations. This is helping them to grow professionally as well as technically.
- **Digitised Archives**: E-content for various courses is now available free on the Web. It has been designed by domain experts to facilitate the teaching-learning-evaluation process.
- **Easy Access:** Difficult geographical conditions like forests, hilly terrains, floods, and other calamities make access to educational institutions difficult but online tutorial provides ease of access.
- **Development of E-Resources:** Development of e-resources has reduced the burden on finance.
- **Disabled Students:** With the help of computers, physically disabled and developmentally different students can compete with normal students.
- **Collaborative Efforts:** To develop the "world of skilled work" teachers are adopting cooperative learning strategies, group learning activities, experimental learning as well problem-based learning in which student's participation is maximum. Students are more engaged by sharing their ideas, creativity by the way of developing audio-video recordings on social media, uploading on portals as well as by creating their e-portfolio.

INITIATIVES BY MHRD FOR DIGITAL EDUCATION

In today's changing times, it is necessary to bring about a change in the Indian education system. It is imperative to incorporate digital learning in the curriculum. Keeping this in mind Indian educational institutions are making new policies to promote digital learning. During the last decade, the government of India has especially focused on the AI and machine learning-based courses in the higher education system as they have realized that the strength of India lies in higher education. Keeping in view the significance of technology in bringing a paradigm shift in the education sector, Govt of India and State Govt is putting continuous efforts. The Ministry of Human Resource Development (MHRD) has also launched various initiatives to give a push to digitalize higher education. With the help of these initatives, educational institutions have been more focused on research, undergraduate teaching, and learning and vocational training. Various policies and plans have been conceptualised and implemented by MHRD to promote digital education. Some of the digital initiatives taken by MHRD are as follows:

- **e-Adhyayan**: e-Adhyayan is a platform to provide 700+ e-Books for the Post-Graduate Courses. All the e-Books are derived from e-PG Pathshala courses. It also provides the facility to listen video content.
- **UGC-MOOCs:** UGC-MOOCs is one of the vertical to produce course on Post Graduate Subjects in SWAYAM (Study Webs of Active learning for Young Aspiring Minds). UGC is the national coordinator of SWAYAM and INFLIBNET is a technical partner for UGC-MOOCs. The portal is offering various online courses for school education and higher education. NCERT is developing course modules for MOOCs.
- **SWAYAM PRABHA:** SWAYAM PRABHA is one of the e-learning initiatives of Govt. of India. It is a collection of 32 channels that are specifically designed to telecast educational video lectures on television. It is very useful for students as e-content related to a particular course and subject is freely available on 24*7 basis. It is also available in the form of an app which can be easily downloaded in mobile through Google app. Students can check the program schedule at regular intervals to get the information at which channel, which topic will be telecasted and at what time. In this way, it is helping students to save time and money.
- **The National Digital Library:** It is a huge collection with more than 75 lakh digital books. Students can use it free of charge. The digital content is available in the form of e-books, lectures, question papers along with their solution.

- **The National Academic Depository:** It is developed to check and verify the certificates issued by institutions as per the requirement of the users.
- **e-Shodh Sindhu:** e-shodh Sindhu is a huge collection of international electronic journals and e-books to facilitate research.
- **e-Yantra:** It is designed to incorporate Robotics into engineering education with a motive to engage students in doing experiments to understand the basic theory of mathematics and computer science in solving real-life problems.
- **e-Kalpa**: It is another MHRD initiative for creating Digital-Learning Environment in India.
- **The Free and Open Source Software for Education (FOSSEE):** The objective of the FOSSEE project is to promote digital learning in educational institutes. Students can take help and use resources anytime free of cost.
- **e-Vidwan:** "Vidwan: Expert Database and National Researcher's Network" is the initiative of INFLIBNET. Its primary objective is to organize profiles of educationists, scientists, researchers, professors working in reputed educational institutes and R&D departments in India and abroad at one place.
- **Virtual Labs:** Virtual labs gives the facility to perform many experiments which are very difficult to perform in real labs due to high risk. It also saves time and maintains the curiosity and innovation among students. It helps in learning by doing method. No specially designed buildings and lab-setup are required for conducting experiments at user premises. A computer with an internet connection is sufficient to perform the experiments remotely. In this way, virtual labs are more effective than real laboratories.
- **e-Pathshala**: e-Pathshala provides NCERT books from class I to XII in different languages in the form of e-books, audio files, and videos. The high-quality e-learning material is uploaded by the ministry on this portal.
- **e-Pathya:** Distant students can easily pursue higher education using e-Pathya as there is no geographical barrier. There is also no restriction on the age limit of learners.
- **IIT Pal:** IIT Pal is online coaching platform for IIT entrance exam preparation. It is providing lectures in the subjects of chemistry, Physics and mathematics at free of cost.

CHALLENGES

However, nothing goes without difficulties faced. Educational institutes are huge buildings where a lot of activities could be carried out by students in groups. Compared to that, digital learning is too boring, mechanical, monotonous, and demanding. The slow speed of internet, expensive data package, lack of classroom fun with interaction, lack of motivation among students are some of the challenges. Online digital learning is best but from an assessment point of view, it is not satisfied. It's just one-way learning. For all those who are living in remote areas, it is not so easy to access online classes. Some people claim that the effect of multimedia, especially the video part drags the attention of the student from the content. Students should be gently introduced to the ethical issues involved in software copying. There should be no place for pirated software in schools and colleges. One big hurdle is the lack of digital infrastructure accompanied by the high cost involved and infect both the teachers and the taught are not mentally ready for the digitization of education.

CONCLUSION

Overall it can be concluded that the future of education supported by artificial intelligence looks promising especially in context with a country like India, as it will be helpful in disseminating educational content and facilitate remote learning to overcome challenges like shortage of teachers and will help to bridge and the digital divide. The purpose of using this technology in higher education is to extend human capabilities and possibilities of teaching, learning and research. The Internet came in a big way and made it possible for the people sitting on a distance to communicate. Discussion groups, real-time chatting, e-mail, telnet are some of the features of the internet, which are very useful in the field of education. Most of the institutions have put their details and journals on their website so that anyone can access this information anytime from anywhere in the world. Thus decentralized proper planning and execution of these innovative and best practices will improve the capacity and capabilities of both teachers as well as students. Although the mechanical teacher could not match the human teacher in terms of intelligence and knowledge, yet many exciting new technologies would continue to transform the world to human welfare. Wholehearted support and enthusiastic participation of educators, students, and parents can make the online teaching-learning venture successful.

REFERENCES

Barta, B.-Z., Telam, M., & Gev, Y. (Eds.). (1995). *Information Technology in Educational Management*. Chapmann and Hall. doi:10.1007/978-0-387-34839-1

Bill, F.(2017). *Intelligent Tutoring Systems: What happened?* Academic Press.

Bitter, G. G. (1989). *Micro Computers in Education Today*. Mitchel Publishing Inc.

Bruner, J. (n.d.). *The Process of Education*. Cambridge, MA: Harvard University Press.

Criswell, E. L. (1989). *The Design of Computer-Based Instruction*. Macmillan Publishing Company.

Fry, E. (1960). Teaching Machine Dichotomy: Skinner vs. Pressey. *Psychological Reports*, (6), 11-14.

Gore, M. S. (1994). *Indian Education –Structure and Process*. Rawat Publication.

Lockard, J., Peter, D. A., & Wesley, A. M. (1987). *Micro Computers for Educators*. Little Brown & Co.

Nayor, P.R., Dave, P.N., & Arora, K. (1982). *The Teacher and Education in Emerging Indian Society*. NCERT.

Ratho, T. N., & Prakash, R. (1995). *Emerging Trends in Teaching of Computer Science*. Kanishkha Publishers.

Siau, K. (2017). Impact of Artificial Intelligence, Robotics, and Automation on Higher Education. *Americas Conference on Information Systems (AMCIS 2017)*, Boston, MA.

Siau, K. (2018). Education in the age of Artificial Intelligence: How will technology shape Learning? *The Global Analyst, 7*(3), 22–24.

Zhu, Z. T., Yu, M. H., & Riezebos, P. (2016). A research framework of smart education. *Smart Learning Environments, 3*(1), 4.

Chapter 4
Artificial Intelligence in Higher Education and Learning

Chander Diwaker
https://orcid.org/0000-0002-3737-9654
UIET, Kurukshetra University, India

Atul Sharma
UIET, Kurukshetra University, India

Pradeep Tomar
Gautam Buddha University, India

ABSTRACT

Artificial intelligence is an emerging technology that is popular in education technology. AI plays a vital role to e-teaching and e-learning in higher education. In this chapter, a major focus is on exploring the wonders of the development of AI in higher education for teaching and learning processes. It analyses the educational ramifications of rising innovations in transit student learning and how organizations instruct and develop. Late inventive degrees of progress and the accelerating new headway in cutting edge training are researched to predict the future thought of cutting-edge instruction in all actuality. The role of AI in higher education is presented in detail by systematic review.

INTRODUCTION

Artificial intelligence (AI) is a division of science that is related withdeveloping smart computational machines that is capable of carry out tasks in the same manner as human intelligence. AI is an interdisciplinary region of science that can be applied

DOI: 10.4018/978-1-7998-4763-2.ch004

to various different discipline of different research area. Machine learning and deep learning are the parts of AI that play important role in visualizing different concepts of research area (Russell and Norvig 2002).

In 1956, John McCarthy presented the term, "artificial intelligence". McCarthy is known as "Father of AI". McCarthy, along with other scientists from IBM, Bell Labs, and Harvard, built the theory of programming machines to utilize language and resolve problems while progressing over time (Buchanan 2005).

ARCHITECTURE OF AI

Fig. 1 shows the usefulness of AI in different area. The major research area includes are speech, natural language processing, expert system, robotics, vision, scheduling, optimization, machine learning etc.

Figure 1. Architecture of AI
(Lucas 2017)

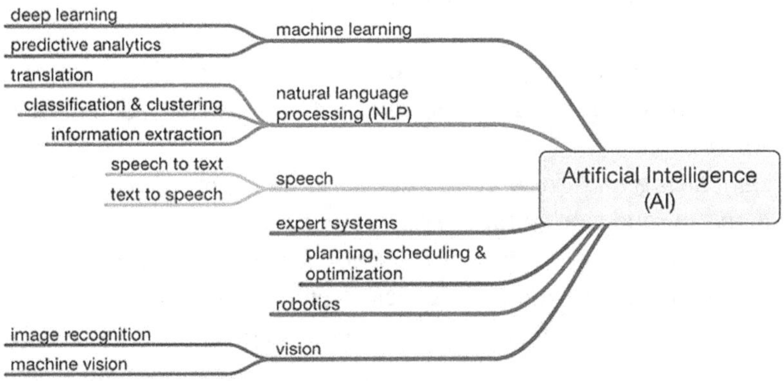

COMPONENTS OF AI

The following are the major components of AI (Arrieta et al. 2020):

1. *Fairness*: Trained data and models should be utilized to avoid unfair action of certain clusters.
2. *Robustness*: Safety and security are important factors while applying AI concepts.

3. *Explain-ability*: The decisions, rules, or suggestions must be clearly understood to users and developers.
4. *Ancestry*: The details of maintenance, deployment and development should be properly documented for future auditing and modification purposes.
5. *Cognitive Abilities*: It is capability of a machine to work like human being.
6. *Database*: The machines should have database that can easily process human query and find solution for humans.
7. *Hardware*: Graphic Processing Units (GPU) is an important part of hardware in AI for user interaction.
8. *Framework*: A good framework requires trained/learn machine to perform better for handing human queries. In present days, Azure Machine Learning Studio, R and Python are utilized.
9. *API*: There is recurrent of API to bring out AI services such as classification of text, classification of images, sentiment analysis etc.

APPLICATIONS OF AI

The various applications of AI are as follows[3]:

1. *Smart assistants*: AI helps in providing smart services like in smart home.
2. *Conversational bots for marketing and customer service*: AI helps in satisfying customer needs.
3. *Manufacturing and drone robots*: Drone robots are utilizing for controlling the activities and storing the current activities.
4. *Optimized, personalized healthcare treatment recommendations*: AI helps in human treatment for a number of deceases and recommends people accordingly.
5. *Social media monitoring tools for dangerous content or false news*: AI helps in monitoring social activities through internet and also check whether the information available through internet is genuine or not.
6. *Robo-advisors for stock trading*: AI helps in stock trading through robo-advisor.
7. *Disease mapping and prediction tools*: AI helps in mapping of different deceases and help in predicting the tools according to deceases.
8. *Spam filters on email*: AI helps in filtering harmful information while accessing internet.
9. *Song or TV show recommendations from Spotify and Netflix*: AI helps in recommendation information according to the test/interest of people accessing internet.

MACHINE LEARNING VS. DEEP LEARNING

Machine learning is an AI-based technique for building systems that learn and change based on experience such as evaluating creative work, operating self-driving cars, developing medical diagnoses, managing investment funds, and performing legal discovery, play games etc. (Lin et al. 2018)

Deep learning is an unsupervised learning in which computer teach itself. It includes performing high-level abstractions and thinking like image recognition (Lin et al. 2018).

All IOT (Internet of Things) devices utilize AI to understand the controlling of a number of devices from a single device with and without human such as Google Nest sensor.

Table 1. Machine learning v/s Deep learning

	Machine Learning	Deep Learning
Training dataset	Small	Large
Choose features	Yes	No
Number of algorithms	Many	Few
Training time	Short	Long

With machine learning, you need less information to prepare the calculation than profound learning. Profound learning requires a broad and various arrangement of information to distinguish the fundamental structure as depicted in table 1. Furthermore, machine learning gives a quicker prepared model. Most exceptional profound learning engineering can take days to seven days to prepare. The benefit of profound learning over machine learning is it is exceptionally precise. You don't have to comprehend what highlights are the best portrayal of the information; the neural system figured out how to choose basic highlights. In machine learning, you have to decide for yourself what highlights to remember for the model.

ROLE OF AI IN HIGHER EDUCATION

A few components should be considered to guarantee that the usage of AI apparatuses is ideal and fair (Zeide 2019):

1. *Procurement*: Give close consideration to the advancements and organizations that will be generally pertinent to your specific student body regarding the authoritative commitments to give information about your students. Ensure that if issues emerge, you have contracted with an organization that will be receptive to your issues.
2. *Training*: Set up those individuals who are going to execute and utilize these instruments, and train them in the advantages and inadequacies of the apparatuses.
3. *Oversight*: Set up a non-stop procedure of looking at whether the instruments are working, regardless of whether they are progressively powerful for specific gatherings of students, and whether they might be giving better numbers yet worse results. This is something that is hard to do however is significant, on the grounds that these instruments can get obsolete rapidly.
4. *Policies and Principles*: Make institutional arrangements encompassing the execution of apparatuses that depend on investigation, and develop rules that make an interpretation of those approaches into operational advances and activities.
5. *Investment*: Get students' and employees' contribution about their interests and what they might want to see from these frameworks. This progression is regularly ignored in light of the fact that it is muddled and can prompt some contention, yet it for the most part makes a superior outcome over the long haul.

At last, to be effective, anybody considering an AI execution inside advanced education ought to pose six basic inquiries (Zeide 2019):

1. *What capacities does the information perform*? You can't simply observe a red, green, and yellow light about student achievement and fully trust that, in any event not on the off chance that you are the one actualizing the frameworks and you need to do so mindfully.
2. *What choices don't we see*? These are choices about the PC preparing as well as about the order and the representation.
3. *Who controls the substance?* Is it you, or is it the innovation supplier? How agreeable would you say you are with that? How agreeable are your educators with that?
4. *How do we check results regarding viability*, as far as circulation, and as far as positive and negative results?
5. *What gets lost with datafication?* This word is utilized to portray doing these things dependent on information instead of on relational or bureaucratic frameworks.

6. *What—and whose—interests do we organize*?

On the basis of above inquires following are the steps to improve learning processes(*Wiley Education Services* 2019):

1. *Student grouping*: School selecting groups will have the option to more readily centre their endeavours by making calculations that can anticipate the candidates well on the way to be acknowledged and enlist, and the states and nations from which they will start. These calculations could likewise decide the selected students who are well on the way to advance, graduate, and become drawn in graduated class. The school confirmations procedure will turn out to be quicker and progressively customized.
2. Via mechanizing numerous managerial exercises during the confirmations procedure, including visa forms, student lodging determination, and course enlistment, schools and colleges will have the option to give adaptable encounters to students.
3. *Student maintenance endeavours will be more proactive than receptive*: By distinguishing early notice signs, warnings, and students who are well on the way to battle scholastically, student achievement staff will have the option to make maintenance designs that foresee, as opposed to respond to, students' troubles.
4. *Affirmations groups will have help tending to "summer soften"*: By giving customized and continuous content informing and correspondence, AI can distinguish acknowledged candidates who paid a store in month of May yet may not join up with September. This distinguishing proof permits confirmations staff to make intercession systems to expand their pre-winter enlistment numbers.
5. The school's essential concern and reputational worth will improve: While understudies don't need to take the course, it could check a difficult present-day lifestyle of school tremendous choice for future understudies.

Coming up next are the issues identified with AI and showing learning process [11]:

1. It is changing how we find and partner with information: We conflictingly in any event, notice the AI structures that sway the data we see and find reliably. Google changes results to clients subject to the spot, Amazon makes recommendations dependent on past buys, Siri adjusts to your essentials and orders, and for all intents and purposes all web advertisements are planned for your inclinations and shopping propensities.

These sorts of sharp frameworks expect a noteworthy movement by they way we cooperate with data in our own and ace lives, and could fundamentally change how we find and use data in schools and the scholarly world as well. Over the range recently decades, AI-based structures have beginning at now altogether changed how we interface with data and with extra uncommon, progressively combined turn of events, understudies later on may have ceaselessly various encounters doing examination and exploring genuine elements than the understudies of today.

2. It could change the movement of educators: There will dependably be an occupation for instructors in training, in any case what that action is and what it incorporates may change because of new advancement as tricky enlisting frameworks. As we've as of late talked about, AI can acknowledge authority over undertakings like investigating, can assist understudies with improving learning, and may even sub for affirmed world coaching. At any rate AI could be changed as per different bits of instructing as well. Man-made knowledge structures could be changed to give authority, filling in as a spot for understudies to introduce demands and discover data or could even trade educators for central course materials. If all else fails, regardless, AI will move the action of the educator to that of facilitator.

Instructors will improve AI works out, help understudies who are doing fighting, and give human alliance and hands-on encounters for understudies. From different viewpoints, improvement is presently driving a touch of these changes in the examination entryway, particularly in schools that are on the web or handle the flipped assessment hall model.

3. Man-made insight can make experimentation learning less disturbing: Experimentation is a fundamental piece of learning, yet for specific understudies, coming up short, or even not knowing the correct response, is incapacitating. Some in a general sense couldn't think about being gotten out before their mates or authority figures like an instructor. A sharp PC framework, proposed to assist understudies with learning, is a liberally less overwhelming approach to manage regulates experimentation. Man-made consciousness could offer understudies an approach to manage test and learn in a generally without judgment condition, particularly when AI associates can offer reactions for development. Without a doubt, AI is the ideal strategy for supporting this sort of learning, as AI frameworks themselves once in a while learn by an experimentation system.
4. Data filled by AI can change how schools discover, educate, and fortify understudies: Keen information gathering, obliged by watchful PC structures,

is beginning at now making changes how universities to talk with exceptional and current understudies. From selecting to helping understudies pick the best courses, sharp PC frameworks are helping make all pieces of the school experience much more positively revamp to understudy needs and targets.

5. PC based insight may change where understudies recognize, who shows them, and how they secure central aptitudes: While critical changes may regardless be several decades later on, really artificial intelligence can significantly change practically all that we think little of about education.

RELATED WORK

Some of the recent works using AI have been discussed below:

In (Hanan Abdullah Mengash 2020), author performed analysis on different decision-making techniques like naïve Bayes, ANN, Decision tree and SVM on real dataset of different students of different universities. The results are evaluated with different performance metrics like precision recall confusion matric etc. This study helps to improve academic performance of students.

In (Wei Zhu, Chao Ma, Xuehua Zhao, Mingjing Wang, Ali Asghar Heidari, Huiling Chen 2020), proposed a compelling OLSCA-KELM half breed model to assess Sino-remote agreeable education ventures.

In (Ruqi Li, Yinwei Li, Zhongyi Meng, Yurong Song 2020), author thought about individual action contrasts and gossip discrediting hubs, and we propose another multifaceted model that can be utilized to all the more likely investigate the procedure of talk spreading practically speaking. The harmony point and the fundamental recovery number R0 of the model are determined by means of the differential elements strategy and the cutting edge framework technique.

In (Ciolacu et al. 2018), introduced an imaginative way to deal with advancing AI in Education 4.0. The point of this contextual analysis is to foresee the last score of students before taking an interest in conclusive assessment.

In (Jing and Shiying 2010), author dismembered the attributes of passionate intelligence information, broke down 804 examples of 5 Chongqing professional Institute utilizing K-implies bunch examination technique. The 5 inward kinds of professional students were uncover, including the fair sort, solid adjustment type, solid assessment type and frail guideline - type, solid adjustment appraisal type, and powerless mindfulness - solid assessment adjustment type, and so forth to give the exploration premise to the improvement of progressively compelling educational systems.

In (Gama et al. 2016), a model was proposed that dependent on the joining in an Intelligent MIS (iMIS) of 5 designs that we are executing in a few HE Institutions (HEI), in Colombia.

In (Irshat, Petr, and Irina 2018), strategy was proposed for choosing of the ideal artificial intelligence innovation by the arrangement of accessible advances for control of versatile robots permits to improve the utilitarian qualities of the robot control framework all in all and its individual subsystems by the ideal inclusion of a lot of undertakings and strategies understood by the robot control framework. The technique depended on the depiction of the underlying data as inclination relations on a lot of choices. As an answer for the issue of choosing an ideal data innovation is received the most nondominant elective.

In (Rao and Liu 2009), many impact elements of educational cost standard were introduced by utilizing the subjective strategy right off the bat, at that point quantitative examination these impact factors by utilizing the technique for dim social investigation, and get three fundamental impact factors. This technique for joining the subjective examination and quantitative investigation is important to apply in the down to earth application.

In (Sandu and Gide 2019), explored the elements which influence the reception of Chatbot innovation to improve the student involvement with the Indian advanced education division. A Quantitative technique was utilized through information assortment from overviews of a portion of the conspicuous advanced education foundations utilizing Chatbot innovation.

In (Tastimur, Karakose, and Akin 2016), an IT-based strategy was proposed which rearranges utilization of the accreditation framework to flights. High effectiveness and increasingly exact outcomes can be acquired by being given outcomes got from proposed strategy as criticism. There are resolved whether achievement accreditation criteria by analysing every one of accreditation criteria with information extricating and preparing systems.

CONCLUSION

In this paper provide systematic review on different existing techniques of artificial intelligence in higher education. The paper presents different factors that are used for artificial intelligence in higher education. All the more critically, this investigation has given an outline of the huge range of potential AI applications in advanced education to help students, employees, and executives. They were depicted in four expansive areas (profiling and expectation, insightful coaching frameworks, appraisal and assessment, and versatile frameworks and personalisation) with 17 sub-classes.

This structure, which was gotten from the precise audit, adds to the comprehension and conceptualisation of AI practice and research.

REFERENCES

Arrieta, A. B., Díaz-Rodríguez, N., Del Ser, J., Bennetot, A., Tabik, S., Barbado, A., García, S., Gil-López, S., Molina, D., Benjamins, R., Chatila, R., & Herrera, F. (2020). Explainable Artificial Intelligence (XAI): Concepts, taxonomies, opportunities and challenges toward responsible AI. *Information Fusion*, *58*, 82–115. doi:10.1016/j.inffus.2019.12.012

Buchanan, B. G. (2005). A (very) brief history of artificial intelligence. *AI Magazine*, ▪▪▪, 26–53.

Ciolacu, M., Tehrani, A. F., Binder, L., & Svasta, P. M. (2018). Education 4.0-Artificial Intelligence Assisted Higher Education: Early recognition System with Machine Learning to support Students' Success. *IEEE 24th Int. Symp. Des. Technol. Electron. Packag.*, 23-30.

Gama, J. A. P., Caro, R., Hernan, C., Alvarado, D. B., Gomez, C. L. C., Gomez, G. H., & Mena, A. M. (2016). Work in progress—New education model based on competencies of higher education and iMIS with architectures. *IEEE Glob. Eng. Educ. Conf.*, 1065-70. 10.1109/EDUCON.2016.7474685

Irshat, K., Petr, R., & Irina, R. (2018). The Selecting of Artificial Intelligence Technology for Control of Mobile Robots. *Int. Multi-Conference Ind. Eng. Mod. Technol.*, 1-4.

Jing, F., & Shiying, K. (2010). Application of data mining for emotional intelligence based on cluster analysis. *IEEE Int. Conf. Artif. Intell. Educ.*, 512-15. 10.1109/ICAIE.2010.5640962

Li, R., Li, Y., Meng, Z., Song, Y., & Jaing, G. (2020). Rumor Spreading Model Considering Individual Activity and Refutation Mechanism Simultaneously. *IEEE Access: Practical Innovations, Open Solutions*, *8*, 63065–63076. doi:10.1109/ACCESS.2020.2983249

Li, Liu, Sun, & Yu. (2020). *Artificial intelligence based method and apparatus for generating information.* Google Patents.

Lin, X., Rivenson, Y., Yardimci, N. T., Veli, M., Luo, Y., Jarrahi, M., & Ozcan, A. (2018). All-optical machine learning using diffractive deep neural networks. *Science*, *361*(6406), 1004–1008. doi:10.1126cience.aat8084 PMID:30049787

Lucas, S. (2017). *Artificial Intelligence (AI) in Architecture. What are the practical applications?* www.futurearchi.org

Mahadevan, S. (2018). Imagination machines: a new challenge for artificial intelligence. *Thirty-Second AAAI Conf. Artif. Intell.*

Marr, B. (2018). How Is AI Used In Education — Real World Examples Of Today And A Peek Into. *Future.*

Mengash, H. A. (2020). Using Data Mining Techniques to Predict Student Performance to Support Decision Making in University Admission Systems. *IEEE Access: Practical Innovations, Open Solutions, 8*, 55462–55470. doi:10.1109/ACCESS.2020.2981905

Ramos, C., Augusto, J. C., & Shapiro, D. (2008). Ambient intelligence—The next step for artificial intelligence. *IEEE Intelligent Systems, 23*(2), 15–18. doi:10.1109/MIS.2008.19

Rao, C., & Liu, H. (2009). Pricing Model of Higher Education Tuition Based on Multivariate Linear Regression. *IEEE Int. Conf. Artif. Intell. Comput. Intell., 4*, 228-31. 10.1109/AICI.2009.355

Russell, S., & Norvig, P. (2002). *Artificial intelligence: a modern approach.* Academic Press.

Sandu, N., & Gide, E. (2019). Adoption of AI-Chatbots to Enhance Student Learning Experience in Higher Education in India. *18th Int. Conf. Inf. Technol. Based High. Educ. Train.*, 1-5. 10.1109/ITHET46829.2019.8937382

Tastimur, C., Karakose, M., & Akin, E. (2016). Improvement of relative accreditation methods based on data mining and artificial intelligence for higher education. *IEEE 15th Int. Conf. Inf. Technol. Based High. Educ. Train.*, 1-7. 10.1109/ITHET.2016.7760736

Writers, S. (2012). *10 Ways Artificial Intelligence Can Reinvent Education.* Academic Press.

Zeide, E. (2019). Artificial Intelligence in Higher Education: Applications, Promise and Perils, and Ethical Questions. *Educause Review.*

Zhu, W., Ma, C., Zhao, X., Wang, M., Heidari, A. A., Chen, H., & Li, C. (2020). Evaluation of Sino Foreign Cooperative Education Project Using Orthogonal Sine Cosine Optimized Kernel Extreme Learning Machine. *IEEE Access: Practical Innovations, Open Solutions, 8*, 61107–61123. doi:10.1109/ACCESS.2020.2981968

Chapter 5
Teaching and Learning With Artificial Intelligence

Libi Shen
University of Phoenix, USA

Irene Chen
https://orcid.org/0000-0001-9358-4460
University of Houston-Downtown, USA

Anne Grey
Concordia University, USA

Anchi Su
UCLA, USA

ABSTRACT

Artificial intelligence (AI) is developing at a fast speed and has incessantly impacted the modern world for decades. AI technologies are beneficial for all kinds of industries, including businesses, economics, transportation, hospitals, schools, universities, and so forth. Many researchers have investigated the development of artificial intelligence in education (AIEd), specifically on how AI assists teaching, learning, assessment, references, and collaboration. Several questions arise. What impact do AI technologies have on education? How do AI technologies assist teaching (e.g., curriculum, assessment, student learning, and teaching practices)? How do teachers cope with AI Technologies in education? What are the ethical concerns of AI technologies? What are the barriers of AI-based learning in education? The purpose of this chapter is to explore the evolution and the challenges of AI technologies in education. Major research on AI from 1999 to 2019 will be reviewed. Problems with AI in education will be raised and solutions for solving the issues will be recommended.

DOI: 10.4018/978-1-7998-4763-2.ch005

INTRODUCTION

While teachers, psychologists, educational leaders, counselors, and parents are debating how much screen time is appropriate for children, the emerging technology named Artificial Intelligence (AI) has surfaced in the classrooms. Jill Watson, an AI-based teaching assistant, has answered students' questions online since 2015, while AI chatbot has assisted recruitment and retention in universities since 2016 (Raths, 2019). Educational robotics has been developed as a tool for students, and has been supporting learning in science, technology, mathematics, informatics, and other school subjects in recent years. Educational robotics has attracted teachers' interest and has been used as a valuable tool to develop social and cognitive skills for students from preschool to high school to support learning in mathematics, science, technology and other subjects at schools (Alimisis, 2013). AI has been applied in the domains of physics, writing, programming, reading, and the development of instructional systems as well.

Earlier, Drigas and Ioannidou (2012) delineated that the typical applications of AI in educational usually include intelligent tutoring, knowledge representation, autonomous agents, and natural language processing. In a decade review, Drigas and Ioannidou (2012) found that AI technology has developed application tools to carry on tasks and to help solve problems in special education, such as Attention Deficit Disorder, Attention Deficit Hyperactivity Disorder, Autistic Spectrum Disorders, dyslexia, physical and sensory impairments, reading/writing/ spelling difficulties, and difficulties in mathematics successfully. Later, Lu and Harris (2018) stated that applications of AI-based educational technology include tutoring (e.g., Intelligence Tutoring Systems), personalizing learning (e.g., adaptive tutors for pace, sequence and difficulty to tailor students' needs; support to special needs students), testing (computer adaptive assessments for different students' mastery levels based on students' answers), and automating tasks (e.g., taking attendance, grading assignments, and generating test questions).

Schroer (2019) reported that seven companies (i.e., Century Tech, Blippar, Knewton, Thinkster Math, Quizlet, Cognii, and Nuance) are using AI in education to enhance classrooms at schools. Learning Management Systems (e.g., Blackboard, Blackboard Ultra, Canvas, and Moodle) have been adopted in higher education to improve the digital learning environment and online classrooms at the universities in U.S. AI in education has been used to increase efficiency and optimize resources (e.g., iTalk2Learn, Third space learning, Duolingo Chatbot, Thinkster Math, and Ed Tech Foundry). The advance of AI technologies has reshaped instruction and learning approaches, since more online programs have been globally developed and implemented. AI in education improved students' learning environments and classroom interaction at universities. It appears that differentiated and individualized learning have become the focus, and instructors' workloads have been reduced. The world is changing because of AI technologies. In this chapter, the researchers will explore the evolution and the challenges of AI in education.

BACKGROUND

Many researchers have devoted efforts to explore artificial intelligence in the past decades. Some researchers examined the development, the innovation, and the applications of artificial intelligence (e.g., Altinay, Karaatmaca, & Altinay, 2019; Andriessen & Sandberg, 1999; Beck, Stern, & Haugsjaa, 2005; Faggella, 2017; Gadanidis, 2017; Gose, 2016; Kumar, 2017; Lu & Harris, 2018; Madda, 2017; Popenici & Kerr, 2017; Poth, 2018; Rajasingham, 2009; Rieland, 2017; Rizzotto, 2017; Saravanan, Sreedevi, & Subhamathi, 2017; Skiba, 2017; Wagner, 2018; Wollowski, Neller, & Boerkoel, 2017). Others focused on the ethical disquietude related to artificial intelligence (e.g., Burton et. al, 2017; Etzioni & Etzioni, 2017; Lambert, 2018; Lee, 2018; McClure, 2018), and the impacts or challenges of educational robotics in instruction (e.g., Alimisis, 2013; Crowe, 2018; Mallawaarachchi, 2017; Oblinger, 2018; Ortiz & Smith, 2015; Renz & Hilbig, 2020).

In education, the major focus of AI is on the development of software to enhance instruction. AI is invaluable to instructional system development, since it assists personalize teaching, enhances student learning experience, responds to student feelings, supplies data for the development of novel education theory, and teaches 21st century skills (i.e., cognitive skills, intrapersonal skills, dialogue systems, interpersonal skills, and inquiry learning) (Woolf, 2015). As Luckin, Holmes, Griffiths, and Forcier (2016) indicated that "AI scientists are currently building on new approaches in machine learning, computer modeling, and probability statistics to improve financial decision making, and are using decision theory and neuroscience to drive the development of more effective medical diagnostics" (p.14). The main purpose of employing AI in education is to help improve teaching and learning in classrooms because AI can help instructors with teaching, classroom work, evaluation, as well as help students learn.

However, some researchers believed that there are disadvantages with AI in education. The negative effects of AI are: AI will replace unskillful people's jobs; AI is in control by the a few people who knows software well; AI is unable to make judgement (Patrizio, 2016). There were six defects of AI; for example, (a) AI may lead to destruction if it is controlled or driven in incorrect way; (b) unemployment rate will be higher if robots start to replace humans in all fields; (c) AI can be changed to implement mass scale destruction; (d) AI may fail to take the programmed instructions if it malfunctions; (e) AI may corrupt the younger generation; and (f)

AI can function only based on its programing and lacks the human touch (Saranya & Phil, 2016). People have concerns that, with AI, students do not need teachers and teaching profession will be obsolete (Madda, 2017).

Additionally, Lee (2018) raised the alert by asserting that technology companies need to stop to pretend that AI won't destroy human's jobs. As Lee (2018) predicted, AI will displace a large number of jobs, which will cause social discontent, and half of our jobs can be done better at almost no cost by AI and robots. Lee (2018) suspected that people are not ready for this AI's fast transition. McClure (2018) pointed out, "an unprecedented number of citizens could lose their jobs to robots and software that can work for cheaper and for longer hours than any human" (p.153). As a matter of fact, new workplace technologies, such as AI and robots, have affected females and non-white minorities more than others, which impacted people's anxiety levels (McClure, 2018). Fear of unemployment and financial insecurity might be the next problem in society.

In Renz and Hilbig's (2020) interviews of 25 EdTech companies in further education and a discursive analysis, they identified some hindrance for implementing AI in instruction; for instance, four major elements (i.e., cultural change, sustainability, individualization, and human-digital-interaction) are inhibiting AI in education. They indicated that,

Cultural change especially follows a diametric relationship. The change is taking place in the tension between a traditional understanding of education and a futuristic idea of education and knowledge transfer. Learning behavior and the requirements for learning methods are constantly changing. In this context, it is evident that an increased circulation of knowledge can be considered by using digital approaches due to the permanent availability of knowledge .... This shows a drastic change in the training and learning culture. While unorganized, often context- and problem dependent real-time training is increasingly gaining importance, the relevance of corporate training is clearly decreasing. Direct access to experts, knowledge and learning freely available online intensifies this trend (Renz & Hilbig, 2020, p.14).

As technology innovation has progressed immensely, the associated possibility of job displacement implies that teachers in education need to reconsider their roles, pedagogies, and curriculum in teaching. In the following, the researchers will review the definitions, evolution, functions, and applications of AI briefly. The models of AI in education and role of teachers with AI in education will be discussed.

Historical Overview of Artificial Intelligence (AI)

In 1956, Professor John McCarthy coined the term "Artificial Intelligence." Based on McCarthy (2006), Artificial Intelligence (AI) involved "expressing knowledge in a computer in logical language and reasoning by logical inference, including no-monotonic inference" and "studying and imitating human neurophysiology" (p.7). The idea embedded in AI was that it can use language, form abstractions, develop concepts, and solve problems for human beings.

Artificial Intelligence was defined as "the science of making machines do things that would require intelligent if done by men" (McCarthy, Minsky, Rochester, & Shannon, 1956), and "the science and engineering of making intelligent machines, especially intelligent computer programs" (McCarthy, 2007). In 1970s, artificial intelligence has been applied to research fields, including expert systems, game theory, mechanical theorem proving, machine translation, machine learning, pattern recognition, robotics, and intelligent control (Pan, 2016). Then, AI became "a modelling science, developing, applying and investigating formalized models of salient aspects pertaining to learning and instruction, allowing reasoning and derivation of new facts, thereby giving the models in use a dynamic flavor" in 1999 (Andriessen & Sandberg, 1999, p.131).

In 2009, Artificial Intelligence was defined as "the science and engineering of making intelligent machines, especially intelligent computer programs" (McCarthy, 2007, p.2). Drigas and Ioannidou (2012) stated, AI could take a physical form of the devices (e.g., humanoid robots) or a software form with 'intellectual' capacity (e.g. a virtual avatar). AI is computer programs that exhibit intelligence (Rajaraman, 2014); it is the computer system designed to interact with the world through capabilities and intelligent behaviors (Luckin, Holmes, Griffiths, & Forcier, 2016). AI has been described as the machines with the ability to think, understand, and learn in a similar way to human beings, which was interpreted as the possibility of using computers to simulate human intelligence.

Luckin, Holmes, Griffiths, and Forcier (2016) noted, AI systems are computer systems that have been designed to interact with the world through capabilities (for example, visual perception and speech recognition) and intelligent behaviors (for example, assessing the available information and then taking the most sensible action to achieve a stated goal) that we would think of as essentially human. Gadanidis (2017) believed that AI is the intelligence in software or machines that can create computers and computer software so that they are capable of intelligent behavior. Saravanan, Sreedevi, and Subhamathi's (2017) perceived artificial Intelligence as the study of "how to make computers do things at which, at the moment, people are better" (p.418). Popenici and Kerr (2017) indicated that AI involves "computing systems that are able to engage in human-like processes such as learning, adapting, synthesizing, self-correction and use of data for complex processing tasks" (p.2).

Today, robots that were equipped with AI have outperformed surgeons with sewing up cuts; assisted credit card companies with fraud detection; performed search and rescuing missions; providing care for children, seniors, and hospital patients; and assisting Amazon's Alexia, Apple's Siri, and Microsoft's Cortana to learn users' behaviors to better serve customers (Etzioni & Etzioni, 2017). Since AI is using computers to understand human intelligence, the essence of AI does not change. AI has the ability to enable a computer to think like people.

In conclusion, most of the definitions remain indistinguishable, but the functions and benefits of AI have proliferated. As Etzioni and Schoenick (2018) noted, AI is a rapidly emerging technology that can potentially change our daily lives with speed in which human beings have never experienced before. Altinay, Karaatmaca, and Altinay (2019) pointed out, AI has become a topic of interest that "deals with methods to ensure that human intelligence is imitated by the computer" (p.330). The current trend of AI is to understand how to develop computers or computer software that are capable of intelligent behavior.

The Development of AI

How was AI developed? There were six stages for the development of AI systems; it started from the Naïve Solution Stage (1950s), the General Method Stage (1970s), the Domain Knowledge Stage (1980s), the Integration Stage (1990s), the Interactive Robots (2000s), to the Natural Language Chatbots (2010s) (Saravanan, Sreedevi, & Subhamathi, 2017). Some of the facets of Artificial Intelligent systems that are already in used included Chat bots, the Intelligent agents, Expert systems and Speech Recognition Systems (Saravanan, Sreedevi, & Subhamathi, 2017), and it's likely that Artificial Intelligence will be spread into almost all the fields by 2030. In other words, AI will be ubiquitous.

The development of AI can also be viewed from researchers' remarks on the classification and foundation of AI. McCarthy (2007) stated that the types of AI comprise common sense knowledge and reasoning, logical AI, search AI, inference, pattern recognition, representation, learning from experience, epistemology, ontology, heuristics, genetic programming, and planning. Gustafson and Gustafson (2016) illustrated, the four foundations of artificial intelligence incorporate search, representation, reasoning, and learning; these include samples of research in AI include autonomous mobile robotics (e.g., rovers on Mars, industrial robots, localization), games (e.g., chess programs), expert systems (e.g., medical diagnosis program), natural language processing (e.g., representation of the syntax and semantics of the language), and perception (e.g., vision-perception programs). Artificial Intelligence

Systems can be categorized into: expert systems (e.g., Amazon Alexa, Apple Siri, Microsoft Cortana, Google Now), robotics (e.g., Asimo, Pepper, Spot, Nao, MyKie), intelligent computer assisted instruction (e.g., Mika from Carnegie's Learning, iTalk2Learn), game playing (e.g., IBM's Deep Blue, Façade, Black and White, Sims, Versu, F.E.A.R.), language translators (e.g., Google Translate, IBM Watson), neural computing (e.g., BrainMaker, NeuralShell Easy, NeuroSolutions, Neural Ware), fuzzy logic (e.g., Massive Software, Vibrobox, Texo Controls), genetic algorithms (Evolver, XpertRule GenAsys), computer vision and scene recognition, intelligent agents, and natural language processing (Saravanan, Sreedevi, & Subhamathi, 2017). AI in education has been developed continuously and effortlessly.

Models of AI in Education

AIEd has focused on the design of digital tutors historically to provide exposition of concepts to be learned and to have the intelligence to respond meaningfully to student behavior, such as offering adaptive support, describing student learning styles, or delivering culturally appropriate communication (Gadanidis, 2017). AI researchers have developed models to represent the emotional, social, and metacognitive aspects of learning in education. There are three key models of AI in education: domain (i.e., knowledge of the subject being learned), learner models (i.e., knowledge of the learner), and pedagogical (i.e., the knowledge and expertise of teaching) (Luckin, Holmes, Griffiths, & Forcier, 2016). These models involved context of the courses,

learner's knowledge, feedback, assessment, a learner's emotional state, and teaching contents. In further details, the **pedagogical model** consists of assessment to inform and measure learning; productive failure (allowing students to explore a concept and make mistakes before being shown the right answer); and feedback (questions, hints, or haptics) triggered by student actions; it is designed to help students ameliorate their learning. The **domain model** comprises causes of World War I; how to add, subtract, or multiply two fractions; Newton's second law (forces); how to structure an argument; and different approaches to reading a text (e.g., for sense or for detail). The **learner model** involves the student's emotional state, previous achievement and difficulties, as well as their engagement in learning (e.g., time-on-task) (Luckin, Holmes, Griffiths, & Forcier, 2016). What functions do AIEd have? Will AI machines surpass human intelligence?

The Application of AI in Education

AI has been applied to understanding natural language, game playing, speech recognition, computer vision, expert systems, and heuristic classification (McCarthy, 2007). In fact, as Rajasingham (2009) explained, the idea of HyperClass is based on HyperReality in which human intelligence and Artificial Intelligence interact to allow people to learn anywhere at any time in virtual universities. Teaching can be done by using *Just in Time Artificially Intelligent Tutors,* and learning can be done by using avatars-online simulacra of themselves to interact as a telepresence in classes in any location. AI is used in four major areas in higher education: student acquisition (e.g., enrollment process), learning and instruction (e.g., grading and resources), student affairs (e.g., personalized degree planning), and institutional efficiency (e.g., guiding administrative decisions, course offerings) (Klutka, Ackerly, & Magda, 2018).

Faggella (2017) also provided examples of how AI is applied in education. The creation and development of **smart content** from digital guides in textbooks to customizable learning digital interfaces are being introduced from elementary to post-secondary, and within corporate environments (Faggella, 2017). AI is used to help disseminate and breakdown textbook content into digestible smart study guides that include chapter summaries, true-false and multiple-choice practice tests and flashcards (Faggella, 2017). *Nextex Learning* "allows educators to design digital curriculum and content across devices, integrating rich media like video and audio, as well as self- or online-instructor assessment" (Faggella, 2017, p.2). Then, **intelligent tutoring systems** (e.g., *Mastery Learning*) is a one-on-one tutoring system to support the effectiveness of individualized instruction in the classroom. For example, Carnegie Learning's Mika software adopted cognitive science and AI technology to provide personalized tutoring and real-time feedback for post-secondary students. Faggella (2017) illustrated, the iTalk2Learn System 16 had an effect on young students' learning fractions; it applied a learner model that explicitly included information about an individual's cognitive needs, mathematics knowledge, emotional state, feedback received, and the students' responses in turn. Additionally, AI connected virtual facilitators and learning environments. The University of Southern California Institute for Creative Technologies created smart virtual environments and applications with AI, 3-D gaming, and computer animation to develop authentic virtual characters and realistic social interactions (Faggella, 2017). The Technologies SimCoach Prototype consisted of initiatives under development (e.g., virtual facilitators, augmented reality, and intelligent tutor in remote learning and training program). It is obvious that AI has paved new learning. AI has paved new learning avenues for the future.

The Intelligent Tutoring Systems in Education

The Intelligent Tutoring Systems (ITS) is the earliest Artificial Intelligence application. These systems were developed to implement traditional methods of teaching and learning in the 1980s. The Intelligent Tutoring Systems consisted of the communication module, the domain knowledge module, the student model, the pedagogical module (Woolf, 1992), as well as the expert model (Beck, Stern, & Haugsjaa, 2005).

The movement from The Intelligent Tutoring Systems (ITS) to the Interactive Learning Environments (ILEs), and later to mixed-initiative systems (a combination of both approaches) in instruction were developed over the decades. ITS is a computer system that provides customized instruction and feedback to students without teacher intervention; it comprises four components: a domain model, a student model, a tutor model, and a user interface model (ITS, 2018). The scope of ITS covered the major AI topics, such as knowledge representation, machine learning, natural language, planning, reasoning, and explanation; the systems formed an interesting test-bed to formalize cognitive theories and to experiment with their operationalization (Andriessen & Sandberg, 1999). ITS replicates teachers' roles and increasingly automates pedagogical functions (e.g., problem generation, problem selection, and feedback generation) to help create new methods and redefine educational goals in education.

The principles of the Interactive Learning Environments (ILEs) are student-centered; it involved student control instead of tutor control; construction instead of instruction; rich feedback generated by the student's interaction with the learning environment, not the tutor; and individualization determined by the student, not the teacher (McArthur, Lewis, & Bishay, 2005). AI in education has continued to evolve and has transferred from ITS to ILEs due to the development and breakthrough in AI. Many examples of ITS have surfaced. For example, there were ActiveMath (a web-based adaptive learning environment for mathematics for improving long-distance learning, completing traditional classroom teaching, and supporting individual lifelong learning), Algebra Tutor (engaging students in problem solving with modern algebraic tools), AutoTutor (helping college students in learning computer hardware, operating systems and the Internet), COLLECT-UML (supporting pairs of students working collaboratively on UML class diagram and providing feedback), Mathematics Tutor (helping students solve word problems using fractions, decimals and percentages), CIRCSIM-Tutor (for medical students to learn about regulating blood pressure), eTeacher (supporting personalized e-learning assistance), ESC101-ITS (an intelligent tutoring system for introductory programming problems) ZOSMAT (addressing all the needs of a real classroom), REALP (enhancing students' reading comprehension by reader-specific lexical practice and personalized practice with authentic materials from the Web), SmartTutor (supporting the needs of continuing education students), SQL-Tutor (teaching students how to retrieve data from databases), and Why2-Atlas (addressing students' writing problems through dialogues and asking them to correct their essays) (ITS, 2018).

However, ITS has its limitations or restrictions. The cost, the evaluation system, and the subject competence might be the constraint for consideration. Since ITS has subject competence limitations, it restricted knowledge of teaching; ITS is expensive to develop and to implement; its immediate feedback and hint sequences failed to develop deep learning for students; it failed to ask questions of the students to explain their actions; evaluation of an ITS is difficult, time-consuming, and costly (ITS, 2018).

The Role of AI in Education

What role does AI in education play? Nowadays, there are online tutors to help with personalized learning and virtual assistants to answer administrative questions and provide analysis for universities or schools. Kumar (2017) has presented ten roles of Artificial Intelligence for education: (1) AI can automate basic activities in education like grading; (2) educational software can be adapted to students' needs; (3) AI can point out places where courses need improvement; (4) students can get additional support from AI tutors; (5) AI-driven programs can give students and educators helpful feedback; (6) AI is altering how we find and interact with information; (7) AI could change the role of teachers; (8) AI can make trial-and-error learning less intimidating; (9) Data powered by AI can change how schools find, teach, and support students; and (10) AI may change where students learn, who teaches them, and how they acquire basic skills.

In addition, Lynch (2018) raised seven roles that artificial intelligence played in education (AIEd): automate grading, allow teachers to act as learning motivators, support teachers, support students, meet a variety of students' needs, provide personalized help, and identify weaknesses in the classroom. Klutka, Ackerly, and Magda (2018) pointed out that the goals for AI in education are: to increase retention, to increase outcomes, to lower cost, to increase access, and to decrease time to completion. It is obvious that the role of teachers has to be changed in higher education with AI in classrooms.

The Benefits of AI in Education

Researchers have also explored the benefits of adopting AI in education. Saranya and Phil (2016) raised three major functions for AI in Ed (AIEd): an agent function, a heuristic function, and an evaluation function. AIEd can offer intelligent support for collaborative learning; AIEd can provide an intelligent, personal tutor for every learner; and AIEd's intelligent virtual reality can support learning in authentic environments, in addition to provide assistance to learners with special education needs, and motivate learners who cannot attend school (Luckin et al., 2016). In other words, no teacher is needed with Intelligent Tutoring Systems (ITS), because the online tutors or the virtual pedagogical agents could be present, acting as teachers, learning facilitators, or student peers in collaborative learning quests for students.

Even though AI might replace human jobs, researchers have witnessed the advantages of AI technology. The positive effects of AI are: (a) machines can do mundane tasks and won't get bored as humans do; (b) AI and cognitive technologies help make faster decisions; (c) AI has the ability of big data processing and machine learning; (d) AI offers error-free processing of data; (e) AI can take the risk doing jobs humans can't do; and (f) AI technology helps achieve better research outcomes (Patrizio, 2016). Additionally, several benefits with AI in education surfaced. AIEd will augment our physical landscape and allow formal classroom content to become the learner's physical reality. AIEd will connect to the Internet of things and permits any network-enabled objects to be interconnected with any other network-enabled machine (Luckin et al., 2016). AIEd will be accustomed to how we feel and how we move. AIEd will furnish just-in-time assessments to shape learning, provide new insights into how learning is progressing, assist us to move beyond 'stop-and-test', embody new insights from the learning sciences, and give us lifelong learning partners (Luckin et al., 2016).

Since AI has the ability to analyze large amounts of data in real time (e.g., students' performance in a particular skill across subjects over the course of a year) and it can automatically provide new content or specific learning parameters to help meet students' needs for continual practice and feedback, it allows teachers to better understand students' performance and construct more effective personalized learning plans (Faggella, 2017). Lambert (2018) illustrated some examples of AI in smarter classrooms, such as Khan Academy's AI that can identify students' strengths and learning gaps and adjust content accordingly; software such as McGraw-Hill Connect and Aplia allow teachers to manage coursework for large classes of students at the same time.

The aforementioned literature review has manifested the definitions, models, benefits, and applications of AI in Education. What challenges do teachers have with AI in Education? What should teachers do to subsist or survive the digital revolution in education with AI? In the following, issues, controversies, problems along with solutions and recommendations will be discussed.

MAIN FOCUS OF THE CHAPTER

Issues, Controversies, Problems

Earlier, Andriessen and Sandberg (1999) found the following trends for AI in education; they are (a) more emphasis on open domains, (b) taking into account the learning environment, (c) collaboration as a didactic strategy, and (d) use of information databases. Later, ITSs was classified into two categories: abstraction of the learning environment and the knowledge type of the instruction (Beck, Stern, & Haugsjaa, 2005). Skiba (2017) pointed out that the short-term trends are blended and collaborative learning; the mid-term trends are the measurement of learning, the use of assessment tools to document academic readiness, learning progress, and educational outcomes; the long-term trends are deeper learning and advancing cultures of innovation. Although there are many benefits to use AI technologies in education, there are several challenges that teachers could face. In the following, possible issues or concerns will be raised and discussed.

1. The Challenges of Utilizing Emerging Technologies

Researchers have noted that there are many challenges with AI in education. Alimisis (2013) explored educational robotics and identified five challenges in educational technology. These five challenges are: technology is everywhere, except in schools; technologies in schools do not support 21st-century learning skills today; there is a need for new and broader perspectives aside from using robotics as servants; learners must be makers rather than just consumers; calls for validation of the impact of robotics (Alimisis, 2013). While classroom instructors can understand students' tones and inflections within a dialogue to provide continual feedback through ongoing dialogue, "Intelligent Tutoring Systems are still limited in dialogue and feedback" (Woolf, 2015, p.43). Woolf, Lane, Chaudhri, and Kolodner (2013) raised five major challenges for AI-based learning systems: (a) creating mentors for every learner; (b) learning 21st century skills; (c) exploring interaction data to support learning; (d) providing universal access to global classrooms; and (e) addressing lifelong and life wide learning.

Additionally, AI can make mistakes while making decisions for students (Rieland, 2017). Skiba (2017) pointed out that, the challenges are improving digital literacy, integrating formal and informal learning, bridging the achievement gap (e.g., how to use data analytics for personalized learning and to connect students with necessary support systems such as writing tutors), and achieving digital equity (e.g., inadequate access to the Internet). Another issue is that users might end up asking AI technology to become more intelligent and capable than teachers, and thus replace teachers in the job market. The fact is that teachers can read students' facial expressions, body languages, and appearance to infer students' emotional status; whereas, AI could struggle with analyzing the complex needs appropriately and immediate cues communicated by a classroom full of students (Lambert, 2018).

Yang et al (2018) summarized ten grand challenges that may have major breakthrough and significant socioeconomical impact for the next five to ten years. These include new materials and fabrication schemes for robot development; biohybrid and bioinspired robots; new power sources, battery technology, and energy-harvesting schemes for long-lasting operation of mobile robots; robot swarms to allow simpler, less expensive, modular units; navigation and exploration in extreme environments; fundamental aspects of artificial intelligence for robotics; brain-computer interfaces; social interaction that understands human social dynamics and moral norms; medical robotics with increasing levels of autonomy; and robot ethics and security (Yang et al., 2018).

Klutka, Ackerly, and Magda (2018) also raised three challenges to view new programs flourish on college campus. They noted,

Accreditation and financial aid requirements should be updated to address the reimagination of academic achievement and instructional support provided by AI. Privacy regulations such as FERPS need to be updated in order to address the ability of AI systems to track data and use it for predictive analytics. If AI takes over some current job responsibilities (e.g., grading, answer students' question), administrators and faculty members will be able to shift their focus to solving more complex problems and connecting with students on deeper levels (p.4).

It seems that there are many challenges for the domain-specific robotics and they need to be tackled, and it requires the collaboration of researchers, teachers, and scientists in higher education. As a result, more research is needed in this field to provide direction, suggestion, or solution while adopting technologies in education. In addition to technologies themselves, another issue is that if school administrators and teachers are ready.

2. Teachers' Insufficient Technology Skills

Do school administrators and teachers have sufficient technology skills to manage or cope with AI in education? Are there enough technicians in each college and university to support an AI system? AI technology in education can assist with communication, differentiation, personalization, exploration, and assessments in the classroom (Poth, 2018). AI technology is reshaping the classrooms all over the world in current decade. It plays an important role in shaping personalized instructions for all students, while teachers are being slowly pushed away from the front of the classroom to assume the roles of coach and facilitator.

Although AI technology can free teachers from mundane tasks like lecturing, grading, creating opportunities for student improvement, and increase more meaningful trial-and-error learning, are teachers ready to accommodate it? Which schools and universities are ready and competent to accommodate AI technology? Teachers can adopt robots with AI as teaching assistants for their classrooms. The challenge involves how teachers can change their roles from instructors to the trainers, explainers, and sustainers. Teacher training might be needed to cope with AI technology development in future, so that teachers will not lose their jobs.

For the development of technologies, there are adaptive learning technologies, mobile learning, the Internet of Things (IOT), next generation learning management system (LMS), natural user interfaces, and Artificial Intelligence (Skiba, 2017). While welcoming AI in education, we have to consider if teachers are prepared and have the technological knowledge/ skills? Do they have sufficient training? How will teachers manage the changes? What do teachers do when AI in education takes over three core components of learning, such as curriculum, instruction, and assessment? What should school administrators and teachers do if AI in education can do all their jobs efficiently?

As Popenici and Kerr (2017) pointed out, "The rise of AI makes it impossible to ignore a serious debate about its future role of teaching and learning in higher education and what type of choices universities will make in regard to this issue" (p.10), although "AI solutions open a new horizon of possibilities for teaching and learning in higher education" (Popenici & Kerr, 2017, p.3). Teacher-bots are "any machine-based software or hardware that assumes the role traditionally performed by a teacher assistant in organizing information and providing fast answers to a wide set of predictable questions; it can be facilitating, monitoring, assessing, and managing student learning within the online learning space" (Popenici & Kerr, 2017, p.10). Teacher-bots are "a complex algorithmic interface able to use artificial intelligence for personalized education, able to provide bespoke content, supervision, and guidance for students and help for teachers" (Popenici & Kerr, 2017, p.10). What do teachers do if there are issues in the classrooms? Are there enough technicians and is the technology team ready to support teachers?

3. Ethical Concerns of AI in Education

Some ethical concerns of AI in education have been raised. What policies have been implemented and what standards have been instilled with AI in education? How will the authority deal with the situation if AIEd goes wrong? Whitby (2013) alerted, when things go wrong, there have been no agreed upon criteria regarding who should be held responsible. Mannino et al. (2015) stated that progress in AI research makes it possible to replace large amounts of human jobs with machines; moreover, many economists assumed that this increasing automation could lead to a massive increase in unemployment within even the next 10-20 years. Mannino et al. (2015) further elucidated, "Many AI experts consider it plausible that this century will witness the creation of AIs whose intelligence surpasses that of humans in all respects" (Mannion et al., 2015, p.2). Robot ethics might become a challenge for teachers. Crowe (2018) raised five major topics for ethical problems: sensitive tasks that require human supervision could be entirely delegated to robots; human beings will no longer take responsibility for failures; unemployment and de-skilling of the workforce; AI could erode human freedom; and using AI in an unethical way. How soon can people solve these ethical problems?

For AI to learn complex tasks on its own with minimal training data is critical. Ethical concerns exist with educational data. There are several questions to be considered. Who owns the education data and who can use the data? Who is accountable and responsible for protecting the data? What role should teachers take if AIEd was used as a classroom spy to monitor, record, and report teachers' performance? Do we still have confidentiality? Our concerns might damage our personal trust and relationships between human beings and machines.

Moreover, there are some critical ethical questions for AI technologies that we have to consider. How should AI behave in our classrooms? What should we do if teaching jobs are in short supply? Should AI systems be allowed to punish students if they do not follow the rules? Should we worry about losing the confidentiality and the possibility of superintelligence? How should we treat AI robots? Since Artificial Intelligence systems are developed by computer software engineers, should ethical considerations be included in AI courses at universities while training those engineers? Should professors who teach AI courses integrate ethical considerations into their curriculum and courses? Should people take precaution to avoid AI malfunctions or possible destruction in the future? Should people adopt some policies to prevent identity theft in case AI systems or AI robots do not do the job to protect them anymore? Who can and will solve the aforementioned problems? Will they become problems for human beings in the long run?

4. Lack of Budget with AI in Education

With job replacement and high costs for higher education, should AI in education be promoted? Does the federal government or the Department of Education have a sufficient budget to support AI in education? Funding is usually an issue in any school project. Who will pay for the costs? "Adopting AI technology comes with a price tag for hardware, software, facilities, and maintenance that universities must absorb. Institutions must also invest in training staff: Adopting AI can mean that staff need to come up a fairly steep learning curve, and it may require hiring staff with new skills" (Oracle, 2018). "The budget implications of using AI in education are unclear, given uncertainties about the cost-effectiveness of the technology. For example, the versatility and scalability of AI might drive some institutions to reduce teaching staff in favor of AI alternatives" (Lu & Harris, 2018, para 1). Universities have to transform to AI friendly units. To find the funding and to control the budget, all authorities have to develop a plan to tackle the issue. What do universities do if the government does not have money to support the project financially? How much will the costs be? Since AI in higher education relies on budget, how would university administrators and leaders solve the funding problem? Who cares and who will support AI in education?

SOLUTIONS AND RECOMMENDATIONS

There are advantages and disadvantages with the development of AI technologies in education. It is of great significance to ensure that the advantages of AI outweigh the disadvantages. In the followings, some recommendations will be presented for researchers, decision-makers, product developers, publishers, teachers, and administrators.

I. Recommendations for Researchers and Decision-Makers

While considering what AI in education will bring to e-classrooms, the approaches and strategies from all respects should be evaluated. For example, AI safety, cooperation among countries, coordination between AI robots and teachers, transparency over new measures, information, training, research, regulation, and policies should be examined. As Mannino et al. (2015) mentioned, it is critical to find additional options and to identify the set of measures with maximum effect; to establish research grants for answering the empirical questions; to build awareness of the risks associated with AI progress for experts working on AI, investors, and decision-makers; to encourage research on AI safety; and to improve international coordination and cooperation to maintain the safety of AI; to promote, fund, and coordinate relevant interdisciplinary research projects; to regulate experiments on living test subjects, and to carry out under the strict supervision of ethics commissions.

II. Recommendations for Publishers and Product Developers

While rethinking what might happen with AI technologies in education, it is essential to understand what publishers, product developers, and educational administrators can do to help solve the problem if there is any. Murphy (2019) stated that publishers, product developers, and educational administrators should focus on applications that leverage the capabilities of AI to help solve important problems in teaching and learning, because AI applications are not well-suited to all content areas or the full array of educational activities that teachers engage currently. Product developers or software engineers need to make the workings and performance of machine learning transparent, especially the limitations and accuracies of their models, the consequence of inaccurate decisions for students and teachers, how the datasets used, and how the models were trained, (Murphy, 2019). Product developers, software designers, and publishers should depict important challenges and concerns, including how to secure access to the relevant training data sets, how to guard against algorithmic bias, how to navigate and comply with data privacy regulations, and how to improve model transparency to increase the confidence and trust of users (Murphy, 2019). With appropriate regulations to limit AI technologies, teachers will feel safe and comfortable employing them.

III. Recommendations for Teachers

The traditional classrooms will likely be replaced with modern e-learning classrooms. What roles do classroom instructors play with the advancement of AI systems in the new classroom environment? As AI systems become more intricate, some job displacement might occur. Three new categories of AI-driven business and technology jobs, such as trainers, explainers, and sustainers will be available (Wilson, Daugherty, & Morini-Bianzino, 2017). Teachers should be ready to take the jobs. Trainers will teach AI systems how they should perform; explainers will provide clarity to bridge the gap between business leaders and technologists; sustainers will help ensure that AI systems are operating as designed and addressing the unintended consequences appropriately (Wilson, Daugherty, & Morini-Bianzino, 2017). Trainers involve customer-language tone and meaning trainer, smart-machine interaction modeler, and worldview trainer; explainers comprise context designer, transparency analyst, and AI usefulness strategist; sustainers consist of automation ethicist, automation economist, and machine relations manager (Wilson, Daugherty, & Morini-Bianzino, 2017). Rieland (2017) suggested that teachers have to serve as data scientists who understand Artificial Intelligence, who can monitor data, who watch the students, and who evaluate the data to identify how students learn.

Allen (2019) pointed out that, if the U.S. is second in the race for AI technology, it will create a situation of national technological and digital inferiority, which could result in national strategic subservience. The question to consider is: are teachers ready to develop into the leaders we will need tomorrow with AI in higher education? What degrees, certificates, or training do teachers need to survive in an AI technology system? In other words, with the innovative progress of AIEd, teachers need to learn technology and communication skills. What should teachers do? Teachers need to have the following three types of skills: (1) foundational literacies (i.e., literacy, numeracy, scientific literacy, information communication, technology literacy, financial literacy, cultural and civic literacy), (2) competencies (critical thinking, problem-solving, communication, and collaboration), and (3) character qualities (i.e., curiosity, initiative, persistence/grit, adaptability, leadership, and social and cultural awareness) (Luckin et al., 2016). Therefore, teachers are encouraged to take additionally training and to prepare for AI-dominated classrooms.

FUTURE RESEARCH DIRECTIONS

In this chapter, the evolution of AI in education, the model of AI in education, the functions of AI in education, and applications of AI in education were briefly reviewed. Future researchers may conduct a quantitative, a qualitative, or a mixed methods study to explore the impact of Artificial Intelligence in higher Education. Research on the impact of AI technologies on K-12 school settings are needed so that they can be evaluated and compared to higher education. How has AI in higher education impact teachers and students in the classrooms? What strategies or approaches should teachers use to cope with the radical changes in the classroom with AI technologies? Is AI in education being developed in the same way across states? How does AI in education help serve the needs for students in higher education? What should be changed in universities, curriculum, content of the courses, assessments, resources, or teachers? How can the government help build classrooms with AI technologies for the entire country? There are many topics to be explored regarding AI in education.

CONCLUSION

The innovation of Internet has contributed to students' self-learning at home; students use Wikipedia, watch YouTube videos, go to social media, listen to TED talks, immerse themselves in the Khan Academy, and explore online news. Technology and human beings are inextricable for now and well into the future. AI will serve as an invaluable tool for the extension of human experts, and help teachers to more effectively and simultaneously meet the diverse needs of many students in multiple locations (Faggella, 2017). Lukman Ramsey, a global solution manager at Google illustrated the vision of AI in higher education for the next five years; he said, AI assisted in students' journeys through higher education, starting from their college search, college enrollment, early intervention for at-risk students, and ending with employment (e.g., matching students' competencies and skills to the jobs) (Castelo, 2020). The advancement and innovation of new AI technologies have contributed to the evolution of teaching methods, curriculum, and materials as well as impacting teaching approaches at universities and students' learning styles. AI technology is reshaping teaching and learning now. Two major influences that are shaping education in the 21st century include: expanding knowledge and technological revolution. It is apparent that the innovation of AI technology has also let to the implementation of AI technology in education; continued development will be swift and incessant.

AI can take over tasks like grading, helping students learn with virtual tutoring, adapting to other aspects of teaching, be programmed to provide expertise, answering students' questions, finding information, and taking the place of teachers for basic course materials (Kumar, 2017). Teachers will supplement AI lessons, assist students who are struggling, and provide human interaction as well as hands-on experiences for students (Kumar, 2017). Teachers are no longer instructors, tutors, or observers; they should serve as facilitators, monitors, and from trainers.

Woolf (2015) suggested two future directions for AIEd to include personalize teaching (e.g., one-to-one attention, supporting learners with decision-making and reasoning in volatile changing environment, responding to student affect) and teaching 21st Century skills (e.g., cognitive skills, interpersonal skills, and intrapersonal skills). "Two AI techniques that can improve teaching for 21st Century skills are dialogue systems and inquiry learning" (Woolf, 2015, p.43). Luckin et al. (2016) predicted that in 15 years many new jobs will be more cognitively demanding than those currently available; social skills will be where humans continue to excel; and teachers have to re-skill large parts of the current workforce – in essence, create a learning society. What would it be like for teachers in the next decade with AI in education? What should the authorities do to help? In the following, researchers' recommendations are gathered.

"Today's robots interact with the physical world. Robotic sensing gives machines the ability to hear through signal processing, see through image processing, and touch through pressure and pattern processing.... this generation of robots can detect and express emotions" (Oblinger, 2018, p.13). What do people do if smart machines can take on all human tasks? How do AI, robotics, and analytics become disciplines in themselves? We need to know what AI can do and what teachers should do in new learning environment with AIEd. "Higher education leaders must consider how

AI, big data, analytics, robotics, and wide-scale collaboration might change the substance of education" (Oblinger, 2018, p.12).

It might not be apparent that AI technologies have already taken over higher education or have great impact in higher education at the moment. However, as Rizzotto (2017) projected, AI in education involves personalized learning (i.e., diverse programs, learning experiences, instructional approaches, and strategies that fit individual student's preferences, interests, inspirations, weaknesses, background), experiential learning (i.e., learning by doing; hands-on experience), and mastery-based learning (i.e., students should move forward with a subject once they've mastered all concepts preceding it since all knowledge is interconnected and cumulative). These types of learning could change education forever in future. Wagner (2018) also foresaw five major shifts for the future AI technology in a blended environment: (1) from stand and deliver instruction to facilitation and coaching; (2) from developers of content to developers of learning experiences; (3) from siloed classrooms to virtual social networks; (4) from textbooks and set curriculum to blended courses and customized design; (5) from a hierarchical top-down network to lateral virtual global network. As a result, teachers need to prepare for the implementation of new e-learning classrooms. Teachers need training and skills to manage or cope with AI technologies in the near future.

REFERENCES

Alimisis, D. (2013). Educational robotics: open questions and new challenges. *Themes in Science & Technology Education, 6*(1), 63-71. Retrieved from https://files.eric.ed.gov/fulltext/EJ1130924.pdf

Allen, J. R. (2019). *Why we need to rethink education in the artificial intelligence age*. Retrieved from https://www.brookings.edu/research/why-we-need-to-rethink-education-in-the-artificial-intelligence-age/

Altinay, F., Karaatmaca, C., Altinay, Z., & Dagli, G. (2019). Developing at a great pace: Studies on artificial intelligence in higher education. *Bucharest, 2*, 330-337. Retrieved from https://search.proquest.com/openview/72ba8c770621633fdb11e1fbaad76430/1?pq-origsite=gscholar&cbl=1876338

Andriessen, J., & Sandberg, J. (1999). Where is education heading and how about AI? *International Journal of Artificial Intelligence in Education, 10*, 130–150.

Beck, J., Stern, M., & Haugsjaa, E. (2005). *Applications of AI in education*. Retrieved from http://citeseerx.ist.psu.edu/viewdoc/download?doi=10.1.1.87.405&rep=rep1&type=pdf

Burton, E., Goldsmith, J., Koenig, S., Kuipers, B., Mattei, N., & Walsh, T. (2017). Ethical considerations in Artificial Intelligence courses. *AI Magazine*, *38*(2), 22–34. doi:10.1609/aimag.v38i2.2731

Castelo, M. (2020). A 5-year vision for artificial intelligence in higher ed. *EdTech: Focus on Higher Education*. Retrieved from https://edtechmagazine.com/higher/article/2020/02/5-year-vision-artificial-intelligence-higher-ed

Crowe, S. (2018). *10 biggest challenges in robotics*. Retrieved from https://www.therobotreport.com/10-biggest-challenges-in-robotics/

Drigas, A. S., & Ioannidou, R. (2012). Artificial Intelligence in special education: A decade review. *International Journal of Engineering Education*, *28*(6), 1366–1372.

Etzioni, A., & Etzioni, O. (2017). Should Artificial Intelligence be regulated? *Issues in Science and Technology*, *33*(4), 32–36. https://papers.ssrn.com/sol3/papers.cfm?abstract_id=2993506

Etzioni, O., & Schoenick, C. (2018). Artificial Intelligence: What educators need to know. *Education Week*, *37*(16), 28–29. https://www.edweek.org/ew/articles/2018/01/10/artificial-intelligence-what-educators-need-to-know.html

Faggella, D. (2017). *Examples of Artificial Intelligence in education*. Retrieved from https://www.techemergence.com/examples-of-artificial-intelligence-in-education/

Gadanidis, G. (2017). Artificial Intelligence, computational thinking, and mathematics education. *The Information Journal of Information and Learning Technology*, *34*(2), 133–139. doi:10.1108/IJILT-09-2016-0048

Gose, B. (2016). When the teaching assistant is a robot: Faculty members experiment with Artificial Intelligence in the classroom. *The Chronicle of Higher Education*. Retrieved from https://www.chronicle.com/article/When-the-Teaching-Assistant-Is/238114

Gustafson, S. M., & Gustafson, D. A. (2016). *Artificial Intelligence*. Retrieved from https://www.accessscience.com/content/artificial-intelligence/053300

Intelligent Tutoring Systems. (2018). *Wikipedia*. Retrieved from https://en.wikipedia.org/wiki/Intelligent_tutoring_system#Limitations

Klutka, J., Ackerly, N., & Magda, A. J. (2018). *Artificial intelligence in higher education: Current uses and future applications*. Retrieved from https://49hk843qjpwu3gfmw73ngy1k-wpengine.netdna-ssl.com/wp-content/uploads/2018/11/201811-AI-in-Higher-Education-TLH.pdf

Kumar, A. (2017). *10 roles for Artificial Intelligence in education*. Retrieved from https://www.linkedin.com/pulse/10-roles-artificial-intelligence-education-anil-kumar

Lambert, K. (2018). Could Artificial Intelligence replace our teachers? *Education World*. Retrieved from https://www.educationworld.com/could-artificial-intelligence-replace-our-teachers

Lee, K. (2018). Tech companies should stop pretending AI won't destroy jobs. *MIT Technology Review*. Retrieved from https://www.technologyreview.com/s/610298/tech-companies-should-stop-pretending-ai-wont-destroy-jobs/

Lu, J. J., & Harris, L. A. (2018). Artificial intelligence (AI) and education. *In Focus*. Retrieved from https://fas.org/sgp/crs/misc/IF10937.pdf

Luckin, R., Holmes, W., Griffiths, M., & Forcier, L. B. (2016). Intelligence unleashed: An argument for AI in education. London: Pearson. Retrieved from file:///C:/Users/Dr.%20S/Desktop/IGI%20(AI%20in%20education)/Intelligence-Unleashed-Publication%202016.pdf

Lynch, M. (2018). *7 roles for artificial intelligence in education*. Retrieved from https://www.thetechedvocate.org/7-roles-for-artificial-intelligence-in-education/

Madda, M. J. (2017). *Educators on Artificial Intelligence: Here's the one thing it can't do well*. Retrieved from https://www.edsurge.com/news/2017-11-20-educators-on-artificial-intelligence-here-s-the-one-thing-it-can-t-do-well

Mallawaarachchi, V. (2017). *Living with robots – the good, the bad and the ugly on humanity*. Retrieved from https://becominghuman.ai/living-with-robots-the-good-the-bad-and-the-ugly-on-humanity-1097f524f936

Mannino, A., Althaus, D., Erhardt, J., Gloor, L., Hutter, A., & Metzinger, T. (2015). *Artificial Intelligence: Opportunities and risks*. Retrieved from https://ea-foundation.org/files/ai-opportunities-and-risks.pdf

McArthur, D., Lewis, M., & Bishay, M. (2005). The role of Artificial Intelligence in education: Current progress and future prospects. *I-manager's Journal of Educational Technology*, *1*(4), 42–80. doi:10.26634/jet.1.4.972

McCarthy, J. (2006). *The philosophy of AI and the AI of philosophy*. Retrieved from http://jmc.stanford.edu/articles/aiphil2.html

McCarthy, J. (2007). *What is Artificial Intelligence?* Retrieved from http://jmc.stanford.edu/artificial-intelligence/index.html

McCarthy, J., Minsky, M. L., Rochester, N., & Shannon, C. E. (2006). A proposal for the Dartmouth summer research project on Artificial Intelligence. *AI Magazine*, *27*(4), 12–14. http://jmc.stanford.edu/articles/dartmouth.html

McCarthy, T., Rosenblum, P., Johnson, B. G., Dittel, J., & Kearns, D. M. (2016). An artificial intelligence tutor: A supplementary tool for teaching and practicing Braille. *Journal of Visual Impairment & Blindness*. Retrieved from https://files.eric.ed.gov/fulltext/EJ1114767.pdf

McClure, P. K. (2018). "You're fired," says the robot: The rise of automation in the workplace, technophobes, and fears of unemployment. *Social Science Computer Review*, *36*(2), 139–156. doi:10.1177/0894439317698637

Murphy, R. F. (2019). *Artificial intelligence applications to support K-12 teachers and teaching: A review of promising applications, opportunities, and challenges*. Retrieved from https://www.rand.org/content/dam/rand/pubs/perspectives/PE300/PE315/RAND_PE315.pdf

Oblinger, D. G. (2018). Smart machines and human expertise: Challenges for higher education. *EDUCAUSE Review*. Retrieved from https://er.educause.edu/articles/2018/8/smart-machines-and-human-expertise-challenges-for-higher-education

Ortiz, A. M., & Shaunna, S. (2015). The power of educational robotics as an integrated STEM learning experience in teacher preparation programs. *Journal of College Science Teaching*, *44*(5), 42–47. doi:10.2505/4/jcst15_044_05_42

Pan, Y. (2016). Heading toward Artificial Intelligence 2.0. *Engineering*, *2*(4), 409–413. doi:10.1016/J.ENG.2016.04.018

Patrizio, A. (2016). *Pros and cons of AI*. Retrieved from https://www.datamation.com/applications/pros-and-cons-of-artificial-intelligence.html

Popenici, S. A. D., & Kerr, S. (2017). Exploring the impact of Artificial Intelligence on teaching and learning in higher education. *Research and Practice in Technology Enhanced Learning, 12*(22), 1-13. Retrieved from https://telrp.springeropen.com/articles/10.1186/s41039-017-0062-8

Poth, R. D. (2018). *Artificial Intelligence: Implications for the future of education*. Retrieved from https://www.gettingsmart.com/2018/01/artificial-intelligence-implications-for-the-future-of-education/

Rajaraman, V. (2014). John McCarthy – Father of Artificial Intelligence. *Resonance: Journal of Science Education.* Retrieved from https://www.ias.ac.in/article/fulltext/reso/019/03/0198-0207

Rajasingham, L. (2009). The impact of Artificial Intelligence systems on future university paradigms. *Journal of Online Learning and Teaching*, *5*(2), 386–394. https://jolt.merlot.org/vol5no2/rajasingham_0609.pdf

Raths, D. (2019). AI's impact on Ed Tech. *Campus Technology*. Retrieved from https://campustechnology.com/articles/2019/01/10/ais-impact-on-ed-tech.aspx

Renz, A., & Hilbig, R. (2020). Prerequisites for artificial intelligence in further education: Identification of drivers, barriers, and business models of educational technology companies. *International Journal of Educational Technology in Higher Education*, *17*(14), 1–21.

Rieland, R. (2017). *Is Artificial Intelligence the key to personalized education?* Retrieved from https://www.smithsonianmag.com/innovation/artificial-intelligence-key-personalized-education-180963172/

Rizzotto, L. (2017). *The future of education: How A.I. and immersive tech will reshape learning forever: How immersive media and Artificial Intelligence can change education forever*. Retrieved from https://tfpodcast.io/2017/08/30/episode-36-the-future-of-education-how-a-i-and-immersive-tech-will-reshape-learning-forever/

Saranya, D., & Phil, M. (2016). A study on Artificial Intelligence and its applications. *International Journal of Advanced Research in Computer and Communication Engineering*, *5*(4), 313–315.

Saravanan, K., Sreedevi, E., & Subhamathi, V. (2017). A review of Artificial Intelligence systems. *International Journal of Advanced Research in Computer Science*, *8*(9), 418–420. doi:10.26483/ijarcs.v8i9.5095

Schroer, A. (2019). *7 companies using AI in education to enhance the classroom*. Retrieved from https://builtin.com/artificial-intelligence/ai-in-education

Skiba, D. J. (2017). Horizon report: Knowledge obsolescence, Artificial Intelligence, and rethinking the education role. *Nursing Education Perspectives*, *38*(3), 165–167. doi:10.1097/01.NEP.0000000000000154

Smith, N. B. (2002). *American reading instruction*. International Reading Association.

Wagner, K. (2018). *A blended environment: The future of AI and education*. Retrieved from https://www.gettingsmart.com/2018/01/a-blended-environment-the-future-of-ai-and-education/

Whitby, B. (2013). *Artificial Intelligence. Encyclopedia of philosophy and the social sciences*. SAGE Publications, Inc.

Wilson, H. J., Daugherty, P. R., & Morini-Bianzino, N. (2017). The jobs that Artificial Intelligence will create. *MIT Sloan Management Review*, *58*(4), 14–16. https://ilp.mit.edu/media/news_articles/smr/2017/58416.pdf

Wollowski, M., Neller, T., & Boerkoel, J. (2017). Artificial Intelligence education. Association for the Advancement of Artificial Intelligence. *AI Magazine*.

Woolf, B. P. (2015). AI and education: Celebrating 30 years of marriage. *AIED 2015 Workshop Proceedings, 4*, 38-47.

Woolf, B. P., Lane, H. C., Chaudhri, V. K., & Kolodner, J. I. (2013). AI grand challenges for education. *AI Magazine*. Retrieved from https://www.aaai.org/ojs/index.php/aimagazine/article/view/2490

Yang, G., Bellingham, J., Dupont, P. E., Fischer, P., Floridi, L., Full, R., . . . Wood, R. (2018). The gra.nd challenges of science robotics Science. *Robotics, 3*(14), 1-14 Retrieved from https://roboticssciencem.agorg/cont.ent/3/14/eaar7650

KEY TERMS AND DEFINITIONS

Artificial Intelligence (AI): The science of making intelligent machine that require human intelligence.

Artificial Intelligence in Education (AIEd): Applying artificial intelligence technology to the field of education and using it in students' learning at schools.

Artificial Intelligence Tutor: AI online learning system such as iTalk2Learn, Third space learning, Duolingo Chatbot, Thinkster Math, and Ed Tech Foundry.

Educational Robotics: Course that teaches the design, analysis, application and operation of robots at schools or universities.

Interactive Learning Environments (ILEs): The settings for a pedagogical approach that incorporates digital technology and virtual communication by students in course design and delivery.

Intelligent Tutoring System (ITS): A computer system that provides customized and immediate instruction and feedback to students without the intervention of a human teacher.

Learning Management System: (LMS): A software application for delivering educational courses, training programs, administration, documentation, training, and learning.

Virtual Facilitators: Online teachers who facilitate virtual classes by using computer software and the Internet to deliver instruction to students.

Chapter 6
Role of Machine Learning in Modern Education and Teaching

Latika Kharb
https://orcid.org/0000-0002-8549-0920
Jagan Institute of Management Studies, India

Prateek Singh
Jagan Institute of Management Studies, India

ABSTRACT

Computers are being utilized in field in education for many years. In last few decades, research within the field of artificial intelligence (AI) is positively affecting educational application. Advanced machine learning and deep learning techniques could be used for extracting knowledgeable information from crude information. In this chapter, the authors have analysed the impact of artificial intelligence in the education domain. The authors will discuss how with the development of machine learning techniques in last few decades, machine learning models can anticipate student performance. By learning about every student, models can identify the shortcomings. Then the authors will propose different approaches to improve student performance. Teachers can also use this model to understand student perception levels in a better way so that they can modulate their lectures according to student perception levels.

DOI: 10.4018/978-1-7998-4763-2.ch006

INTRODUCTION

Computers are being utilized in field in Education for many years. In the last few years research within the domain of Artificial Intelligence (AI) is positively affecting educational application. Artificial Intelligence is a mixture of Big data, Machine Learning, Combinatorial Optimization, and Natural Language Processing. It is the new generation of technology which will help out modern society and education in many ways. Different technologies are already using these techniques to provide more functionality in their applications. Advanced machine learning and deep learning techniques could be used for extracting knowledgeable information from crude information. By learning about every student, models can identify the shortcomings and then authors will propose different approaches to improve student performance. Teachers can also use this model to understand students' perception level in a better way so that they can modulate their lectures according to the student's perception level.

Artificial Intelligence is progressing at an accelerated pace, it already fabricates the intelligent nature of services in the education domain. Some AI solutions are dependent on programming, whereas some have capability to find patterns and make predictions regarding the given problem. Example: Recently French song writer Benoît Carré has worked together with an AI music program called Flow Machines to create an EuroPop Album. Authors describe Machine Learning as a subfield of AI that joins programming prepared to perceive designs, make predictions, and apply recently discovered examples to conditions that were rejected or secured by their underlying plan. To Understand Artificial Intelligence better let us know about the basics of Artificial Intelligence:

- Big Data:- Large data sets that are analyzed by using patter revelation, trends, associations which will help in relating to human behaviour and interactions. It deals with very large data sets that are too complex to be solved with traditional data processing software.
- Machine Learning: - It's an application of artificial intelligence that deliversintelligence to computers so that they learn repeatedly from training sets and test the predictions on test data to check accuracy and along with other statistical parameters. It mainly focuses on applications that grant rights to use data and use it for machine learning tasks.
- Combinatorial Optimization:- it is an emerging field of theoretical computer science that uses combinatorial techniques that aims to solve discrete optimization problems. It finds the best possible solution from a finite set of problems.

- Natural Language Processing (NLP):- It involves machines or robots to understand and replicate the language that humans speak. It also tries to understand the emotions and reactions of human beings.

The future of cutting edge education systems is naturally associated with improvement of new advancements and computing capacity of new astute machines. Machine learning can help to fill the needs gaps in learning and teaching. Teachers can predict student's performance and can also classify confusion levels of students whether a particular topic will be clear to the cluster of students or not.

In this chapter, authors have analysed the impact of Artificial Intelligence in the education domain. Authors will discuss how with the development of Machine Learning techniques in last few decades, machines learning models can anticipate student performance. The objective of our chapter is to study the student's performance based on current real world data (viz. student grade, demographic area data, social activity features and school related features). In this chapter, several machine learning models (Support Vector Machine, Logistic Regression, Decision Tree Classifier, Naive Bayes) by (Islam & Zhang, 2018) are applied to investigate the performance of students. (Kharb, Aggarwal & Chahal, 2020)Big data faces various difficulties, for example, data storage, data capturing, data analysis, sharing data reports, searching, transferable data, data visualization, tossing queries on it, updation, security. Dataset is collected from the University of California Irvine (UCI) machine learning repository in (Namayanja & Janeja 2012) and (Frank & Asuncion, 2010); it holds 649 instances and 33 attributes.

The data approach student accomplishment in advance education of two Portuguese schools. Two datasets are given with respect to two different subjects (i.e. Mathematics and Portuguese language). Also four machine learning regression models (i.e. Linear Regression, Support Vector Regression, Decision Tree Regression and Random Forest Regression by (Cortez & Silva, 2008)) are used to predict final year student performance. Parting of dataset is finished utilizing Cross Validation method (i.e. K-Fold Cross Validation).

Figure 1. Some feature samples from dataset

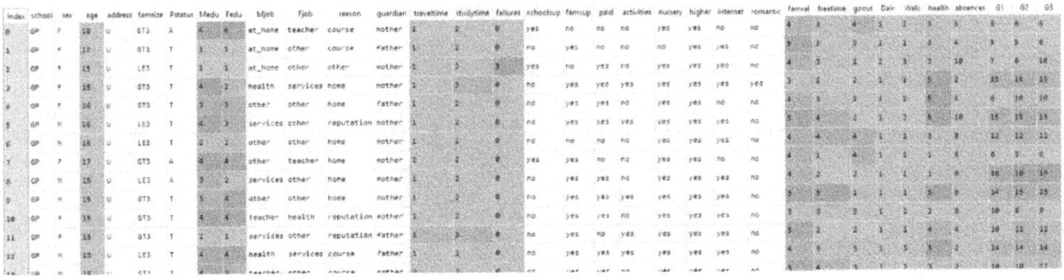

Index	school	sex	age	address	famsize	Pstatus	Medu	Fedu	Mjob	Fjob	reason	guardian	traveltime	studytime	failures	schoolsup	famsup	paid	activities	nursery	higher	internet	romantic	famrel	freetime	goout	Dalc	Walc	health	absences	G1	G2	G3
0	GP	F	18	U	GT3	A	4	4	at_home	teacher	course	mother	2	2	0	yes	no	no	no	yes	yes	no	no	4	3	4	1	1	3	6	5	6	6
1	GP	F	17	U	GT3	T	1	1	at_home	other	course	father	1	2	0	no	yes	no	no	no	yes	yes	no	5	3	3	1	1	3	4	5	5	6
2	GP	F	15	U	LE3	T	1	1	at_home	other	other	mother	1	2	3	yes	no	yes	no	yes	yes	yes	no	4	3	2	2	3	3	10	7	8	10
3	GP	F	15	U	GT3	T	4	2	health	services	home	mother	1	3	0	no	yes	yes	yes	yes	yes	yes	yes	3	2	2	1	1	5	2	15	14	15
4	GP	F	16	U	GT3	T	3	3	other	other	home	father	1	2	0	no	yes	yes	no	yes	yes	no	no	4	3	2	1	2	5	4	6	10	10
5	GP	M	16	U	LE3	T	4	3	services	other	reputation	mother	1	2	0	no	yes	yes	yes	yes	yes	yes	no	5	4	2	1	2	5	10	15	15	15
6	GP	M	16	U	LE3	T	2	2	other	other	home	mother	1	2	0	no	no	no	no	yes	yes	yes	no	4	4	4	1	1	3	0	12	12	11
7	GP	F	17	U	GT3	A	4	4	other	teacher	home	mother	2	2	0	yes	yes	no	no	yes	yes	no	no	4	1	4	1	1	1	6	6	5	6
8	GP	M	15	U	LE3	A	3	2	services	other	home	mother	1	2	0	no	yes	yes	no	yes	yes	yes	no	4	2	2	1	1	1	0	16	18	19
9	GP	M	15	U	GT3	T	3	4	other	other	home	mother	1	2	0	no	yes	yes	yes	yes	yes	yes	no	5	5	1	1	1	5	0	14	15	15
10	GP	F	15	U	GT3	T	4	4	teacher	health	reputation	mother	1	2	0	no	yes	yes	no	yes	yes	yes	no	3	3	3	1	2	2	0	10	8	9
11	GP	F	15	U	GT3	T	2	1	services	other	reputation	father	3	3	0	no	yes	no	yes	yes	yes	yes	no	5	2	2	1	1	4	4	10	12	12
12	GP	M	15	U	LE3	T	4	4	health	services	course	father	1	1	0	no	yes	yes	yes	yes	yes	yes	no	4	3	3	1	3	5	2	14	14	14

Dataset Information

The used dataset has been taken from University of California Irvine (UCI) machine learning repository (Namayanja et. al, 2012) where it was donated by Paulo Cortez, University of Minho. Dataset approach student achievement in advance education of two Portuguese schools (i.e. Gabriel Pereira and Mousinho da Silveira). (Berwick, 2003) stated that like several others (e.g. France and Venezuela) Portugal also uses a 20 point evaluating scale, where 0 is considered as most minimal evaluation and 20 is considered as Excellent grade. Amid the school year, students are surveyed in three periods and the last assessment relates to the last grade(G3). Information gathered during the 2005-06 academic year from two public schools in the Alentejo area in Portugal. Data is collected from two sources: School Report Cards and Questionnaires.

Table 1. Machine Learning Applications In Education

Adaptive Learning	Learning Analytics	Predictive Analytics
Adaptive learning breaks down an students presentation progressively, alters instructing strategies and the educational program dependent on that data. It helps with having a customized commitment and tries to adapt to the individual for a better education..	Ordinarily it happens that the educator additionally stalls out while teaching. Along these lines, the bits of information and substance aren't fittingly appreciated by the understudies. With learning investigation, the instructor can pick up understanding into information and can perform significant dives into data.	Predictive analytics in training assists with making decisions about the things that may occur later on. This enables the staff and the guardians to get caution and take to suitable measures. Through this, a student can benefit from outside assistance in a superior manner and can take a shot at his feeble subjects.
Personalized Learning	**Increasing Efficiency**	**Evaluating Assessments**
This one is the best use that AI gives. It is customization and individual essentials are being managed through this. Through this educational model, the understudies can coordinate their own learning. They can have their own pace and can choose decisions about what to acknowledge and how to learn. They can pick the subjects they are enthusiastic about, the teacher they have to pick up from and what instructive program, rules and model they have to follow.	Machine learning has the capacity of better substance and educational program association and the executives. It assists with bifurcating the work as needs be and comprehends the capability of everybody. This assists with breaking down what work is most appropriate for the instructor and what works for the understudy. It makes work of instructors and students simpler and that makes them cheerful and alright with training. This likewise builds the contribution and their affection towards interest and learning. Along these lines, expanding the proficiency of instruction.	Machine learning has the capacity of better substance and educational plan association and the executives. It assists with bifurcating the work as needs be and comprehends the capability of everybody. This assists with breaking down what work is most appropriate for the teachers and what works for the students. It makes work by educators and students less complex and that makes them merry and OK with preparing. This in like manner grows the consideration and their affection towards collaboration and learning. Along these lines, expanding the productivity of instruction

The final data is integrated in two datasets mainly focused on two main subjects Mathematics (contains 395 records) and Portuguese (contains 649 records). Total 33 attributes have been used in both dataset for predicting student performance.

Exploratory Data Analysis (EDA)

See Table 2 and Figures 2-11.

Table 2. Student related attributes

Attributes	Description
sex	Describe gender of student (Male or Female)
age	Describe age of student (15 to 22)
school	Describe student school (Gabriel Pereira or Mousinho da Silveira)
address	Describe student home address (urban or rural)
Pstatus	Describe parents cohabitation status(Living together or Apart)
Medu	Describe student's mother qualification (0 to 4)
Mjob	Describe student's mother profession
Fedu	Describe student's father qualification (0 to 4)
Fjob	Describe student's father qualification
guardian	Describe student's guardian (mother, father or other)
famsize	Describe student's family size
famrel	Describe student's family relation rating(1 (very bad) to 5 (Excellent))
reason	Reason for choosing school
traveltime	Travelling time from home to school
studytime	Weekly time spend on studying
failures	Number of past classes failures
schoolsup	Extra educational school support (Yes or No)
famsup	Family educational support (Yes or No)
activities	Extracurricular activities (Yes or No)
paidclass	Extra paid tuitions (Yes or No)
internet	Internet access at home (Yes or No)
nursery	Attended nursery schooling (Yes or No)
higher	Plan for pursuing higher education (Yes or No)
romantic	Committed (Yes or No)
freetime	Free time after school (1 (very less) to 5 (very high))
gout	Hanging out with friends (1 (very less) to 5 (very high))
Walc	Weekend alcohol consumption (1 (very less) to 5 (very high))
Dalc	Weekday alcohol consumption (1 (very less) to 5 (very high))
health	Current fitness level (1 (very bad) to 5 (very good))
absence	Number of school absence (0 to 93)
G1	First period grade (0 to 20)
G2	Second period grade (0 to 20)
G3	Final grade (0 to 20)

Figure 2. Statistical Description of Mathematics Dataset

Index	age	Medu	Fedu	traveltime	studytime	failures	famrel	freetime	goout	Dalc	Walc	health	absences	G1	G2	G3
count	395	395	395	395	395	395	395	395	395	395	395	395	395	395	395	395
mean	16.6962	2.74937	2.52152	1.4481	2.03544	0.334177	3.9443	3.23544	3.10886	1.48101	2.29114	3.55443	5.70886	10.9089	10.7139	10.4152
std	1.27604	1.09474	1.0882	0.697505	0.83924	0.743651	0.896659	0.998862	1.11328	0.890741	1.2879	1.3903	8.0031	3.31919	3.7615	4.58144
min	15	0	0	1	1	0	1	1	1	1	1	1	0	3	0	0
25%	16	2	2	1	1	0	4	3	2	1	1	3	0	8	9	8
50%	17	3	2	1	2	0	4	3	3	1	2	4	4	11	11	11
75%	18	4	3	2	2	0	5	4	4	2	3	5	8	13	13	14
max	22	4	4	4	4	3	5	5	5	5	5	5	75	19	19	20

Figure 3. Statistical Description of Portuguese Dataset

Index	age	Medu	Fedu	traveltime	studytime	failures	famrel	freetime	goout	Dalc	Walc	health	absences	G1	G2	G3
count	649	649	649	649	649	649	649	649	649	649	649	649	649	649	649	649
mean	16.7442	2.51464	2.30663	1.56857	1.93066	0.22188	3.93066	3.18028	3.1849	1.50231	2.28043	3.53621	3.65948	11.3991	11.5701	11.906
std	1.21814	1.13455	1.09993	0.74866	0.82951	0.593235	0.955717	1.05109	1.17577	0.924834	1.28438	1.44626	4.64076	2.74527	2.91364	3.23066
min	15	0	0	1	1	0	1	1	1	1	1	1	0	0	0	0
25%	16	2	1	1	1	0	4	3	2	1	1	2	0	10	10	10
50%	17	2	2	1	2	0	4	3	3	1	2	4	2	11	11	12
75%	18	4	3	2	2	0	5	4	4	2	3	5	6	13	13	14
max	22	4	4	4	4	3	5	5	5	5	5	5	32	19	19	19

Proposed Techniques

For evaluating student's performance, authors used four Machine Learning regression models in this chapter. Datasets has been split using the k-fold cross validation method. Label Encoder is used for translating non- numeric values to numeric values. Figure 12 represents the architectural diagram for our model.

Encoding Methods -Labels

The process of converting categorical i.e. non-numeric data values to numeric form of feature representation. Label Encoding is used to make data ready for the model. Models don't accept textual data i.e. it is necessary to encode or convert such data to numeric data. Two most common encoding methods are: OneHotEncoder and Label Encoder.

In this chapter LabelEncoder method is used for conversion of textual data to numeric form of data. This method can be used using scikit-learn library sklearn in python. It encodes labels within range of 0 to n_classes – 1, where n = distinct number of labels. If a particular label value reappears it simply assigns the same value to label as assigned earlier.

Figure 4. Number of null values in Mathematics Dataset

```
In [6]: dataset_Maths.isnull().sum()

Out[6]: school        0
        sex           0
        age           0
        address       0
        famsize       0
        Pstatus       0
        Medu          0
        Fedu          0
        Mjob          0
        Fjob          0
        reason        0
        guardian      0
        traveltime    0
        studytime     0
        failures      0
        schoolsup     0
        famsup        0
        paid          0
        activities    0
        nursery       0
        higher        0
        internet      0
        romantic      0
        famrel        0
        freetime      0
        goout         0
        Dalc          0
        Walc          0
        health        0
        absences      0
        G1            0
        G2            0
        G3            0
        dtype: int64
```

Cross Validation

Cross Validation is basically utilized in applied machine learning to calculate the expertise of machine learning models on concealed data. Finite number of samples is used in order to calculate how a model is expected to perform in general when it is used to make predictions on a given set of data.

There are several cross validation methods available for machine learning models. In this chapter authors have used k-fold cross validation. The methodology has a binary parameter k that represents the number of groups a given data sample has to be split into.

Figure 5. Number of null values in Portuguese Dataset

```
In [7]: dataset_Por.isnull().sum()

Out[7]: school        0
        sex           0
        age           0
        address       0
        famsize       0
        Pstatus       0
        Medu          0
        Fedu          0
        Mjob          0
        Fjob          0
        reason        0
        guardian      0
        traveltime    0
        studytime     0
        failures      0
        schoolsup     0
        famsup        0
        paid          0
        activities    0
        nursery       0
        higher        0
        internet      0
        romantic      0
        famrel        0
        freetime      0
        goout         0
        Dalc          0
        Walc          0
        health        0
        absences      0
        G1            0
        G2            0
        G3            0
        dtype: int64
```

Linear Regression

Linear regression is a commonly used machine learning regression model. It is generally used for predicting target variables or dependent variables based on a set of independent variables. It is generally used to find relation within variables and forecasting target variable. Hypothesis function for linear regression:

$$y = \theta_1 + \theta_2 \cdot x$$

Figure 6. Number of Males and Females

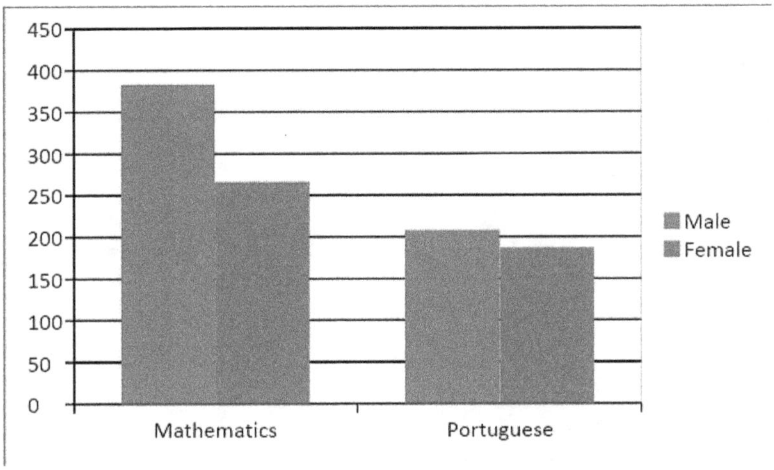

Figure 7. Residency of students

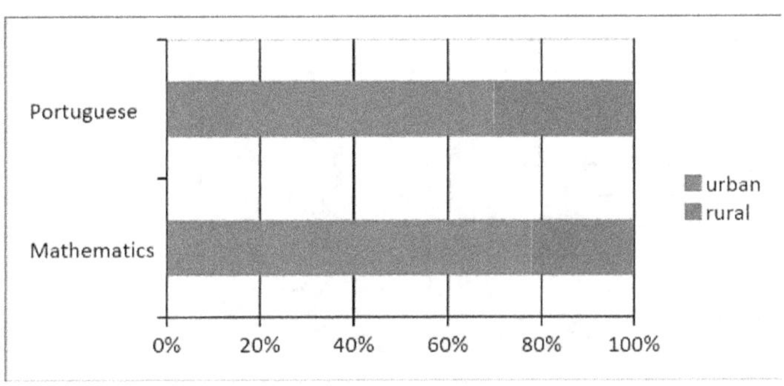

Cost function of linear regression can be used to evaluate accuracy of our hypothesis. Cost function takes average distinction of all the results of hypothesis with inputs independent features variables and actual output dependent variable.

$$J\left(\theta_0,\theta_1\right)=\frac{1}{2m}\sum_{i=1}^{m}\left(\hat{y}_i-y_i\right)^2=\frac{1}{2m}\sum_{i=1}^{m}(h_\theta\left(x_i\right)-y_i)^2$$

$m = number\ of\ training\ examples$

Figure 8. Family size of students

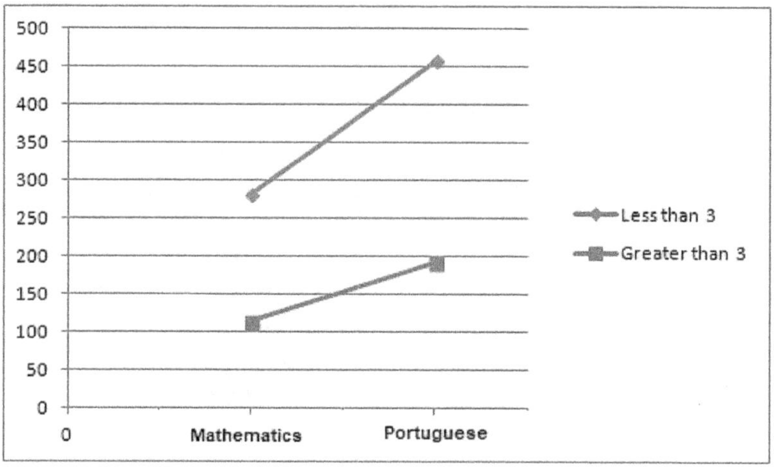

Figure 9. Mother Qualification of students

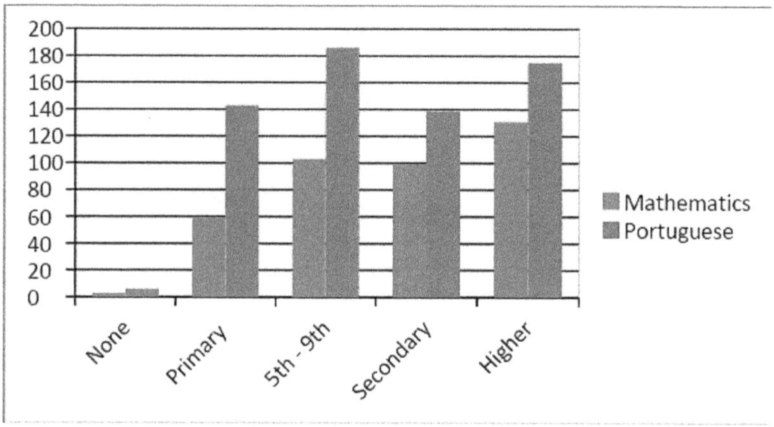

Support Vector Regression

Support Vector Machine is a widely used machine learning algorithm utilized for both regressions as well as for classification problems. Support Vector Regression uses the same hypothesis as support vector machine uses for classification problems. As per (Cortez et.al, 2008), there is no significant contrast in working of Support Vector Classifier (SVC) and Support Vector Regression (SVR). As per (Oddershede& Petersen, 2015), Support Vectors are the information focuses that lie nearest to the

Figure 10. Father Qualification of students

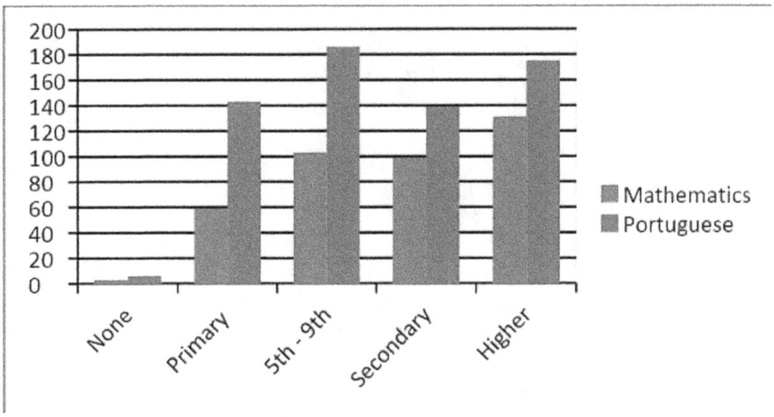

Figure 11. Health of students

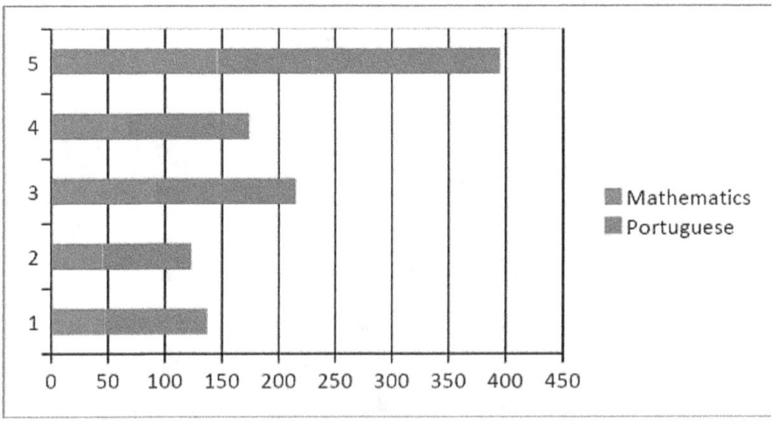

decision surface (hyperplane). The Main target of SVM is to find hyperplanes in N-Dimensional space (Number of Features) that particularly classifies the data points. Support Vectors closer to hyperplane impact the position and introduction of hyperplane. To maximise the border within the datapoints and hyperplane, authors use loss function to maximise the border

$$c\left(x, y, f\left(x\right)\right) = \begin{cases} 0, & if\, y * f\left(x\right) \geq 1 \\ 1 - y * f\left(x\right), & else \end{cases}$$

Figure 12. Architectural diagram

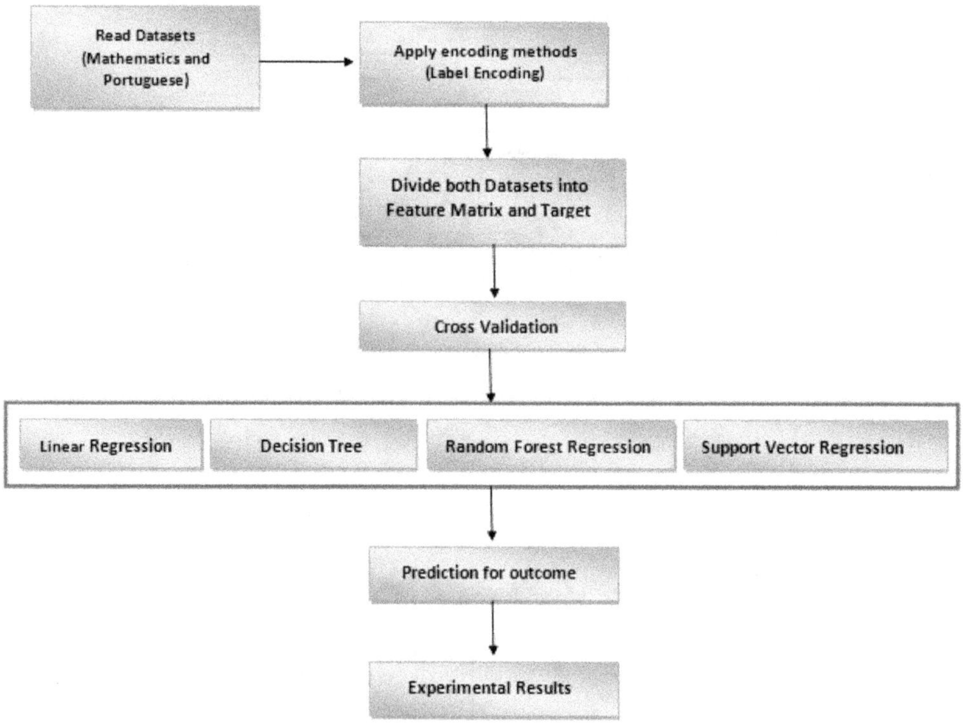

Figure 13. Sample of textual data from Mathematics dataset

Index	school	sex	age	address	famsize	Pstatus	Medu	Fedu	Mjob	Fjob	reason	guardian	traveltime	studytime	failures	schoolsup	famsup	paid	activities	nursery	higher	internet	romantic	famrel	fre
0	GP	F	18	U	GT3	A	4	4	at_home	teacher	course	mother	2	2	0	yes	no	no	no	yes	yes	no	no	4	3
1	GP	F	17	U	GT3	T	1	1	at_home	other	course	father	1	2	0	no	yes	no	no	no	yes	yes	no	5	3
2	GP	F	15	U	LE3	T	1	1	at_home	other	other	mother	1	2	3	yes	no	yes	no	yes	yes	yes	no	4	3
3	GP	F	15	U	GT3	T	4	2	health	services	home	mother	1	3	0	no	yes	yes	yes	yes	yes	yes	yes	3	2
4	GP	F	16	U	GT3	T	3	3	other	other	home	father	1	2	0	no	yes	yes	no	yes	yes	no	no	4	3
5	GP	M	16	U	LE3	T	4	3	services	other	reputation	mother	1	2	0	no	yes	yes	yes	yes	yes	yes	no	5	4
6	GP	M	16	U	LE3	T	2	2	other	other	home	mother	1	2	0	no	no	no	no	yes	yes	yes	no	4	4
7	GP	F	17	U	GT3	A	4	4	other	teacher	home	mother	2	2	0	yes	yes	no	no	yes	yes	no	no	4	1
8	GP	M	15	U	LE3	A	3	2	services	other	home	mother	1	2	0	no	yes	yes	no	yes	yes	yes	no	4	2
9	GP	M	15	U	GT3	T	3	4	other	other	home	mother	1	2	0	no	yes	yes	yes	yes	yes	yes	no	5	5
10	GP	F	15	U	GT3	T	4	4	teacher	health	reputation	mother	1	2	0	no	yes	yes	no	yes	yes	yes	no	3	3

Figure 14. Label Encoding for Mathematics and Portuguese dataset

```
In [17]: from sklearn.preprocessing import LabelEncoder
         Features = dataset_Maths.drop('G3',axis=1)
         Target = dataset_Maths['G3']
         label = LabelEncoder()
         Cat_Colums = Features.dtypes.pipe(lambda Features: Features[Features=='object']).index
         for col in Cat_Colums:
             Features[col] = label.fit_transform(Features[col])
```

```
In [18]: from sklearn.preprocessing import LabelEncoder
         Features_Por = dataset_Por.drop('G3',axis=1)
         Target_Por = dataset_Maths['G3']
         label = LabelEncoder()
         Cat_Colums_Por = Features_Por.dtypes.pipe(lambda Features_Por: Features_Por[Features_Por=='object']).index
         for col in Cat_Colums_Por:
             Features_Por[col] = label.fit_transform(Features_Por[col])
```

Figure 15. After applying label encoding method

Index	school	sex	age	address	famsize	Pstatus	Medu	Fedu	Mjob	Fjob	reason	guardian	traveltime	studytime	failures	schoolsup	famsup	paid	activities	nursery	higher	internet	romantic	famrel	freetime	goout
0	0	0	18	1	0	0	4	4	0	4	0	1	2	2	0	1	0	0	0	1	1	0	0	4	3	4
1	0	0	17	1	0	1	1	1	0	2	0	0	1	2	0	0	1	0	0	0	1	1	0	5	3	3
2	0	0	15	1	1	1	1	1	0	2	2	1	1	2	3	1	0	1	0	1	1	1	0	4	3	2
3	0	0	15	1	0	1	4	2	1	3	1	1	1	3	0	0	1	1	1	1	1	1	1	3	2	2
4	0	0	16	1	0	1	3	3	2	2	1	0	1	2	0	0	1	1	0	1	1	0	0	4	3	2
5	0	1	16	1	1	1	4	3	3	2	3	1	1	2	0	0	1	1	1	1	1	1	0	5	4	2
6	0	1	16	1	1	1	2	2	2	2	1	1	1	2	0	0	0	0	0	1	1	1	0	4	4	4
7	0	0	17	1	0	0	4	4	2	4	1	1	2	2	0	1	1	0	0	1	1	0	0	4	1	4
8	0	1	15	1	1	0	3	2	3	2	1	1	1	2	0	0	1	1	0	1	1	1	0	4	2	2
9	0	1	15	1	0	1	3	4	2	2	1	1	1	2	0	0	1	1	1	1	1	1	0	5	5	1
10	0	0	15	1	0	1	4	4	4	1	3	1	1	2	0	0	1	1	0	1	1	1	0	3	3	3

Figure 16. K-fold cross validation

```
In [23]: #Mathematics
         from sklearn.model_selection import KFold
         kf = KFold(n_splits=20)
         kf.get_n_splits(X_Maths)
         #print(kf)
         for train_index, test_index in kf.split(X_Maths):
           #  print("train:", train_index, "TEST:", test_index)
             X_train_M, X_test_M = X_Maths[train_index], X_Maths[test_index]
             y_train_M, y_test_M = Y_Maths[train_index], Y_Maths[test_index]
```

```
In [25]: #Portuguese
         from sklearn.model_selection import KFold
         kf = KFold(n_splits=20)
         kf.get_n_splits(X_Por)
         print(kf)
         for train_index, test_index in kf.split(X_Por):
             print("train:", train_index, "TEST:", test_index)
             X_train_P, X_test_P = X_Por[train_index], X_Por[test_index]
             y_train_P, y_test_P = Y_Por[train_index], Y_Por[test_index]

         KFold(n_splits=20, random_state=None, shuffle=False)
         train: [ 33  34  35  36  37  38  39  40  41  42  43  44  45  46  47  48  49
           51  52  53  54  55  56  57  58  59  60  61  62  63  64  65  66  67  68
           69  70  71  72  73  74  75  76  77  78  79  80  81  82  83  84  85  86
           87  88  89  90  91  92  93  94  95  96  97  98  99 100 101 102 103 104
```

Figure 17. Linear Regression model for Mathematics and Portuguese dataset

```
In [26]: #Mathematics
         from sklearn.linear_model import LinearRegression
         regressor = LinearRegression()
         regressor.fit(X_train_M,y_train_M)
         Y_pred_M_LR = regressor.predict(X_test_M)

In [ ]:  #Portugese
         regressor.fit(X_train_P,y_train_P)
         Y_pred_P_LR = regressor.predict(X_test_P)
```

Hinge loss function can also be represented as:

$$c\left(x, y, f\left(x\right)\right) = \left(1 * y * f\left(x\right)\right)_{+}$$

Loss function for SVM:

$$\min_{w} \lambda \left\|w\right\|^{2} + \sum_{i=1}^{n} \left(1 - y_{i}\left\langle x_{i}, w\right\rangle\right)_{+}$$

Gradient descent can be used for weight updating in given set of features:-

$$\frac{\delta}{\delta w_{k}}\left(1 - y_{i}\left\langle x_{i}, w\right\rangle\right)_{+} = \begin{cases} 0, & if\, y_{i}\left\langle x_{i}, w\right\rangle \geq 1 \\ -y_{i}x_{ik}, & else \end{cases}$$

Figure 18. Support Vector Regression

```
In [ ]:  #Mathematics
         from sklearn.svm import SVR
         regressor = SVR()
         regressor.fit(X_train_M,y_train_M)
         pred_SVR_M = regressor.predict(X_test_M)

In [ ]:  #Portuguese
         regressor.fit(X_train_P,y_train_P)
         pred_SVR_P = regressor.predict(X_test_P)
```

Decision Tree Regression (Oddershede et.al, 2015)

Decision tree build a flow chart type structure (tree structure) to deal with classification and regression problems. Dataset is divided into small subsets while on other hand analogous decision trees are incrementally developed. The tree is the combination of leaf nodes and decision nodes. Decision nodes can have two or more branches each representing an attribute assigned to it. Leaf nodes constitute a decision on the numerical target, leaf nodes don't have any further branches. Decision tree is formed following 2 major steps: Induction and Pruning. Induction is when authors actually collect a tree for example set larger part of different leveled decision limits reliant on our data. Pruning is the route towards removing the silly structure from a decision tree. Simple squared error can be used as our cost function:

$$E = \sum (Y - \hat{Y})^2$$

Figure 19. Structure of Decision Tree

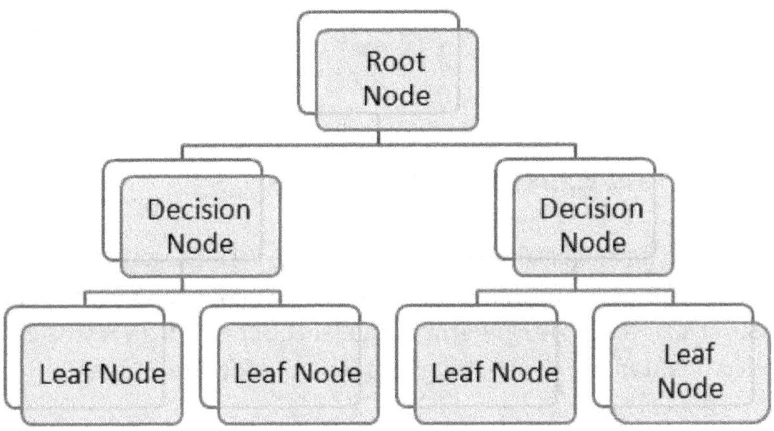

Figure 20. Decision Tree Regression

```
In [32]: #Mathematics
         from sklearn.tree import DecisionTreeRegressor
         DCT = DecisionTreeRegressor(random_state = 0)
         DCT.fit(X_train_M, y_train_M)
         pred_DCT_M = DCT.predict(X_test_M)

In [33]: #Portuguese
         DCT.fit(X_train_P, y_train_P)
         pred_DCT_P = DCT.predict(X_test_P)
```

Random Forest Regression

Random forest is capable of dealing with both classifications as well as with regression problems. Random forest uses multiple machine learning models to make predictions i.e. it uses multiple decision trees. As per (Burkart, Robert &Huber, 2020), random forest uses bagging which involves training each decision tree on a different data sample. Rather than relying on a single decision tree random forest uses multiple decision trees to determine its output. Scikit-learn recently changed the default value of n_estimators(n number of decision trees) from 10 to 100 with the release of version 0.22 .

Figure 21. Random Forest Regression

```
In [ ]: #Mathematics
        from sklearn.ensemble import RandomForestRegressor
        rfr = RandomForestRegressor()
        rfr.fit(X_train_M, y_train_M)
        pred_RFR_M = rfr.predict(X_test_M)

In [ ]: #Portuguese
        rfr.fit(X_train_P, y_train_P)
        pred_RFR_P = rfr.predict(X_test_P)
```

Performance and Experimental Results

The basic performance measurement is done using various statistical methods (i.e. mean squared error, mean absolute error, explained variance score, r2 score, rooted square mean error (RMSE)) as given by (Oddershede et.al, 2015). Statistical methods were applied on all machines learning regression models used in this chapter.

- **Explained Variance Score:** Variance can be described as how far data has been spread out if variance is zero it means data contains same values. Variance is average of squared differences from mean is known as total variance of data. After applying regression model, the difference between predicted and actual data is called residual variance. Difference between total variance and residual variance is known as explained variance.

$$ExplainedVariance = TotalVariance - ResidualVariance$$

Figure 22. Explained Variance for Linear Regression

```
In [56]: #Mathematics
         print(explained_variance_score(y_test_M,Y_pred_M_LR))

         #Portuguese
         print(explained_variance_score(y_test_P,Y_pred_P_LR))

0.8426824839290784
0.7915345521711494
```

Figure 23. Explained Variance for Decision Tree

```
In [55]: #Mathematics
         print(explained_variance_score(y_test_M,pred_DCT_M))

         #Portuguese
         print(explained_variance_score(y_test_P,pred_DCT_P))

0.8467388325568649
0.6539560635827828
```

Figure 24. Explained Variance for Random Forest

```
In [57]: #Mathematics
         print(explained_variance_score(y_test_M,pred_RFR_M))

         #Portuguese
         print(explained_variance_score(y_test_P,pred_RFR_P))

0.9360338448890106
0.7473642614752636
```

Figure 25. Explained Variance for Support Vector Machine

```
In [58]: #Mathematics
         print(explained_variance_score(y_test_M,pred_SVR_M))

         #Portuguese
         print(explained_variance_score(y_test_P,pred_SVR_P))

0.6824696138964645
0.6122263106805212
```

Figure 26. Performance of explained variance on both datasets

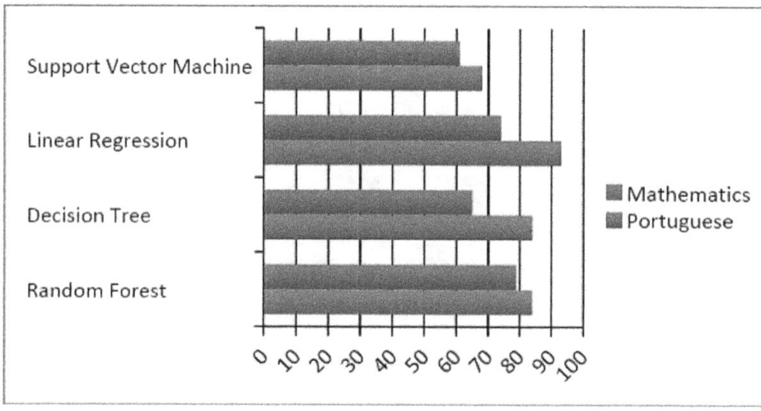

- **Mean Squared Error:** Mean squared error simply represents how close is a regression line is to a set of data points. It simply calculates the distance from the data point to the regression line(this distance is considered as errors) furthermore, squaring them, squaring is done to remove negative signs; it additionally gives more weight to bigger contrasts. Thus it is known as mean squared error.

$$Mean\,Squared\,Error = \frac{1}{n}\sum\nolimits_{i=1}^{n}(y_i - \hat{y}_i)^2$$

Figure 27. Mean Squared Error for Linear Regression

```
In [59]: from sklearn import metrics

         #Mathematics
         print(metrics.mean_squared_error(y_test_M, Y_pred_M_LR))

         #Portuguese
         print(metrics.mean_squared_error(y_test_P, Y_pred_P_LR))

         3.3967629278446108
         5.748580383151158
```

Figure 28. Mean Squared Error Decision Tree Regression

```
In [60]: #Mathematics
         print(metrics.mean_squared_error(y_test_M, pred_DCT_M))

         #Portuguese
         print(metrics.mean_squared_error(y_test_P, pred_DCT_P))

         3.3461538461538463
         8.55813953488372
```

Figure 29. Mean Squared Error Random Forest Regression

```
In [61]: #Mathematics
         print(metrics.mean_squared_error(y_test_M, pred_RFR_M))

         #Portuguese
         print(metrics.mean_squared_error(y_test_P, pred_RFR_P))

         1.3903846153846153
         6.466279069767442
```

Figure 30. Mean Squared Error Support Vector Regression

```
In [63]: #Mathematics
         print(metrics.mean_squared_error(y_test_M, pred_SVR_M))

         #Portuguese
         print(metrics.mean_squared_error(y_test_P, pred_SVR_P))

         7.362759853334634
         10.425343299051177
```

Figure 31. Performance of mean squared error in both datasets

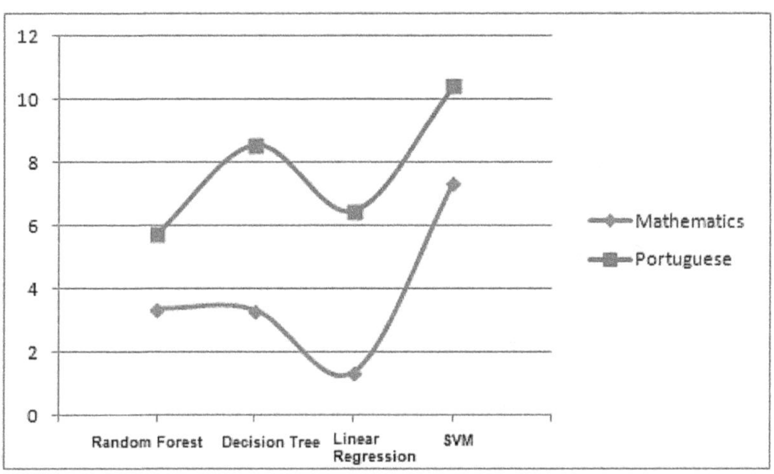

- **Mean Absolute Error(Burkart et. al, 2020):** It weighs the average magnitude of the error in predictionsIt keeps normal over the test sample data of absolute difference between actual and predicted value where every single individual distinction has a similar weight. Absolute values are taken to remove the signs of error.

$$Mean\ Absolute\ Error = \frac{1}{n}\sum_{j=1}^{n}\left|y_j - \hat{y}_j\right|$$

Figure 32. Mean Absolute Error Linear Regression

```
In [64]: #Mathematics
         print(metrics.mean_absolute_error(y_test_M, Y_pred_M_LR))

         #Portuguese
         print(metrics.mean_absolute_error(y_test_P, Y_pred_P_LR))

         1.2943528117617196
         1.2735872563805746
```

Figure 33. Mean Absolute Error Decision Tree Regression

```
In [65]: #Mathematics
         print(metrics.mean_absolute_error(y_test_M, pred_DCT_M))

         #Portuguese
         print(metrics.mean_absolute_error(y_test_P, pred_DCT_P))

         0.9615384615384616
         1.8604651162790697
```

Figure 34. Mean Absolute Error Random Forest Regression

```
In [66]: #Mathematics
         print(metrics.mean_absolute_error(y_test_M, pred_RFR_M))

         #Portuguese
         print(metrics.mean_absolute_error(y_test_P, pred_RFR_P))

         0.9346153846153846
         1.4627906976744187
```

Figure 35. Mean Absolute Error SVM

```
In [68]: #Mathematics
         print(metrics.mean_absolute_error(y_test_M, pred_SVR_M))

         #Portuguese
         print(metrics.mean_absolute_error(y_test_P, pred_SVR_P))

         1.989839563245233
         1.8189211314271718
```

- **Rooted Square Mean Error (RSME):** Residuals count the distance between data point and regression line. RSME can be said as standard deviation of residuals. It represents the concentration of data around the best fit regression line. RSME gives a measurement of how spreads out residuals are.

$$RSME = \sqrt{\frac{1}{n}\sum_{j=1}^{n}\left(y_j - \widehat{y_j}\right)}$$

Figure 36. Performance of mean absolute error in both datasets

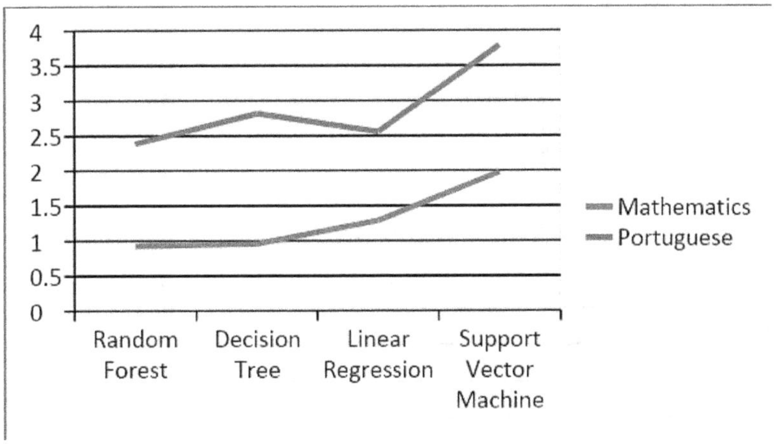

Figure 37. Rooted Square Mean ErrorLinear Regression

```
In [69]: #Mathematics
         print(np.sqrt(metrics.mean_squared_error(y_test_M, Y_pred_M_LR)))

         #Portuguese
         print(np.sqrt(metrics.mean_squared_error(y_test_P, Y_pred_P_LR)))

         1.8430309080003544
         2.397619732808178
```

Figure 38. Rooted Square Mean ErrorDecision Tree Regression

```
In [72]: #Mathematics
         print(np.sqrt(metrics.mean_squared_error(y_test_M, pred_DCT_M)))

         #Portuguese
         print(np.sqrt(metrics.mean_squared_error(y_test_P, pred_DCT_P)))

         1.8292495308606331
         2.925429803444909
```

Figure 39. Rooted Square Mean ErrorRandom Forest Regression

```
In [73]: #Mathematics
         print(np.sqrt(metrics.mean_squared_error(y_test_M, pred_RFR_M)))

         #Portuguese
         print(np.sqrt(metrics.mean_squared_error(y_test_P, pred_RFR_P)))

         1.1791457142289987
         2.5428879388929904
```

Figure 40. Rooted Square Mean ErrorSupport Vector Machine

```
In [74]: #Mathematics
         print(np.sqrt(metrics.mean_squared_error(y_test_M, pred_SVR_M)))

         #Portuguese
         print(np.sqrt(metrics.mean_squared_error(y_test_P, pred_SVR_P)))

         2.7134405932938046
         3.2288300201545415
```

Figure 41. Performance of Rooted Square Mean Errorin both datasets

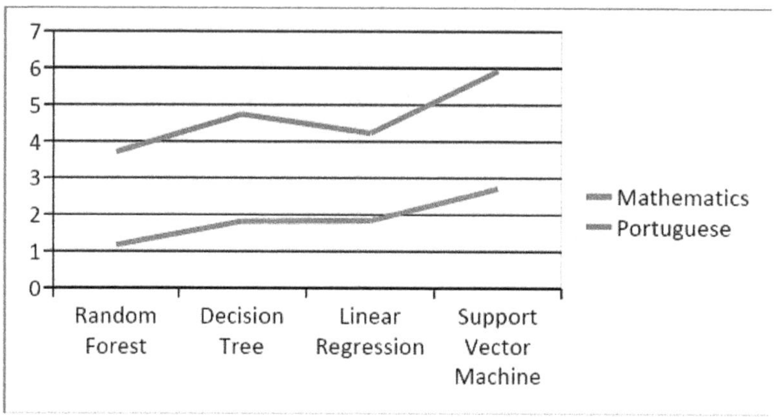

- **R-Squared (R^2):** It is a statistical measurement that addresses to the extent of the difference for a dependent variable that is clarified by an independent variable or other variables in the regression model. R-Squared represents the variance of one variable representing the variance of another variable in a regression model.

$$R^2 = 1 - \frac{Explained\,Variation}{Total\,Variation}$$

Figure 42. R-SquaredLinear Regression

```
In [76]: #Mathematics
         print(metrics.r2_score(y_test_M, Y_pred_M_LR))

         #Portuguese
         print(metrics.r2_score(y_test_P, Y_pred_P_LR))

         0.8426821225525516
         0.762700367734272
```

Figure 43. R-SquaredDecision Tree Regression

```
In [77]: #Mathematics
         print(metrics.r2_score(y_test_M, pred_DCT_M))

         #Portuguese
         print(metrics.r2_score(y_test_P, pred_DCT_P))

         0.8450260345300082
         0.6467226290409002
```

Figure 44. R-SquaredRandom Forest Regression

```
In [78]: #Mathematics
         print(metrics.r2_score(y_test_M, pred_RFR_M))

         #Portuguese
         print(metrics.r2_score(y_test_P, pred_RFR_P))

         0.9356056453822965
         0.7330739864261475
```

Figure 45. R-SquaredSupport Vector Regression

```
In [79]: #Mathematics
         print(metrics.r2_score(y_test_M, pred_SVR_M))

         #Portuguese
         print(metrics.r2_score(y_test_P, pred_SVR_P))

         0.6590007083547402
         0.5696450312567953
```

Figure 46. Performance of R-Squared in both

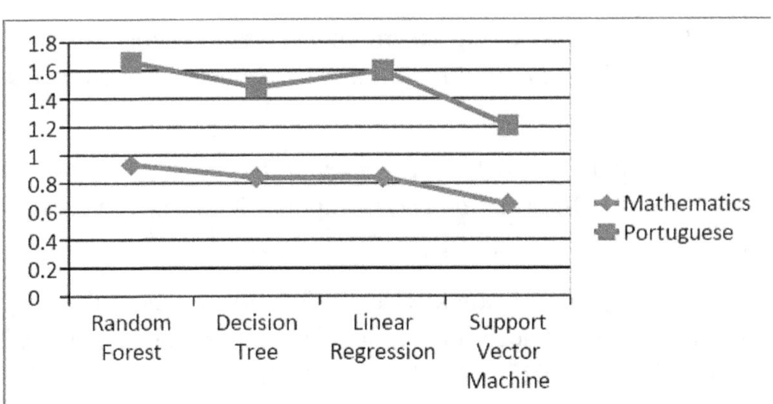

Various machine learning models werediscussed (Singh, Chahal &Kharb 2020) and were used to detect the perception level of students that can be utilized by educators for enhancement of education standards.

CONCLUSION

In this chapter, we have discussed how machine learning can be utilized in modernizing the education system. To evaluate the performance of our model, we used several statistical parameters for the proposed system. With the help of statistical methods and machine learning algorithms, a model is proposed that helps teachers to understand the perception of students and can predict performance of students. These predictions can be utilized by educators in several perspectives in modulating their lectures so that students get maximum output from their lecture. In the above model we utilised datasets of two different subjects (i.e. Mathematics and Portuguese) and predicted students' performance based on several parameters like their demographic data to better understand their perception. Different data pre-processing techniques and machine learning models have been used for predicting students' performance.

REFERENCES

Berwick, R. (2003). *An Idiot's guide to Support vector machines (SVMs).* Academic Press.

Burkart, N., Robert, S., & Huber, M. F. (2020). Are you sure? Prediction revision in automated decision making. *Expert Systems: International Journal of Knowledge Engineering and Neural Networks*, *2020*, 1–19. doi:10.1111/exsy.12577

Cortez, P., & Silva, A. (2008). Using data mining to predict secondary school student performance. *Proceedings of 5th Annual Future Business Technology Conference*, 5-12.

Frank, A., & Asuncion, A. (2010). *UCI machine learning repository.* University of California, School of Information and Computer Science, Irvine. http://archive.ics.uci.edu/ml

Islam, J., & Zhang, Y. (2018). Brain MRI analysis for Alzheimer's disease diagnosis using an ensemble system of deep convolutional neural networks. *Brain Informatics*, *5*(2), 2. doi:10.118640708-018-0080-3 PMID:29881892

Kharb, L., Aggarwal, L., & Chahal, D. (2020). A Contingent Exploration on Big Data Tools. *Lecture Notes in Electrical Engineering, 637*. 10.1007/978-981-15-2612-1_71

Namayanja, J., & Janeja, V. P. (2012). An Assessment of Patient Behavior Over Time–Periods: A Case Study of Managing Type 2 Diabetes Through Blood Glucose Readings and Insulin Doses. *Journal of Medical Systems*, *36*(S1), 65–80. doi:10.100710916-012-9894-3 PMID:23104240

Oddershede, L., & Petersen, K. D. (2015). Adjustment of foreign EQ-5D-3L utilities can increase their transferability. *Clin Outcomes Res*, *7*, 629–639. doi:10.2147/CEOR.S93280 PMID:26719715

Singh, P., Chahal, D., & Kharb, L. (2020). Predictive Strength of Selected Classification Algorithms for Diagnosis of Liver Disease. *Lecture Notes in Electrical Engineering, 597*. 10.1007/978-3-030-29407-6_19

Chapter 7
Self-Learning System for Child Development Using Conversational AI and Natural Language Processing (NLP)

Amit Mishra
ST Microelectronics, India

ABSTRACT

Education and learning are the most important aspects of the evolution of societies. They have been a favorite subject for philosophers and psychologists to work upon. Same questions are now being re-dealt by computer scientists in current scenarios. Although evolution is a continuous process, the pace of evolution is not a linear graph. Children acquire a huge amount of knowledge with very little input from teachers, friends, parents, and surroundings. Understanding how human brain works and more precisely, how the child brain actually functions is opening the path of researches in artificial intelligence (AI).

INTRODUCTION

Several researchers and companies are working intensely on machine learning and related applications. They worked to realize robots as partners for people (T. Kanda et al. 2004). The concept of a partner robot is really emerging as favorite topic of research for data scientists. These are visually human like robots equipped with human like skeleton body and various sensors used to interact with people in possibly most natural way. This way the partner robots imitate as a peer for day to day life.

DOI: 10.4018/978-1-7998-4763-2.ch007

Artificial Intelligence (AI) scientists (Sakagami et al. 2002) elaborated on use of humanoid robots in the field of hotel industry, office visitors, hospitals etc. to do human like interactions with visitors arriving and needing guidance. It is more to replace the front office today or "May I help you desk?". It interacts not only with speech but also through eye contacts, hand gestures etc. But these humanoids are with very limited capabilities or with limited intelligence.

Current discussion is next level of advancement in the sense to have trained machines with real child like learnings in different environments. Later these learned machines become capable of propagating the learning they got in most natural way to peer children. Based on the activities and speeches of human children robot will decide exhibiting the suitable aged behavior. Final aim of the research discussion is to develop humanoid child intelligent robot. However, in the first phase of the discussion will focus only on the intelligent software module. This software module will be equipped for speech recognition and scene recognition capabilities which will help to train the system with these as training data. In this phase, of development the system will be a software which will interact with child through a computer or tab like screen with suitable dummy photo. Once, building blocks are read, the final development can be extended. Training of the system would be done by neural networks using deep learning algorithms.

CONVERSATIONAL AI AND SERVICE ROBOTS

Going through the available literature around the subject, several works have been done in the field of Artificial Intelligence (AI). In year 2002 NEC Corporation has done a prototype personal robot. Trained and equipped to deploy in a specific family. It had the capabilities to recognize faces of family members, greets and entertains family members. It does some personal works of family members, set TV channels suitable to individual's interest. In the same year (Dautenhahn and Werry, 2002) robots were used to treat people with developmental disorders, so a kind of robotic autism therapy. With this in place now many at times robots start to work as partner and participating as agent in human society. They perform several functions which human partners are expecting to their robot partner.

There are researches where robots are used not only to teach students but also entered to the next levels. That is robots acting as teacher for teachers with the concept of train the trainers. Human and computer interaction is consistently the most important factor. Specially in robot-based learning, it plays a crucial role in learning. Turing test determines the degree of machine response imitating human, and to distinguish robots from human two main functions were suggested by (Sakagami et al. 2002). These two functions are Mobility and Human Robot Interaction (HRI).

Also, it has been elaborated in study by (Magne Jorgensen et al.,2007) as a factor by which robot is detected by robot user i.e. by human. However, this work has been accomplished only up to experimental levels. Where in children interacted to robots only for short clippings and not in continuous seamless interaction. These experiments focused on children who were primary sections only. This limitation affected the information on the perception of children for the robots. Hence this is not giving real use case of robots in actual education fields but still a good level of achievement in early development of this field. With the advancement of technology, it has became common to be able to recognize or identify a person interacting from the voice attributes, face recognitions and retina identifications. One time tagging of partner child would be required (Guillaume Klein et al. 2017). Challenge is to respond a child in childish manner. Another challenge is the kind of personality trait exhibited by the machine or software. Like interaction of a child with another child may differ from child to child, the trained machine will exhibit a particular behavior based on the training set provided. System may be put for learning from different class of children and system can be set to a particular type of personality trait while being set for interaction for a child training. This means a child under training may be exposed to an introvert personality machine or to and extrovert child. With the increased computing power, neural networks and deep learning algorithms it has been made now very much possible to train such a system.

As part of open innovation and to advance the technologies supporting conversational AI, Amazon has organized the Alexa Prize event. It was a 2.5-million-dollar open innovation challenge and competition. Sixteen qualified universities participated to this challenge event with the objective to build conversational AI agents. Later these conversational AI agents are known as "socialbots". The competition had objective to do conversation coherently and engagingly with humans on set of pre-determined topics including Science & Technology, Politics, Sports, Entertainment and Fashion for 20 minutes. None could achieve 20 minutes long engaged conversation (Amazon AI Team,2019).

IMPLEMENTATION INSIGHT

Acoustic and speech recognition is used to prepare training data for such systems. Interaction of 2 kids are recorded for different environments and over different age categories. Data is stored for the kids interaction of say age of 3 years till 8 years, when maximum childhood learning is achieved. Main focus for the system is educational and speaking power enrichment. One child in recording is treated as input and the response from the other child is used as labeled response to the input. NLP is used to organize the training data. Speech is converted to text and text is processed to prepare the classification. When working for child education with the final aim to develop a robot which will interact with child as a humanoid.

Ninety percent of the same data is put as part of training data set, while the remaining 10% of recording data is used as the test data for the system. Test will certify the response to the unseen input by the learned system. Algorithm we use will be convolutional neural networks with deep learning algorithms. Algorithm and code still to be done. Small chunk of basic units of algorithm however has already been tested and can be demonstrated.

Language and Libraries Suggested for Implementation

Python language have been used in the base of practical aspects in this chapter for implementation of algorithms. Use recognizer class and instantiate to use google APIs. "speech_recognition" is used to do the speech recognition using microphones. This is instrumental to build a system for training the child educational robots. NLTK libraries are available to build all sort of text and paragraph processing e.g. tokenization and classifications of text etc.

High Level Implementation Approaches

Figure 1. Basic Packages to be Imported for NLP on Child Educational Robots

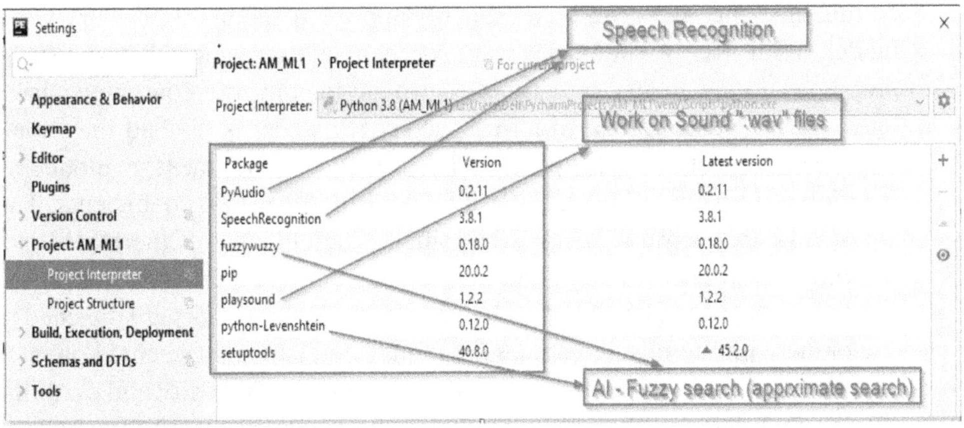

Implementation is addressed through 2 main approaches –

Approach-1: Primarily based on existing Amazon's Alexa Skill Kit (ASK) and Tensorflow (Ian Beaver and Cynthia Freeman, 2020) and (Amazon Alexa Team,2019)

- Alexa Skills Kit (ASK) – APIs Framework for socialbots implementation
- Alexa Automatic Speech Recognition (ASR) to create sound files ".wav" file payload containing the user utterance
- Alexa Text-to-Speech (TTS) for Natural Language Generation NLG
- AWS Lambda to do the dialog management and other processing to retrieve or generate a response to ASK for TTS

Approach-2: Alternate conversational AI, classification & approximate search with continuous learning

Approach-1, at high-level implementation is explained as follows:

Step 1: Speech Recognition

As all the training data and test data has to be from the audio conversations, this work requires speech recognitions with AI using deep Neural Networks. Python library ***"SpeechRecognition"*** library is to be used for treating sound wave files.

- **Science of Converting Speech to Text:** In general speech recognition systems are not easy to implement without using "SpeechRecognition" package of Python. Using this package we avoided all complexities of science of sound waves. These waves rely on Hidden Markov Model (HMM). HMM assumes that a speech signal, which is continuous wave can be viewed on very short timescales. Such small intervals could be ten milliseconds, or even smaller. At this time slice they can be reasonably approximated to a stationary wave model. With such a stationary wave we can safely assume that statistical properties do not change over time. As we are to convert a continuous wave into a discrete data signal. In HMM the speech signal is divided into small time scale fragments. This spectrum of each slice or fragment, is plotted as function of frequency - F(v). Later it is mapped as cepstral coefficients. The measure of this cepstral is very-very small. The outcome of the HMM is a combination of these vectors and hence discrete numbers. These sequences are then used to decipher the speech into text, groups of vectors are matched to one or more **phonemes.** Phonemes are fundamental unit of speech. Phonemes vary from speaker to speaker which adds additional complexity and even this variation takes place from one utterance to another even for the same person speaking another statement. To filter out noise and reduction of audio signals to the portion which contains only speech portion. This technique is known as, Voice activity detectors (VADs).

Implementing full science of sound and waves is not under scope of the discussion under this chapter. Python language has been used in the base of practical aspects in this chapter for implementation of algorithms. Use recognizer class and instantiate to use google APIs.

```
import os     è Various file operations
from playsound import playsound  è To play the Sound ".wav"
files
from fuzzywuzzy import fuzz        è To do "Fuzzy Search not
exact"
import speech_recognition as sr   è Speech Recognition through
Microphone
r1=sr.Recognizer()
while (1==1):
    with sr.Microphone() as source:
        print('Child speak now')
        audio=r1.listen(source)
        try:
            get=r1.recognize_google(audio)
            print(get)
            str1=get
            print('Question Asked: '+ str1)
```

Input sound can be taken through microphone. For the prototype implementation, the wave sound file types ".wav" extension, can be used. Sound data extracted from these wave files into text using recognize_google method. This is online API method, which works when connected through Internet only.

```
>>> TrainChild= sr.AudioFile('TrainChild.wav')
>>> with TrainChild as source:
Audio=r.record(source) # record method reads data
>>> r.reconize_google(audio,s) # reads "s" second data from the
".wav" file.
```

Step 2: Conversational AI & Intelligent Virtual Agents (IVAs)

To be used for emulating the child behavior in terms of applying relational strategies in conversation. Analysis has to go at intent of speech and classifications like Greetings,

Anger, Happiness, Backstory etc. Conversational AI however is still in it's primitive stage even with big players. For example today industry popular such agents are -

Amazon Alexa, Apple's Siri and Google Assistant. They are also limited to small task oriented conversation only and not the full fledged Natural Language Understanding (NLU) and Natural Language Generation (NLG).

Step 3: From Conversational AI to Socialbots

To accomplish the big task of learned child system it needs to be achieved in steps of several socialbots on specific topics such as Playing Games, toddlers classroom, argument on dresses children wore, fight and crying, mom demands, sibling fights etc. Once these social bots are refined and achieve high acceotability level of conversation they can be used to train the child in bits and pieces. Later the same will emerge as full integrated learned system.

NLTK libraries are used to work for developing socialbots using deep neural networks. It uses the supervised learning approach to mark labels to the training data. Response is then generated determining the label for the test data.

Step 4: Training Socialbots

Each classified socialbots are to be trained specifically. Conversations of children are to be recorded through microphones for all shorts of identified target socialbots. This has to be from play ground, classrooms, with parents, siblings etc. To prepare unbiased data special care has to be taken so that children are not aware about any recordings or being observed. Such sound files labeled under classifications to be sued for training the system.

- **Alternate Conversational AI approach:** Apart from above stated approach based on established AI approaches we are going to implement another conversational approach. Benefit of this approach is simplification of machine learning rules by training the system with huge set of conversations. It works on the hypothesis that learned machine is having such a rich knowledge base that it can determine the reply conversation, looking the knowledge base and finding it's associated conversation and answering based on already existing knowledge. While finding the associated answer based on input query, the reply should be based on exact match or approximate match. If the match is below certain threshold (say 70%) then knowledge base to record new conversation inside knowledge base. Python code excerpts:

```
with open(filed,'r') as f:
    str2=f.read()
    f.close()
    ratio=fuzz.ratio(str1,str2)
    if ratio > 70:
        print('Question: '+str2+str(ratio))
        ansfile='C:/ED_ROBOT/ML/'+'ans'+file
        with open(ansfile,'r') as f:
            str3=f.read()
            print(str3)
            f.close()
            ansfile_sound=ansfile.replace('txt','wav')
            playsound(ansfile_sound)
```

CONCLUSION

In conclusion, what is important is that educational Systems or robots are already there but system trained to respond in childish way is still a dream. Today's systems to be extended further from contents and functions to promote the social and emotional interaction level with child. Feature has to focus first on the speaking interaction on general topics (not domain specific) and on educational boundary. Idea is also that system keeps learning while in use. Intelligence will keep on increasing. Machine being immortal will capture immense experience still remaining as child hence it will become a superchild which will groom well the child interacting with such a system. Limitation is that all the training of the system is done using only 2 party conversations which is little far from reality. Overall developing this system is a big project for very long duration and investment. As Amazon's Alexa even for simple task oriented machine learning involved efforts of many universities and tech giants to reach this level.

Limitations –

- Implementation discussed in this chapter has assumed the training of the system is using **only 2 party conversations** which is little far from reality.
- Approach to be enhanced to consider multipoint conversations.
- Implementation considers autodetection of language being used by child but in case child is switching the languages in between, approach is not defined

Figure 2. Alternate Conversational AI approach

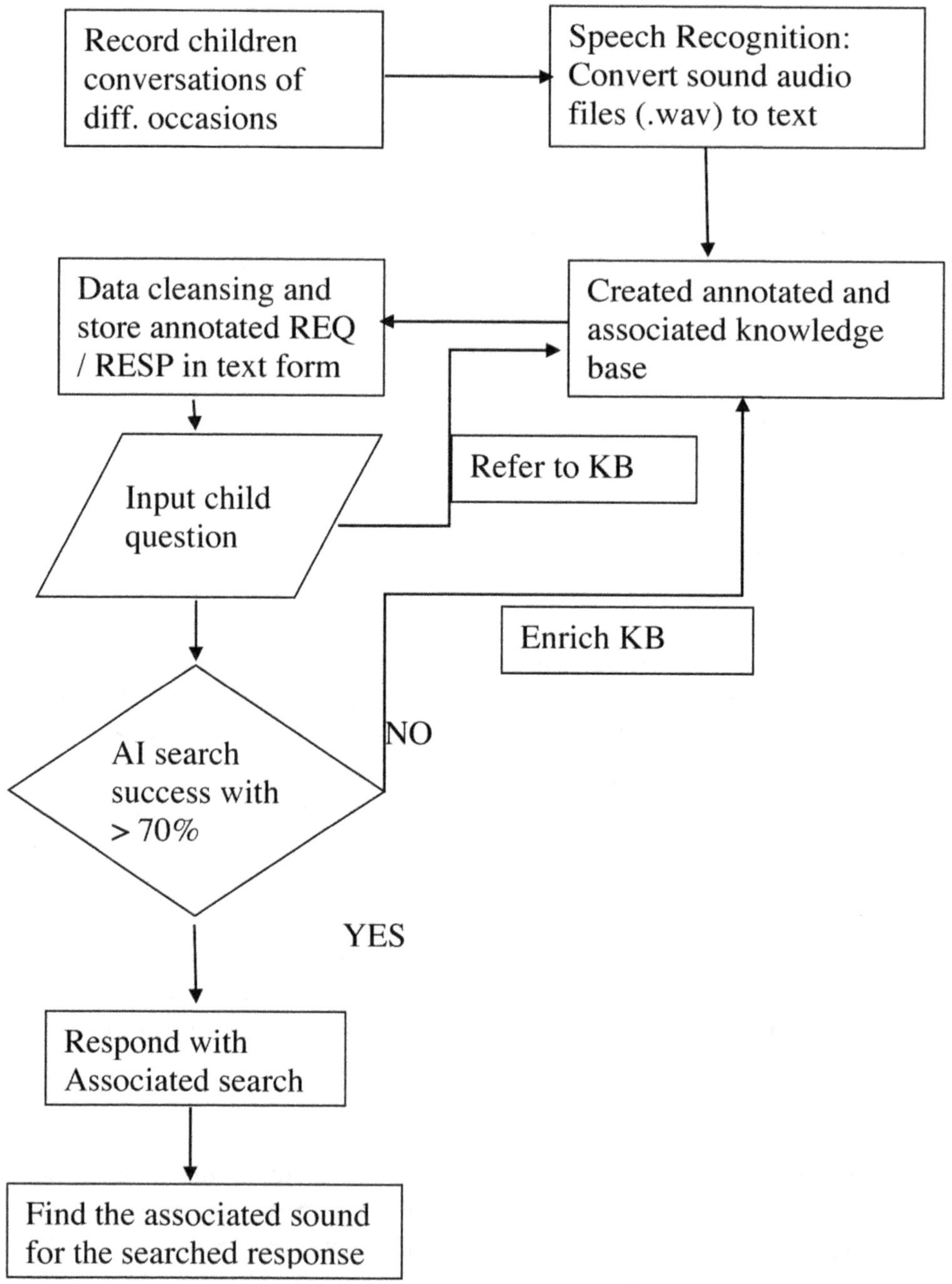

REFERENCES

Ali, A. M., & Gonzalez, A. J. (2017). Machine Learning from Conversation with Humans. *Proceedings of the Thirtieth International Florida Artificial Intelligence Research Society Conference*.

Amazon AI Team. (2019). *Conversational AI: The Science Behind the Alexa Prize*. Author.

Ballantyne, D. (2004). Dialogue and its role in the development of relationship specific knowledge. *Journal of Business & Industrial Marketing, 9*(2), 114–123.

Beaver & Freeman. (2020). *Towards Awareness of Human Relational Strategies in Virtual Agents*. Academic Press.

Jorgensen, M., & Shepperd, M. (2007). A Systematic Review of Software Development Cost Estimation Studies. *IEEE Transactions on Software Engineering, 33*(1), 33–53. doi:10.1109/TSE.2007.256943

Kanda, T., Hirano, T., Eaton, D., & Ishiguro, H. (2004). Interactive robots as social partners and peer tutors for children: A field trial. *Human-Computer Interaction, 19*(1), 61–84. doi:10.120715327051hci1901&2_4

Klein, Kim, Deng, Senellart, & Rush. (2107). *Opennmt: "Open-source toolkit for neural machine translation."* Academic Press.

Ng, H.-W., Nguyen, V. D., Vonikakis, V., & Winkler, S. (2015). Deep learning for emotion recognition on small datasets using transfer learning. In *Proceedings of the 2015 ACM on international conference on multimodal interaction*, (pp. 443–449). ACM.- 2015. 10.1145/2818346.2830593

Sakagasmi, Y., Watanabe, R., Aoyama, C., Matsunaga, S., Higaki, N., & Fujimura, K. (2002). The intelligent ASIMO: System overview and integration. In *Proceedings of the IEEE/RSJ International Conference on Intelligent Robots and Systems*. New York: IEEE. 10.1109/IRDS.2002.1041641

Chapter 8
Artificial Intelligence-Based Knowledge Representation and Reasoning

Dimpal Tomar
Gautam Buddha University, India

Pradeep Tomar
Gautam Buddha University, India

ABSTRACT

The quality of higher education can be enhanced only by upgrading the content and skills towards knowledge. Hence, knowledge representation and reasoning play a chief role to represent the facts, beliefs, and information, and inferring the logical interpretation of represented knowledge stored in the knowledge bases. This chapter provide a broad overview of knowledge, representation, and reasoning along with the related art of study in the field of higher education. Various artificial intelligent-based knowledge representation and reasoning techniques and schemes are provided for better representation of facts, beliefs, and information. Various reasoning types are discussed in order to infer the right meaning of the knowledge followed by various issues of knowledge representation and reasoning. .

1. INTRODUCTION

Intelligence is one of the complex phenomena as stated by the individuals that is clearly governed by the knowledge. For example, a person can take a decision about what has to do on the basis of what we believe or no effortlessly. Artificial Intelligence

DOI: 10.4018/978-1-7998-4763-2.ch008

(AI) is the study of intelligence and behaviour governed by the machines through computational means in contrast to natural intelligence.In artificial intelligence, knowledge representation and reasoning act as a central aspect which is concerned with how a machine represent a human knowledge and use it in order to decide what to do.

Knowledge representation and reasoning plays a vital role in several domain of learning, teaching and research. For instance, in higher education, development of an intelligent educational system and intelligent tutoring system encompassing intelligences by offering adaptive representation and navigation of teaching contents. The crucial aspect while developing the system is how knowledge has to be represented and how the meaning is accomplished for making decisions (Hatzilygeroudis & Prentzas, 2006).

This section will try to address an overview on understanding what is knowledge, representation and reasoning.Why these concepts are important in artificial intelligence followed by the artificial intelligence knowledge cycle.

1.1 Overview

Human knows and understand best of what is knowledge and based on their knowledge, they can make decisions and perform various activities. But, how does a machine can perform all these actions is all comes under the umbrella of "knowledge representation and reasoning".

Knowledge representation and reasoning can be defined as a process which explains how a knowledge be represented in artificial intelligence.It is not just a process of storing the information into the database but also responsible for how an intelligent agent in enable to learn from the obtained knowledge and behave intelligently.

1.1.1 Knowledge

Now, what do you understand by knowledge here? This question has been taken up since long time and still not been exposed totally. In general, knowledge can be explained as aninformation received from the environment in terms of experiences, situations and data or information which can be articulated in proposition form (Grosan and Abraham, 2011).

Let's take an example to understand this. First notice how we talk about something, let's say. "Sam knows that..."

Now fill that blanks with the simple statement like "Sam knows that John will come to play basketball" or "Sam knows that Washington is the capital of United State".This shows that relationship that exist between a knower and the proposition represent a "knowledge". Here, in the above declarative sentences,

Knower: Sam
Proposition: John will come to play basketball. (It is an idea expressed by the simple statement).

The preposition can be true or false, right or wrong, may holds same content with different attitude and other forms of propositional attributes.

Knowledge can be differentiated into several categories, are as follows: declarative knowledge, procedural knowledge, structural knowledge, heuristic knowledge and meta knowledge (Jaiswal, n.d.)(Chakarborty, 2010).

1. *Declarative knowledge:* It is all about "knowledge about something" that can be articulated. In other words, information about something can be true or false. For example RAM is younger than Shyam. Basically, Declarative knowledge deals with object and events representation facts and relationship.
2. *Procedural knowledge:* It deals with "how to do something" and can be applied directly to any task in order to achieve a particular goal. It includes models, agendas, procedures, strategies and rules.
3. *Structural knowledge:*Knowledge about to problem solving. It deals with relation among concepts and objects like part-of, type-of, kind-of etc.
4. *Heuristic knowledge:*Knowledge about expert in an area. It deals with the accurate judgement, practical approach one's ability of guessing and evaluation ability.
5. *Meta knowledge:*Knowledge about knowledge.

1.1.2 Representation

Representation, in a generic way, can be explained as symbol which are used to represent the propositions. Basically, representation is the procedure in which the knowledge is encoded and enable to define the performance of the system in doing something (Jaiswal, n.d.).For example,"+" symbol is used for first aid.

Hence, a good knowledge representation facilitates accurate and fast accessibility to the information and proper interpretation of the content.

1.1.3 Reasoning

Reasoning can be defined as a manipulation of symbols (a collection of encoded proposition) in order to create representation of newly formed propositions. Reasoning is also represented as a calculation over symbols rather than numeric values, unlike in arithmetic.

E.g: 1011+10 ->110 implies Eleven +two= thirteen

Basically, reasoning plays the role of bridge to fill the gap exist between what is believed and what is presented (Brachman and Levesque, 2004).

1.2 Review of Literature

Artificial intelligence putting a lot of efforts in the domain of education by developing and evaluating various software that are capable of dealing with the more improved learning and teaching process. Out of which, presenting the information with the right interpretation by various teaching and learning models through the AI-based knowledge representation and reasoning has gained the attention. However, researchers and industry experts have devoted a lot of focus towards improving the knowledge representation and reasoning in AI systems.

Hatzilygeroudis & Prentzas(2006)tried to identify the knowledge representation and reasoning requirements in an Intelligent Educational System (IES) based on three aspects of system that is, stages of system, types of user and modulus. Also, author did a comparative study of knowledge representation schemes in which their findings states that hybrid approach can satisfy the requirements to knowledge representation with the higher degree.

Katalnikovaet. al. (2017) proposed a collaborative system for intelligent education. Author considered various knowledge representation models and use them in context to intelligent education system and later compare them.

Ramirezand Valdes(2012) discovered various concepts of knowledge representation and proposed a knowledge representation model known as memory map which combines skills and concepts dynamically of various domains represent the knowledge as per the context. Author compared their model with the other models such as Multinet and OAR in order to obtain the differences and similarities with respect to representation

Lardjane and Nuutinen(2014), presented an overview of knowledge representation tools in order to enable the high quality learning which helps in promoting better learning and teaching process in higher education.

Al-Fedaghi(2016) proposed teaching syllogism tool for improve teaching process to students, illustrative and educational purpose in logic.Singh et. al. (2004) discussed evolution, architecture and operation of common sense knowledge representation and reasoning system that is conceptNet, lifeNet and storyNet. Also, author put a light on the integration of these systems which enable deep understanding of problem and their solution.

Breuker and Muntjewerff(1999), designed educational system for constructing ontologies. Author exemplified the system used in in three different domains that is information processing system, law and ecology.

Masood and Mokmin(2017) presented intelligent tutoring system which uses case-based reasoning enabling recommendations for learning material based on students profile to the target students.

As the innovation progressed in the domain of artificial intelligence immensely. Artificial intelligence based agents improve intelligent behaviour day by day with new techniques in the field of education with respect to learning and teaching. For such behaviour, knowledge representation and reasoning plays a vital role in AI systems to use their knowledge and enable to take decisions.

1.3 Artificial Intelligence Knowledge Cycle

For an agent to display its intelligent behaviour, it has the following component in its knowledge cycle as shown in the figure 1.

Figure 1. Artificial Intelligence-Based Knowledge Cycle

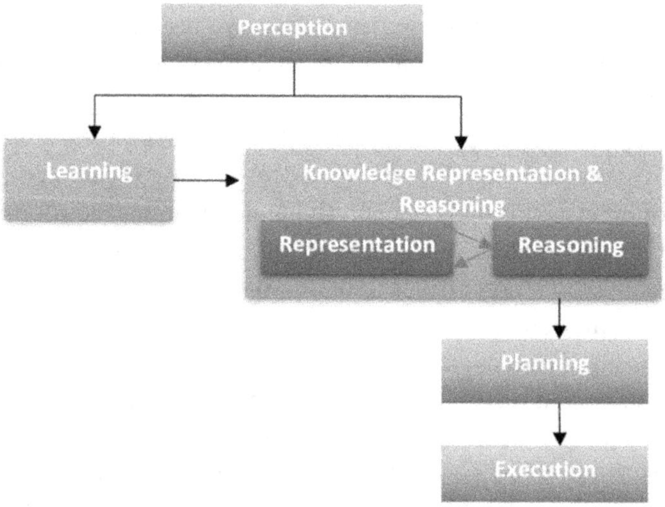

- Perception: Retrieves information from the surroundings such as audio, visual or sensory inputs.
- Learning: learn from the data captured by the perception component.

- Knowledge representation and reasoning:Responsible for displaying intelligent behaviour like human brain.
- Planning and execution:Both the components rely upon the analysis done by knowledge representation and reasoning component.

2. KNOWLEDGE REPRESENTATION SCHEME

2.1 Relational Knowledge

It can also be conceptualized as a connection exist among the elements of one domain to another. Relational knowledge representation binds relational symbols to a set of order tuples of elements (Goodwin and Johnson-Laird, 2004) (Halford et. al.,1998). The relational symbol indicate the "intension of relation" by specifying which relation is intended. Whereas, the set of ordered tuples of elements signifies the extension of relation by providing knowledge from the statistics and experience received from the world (Jaiswal, n.d.). Basically, it is composed of objects, attributes and their associated tuple values. This representation approach is quite popular in database systems where relation among various attributes has been presented. Following table 1, shows the relational representation where the attribute of objects are arranged in columns systematically by providing little opportunity for inference (Chakarborty, 2010).

2.2 Inheritable Knowledge Representation

In this scheme, "phenomena of inheritance" has been applied where elements inherited the properties and values from their parent classes. In artificial intelligence, it is the knowledge that can be passed on. The representation in hierarchical manner is a collection of frames, also known as semantic network or slot and filter structure which justify the property of inheritance and allowed the addition of new knowledge. Following figure 2 shows the example of inference knowledge representation, where nodes represents objects & values of attributes and directed arrows describes attributes.

2.3 Inferential Knowledge Representation

In this scheme of knowledge representation, new facts or knowledge can be derived by analysing the already existed knowledge. This type of knowledge can berepresented as a formal logic.

For example:

Figure 2. Inheritable Knowledge Representation Example

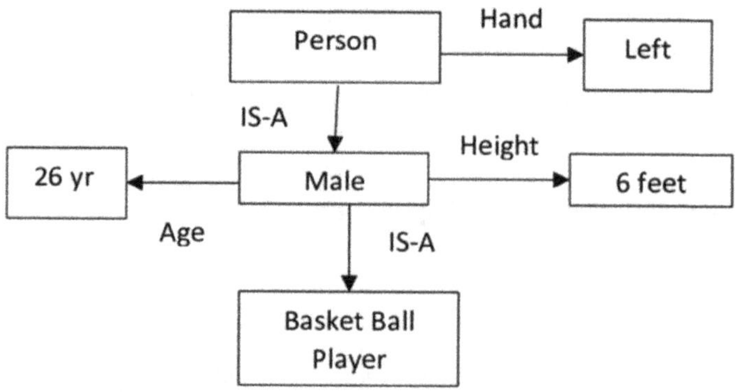

Krauss is a name of the dog.

All dogs belongs to the mammal class.

All mammals either live on land or water.

From the all the above three sentences, inference is derived as: "Krauss lives either on land or in water". If more knowledge is provided about these objects and relations then more inferencing can be obtained.

2.4 Declarative Knowledge Representation

In this scheme, a collection of factual information and assertions (Vincent, Kovarik, 2009). It deals with the state of knowing about the facts, being familiar or acquainted with, apprehending facts, recognising or aware of and so on with respect to the concept of higher education. This scheme is more focused upon the rhetoricalability like giving answers to the questions related to the facts, principles, theorems and rules. Declarative knowledge is all about "knowing that".For example, world history, mathematical theorem, rules and formulas are all fall into the declaration of knowledge.

3. KNOWLEDGE REPRESENTATION AND REASONING TECHNIQUES

Intelligent behaviour is one of the striking aspect that is conditioned by the "knowledge and reasoning". Human brain has its own way to represent any information on knowledge and to implement actions. Human brain will use that knowledge to take the proper decision. Similarly, machines for computers require a need for good knowledge representation and reasoning techniques which helps in designing machine representations that will be able to solve complex problems by using captured knowledge. Broadly, knowledge representationand reasoning techniques are fallen into four categories, they are as follows: logical representation, semantic network representation, frame representation and production rules.

3.1 Logic Representation

In this techniques, information has been processed along with certain concrete rules that manages prepositions and assure to represent precisely in any other language. Logic-based representation deals with the following components; facts and premises, drawing conclusions, rules of propositional logic and predicate calculus followed by measure of certainty (Knowledge representation techniques, n.d.). It's all about specifically defined aspects that will support the inference i.e. syntax and semantics. Usingthese two aspects, every declarative statement has to be transformed into logics.

- Syntax: Well-formed rules helps in deciding how to form a sentence in the logic by identify a group of symbols and arrange them in what way, they drive a properly formed statement.
- Semantic: Well-formed rulesspecifying how to form sentence are proposed to be expressed. Basically, it helps in interpreting the statement in the logic.

The logic representation are further categorised into two different types of logics, they are propositional logic and predicate logic.

*Propositional logic:*It focus on the ways of combining or modifying entire declarative sentences in order to form more complex prepositions or sentences along with the logical associations and properties which are formed from the joining or altering statements method. It is also termed with other names also known as Boolean algebra, propositional calculus or sentential calculus. Propositional logic deals with the true or false but not both. Propositions are nothing, "sentences" which is the smallest unit.

E.g.

Grass is green. (Truth value is TRUE, hence Proposition is TRUE)

2+2=5 (Truth value is FALSE, hence Proposition is TRUE)

*Predicate logic:*This form of logic is built upon the ideas of propositional logic and is powerful enough for all types of assertion expression and reasoning. Predicate logic enable to express the attributes of objects or a relationship between objects.

E.g.

All men are mortal.

Socrates is a man.

Then Socrates is mortal.

Advantage:

- Helps in enabling logical reasoning.
- Basics for programming language.

Disadvantage:

- Imposes certain restrictions making difficult to work with it
- Inferencing might not be so efficient.

3.2 Semantic Network Representation

In semantic network representation, the meaning of concept has been derived based on their relationship among other concepts. However, concepts are being denoted as nodes with labelled links which represents relationship between nodes. For example IS-A or PART OF. Hence, knowledge insemantic network is a blend of information related to object or concepts and how these objects related to each other (Foltz,2001). Semantic networks are quite influencing, easy to understand and can easily be extended by representing or knowledge in the form of graphical network (Jaiswal, n.d.). For example,

Krauss is a dog.

A dog is a living being.

Advantage:

- Transparency while interpreting process
- Simple and easy to understand.

Disadvantage:

- Take more computation time while running.
- Do not have any equivalent quantifier,so they are in educate to work with.
- No standard definition for linked name.
- Not quite intelligent.

3.3 Frame Representation

In this formalism, the concept of inheritance is described. This technique consists of frames cluster and links related to each other. A frame is defined as more than a record or simply called a data structure that is a combination of attributes and its values. Every frame represent both class and instances and link represent relationships. Knowledge is arranged in slots. Slots have name and values known as facets. This method is also known as slot-filler knowledge representation.For example, take a frame of literature book shown in table 1.

Table 1. Frame of literature book

Slots	Filler
Title of the Book	Julius Caesar
Genre	English Literature
Author Name	William Shakespeare9
Page	168
Year of Publication	2017

Advantages:

- Frame knowledge representation group the related objects making the programming easier.
- Quite flexible and applicablein various application areas of artificial intelligence as compared to other knowledge representation method.
- Easy to understand.
- New slots can be added for new attributes and relations.
- Provide simple ways to find missing values.

Disadvantages:

- Difficult to access the frame system in a program.
- Inferencing answering may not be smoothly process.

3.4 Production Rule

This representation technique consists of initial state, goal state, legal operators and operators restrictions. This technique is used for a specific problem solving contents. Production rules consist of if-then or situation-action pairs. In this representation, agents verify the condition and if specified condition exist then corresponding production rule fires and accordingly action is carried out. "The condition" determines rule to be imposed on the problem. "The action"determines associated task to solve the problem. For example,IF (at railway station AND train arrives)THEN action (get into the train).

Advantage:

- Highly modular.
- Expressible in natural way of representation.
- Easy insertion, deletion or modification of individual rule is possible.

Disadvantage:

- Do not exhibit learning ability.
- Inefficient.

4. TYPES OF REASONING

In the previous section, various knowledge representation in artificial intelligence schemes and techniques have been discussed. In this section, focus is on the number of approaches that are the reason on this knowledge.

Reasoning is the process to infer for a logical meaning from the existing or feasible facts knowledge or beliefs. It is essential in artificial intelligence in order to make machines to think in a rational way so that they are able to derive conclusions like a human brain. Reasoning, in AI, can be categorised into the following types, they are: deductive reasoning, inductive reasoning, abductive reasoning, common sense reasoning, monotonic reasoning and nonmonotonic reasoning.

4.1 Inductive Reasoning

In inductive reasoning, no conclusions have been necessarily derived from the existing data which means moment of truth for conclusions does not guaranteed (Klix, 2001). Based on insubstantial information, a conclusion is being derived using generalisation process in which it starts from the little set of definite facts then finally reaches to some conclusion. Basically, it belongs to the propositional logic dealing with cause-effect manner. It process the data in a bottom-up fashion in order to reach the conclusion.The process of inductive reasoning has been represented by the four stages; observation, pattern, hypothesis and theory. Example of Inductive reasoning,

Premise: All the tiger have seen in the zoo are white.
Conclusion: Hence, we are expecting that all tigers to be white.

4.2 Deductive Reasoning

In this type of reasoning, from the new logical information is figured out from the already existing logically related data sets and rules which means true premises does guarantee the truthiness of the derived conclusion. The reasoning process has been carried out in a top-down manner. For example,

Premises 1: All the cats drink milk.
Premises 2: Poly is a cat.
Conclusion: Poly drinks milk.

The general deductive reasoning process is carried out in 4 steps theory, hypothesis, pattern followed by true conclusion.

4.3 Abductive Reasoning

In abductive reasoning, the best conclusion can be drawn from the series of observations (Crowder et. al., 2020). Unlike deductive inferencing, it is not necessary that if premises are true then conclusion is also drawn to be true as it does not guarantee. For example,

Premise 1: pitch is wet if it is raining.
Premise 2: pitch is wet.
Conclusion: It is raining.

4.4 Common Sense Reasoning:

An informal way of reasoning in which best judgement has been taken based on experiences. In AI, machines used heuristic knowledge and rules to derive the good judgement. For instance, robotsrequired the need for common sense reasoning to work in an uncontrolled environment appropriately. However, there are numerous application areas in which commonsense reasoning is applicable like natural language processing, robotics computer vision etc (Davis& Marcus, 2015). Theorem proving is an example of common sense reasoning.

4.5 Monotonic Reasoning

In this reasoning approach, addition of new data to the available data in the knowledge base does not affect the already derived conclusion. Such type of reasoning is not suitable for real time systems.

4.6 Non monotonic Reasoning

Unlike monotonic reasoning, newly added knowledge to the bases is capable to invalidate the derived conclusions. Such reasonings is capable to handle the uncertain and incomplete modes, real time systems like robot navigation. For example, human perception for a particular situation in a life.

5. ISSUES IN KNOWLEDGE REPRESENTATION AND REASONING TECHNIQUES

The knowledge representation and reasoning holds a primary aspiration of facilitating true conclusions or inference based on the knowledge. But, this process of driving good judgement leads to the rise of several issues while applying knowledge representation techniques, which are being discussed in this section (Chakarborty, 2010).

5.1 Foremost Attributes

Is there any attribute that may occur in various domains off problem? That means, there are general significance of attributes which are in two forms IS-A and Instance as they support the property of inheritance.

5.2 Association Between Attributes of Objects

Identify the relationship exist among the attributes. The existing relationship is independent of specified information that they encoded in itself and may carry properties such as single valued attributes, be a part of, is-a hierarchy, inverse and various techniques for reasoning about value.

- Inverse deals with consistency check.
- Is-a Hierarchy deals with generalization specialisation process.
- Reasoning about value deals with reasoning attribute values.
- Atomic valued attribute is a specific attribute that will hold unique value.

5.3 Granularity

This explains what is the scale on level of detail in the knowledge has to be represented. It also deals with the primitives whether they should in small or large of low or high level facts. As there arisea further issues like if high level primitives used then they may not be adequate for conclusions whereas low level one deals with lot of storage issue.

5.4 Set of Objects

An individual object does not justify some of its properties as it justified them being a member of objects set.

5.5 Discover Right Structure

It is required to select a proper and correct structure in order to find the solution to the following problems such as

- how to select an appropriate structure,
- how to introduce correct details,
- if current structure turn out to be a bad choice then how do find a better one,
- what if none of the existing structure is suitable.

These are some genuine problem which are not yet solved by all the knowledge representation techniques, only some of the techniques are able to solve out of these problems.

CONCLUSION

Nowadays, education set up as a joint cause and course for the youngsters. For instance, schools college and universities are becoming more focused and open towards innovation with improved learning and teaching process. Artificial intelligence plays a central role in educational transition by providing enhanced knowledge representation and reasoning model in the teaching and learning systems. This chapter provide all the necessary schemes and techniques used in AI- based knowledge representation and reasoning useful for designing and development of artificial intelligent educational agents which will help in more enhanced learning and teaching process and changing the outlook towards education sector.

REFERENCES

Al-Fedaghi, S. S. (2016). Knowledge representation in education: Diagramming Carroll's syllogisms. *Proceedings of the 2016 IEEE International Conference on Knowledge Engineering and Applications (ICKEA)*, 150-154. 10.1109/ ICKEA.2016.7803009

Brachman, R. J., & Levesque, H. J. (2004). Knowledge Representation and Reasoning. Elsevier.

Breuker, J., & Muntjewerff, A. (1999). Ontological Modelling for Designing Educational Systems. *Proceedings of the AI & Education*, 101-122.

Chakarborty, R. C. (2010). *Knowledge Representation*. Retrieved from http://www.myreaders.info/03_Knowledge_Representations.pdf

Crowder, J., Carbone, J., & Friess, S. (2020). Abductive Artificial Intelligence Learning Models. In *Artificial Psychology* (pp. 51–63). Springer. doi:10.1007/978-3-030-17081-3_5

Davis, E., & Marcus, G. (2015). Commonsense Reasoning and Commonsense Knowledge in Artificial Intelligence. *Communications of the ACM*, *58*(9), 92–103. doi:10.1145/2701413

Foltz, P. W. (2001). Semantic Processing: Statistical Approaches. In International Encyclopedia of the Social & Behavioral Sciences (pp. 13873-13878). Elsevier.

Goodwin, G. P., & Johnson-Laird, P. N. (2005). Reasoning about relations. *Psychological Review*, *112*(2), 468–493. doi:10.1037/0033-295X.112.2.468 PMID:15783294

Grosan, C., & Abraham, A. (2011) Knowledge Representation and Reasoning. Intelligent Systems. Intelligent Systems Reference Library, 17. doi:10.1007/978-3-642-21004-4_6

Halford, G. S., Wilson, W. H., & Phillips, S. (1998). Processing capacity defined by relational complexity: Implications for comparative, developmental, and cognitive psychology. *Behavioral and Brain Sciences*, *21*(6), 803–831. doi:10.1017/S0140525X98001769 PMID:10191879

Hatzilygeroudis, I., & Prentzas, J. (2006). Knowledge Representation in Intelligent Educational Systems. In Web-based Intelligent E-learning Systems: Technologies and Applications (pp.175-192). IGI Global. Doi:10.4018/978-1-59140-729-4.ch009

Jaiswal, S. (n.d.). *Knowledge represent.* Retrieved from https://www.javatpoint.com/knowledge-representation-in-ai

Katalnikova, S., Novickis, L., Prokofyeva, N., Uskov, V., & Heinemann, C. (2017). Intelligent Collaborative Educational Systems and Knowledge Representation. *Procedia Computer Science*, *104*, 166–173. doi:10.1016/j.procs.2017.01.097

Klix, F. (2001). Problem Solving: Deduction, Induction, and Analogical Reasoning. In International Encyclopedia of the Social & Behavioral Sciences (pp. 12123-12130). Elsevier.

Knowledge representation techniques. AI lectures. (n.d.). Retrieved from http://www.hbcse.tifr.res.in/jrmcont/notespart1/node38.html

Kovarik. (2009). Cognitive Research: Knowledge Representation and Learning. Cognitive Radio Technology, 367-399. doi:10.1016/B978-0-12-374535-4.00012-6

Lardjane, S., & Anna Nuutinen, M. (2014). *Knowledge Representation for High Quality Learning. hal-01098521f.* Retrieved from https://hal.archives-ouvertes.fr/hal-01098521/document

Masood, M., & Mokmin, N. A. (2017). Case-based Reasoning Intelligent Tutoring System: An Application of Big Data and IoT. *Proceedings of the 2017 International Conference on Big Data Research*, 28-32. 10.1145/3152723.3152735

Ramirez, C., & Valdes, B. (n.d.). *A General Knowledge Representation Model of Concepts.* Retrieved from https://cdn.intechopen.com/pdfs/36656/InTech-A_general_knowledge_representation_model_of_concepts.pdf

Singh, P., Barry, B., & Liu, H. (2004). Teaching Machines about Everyday Life. *BT Technology Journal*, *22*(4), 227–240. doi:10.1023/B:BTTJ.0000047601.53388.74

Chapter 9
Simulation of Human Brain:
Artificial Intelligence-Based Learning

Navita Malik
Galgotias University, India

Arun Solanki
Gautam Buddha University, India

ABSTRACT

AI is a branch of computer science that gives the ability to a computer to think and make decisions like humans. It stimulates the human brain in the computer and makes appropriate decisions when required. AI-enabled education impacts the designing of curriculum, mode of instruction, and many more. The use of these tools revolutionizing the education sector with the progression of ICT tools have now become AI-enabled. The main feature of an AI-enabled tool is personalization. These AI-enabled tools work like intelligent assistants for the students. The intelligent system having features like answer the queries of the students, give assistance, support learning, provide or take assignments, and provide reinforcement material according to their opted courses. A teacher has a minimum intervention with this process and has the role of a facilitator only. This chapter concludes that the AI-enabled teaching-learning process can't replace the classroom teaching; instead, it is handy. In the future, AI could replace the need of a teacher in class to some extent.

DOI: 10.4018/978-1-7998-4763-2.ch009

1. INTRODUCTION

In many science fiction movies, we have seen the role of AI. In the education domain, AI is more than science fiction (Subrahmanyam,2018). There are credit systems in each education domain, and it has been offered by the MHRD in India to pass a course on the Swayam portal that is equal to the credit of an Indian university program of language education (Kashtwari,2019). Education using AI is much smarter than language learning and educational technology. Countries like the USA and China are in front of AI centered education and put AI in the classroom, too. As time passes, the education system realizes the role of AI in Education and find that teaching using AI techniques affect the way of teaching and learning. The AI may impact the designing of curriculum, mode of instruction, assessment preparation, and submission, but the advanced education tool of AI may or may not be capable of understanding and integrating the product and services of the system in the future (Hammond,2019).

In today's scenario, we are going rapidly towards automation in every domain, and the education sector is also not untouched from this transition. The education sector is also using the online tutorials, smart boards, intelligent tutorial systems, chatbots, robots in the classroom to teach the students as technological advancements. This technological advancement is producing new opportunities for different sectors. Technological progress always raises the question of whether it is capable of revolutionizing higher education. This progress gives a fear which arises due to these applications of Artificial Intelligence. Different parameters are used in the education sector. These parameters should always be taken into account before putting theses AI advancements in the education sector before benefitting the teachers and students.

A learner starts its education when he or she is an infant and ends as a higher education student. The AI will impact the individual learning application as a teacher and learner.

This technological advancement of AI, start with the birth of ICT when the education system was using different ICT tools in the domain (Lieto, 2016). These ICT tools make the stakeholders i.e., teachers and students, curious to enhance the capability of existing tools as AI-enabled. In point of view of a single stakeholder, AI tools provide a viable solution in a certain way, to give the automated assistance. AI provides virtual support, which is helpful to stakeholders as it is available according to the time of the individual. This AI-enabled education gives us a rethink scenario as it is creating an impact on our convolution learning. Newly developed AI-based applications will provide a chance to introduce the new versatile curriculum to the education system. In the last decade, these changes taken place gradually and not noticeable significantly by the majority of universities. The impact of these changes used in many decision-making of education systems in the whole of the world.

Nowadays, the role of this Artificial intelligence policy is going to revolutionize the education system in the entirety of the word (Ventura,2017). This chapter discusses the different aspects of the usage of AI in the higher education sector, covering the teacher and learner collaboration using AI, Human Intelligence and Artificial Intelligence, Intelligent Assistants in AI, importance, and role of AI in education, etc. After reading this chapter, the learner will be well aware of the current and future impact of AI in higher education.

2. TEACHER AND AI COLLABORATION

Many tools of Artificial Intelligence is used to enhance the skills and testing of primary students. AI-enabled educational tools are in their evolving stage, so students and teachers are also in the learning phase and trying to do differently and more using these tools. These tools give the freedom to teachers and help them in a personalized manner. These AI tools have a uniquely human capability where an automated machine lacks. This combination, i.e., AI-enabled tools and teachers become the best and give the best outcome for the students. Artificial Intelligence is a sun rising technology, and a lot of future work will be completed using this, so it will be suitable for our students that they will be exposed to this technique (Holstein, 2016).

3. HUMAN INTELLIGENCE AND ARTIFICIAL INTELLIGENCE

Human Intelligence is the sum of those cognitive abilities that give the human being a relative autonomy, which can be categorized as "intelligence profiles" or "multiple intelligences (Shabbir, 2015). Computational intelligence (Manju, 2014) is known as superior to Human Intelligence due to its memory capacity, but Computational intelligence is not capable of interpreting meanings. Hence Computational Intelligence is used for information processing but doesn't know what is processed. On the other side, the human brain has the capacity of processing with the knowledge of processed data. So to give the intelligence capability to the computer system, the term Artificial Intelligence comes into existence (Vassileva, 2008). AI is a branch of computer science that is used to design and develop an intelligent system, i.e., the systems which behave and make decisions like a human (Xia, 2020).

The term AI was come into existence in 1956, at a conference at Dartmouth College, in Hanover. The AI was started with the development of "Turing Machine" by the famous scientist Alan Turing (Saygin,2003). This machine was capable of processing different types of calculations. Alan Turing also developed a Turing machine test in which a machine thinks and makes a decision like the human, and an observer cant found whether the decision was taken by machine or a person. Other scientists named McCulloch, Turing, von Neumann, Wiener, and Pitts, Gardner, also contributed to the development of AI techniques in the early phase (Mainzer, 2020). There are two types of AI, i.e., Weak AI and Strong AI. Weak AI is only restricted to the use of computers to study the cognitive possibilities of the human being; and a strong AI, which is oriented to linking the AI and human intelligence, and seeking ways to connect them even more (Shabbir, 2015).

4. INTELLIGENT ASSISTANTS IN EDUCATION

AI-enabled educational tolls comprise the smart tutoring system, conversational educational system, chatbots, and robots (Heo, 2019). These educational tools can answer the queries of the students, give assistance, support learning, provide or take assignments, and provide reinforcement material according to their programs. These tools offer a personalized experience for each student, i.e., educational material changes according to the pace and behavior of the student. These assistants gather the individual learner data and predict the success and failure of the student. These assistants also identify the learning gaps, highlight the weakness and strength of the student, and give suggestions to overcome the weakness. Assistants can work individually or with the collaboration of human teachers. It has customized exercises, learning curriculum, attendance, and sessional marks for each student. An Assistant can work independently, but a teacher needs to monitor. In this way, AI and teacher will create an immersive learning experience together for the students (Duque, 2018).

4.1 Voice Assistants

Nowadays, the teachers are using the voice assistants in the classroom. Voice assistants such as Amazon Alexa, Google Home, Apple Siri, and Microsoft Cortana are some examples that are used by the students to interact with educational material without the interaction of the teacher. The students use these devices with teaching material and additional educational assistance at the home place or in educational institutes. In the higher education scenario, Universities are also giving voice assistant to the students in place of their books and E-resources. Many universities in the world are giving the Amazon Alexa voice assistant to complete the educational and campus needs. Alexa provides a personalized environment for the student and provides the answers to the student query regarding the education and campus of the university. This voice assistant reduces the human intervention and cost of hard books, which can be out of date in the future. In the future, more students and teachers will use these voice assistants and will be the need of the hour (Callaghan, 2019).

4.2 Chatbots

Chatbots are the software that answers the queries of the user without the intervention of humans. Many domains like banking, telecommunication, and others are using the chatbots in place of humans. In the education sector, chatbots are also used in the different process like admission, career counselling, etc. Niaa is the example of a chatbot that helps the aspirant to get admission in an educational institute. Niaa is a brilliant fusion of advanced Artificial Intelligence and personalized Machine Learning, Niaa is built to intelligently engage your prospects based on their journey, providing them with delightful counseling experience. Unlike other chatbots for education, Niaa is built to strike a real conversation with aspirants prospects. So instead of relying on plain chat workflows, Niaa draws its learnings from the tightly coupled NoPaperForms platform and provides an experience like no other (Shafi, 2020), (Anshu, 2019).

4.3 Recommendation System

The software which retrieves and filters the data from the existing content according to the user profile, behaviour, and past browsing is called the recommendation system. The Recommendation system usually covers the e-commerce domain. Amazon, Facebook, youtube, Flipkart, Netflix are the leading website which uses the recommendation system and gives the suggestion to the user. In the education domain, the first use of recommendation systems is to assist the students in their educational choices, i.e., where a student gets the admission, the information about the recommended university, teachers, or, moreover, support choices of speciðc academic courses or disciplines. The recommendation system also recommends specific E-learning or online courses (Zhu, 2008), (Ahuja, 2019).

5. ROLE OF AI IN EDUCATION SYSTEM

Overall the integration of AI-enabled education drives positive outcomes in the domain. But an individual may have different effects of AI-based education. AI in education can be grouped into five general roles:

1. **Automation:** The most straightforward role of AI is the automation of students related activities which involves grading, digital asset categorization, or timetable scheduling. The teachers can spend more time with the students.
2. **Integration:** AI, with the combination of Machine Learning or IoT (Priyadarshni, 2019), (Rajput, 2016), (Tayal, 2019), (Pandey, 2019), (Solanki, 2018), (Rameshwar, 2020) can give a personalized experience to the students.
3. **Acclimation:** Nowadays, students are spending their time online. With these new conditions, AI-enabled education can help students to the pace of technological change.
4. **Delineation:** The learning of every student is different from the other students. We change educational policy and curriculum according to the student's needs. But it is always tricky to find whether a teacher is delivering the content according to the students. AI-based analytics helps to spot critical trends and helps the teachers to design the most effective classroom experience.
5. **Identification:** Using AI-enabled education in a classroom helps to identify critical areas for student and teacher performance. AI can help spot and remedy potential problems in their formative stages.

6. IMPORTANCE OF AI-ENABLED TEACHING

The Artificial Intelligence-based educational system is giving positive outcomes in many countries. Following are the essence of AI-based education system (Nichols, 2006).

1. **Adaptive Nature:** AI-based education learning's most prominent importance is its personalization, according to the individual learner. Some of this is already happening through growing numbers of adaptive learning programs, games, and software. These systems give recommendations according to the need of the learner, assist in learning tuff topics or topics where the student lacks on with the student pace and time. The teacher only intervenes when it's required. Adaptive learning has already had a significant impression on the education system across the world. As AI advances in the coming decades, adaptive programs will likely only improve and expand.
2. **Improvement in existing courses:** Every teacher is not an expert in delivering the content and doesn't know the gaps in his/her lectures. The educational material which is provided to the student may be confusing to the students about the different concepts. AI-enabled education can quickly solve this problem. Simplilearn and Coursera are the E-learning platforms that are addressing these problems using AI-enabled teaching. AI-enabled education system sent

an alarm to the teachers that most of the students make the same mistake when an assignment is submitted. Then the teacher gives a hint to the students, how this mistake can be resolved. This type of AI-enabled education finds the gaps and suggest the teacher overcome these problems. The system also considers the fundamental problem of the students where they are lacking.

3. **Additional support from AI tutors:** Classroom teaching can not be replaced by online teaching. The classroom instructor or tutor delivers the lectures, and the machines can not offer this type of talk. However, due to lack o time and spending more time on the internet, in the future, we will find more tutors online in the comparison of classes. Some AI-enabled tutoring programs already exist, which are helping the students in different subjects. These tutorials only teach the fundamentals. However, it can not cover the high-order thinking and research problems. This type of problem can be solved by real-time or classroom tutorials. But in the future, it will be covered by AI tools.
4. **Feedback System:** The AI system provides feedback about the success and failure of the courses opted by the students. The online AI system shows you the performance of a student and gives feedback to the students about the lack of the student. These lacks can be improved under the guidance of the teacher.
5. **Usage in Daily Life:** Most of the stakeholders don't notice that they are getting regular information using AI-enabled system like google and amazon. Google gives information based on GPS location, and amazon provides recommendations based on past purchases. Siri provides suggestions according to your commands. Facebook sends ads on your page according to your interest. If a student is interested in any online course and browsed one time or search that course, then all of these tools will give you the specific recommendation. This kind of smart system affects your personal, professional, and academic as well. In the future, the student will have a more personalized experience in comparison to today as technology advances.
6. **Role of Teachers:** The role of the teacher is changing in education with the advancement of intelligent technologies. AI system is already taking assignments, giving tutorials, improving student skills, as discussed in section 3. In the future, AI could replace the need of a teacher in class to some extent. In future teacher will be known as a facilitator.

7. CONCLUSION

The chapter starts with the introduction of artificial intelligence and the current scenario of AI-based education in different countries like India, China, and the USA. The AI-enabled education impacts the designing of curriculum, mode of instruction, assessment preparation, and submission. Every sector, including education, is automated, using online tutorials, smart boards, intelligent tutorial systems, chatbots, and robots in the classroom. This advancement in education is revolutionizing higher education. This revolution was started with the birth of ICT. As the ICT tools advances, teachers and learners become curious to make it more user-friendly and self-decision support. Nowadays, there are a lot of AI-enabled tools that support self-decision. This support and decision are available according to the time of the individual. Nowadays, the role of this Artificial intelligence policy is going to revolutionize the education system's entire word. Many AI-enabled educational tools are in the development of their primary stage, so not well known to students and teachers. These AI tools work in a personalized manner. These AI tools simulate human brain decision-making powers. The system which possesses such capabilities is known as an intelligent system and can assist the different student in a personalized manner. The intelligent assistant system can answer the queries of the students, give assistance, support learning, provide or take assignments, and provide reinforcement material according to their opted courses. These assistants are used to predict the success and failure of the student in his/her academic carrier. A teacher has only to monitor the teaching assistant. In this way, AI and teacher will create an immersive learning experience together for the students. Some examples of these intelligent assistants are voice assistant, chatbot, and recommendation system, etc. This chapter also highlights the role of AI, which covers automation, integration, Acclimation, Delineation, and Identification. The end section of this chapter the importance of AI-enabled teaching importance in current and future prospectives, which covers the adaptive nature of AI system, Improvement in existing courses, support for AI tutors, feedback system, and daily usage of AI in the education sector. In the last, the role of the teacher will be changed as technology advances. In the future, AI could replace the need of a teacher in class to some extent. In the future, teachers will be known as the only facilitator.

REFERENCES

Ahuja, R., & Solanki, A. (2019). Movie Recommender System Using K-Means Clustering AND K-Nearest Neighbor. In *Confluence-2019:9th International Conference on Cloud Computing, Data Science & Engineering*. Amity Universty. DOI: 10.1109/CONFLUENCE.2019.8776969

Anshu, K., Gaur, L., & Solanki, A. (2019). Impact of Chatbot in Transforming the Face of Retailing- An Empirical Model of Antecedents and Outcomes. *Recent Patents on Computer Science, 12*. Advance online publication. doi:10.2174/22132 75912666190809110804

Callaghan, M. J. (2019). Voice Driven Virtual Assistant Tutor in Virtual Reality for Electronic Engineering Remote Laboratories. In M. Auer & R. Langmann (Eds.), *Smart Industry & Smart Education. Lecture Notes in Networks and Systems* (Vol. 47). Springer. doi:10.1007/978-3-319-95678-7_63

Duque Méndez, N. D., Rodríguez Marín, P. A., & Ovalle Carranza, D. A. (2018). Intelligent Personal Assistant for Educational Material Recommendation Based on CBR. In A. Costa, V. Julian, & P. Novais (Eds.), *Personal Assistants: Emerging Computational Technologies. Intelligent Systems Reference Library* (Vol. 132). Springer. doi:10.1007/978-3-319-62530-0_7

Hammond, L.D., Flook, L., Harvey, C. C., Barron, B., & Osher, D. (2019). *Implications for educational practice of the science of learning and development*. doi:10.1080/10888691.2018.1537791

Heo, J., & Lee, J. (2019). CiSA: An Inclusive Chatbot Service for International Students and Academics. In C. Stephanidis (Ed.), Lecture Notes in Computer Science: Vol. 11786. *HCI International 2019 – Late Breaking Papers*. Springer. doi:10.1007/978-3-030-30033-3_12

Holstein, K., McLaren, B. M., & Aleven, V. (2017). Intelligent tutors as teachers' aides. In *Proceedings of the Seventh International Learning Analytics & Knowledge Conference on -LAK 2017*. New York: ACM Press.

Kashtwari, D.M., & Wani, Z.A. (2019). *MOOCS: the Indian journey so far: Ubiquitous Inclusive Learning in a Digital Era*. Doi:10.4018/978-1-5225-6292-4.ch002

Lieto, A., & Radicioni, D. P. (2016). From human to artificial cognition and back, new perspectives on cognitively inspired AI systems. *Cognitive Systems Research, 39*, 1–3. Advance online publication. doi:10.1016/j.cogsys.2016.02.002

Mainzer, K. (2020). A Short History of the AI. In *Artificial intelligence - When do machines take over? Technik im Fokus*. Springer., doi:10.1007/978-3-662-59717-0_2

Manju, A., & Nigam, M. J. (2014). Applications of quantum-inspired computational intelligence: A survey. *Artificial Intelligence Review, 42*(1), 79–156. doi:10.100710462-012-9330-6

Nichols, J., & Goul, M. (2006). Synergizing the Artificial Intelligence and Decision Support Research Streams: Over a Decade of Progress with New Challenges on the Horizon. In *Intelligent Decision-making Support Systems. Decision Engineering*. Springer. doi:10.1007/1-84628-231-4_3

Pandey, S., & Solanki, A. (2019). Music Instrument Recognition using Deep Convolutional Neural Networks. *International Journal of Information Technology*. doi:10.100741870-019-00285-y

Priyadarshni, V., Nayyar, A., Solanki, A., & Anuragi, A. (2019). Human Age Classification System Using K-NN Classifier. In A. Luhach, D. Jat, K. Hawari, X. Z. Gao, & P. Lingras (Eds.), *Advanced Informatics for Computing Research. ICAICR 2019. Communications in Computer and Information Science* (Vol. 1075). Springer. doi:10.1007/978-981-15-0108-1_28

Rajput, R., & Solanki, A. (2016). Real Time Analysis of Tweets using Machine Learning and Semantic Analysis. In *International Conference on Communication and Computing Systems(ICCCS-2016)*. Taylor and Francis. 10.1201/9781315364094-123

Rameshwar, R., Solanki, A., Nayyar, A., & Mahapatra, B. (2020). *Green and Smart Buildings: A Key to Sustainable Global Solutions*. Green Building Management and Smart Automation with IGI Global USA. doi:10.4018/978-1-5225-9754-4.ch007

Saygin, A. P., Cicekli, I., & Akman, V. (2003). Turing Test: 50 Years Later. In J. H. Moor (Ed.), *The Turing Test. Studies in Cognitive Systems* (Vol. 30). Springer.

Shabbir, J., & Anwer, T. (2015). Artificial Intelligence and its Role in Near Future. *Journal Of Latex Class Files. VOL, 14*(8).

Shafi, P. M., Jawalkar, G. S., Kadam, M. A., Ambawale, R. R., & Bankar, S. V. (2020). AI—Assisted Chatbot for E-Commerce to Address Selection of Products from Multiple Products. In N. Dey, P. Mahalle, P. Shafi, V. Kimabahune, & A. Hassanien (Eds.), *Internet of Things, Smart Computing and Technology: A Roadmap Ahead. Studies in Systems, Decision and Control* (Vol. 266). Springer. doi:10.1007/978-3-030-39047-1_3

Solanki, A., & Nayyar, A. (2018). Green Internet of Things (G-IoT)- ICT Technologies, Principles, Applications, Projects, and Challenges: Green Internet of Things. In Handbook of Research on Big Data and the IoT. IGI Global. doi:10.4018/978-1-5225-7432-3.ch021

Subrahmanyam, V. V., & Swathi, K. (2018). Artificial Intelligence and its Implications in Education. *International Conference on Improved Access to Distance Higher Education Focus on Underserved Communities and Uncovered Regions.*

Tayal, A., Kose, U., Solanki, A., Nayyar, A., & Saucedo, J. A. M. (2019). *Efficiency analysis for stochastic dynamic facility layout problem using meta-heuristic, data envelopment analysis and machine learning. Computational Intelligence*. SCI Publication. Wiley Online Library., doi:10.1111/coin.12251

Vassileva, J. (2008). Social Learning Environments: New Challenges for AI in Education. In B. P. Woolf, E. Aïmeur, R. Nkambou, & S. Lajoie (Eds.), Lecture Notes in Computer Science: Vol. 5091. *Intelligent Tutoring Systems*. Springer. doi:10.1007/978-3-540-69132-7_5

Ventura, M. D. (2017). Creating inspiring learning environments by means of digital technologies: a case study of the effectiveness of whatsapp in music education. *EAI Endorsed Trans. e-Learn., 4,* 1–9. https://eudl.eu/pdf/10.4108/eai.26-7-2017.152906

Xia, P. (2020). Application Scenario of Artificial Intelligence Technology in Higher Education. In *International Conference on Applications and Techniques in Cyber Intelligence ATCI 2019. ATCI 2019. Advances in Intelligent Systems and Computing*, (vol. 1017). Springer. 10.1007/978-3-030-25128-4_29

Zhu, F., Ip, H. H. S., Fok, A. W. P., & Cao, J. (2008). PeRES: A Personalized Recommendation Education System Based on Multi-agents & SCORM. In H. Leung, F. Li, R. Lau, & Q. Li (Eds.), Lecture Notes in Computer Science: Vol. 4823. *Advances in Web Based Learning – ICWL 2007. ICWL 2007*. Springer. doi:10.1007/978-3-540-78139-4_4

Chapter 10
Influence of Artificial Intelligent-Based Vocational Courses on Self-Concept of Students

Shivani Verma
Mayawati Government Girls Post Graduate College, India

Pradeep Tomar
Gautam Buddha University, India

ABSTRACT

Artificial intelligence (AI) these days is becoming a more popular choice among students because of its large scope in different fields of life and career. The chapter is based on how the vocational courses of AI have its effect on the students' self-concept. The two groups of students have been taken for the study: one group having vocational trade as AI and basics (150 students) and another group having non-vocational subjects (150). The chapter has two goals: to compare level of self-concept of students with AI-based vocational trade subject and students without any vocational courses and to analyze gender difference among students in relation to self-concept. The samples were selected by simple random sampling. T-test analysis showed that the two groups had significant difference between their levels of self-concept. The students with AI-based vocational subject have a higher self-concept than that of students of non-vocational subjects.

DOI: 10.4018/978-1-7998-4763-2.ch010

1. INTRODUCTION

The term 'Self Concept' itself is explanatory of its meaning as it gives reflection of self. Among the non-cognitive aspects of personality disposition self-Concept has been considered to be a key point in the understanding of human behaviour and it has been found to be an important factor affecting various areas of development and achievement including social development and academic achievement. As pointed out by *(Roggers, 1994)*, much of the child's academic behaviour is influenced by his 'Self Perception'. There are several terms those are virtually synonymous with Self-Concept; among them are "Self-image", "the Ego", "Self understanding", "Self perception", and "Phenomenal self". The Self-Concept is not inherited; rather, it is development formation in the psychological make-up of the individual. The Self-Concept formed through experiences with his environment and are influenced especially by environmental reinforcement and significant others. A person's awareness of himself is established largely by the acceptance and rejection of the other people. The adolescence is the age when a child starts viewing itself as more matured and responsible person. Graduation year is the transition phase in which a student prepare himself for his/her career. And, type of higher education depends upon the subject choices in intermediate classes. The subjects of study influence the personality characteristics of children. Sometimes, some subjects have positive impact on personality traits but sometimes they may have negative impact. Artificial Intelligence courses these days are becoming more popular choice among students because of its large scope in different field of life and career. Especially the school students are fascinated with the AI more. Sometimes, having smart and artificially intelligent devices becomes status symbol among themselves. A person develops his Self-Concept on the basis of what he thinks, the significant others think of himself and it affects his behavior in turn. This is known as reflected Self-Concept. It has been seen that the individuals from disadvantaged group have poor Self-Concept they take negative feeling about their performances in different fields, like students' academic performance can be poor due to low Self-Concept. In the present chapter Self-Concept of adolescents has been measured. Adolescence is a period of life with its own peculiar characteristics and problems. Hence for deep penetration into their perception, their own physical, social, temporal, educational, moral, and intellectual sphere of Self-Concept need to be explored. Proposing that the self is the result or by product of social interchange which makes it necessary to examine not only the "systems of communication and relationship that becomes built-into the self but also the concept in which such communications suited *(Gerger, 1994)*. The picture, an individual has of himself is called the concept of self. He may possess honesty, confidence, extravagance etc. These several traits form a personality but the Self-Concept covers beliefs, convictions and values; further, it includes the attitudes as a person has been concerned with himself. The courses studied at school age have their effect on the career chosen for future because these courses become the basic prerequisites thereafter. The interest of the child is also represented through these subjects. The smart and artificially intelligent devices are found to be very interesting by the college going youngsters so most often they opt for AI based courses at graduate level courses. If the students chose the course of their interest the confidence level automatically is increased. Thus helps in balancing the personality and self-concept.

2. THE DEVELOPMENT OF SELF-CONCEPT

The sense of self grows slowly. It begins in infancy, with Self Awareness, when a child recognizes itself; the first moment of self-recognition comes. The next step is Self -Definition. This comes when the child identifies the characteristics it considers important to describe it. A little girl can think herself in terms of externals as her pony tailed hair, her neat house, and her activities in school. Until about age 6 or 7 the child begins to define in psychological terms. He/She now develops a concept of who he/she (the real self) and also of who he/she would like to be (the ideal self). By the time he/she achieves self-understanding (Hurlock, 1978).

It is referred as one's attitude towards self. This is a dominant element in personality pattern of an individual because how a person feels and takes himself herself in life, determines the personality. Intercultural study of self image of teenagers of Finland, the United States and Germany in the age group of 12-19 yrs. By *(Erkolahti et. al., 1991)* found more similarities among three groups than differences. The biggest differences emerged in emotional tone and mood, where Finish Ss had the highest scores, vocational and educational goals and superior adjustment skills were higher among Ss from the US and West Germany. Using Tennessee Self Concept Scale with the interethnic sample of 35 subjects having one parent of Asian Indian descent and one of the non Asian Indian descent and the intra-ethnic sample of 30 subjects having both parents of Asian Indian descent *(Grover, 1989)* found higher scores on the self concept identity and psychological adjustment scaled of the TSCs than did the intra-ethnic subjects. The majority of the interethnic subjects chooses a dual ethnic identity with which to identity and reported they were satisfied in having dual ethnic backgrounds.

There is great the influence of environmental factors on Self Concept of children especially on the adolescents. Self-concept changes, by changing the environment *(Giordanella, 1996)*. His study was done to probe the relationships between educational placement and perceived self concept of individuals with learning disabilities after mainstreaming. A pretest-post test one way analysis of variance, group design study was used. No difference was found in the academic variables of individuals after mainstreaming but significant difference was found for the self-concept variables of happiness and popularity. Self-concept differentiation is the degree to which separate domains of the self-concept are differentiated from one another. *(Heath and Brown, 1999)* studied on children's self-reported depressive symptomatology and self-concept differentiation; and found higher level of differentiation associated with depressive symptomatology, which showed that the extent of influence of depressive symptomatology is different on different domains of self-concept is affected differently by different factors.

Although there are various influencing factors which affect differently the child's personality traits and self- concept but gender may not affect self- concept of the teenagers *(Coner and Miranda, 2002)*. They sought to identify the array of motivational and environmental predictor variables that produce high mathematics achievement. The results disclosed that both genders within all four races, Asian, Hispanic, Black non-Hispanic and white closely parallel each other within intact and non-intact households. The best predictor of achievement was prior ability followed by negligible influence of Socio Economic Status (SES). Findings also revealed the lack of influence of self-concept, and the students' perceptions of performance and effort on the criterion mathematics achievement. According to *(Delphine, et al., 2002)*, academic achievement is related to self-concept of individuals. In their research, they examined French students of different academic levels to use Self-Concept Questionnaire, the prototype matching strategy in two studies. In study one, 30 students of eight grades were selected who were high achievers academically. In study two, 60 students of three categories were selected - (i) High Academic Achievers, (ii) Average, (iii) and Low Achievers. ANOVA revealed the main effects of academic level on the formation of self- concept. Only high achieving students possessed well-structured academic self- concept. In *(Kanchana M., 2002)* study, an attempt is made to compare 196 college students from North America and 150 from India on the following dimensions: (i) Self-concept and Career Decision Making self-Efficiency (CDMSE).(ii) Gender differences in self-concept and CDMSE. Tools used were self-description Questionnaire career decision making self-Efficacy Scale by Nancy E. Betz. The data obtained was analyzed using t -test. Results of the study shows: Indian college students have lower self-concept and CDMSE than American students. Some gender differences were seen in self-concept, both among American and Indian students. There is no gender difference in CDMSE in both the samples. Thus the culture has a great impact on the self-concept of the individuals.

The scarcity of women in ICT-related studies has been systematically reported by the scientific community for many years. The study of *(Milagros Sainz and Jacquelynne Eccles, 2011)* had three goals: to analyze gender differences in self-concept of computer and math abilities along with math performance in two consecutive academic years; to study the ontogeny of gender differences in self-concept of computer and of math abilities and math performance across subject areas; and to contrast the role these variables play in predicting ICT-related studies over 2 years. Spanish secondary students participated at both times. Self concept of computer ability is higher in boys at both times; furthermore it decreases in girls and increases in boys across time. At time 2, boys have a higher self-concept of math ability, despite the lack of gender differences in math performance. Participants have a higher self-concept of math ability and math performance at time 1 than at time 2. Self-concepts of computer ability predict the intention to pursue ICT-related studies and mediate the association of gender with the intention to pursue ICT-studies. From the different studies, it is clear that there are different concrete and discrete influencing factors which can increase and decrease Self- Concept of students in adolescent years. A senior secondary student's Self Concept can be affected differently by different choices of subject at 10+2 standard, be it a favourite subject like computer or the culture. Following were the objectives and hypothesis of the present study:

3. OBJECTIVES OF THE STUDY

- To compare the Self-Concept of Students of Artificial Intelligence based vocational courses and students of non vocational courses at college level.
- To study the gender difference in students at in relation to their self concept.

4. HYPOTHESIS

- There is no significant difference between AI based vocational education students and non vocational students in relation to Self-Concept.
- There is no significant difference due to their gender in students of in relation to their self concept.

5. TOOLS AND TECHNIQUES USED

The present study is based on the descriptive study of self-concept of AI based vocational stream students and non vocational students. The investigation was conducted through survey method. The population comprised of students of Colleges, in Gautam Budh Nagar, Uttar Pradesh, India. The students were taken from vocational courses of Artificial Intelligence and from Non- vocational courses. Random sampling technique was used to collect data. Total 300 senior secondary students were selected. Out of this, 150 students of vocational (AI) and 150 students of non vocational subjects were randomly selected from nine schools. Self Concept Questionnaire by Mr. R.K. Saraswat was selected for the study. This self concept inventory provides six separate dimensions of self-concept, viz. **Physical, Social, Intellectual, Moral, Educational and Temperamental self concept**. Percentage, Mean and 't' test statistical techniques were used to describe the results.

6. FINDINGS

- Most of the students with Artificial Intelligence courses showed High Self Concept and students of non-vocational courses showed above average self concept. *Table 1* represents the level of Self Concept among college going students. It is exhibited in the table that all the students are having either High or above average Self Concept. This indicates that the adolescents start to think logically and have real sense of self concept. *Table 1* also explains that most of the students at this stage have clear idea of themselves, which means that they know what they are and what they want from life. The positive self concept is developed due to the support of parents, teacher and peer group *(Orgell, 1992)*. The groups studied are found homogeneous in relation to self-concept as all the respondents are having positive self concept. In adolescent years, children tend to think as adults do. Therefore confidence is raised, resulting in increasing their level of self-concept.

Table 1. Percentage distribution of students according to category of Self Concept.

S. No.	Category of Self Concept	AI Students (n=150)		Non Vocational Students (n=150)		Total Respondents (n=300)	
		N	%	N	%	N	%
1.	High Self Concept	56	37.3	14	9.3	70	23.3
2.	Above Average Self Concept	94	62.6	136	90.6	230	76.6
3.	Average Self Concept	00	00	00	00	00	00
4.	Below Average Self Concept	00	00	00	00	00	00
5.	Low Self Concept	00	00	00	00	00	00

- *Table 2* presents the distribution of respondents under the category of Self-Concept, dimensions wise separately. It is indicated in the table that all the 300 respondents have positive self concept but the level of their self concept is different for different dimensions of self concept. 77.3 percent respondents' physical self comes under 'Above Average' category. This category's percentages of students are 76%, 61%, 45%, 41% and 72% for social, temperamental, educational, moral and intellectual self respectively. When educational self is measured it is found that most of the respondents (58.6%) fall in 'High Self Concept' category whereas according to Intellectual Self, only 18.6 percent students are found in this category.

Table 2. Percentage distribution of respondents according to the dimensions of their self-concept (N=300)

Category of Self Concept	A		B		C		D		E		F		T	
	n	%	n	%	n	%	n	%	n	%	n	%	n	%
High	59	19.6	70	23.3	112	37.3	160	53.5	176	58.6	56	18.6	70	23.3
Above Average	232	77.3	228	76	183	61	137	45.6	124	41.3	216	72	230	76.6
Average	09	3	02	.6	5	1.6	05	1.6	0	0	28	9.3	00	0
Below Average	00	00	00	00	0	0	0	0	0	0	0	0	00	0
Low	00	00	00	00	0	0	0	0	0	0	0	0	00	0

A = Physical Self, B = Social Self, C = Temperamental Self, D = Educational Self, E = Moral Self, F = Intellectual Self, T = Total (Overall) Self Concept

This is understood from these results that there may be different influencing factors to affect all the dimensions differently. The similar findings are also drawn from the study of *(Heath and Brown, 1999)* as they came to conclude that all the domains of self-concept are affected differently by different factors.

- The comparison between Self-Concept of both the groups of study indicates the highly significant difference in the mean values of AI (187.71) and Non AI stream (178.27) students *Table 3*. As one value come under category of 'High Self Concept' and another in 'Above Average'. The t-value calculated is 5.89 between the two groups. This shows the heterogeneity of the groups in the regard of the variable of Self Concept.

Table 3. Comparison between Self Concept of Vocational and Non Vocational courses Students

S. No.	Group of Study	N	Mean	Sd	t-Value	Significance
1.	AI vocational courses	150	187.71	1.32	5.89**	Significant
2.	Non vocational courses	150	178.27	.894		

This difference in the Self Concept of the respondents also reveals that there is impact of stream of study on the Self Concept of students. The subjects during XI and XII classes influence their perception of selves and explain how they take and think of themselves. This may be because choosing a AI based Vocational trade makes the students more career oriented and increases their understanding of 'Self' and thus helps in attainment of Higher Self Concept.

- When correlation is calculated between dimensions of Self Concept of AI based Vocational and non vocational students, it is seen that in some of the dimensions two groups of study are significantly different *Table 4* the level of physical self in vocational trade students shows highly significant difference with that of Non Vocational students. The similar pattern of difference is obtained for their social and temperamental selves. Educational self is also found to be different significantly in the two groups as t-value is calculated as 2.7. But on the contrary, moral and intellectual selves are investigated as non-significantly different in both vocational and Non Vocational students cleared from the t-values calculated i.e. 1.5 and 1.09 for Moral and Intellectual selves respectively. It is exhibited through findings that physical, social and temperamental dimensions of Self- Concept are influenced by the subjects (AI based Vocational trade and Non Vocational) chosen for the study at college level. Again, highly significant difference is analysed between the total self concept of both the groups of students i.e. AI based Vocational course and Non Vocational courses.

Table 4. Difference among dimension of Self-Concept of Vocational Education and Non Vocational students

S. No.	Dimensions of Self Concept	Vocational (AI) Course Students (N=150)		Non Vocational Students (N=150)		t
		Mean	Sd	Mean	Sd	
1.	A	**30.6**	**.28**	28.7	.20	5.5**
2.	B	**30.8**	**.26**	28.3	.25	6.7**
3.	C	**31.8**	**.28**	30.1	.32	3.8**
4.	D	**33.06**	**.28**	31.9	.27	2.7*
5.	E	**32.64**	**.24**	32.16	.19	1.5ns
6.	F	**28.4**	**.24**	28.05	.29	1.09ns
7.	T	**187.7**	**1.32**	178.27	.89	5.89**

7. GENDER DIFFERENCE

- The gender difference has also been calculated and analysed among the respondents of the study on the basis of their Self-Concept. *Table 5* reveals no significant difference between the boys and girls when compared. Although, respondents were selected randomly and sample is heterogeneous in respect of their gender but it is found to be homogeneous in relation to their aspects of self-concept *Table 5*. Thus the study reveals that both the gender follows same developmental pattern and have same influencing factors.

Table 5. Difference of Self Concept due to gender among the respondents

Variable	Boys		Girls		t	Difference
	m	σ	M	σ		
Self Concept	189.8	2.2	**187.02**	**1.5**	.90	Non significant

Some of the previous studies also support the findings of present investigations. As, *(Asci et. al., 2001)* examined the gender difference in adolescents' social competence and analysed no significant difference among them in respect to their gender, which supports the result of the present study. Similarly findings were also obtained by *(Garg, 1987)*, *(Desai, 1979)*, *(Sharma, 1977)*, *(Schmitz, 1972)* and *(Jury, 1976)* as they found no difference in Self Concepts of male and female subjects of their studies.

8. CONCLUSION

The study concludes the following points: The AI based Vocational trade subject taken by the students has great and positive effect on their self- concept. The Self-Concept of these students with Vocational subject is higher than that of the students of Non vocational subjects. Gender does not play any role in building self- concept in students. Both girls and boys show similar pattern of self- concept.

REFERENCES

Asci, F. H., Kosar, S. H., & Isler, A. K. (2001). The relationship of self-concept and perceived athletic competence to physical activity level and gender among Turkish early adolescent. *Adolescence.* Libra publications. *San Digego*, *36*(143), 499–507. PMID:11817631

Conner & Miranda. (2002). The linkage among family structure, self-concept, effort and performance on mathematics achievement of American High School students by race. *American Secondary Education*, *31*(1), 72-92.

Desai, G.H. (1979). A study of creativity in school teachers as measured by Mehdi's test in relation to their self-concept toward teaching, *M.U. Ind. Edu. Review*, *22*(1).

Erkolahti, R., Jonsson, J., Offer, D., & Steinhouser, H.C. (1992). Comparison of the self –mage of teenagers in Fineland, the united states and Germany. *Switzerland Journal of Adolescent Health*, *13*(5), 392–395. doi:10.1016/1054-139X(92)90036-B PMID:1390794

Gergen, K. J. (1994). Toward a post modern psychology. In S. Kavale (Ed.), *Psychlogy and Postmodernism*. Sage Publications.

Giordanella, K. B. (1996). *Self- concept in individual with learning disabilities: Influence of educational placement. (Ed.D.)*. Columbia University Teachers College.

Heath, N. L., & Brown, A. E. (1999). Self-concept differentiation and depressive symptomatology in children. *International Journal of Psychology*, *34*(2), 95–105. doi:10.1080/002075999399990

Jury, L. E., Willower, D. J., & Delacy, W. J. (1976). Teacher self-concept and pupil control ecology. *The Alberta Journal of Educational Research*, *21*(4), 295–300.

Kanchana, M. (2002). Self - concept and Career decision –marking self- efficacy of under graduate College students; Indian and American comparisons. *Journal of Psychological Researched*, *46*(1), 17–26.

Rodriguez, M. (1994). Changes in academic self-concept self- confidence, and grade point average of migrant Mexican and Mexican American. Community College students who saved as mentors (Ed.D.). University of Southern California.

Roggers, C. R. (1994). *The facilitation of significant learning*. Speech, West Behaviour Science Institution.

Sainz, M., & Eccles, J. (2011). Self-concept of computer and math ability: Gender implications across time and within ICT studies. *Journal of Vocational Behavior*, *30*, 14.

Schmitz, H.V. (1972). Performance of self actualized college students in operant based methods of instruction, and of indices of study habits, extracurricular involvement and teaching vocational interest. *Dissertation Abstracts International*, *33*(1), 198-A.

Sharma, R. R. (1977). *Self concept, level of aspiration and mental health as factors in academic achievement (Ph.D. Psy)*. B.H.U.

Chapter 11
Impact and Latest Trends of Intelligent Learning With Artificial Intelligence

Aditi Sakalle
Gautam Buddha University, India

Pradeep Tomar
Gautam Buddha University, India

Harshit Bhardwaj
Gautam Buddha University, India

Uttam Sharma
Gautam Buddha University, India

ABSTRACT

Artificial intelligence (AI) has been used mainly on education in some methods that contribute to the development of competencies and test systems. With the continued development of educational AI solutions, it is hoped that AI will help address the need for learning, education, and teaching. AI can enhance performance, personalization, and streamline administrative tasks in order to give teachers time and freedom to learn and adapt—uniquely human skills that would battle on machines. The AI dream of education is one where the best results for students are obtained, based on the best qualities of machinery and teachers. The development of curriculum based on the specific needs of individual students has been a concern for educators for many years, but the AI presents teachers with an unprecedented degree of distinction to handle 30 students in each class. With AI many possibilities can be seen in the teaching and learning system considering interest and understanding of an individual, which will increase efficiency of the education system.

DOI: 10.4018/978-1-7998-4763-2.ch011

INTRODUCTION

AI can be difficult to describe, particularly for practitioners. One explanation is that AI is continually evolving. Nick Bostrom, a leading AI researcher at the University of Oxford, states "A number of cutting-edge AIs have been introduced into general implementations, often without being referred to as AIs, because it is generally fairly and widely no longer called AI" Rather, the software or an algorithm or method is called a machine but not an AI. The interdisciplinary existence of the field is another reason for the difficulties of describing the AI. Everyone contributes to the field of AI and each category carries its own experience and terms, anthropologists, biologists, computer scientists, linguists, historians, psychologists, and neuroscientists.

One way to describe AI is as computer systems programmed to communicate with the environment by skill, for example, visual perception and speech recognition, and smart behavior (e.g. analyzing the knowledge available and taking the most appropriate steps to accomplish a given objective) which we find to be inherently humane. AI is used more and more easily in our everyday lives. To order to improve financial decision-making, for instance, Scientists are now drawing on emerging methods to machine learning, statistical simulation, and probability statistics, to using decision analysis to neuroscience to create more successful medical diagnostics. And it is expected this growth to begin at an early stage–particularly, we believe, with OpenAI, a non-profit artificial intelligence testing company with a nominal $1B investment.

The AI use in education and learning will rise by 47.5% by 2021, as a result of a report released by eSchool news. Across the lowest education level to higher education institutions, the impact of this development is felt. It enables personalized coaching strategies for the enhancement of student environments. Artificial intelligence will let the students know how their career choices rely on their goals to support them above and beyond academics. The impact of AI is Intelligent learning and is visible with time.

Is AI Trying to Run Over People?

Many scientists are concerned that AI is a Pandora box with harmful results. Back in 1993, informatician Vernon Vinge popularized the notion of singularity that makes an AI computer or robot to reinvent and develop itself or construct AI more advanced than itself. It's likely, it is claimed, that this will lead to AI which far exceeds human intellect, intellect, and power (*Vinge,1993*). Most recently Stuart Russell, Max Tegmark, and Frank Wilczek, including Stephen Hawking and other leading scientists, have warned us of AI's potentials being too smart (*Hawking et al.,2014*). For many decades, after 2001, this troubling notion has fuelled Hollywood films:

Space Odyssey in the' 60s, the Terminator of the 1980s, and the new transcendencies-all reflecting an out-of-control AI vision of the Dystopian universe. Yet it's worth remembering the emerging capabilities of artificial intelligence before we get too worried. Great improvement in' general IA' would be required for any singularity to arise if it would effectively fulfill any analytical function that a person may have. And General AI isn't currently available. General AI is somewhat different from the "site AI" that most of us know about. These domain-specific AIs are based on one thing-e.g. mastering chess (Deep Blue or Go (Google's Deep Mind), driving a car (Google's cars), or recognizing that a passport photograph is a person's picture.

AI in Education and Learning

For more than 30 years scientific research has been focused on the application of artificial intelligentsia to education. To promote quality schooling and lifelong learning, the sector explores how it is performed in conventional schools or workplaces. This unites interdisciplinary AIs and technology (educations, psychology, biology, linguistics, sociology, and anthropology) to enable the creation of scalable, accessible, customized, appealing, and efficient learning systems and artificial intelligence. The empirical aim "to make correct and concrete quantitative aspects of teaching, psychology and the psychological awareness that are still left unconscious," is at the core of artificial intelligence teaching (*Self, 1999*). This is, in addition to being a driving force behind other' intelligent' technologies, the AI for learning and education is a powerful tool which provides us with more knowledge about how learning happens (such as how it is influenced by the socioeconomic and physical background of the learner or by technologies) and opens up what is often known as the' tiny black box' of learning. This information can also be used in the development of potential AI for learning and Education applications and can guide learning strategies that don't require technology. For example, AI for learning and Education will help us in seeing and interpreting the micro-steps students to follow in physics or other specific misunderstandings (*Vanlehn et al., 2005*). These observations will then be used by teachers in the classroom.

Artificial Intelligence Transforms the Educational Cycle!

The artificial intelligence is completely revolutionizing the educational teaching process by making teachers focus on forming the minds of students instead of reviewing copies to tailoring the learning experience for any student.

Learning with the AI system is setting examples in this difficult time when everything has been lockdown against novel corona vires (2019-2020). Schools, colleges, and universities have opted for online classes so that students can learn sitting at home with a laptop and understand with their understanding level by creative AI systems designed for education and learning. AI is simplifying administrative tasks as well. Maintaining attendance and other data is also easier than before.

BACKGROUND

The impact of AI systems for teaching is getting the learning world more relaxed and tailored. This changed the way people learn as learning resources became available to everyone by intelligent tools and computers. Today, students do not need physical classrooms to prepare if laptops and Internet access are available. AI also allows manual activities to be streamlined, meaning that schools can reduce the time required to carry out challenging duties and allow educators and spend more time with their students. Now is the time to explore AI's educational transitions.

Major Impact:

- AI will optimize the expedition of administrative tasks for teachers and academic institutions. Trying to simplify administrative tasks
- AI and education go hand in hand and new approaches will be required to ensure the overall academic achievement of all students. Standard syllabuses are used by AI systems to build personalized textbooks for such subjects. The consequence is the digitization of textbooks and the development of modern learning technologies to support students of all grades and ages. Creating intelligent content.
- AI customizes all classroom assignments and final tests to ensure students get the best possible support. Evidence shows that direct feedback is a gateway to effective tutoring. Students get personalized, tailored answers from their teachers via AI-enabled applications. Learning based on Specific research.
- There are no limitations of global education and AI trying to eliminate constraints.
- IT systems are strengthened, and new efficiencies are unleashed. Schools should determine appropriate measures to prevent the lack of students in crowds in corridors. AI giving new productivity.

A summary of recent AI approaches for advanced training programs. The importance of the various models of an optimal online learning environment is stressed by adaptive educational systems. Identification and adaptation to the needs and strengths of individual learners are essential to progress in the development of integrated e-learning programs (*Shute et al., 2012*). Accurate student profiles and behaviors based on observations of their affective states, information level, and form, personality characteristics, and skills are also important. These data can then be used to build an integrated learning environment efficiently (*Shute et al., 2012*). The data collected must be used and used successfully to build an integrated learning environment. These templates and data can be seen in two ways after they have been obtained. The first is to educate the pedagogy of the integrated curriculum program suggested by researchers and designers.

The mining of educational data and the analytics of learners are two key fields that overlap and can affect the origination of these skills. Models for artificial intelligence are also useful to build and mimic the human decision-making process to reach such capabilities.

The latest and related topics in digital learning circles such as massive open online courses (MOOCs), pédagogical data mining, learner analytics, and associated artificial intelligence strategies will also be studied and further explored.

MASSIVE OPEN ONLINE COURSES

MOOCs are a phenomenon that was developed in 2008. This kind of open method of learning has quickly become popular (*Haggard, 2013*). There must be two elements in each MOOC: free and available to any user (*Chen et al., 2013*). MOOCs have recently been made available for learning by major universities and schools, including Stanford and Harvard (*Chen et al., 2013*). The number of individuals registered will range from a thousand to millions— that is, many users can be registered (*Chen et al., 2013*). The biggest challenge for MOOCs is to gather large data sets from student encounters with their learning environments and to integrate them with technologies of artificial intelligence to gain insights into efficient human education (*Haggard, 2013*). When we could use these approaches to forecast performance so analytics could be the next critical step in implementing personalized programs that are adapted to the needs of students based on the patterns observed by students as well as evidence from past students (*Haggard, 2013*). The number of students enrolled in large free online courses is, according to (*Onah et al., 2014*), strong drop-out rates and the graduation rates for these courses are less than 13%. The alternative may be to change the curriculum based on student behavior analysis.

The alternative may be to change the curriculum based on student behavior analysis. The study of learning experiences is not only useful for academic reasons; it also allows students to get feedback on their success and modes of learning (*Fournier et al., 2011*). Nevertheless, the human understanding of data is needed (*Fournier et al., 2011*), given the capabilities of learning research technologies and software. A comprehensive survey on MOOCs ' artificial intelligence technology and data mining applications has been published by Fauvel and Yu (*Fauvel et al., 2016*).

Mining of School Data and Monitoring of Learners

Examples include Sakai, Moodle and ILAS, and portals on learning, such as the Dreambox, Knewton, or huge online open courses, which provide courses on e-learning (*Lin and Prez, 2015*). Numerous LMS (Learning Management Systems) are available. These courses feature the quality, which is stored in a massive quantity of data. The student's personal qualities and appraisal of his results determine each stage of the process (*Lin and Prez, 2015*).

The study of this data is based on two research fields:

Educational Data Mining (EDM) and LA (Learning Analytics) (*Lin and Prez, 2015*). Similar parallels occur in the classification of EDM and LAK categories. According to the International Data Mining Company (IDM), EDM is defined as an additional field of research aimed at planning techniques to analyze and apply the world where expert expertise comes from the educational sector (*Siemens and Baker 2012*).

Learning Analytics (LA), as described by The Society for Learning Analytics Research, is to collect, measure, evaluate and inform students of their characteristics in which, along with the context in which it takes place, the student's learning processes can be well understood and improved (*Siemens and Baker 2012).*

These approaches are particularly common because of the following factors:

- As in industrial or empirical research, the propensity for using a data processing methodology is increasing to make better decisions (*Lin and Prez, 2015*) (*Haralabus et al., 2010).*
- Powerful machine learning, statistical and data extraction methods, and procedures are available, which can detect correlations in data and create decision-making rules and predictive models which are obtained from the educational sector.
- Compilation of facts and information has become simpler and modern-day computers have enough memory to process and store the information.
- Because of the budget pressures and increasing demand, education institutions were forced to cut expenses and raise additional revenue by tap into developed countries ' growing education markets, forcing students to pursue their courses and provide improved quality standards (*Lin and Prez, 2015*).

The key goal of both LA and EDM is to look for appropriate knowledge from information gathered in the field of education to facilitate decision-making in this area. The proof must be framed in such a way that the various parties involved in the process will respond to their needs (*Lin and Prez, 2015*) (*Daradoumis et al., 2010*).

The input provided by the donors helps the instructors assess the quality of the research and the progress of the learning process. When a student's success is constantly tracked, any student having difficulties with learning the course content will early be noticed and can also help figure out other aspects of the course that create further trouble.

If the right methods are not usable, then the whole cycle is tougher and takes longer (*Lin and Prez, 2015*) (*Juan et al., 2009*). Students will have a facility to be directed by the required tools, following their priorities and expectations, their inspiration and their performance; they will be able to graphically display the learning outcomes and see where they are alongside their colleagues, and they will imagine their contributions and accomplishments concerning shared education initiatives.

In a nutshell, in a scalable educational program system can be used in various ways:

- Modelling users ' behavior, level of expertise and experience,
- User profile,
- Modelling of essential concepts in every area, as well as modelling of domain information components,
- Pattern research empirical. Another area where these approaches can be applied is the use of automation to adjust the method according to or according to the users ' desires and needs (*Prakash et al., 2014*).

Nevertheless, the greatest impediment to the successful use of LA and EDM is a lack of knowledge and understanding (*Lin and Prez, 2015*), a great many curriculum practitioners are unable to accurately interpret the results, translate the conclusions adequately or agree on the topic of a significant variety of realistic and principle terms. To find a solution to this issue, a constructive atmosphere must be developed and a data-based approach (data-focused approach) must be promoted in the education sector (*Romero et al., 2013*). (*Romero et al., 2007*), (*Romero et al., 2010*), (*Pea-Ayala, 2014.*) and list surveys of the dream of learning empirical studies and data mining and their use for educational purposes, as well as for the development of innovative e-learning systems.

LATEST TREADS IN LEARNING WITH AL SYSTEM

What AI Can Offer for Learning Right Now?

In our schools and colleges, a multitude of AI-driven devices is already used. A lot of the techniques are used to track student behavior, such as gathering statistics on school attendance and application to recognize and help students at risk of dropping out of their research, for example. They are used to monitor student behaviors.

AI developers are developing new user interfaces, such as natural speech and movement recognition, eye tracking, and other psychological features that can also be used for the extension of applications such as AI for Education and Non-AI for Education.

Here, though, we focus on three types of AI for Education tech programs intended to more specifically benefit learning: tutors to each learner, smart social learning assistance, and intelligent virtual reality.

AI for the Education system should provide every student with a knowledgeable, personal tutor.

Tutoring one-on-one for persons has long been recognized as the most successful teaching and learning method (because Aristotle tutors Alexander the Great at least!). There won't be just enough individual tutors, there won't be free. All this begs the question: how do we support all learners across subjects with the positive effects of one-to-one tutoring?

Intelligent tutoring systems (ITS) are used for this purpose. ITS use AI-Techniques to replicate one-to-one human tutoring, to execute learning tasks better suited to the cognitive needs of the learner, and to offer personalized and timely input. There are ITS that help students develop self-regulatory skills to monitor their learning; some use pedagogical techniques to reach into the lessons so that students are sufficiently encouraged to assist.

The 1970s offered individualized and integrated programming for some of the first AI programs. For instance, BUGGY (*Brown et al.,1978*), a pioneering method for teaching simple addition and subtraction, uses a pattern of myths that can be encountered in their formal arithmetic by students. This' bug collection' was used to diagnose any mistake a student made, essentially the domain model of the program

That could provide appropriate tutoring. At first, the bugs which could be found, those used in the initial code, were small. Further misunderstandings were uncovered and applied to the library over time.

Most recent ITS models are focused on machine learning methods, self-training algorithms focused on vast collections of data and neural networks, which allow them to make the right decision as to what learning material the learner will have. Yet the reasoning behind such decisions cannot be made clear in this approach.

New hybrid models should be even more robust. They require clear and understandable human reasoning for each judgment of the program (and thus theoretically applicable to teaching in the classroom). In the past decade, several innovative tutors to promote the individualization of learning have implemented more mature pupils, pedagogical models, and subject modelling.

The iTalk2Learn system (http://www.italk2learn.e), for example, has been developed to help young people learn fractions, which uses a learner model with details about the math skills of people, their academic challenges, their emotional state, their input which their responses.

Distance Learning and Education

Although the hindrances and problems in building distance-learning environments were and are still various, distance education is here to stay. "Exploring educational frontiers on the Web frightens some professors and maybe some students, but it can also generate unusual levels of motivation and pride in creating something new", says Shneiderman. Many universities offer course modules, whole courses, or even degrees online. Moreover, many companies offer all sorts of education-oriented material and educational software via the WWW.

Education applications may usually be built from scratch, applied, or constructed with general-purpose authorship instruments. Here, it becomes evident one of the new positions of teachers as readers. The product may be designed from scratch or developed using commercial products and freeware software by teachers/training designers.

Therefore, teachers must either opt to create their online courses (*Kaplan, 1998*) off-the-shelf or to choose from various online resources, such as WebCT, Blackboard, eCollege.com... The optimal compromise of instructional features, educator resources, teaching functions, student resources, technical assistance, administrator tools, administrative features, program costs, and computer equipment specifications will be determined of teachers ‘ selection.

Several colleges have planned to build tools for their teachers (*Collis, 1999*) with their authoring software. While the tools make it simpler for you to write online courses, one key issue is that they "still give the same look and sound," while off-stage part software should, according to Kaplan, "imitate the style of the classroom"(*Kaplan, 1998*). In comparison, streamlined packages simply demand more teacher preparation time and do not allow experienced users to be innovative enough.

However, we don't see a good function to emulate the traditional classroom. We expect that this pattern in copying will vanish over time–while this can be beneficial in the present creation in distance learning opportunities for both teachers and students and will assist in the context of the transition to web-based education. As other scholars have pointed out (*Synnes et al., 1999*), it makes no sense to simply seek to build a replica of the traditional instructional method, which will only yield weak outcomes because it is an imperfect replication. Nevertheless, it is a much easier way of making use of the opportunities that the modern world offers.

- Distance learning on the cloud has, as is well known, key benefits, features from–anywhere to anywhere at any time. Free education also exists as well, but much of the education applications available today aren't free and, in many schools, distance-learning services are available at a premium.
- Quick, text-based teaching materials no longer suffice. The very recent improvements in bandwidth permitted greater speech, Internet pictures are commonplace and the volume in soundtracks and images, and other (multiple) media forms have developed (animation, etc.).
- Appropriate teaching techniques and generally (intelligent) adaptation to the use of ITS (*Woods et al., 1996*) are built based on learner modelling (*Paiva,1996*) which is also defined in the following section. More recently, at the intersection of hypertext (hypermedia) and user modelling, the area of adaptive hypermedia emerged.

ITS: Learner Models, Domain Models; ITS on the Web

"Modern ITS has too little versatility concerning their pedagogical approach." Besides, "ITS is typically built according to an existing technique practically applicable to all students" (*Abou-Jaoude et al.,1998*). Moreover, "most ILEs provide a range of functionalities without their importance in the learning process being taken into consideration" (*Nkambou, et al., 1998*). An instructional purpose e.g. encourages and/or more thorough interpretation of the content material due to the use of ITS and/or adaptive/interactive approaches and (smart) techniques would be the only justification. A potential way of change is to switch between pedagogical approaches, cooperative strategy contexts (*Abou-Jaoude et al.,1998*).

Pedagogical Strategies and Explanation

- Tutor-tutee Traditional: computer is a teacher, the user is student
- Learning companion: A computer-simulated learner, to accompany the user (*Gilmore et al., 1988).*
- Learning by disturbing: Learning with a simulated troublemaker (*Frasson and Aimeur, 1996*).
- Learning by teaching: Human student teaches the simulated companion. (*Kasai and Okamoto, 1999).*
- Learning with a co-teacher: Both simulated teacher and co-teacher

In these contexts, there are guided strategies: learning with examples, learning through sharing stories, learning with games, learning through inference, learning through discovery, learning through intuition and deduction, etc. In these theoretical contexts.

A learner model is expected to move between strategies (*Okamoto et al., 2000*). Already in 1996 Greer (*Greer, 1996*) pointed to the relevance of the student's values; he said that it was important to provide tailor-made programs, to elicit appropriate input, to promote student contact and assistance. The "pupil beliefs, metacognition, and input expectations of the learner" must be sufficiently established for the correct option, however (*Nkambou et al.,1998*). In the end, the student model will be compared to the model of the area of information. This above is the concept of learning material which (naturally) relies on the context.

The more recent models include a classic and cognitive learner appraisal based on a learning profile or program, beginning from a classical awareness and cognitive model stage. The last layer to be applied is the integrity and emotional layer which is meant to point to the right pedagogical approach to learners, if correctly interpreted.

How the system acquires learner knowledge varies:

- The simplest way is through questionnaires, e.g. single/various choices where the learner inserts his / her preferences, opinions about his / her level of knowledge, learning profiles, emotional profile, etc. The user's choice can be tested in the same transparent way through the learning method choices (e.g. clicking the "utterance" or "request" button, after any text feedback, etc. (*Inaba and Okamoto, 1997*)). The context configuration settings such as background color, desired text type, color scheme, frame arrangement, etc. all belong to the same group.
- A method to assess the learner to create his / her profile can be used independently or along with the previous one. Such assessments can range from scientific testing to IQ testing, or personality testing.
- The last and best of these approaches is to follow the actions of learners and to turn the user's choices into a student model (*Cristea et al., 2000*) (*Kayama et al., 2000*). You will use this student guide to pick a learning approach, etc.

To obtain knowledge about the subject, the procedure for interviewing and checking directly benefits from the accuracy of the information (if the student does not know himself). The development of the interface model is straightforward for the learner, who may control it directly.

Since the conceptual basis of user, modelling is not yet clearly established, it is also best that the user exercises considerable control on modelling and correct any misunderstandings because of the nature of the actual person's mental profile. Such specific knowledge gathering also contributes to higher overhead, although it is simpler on the automated processing side. Aside from learning how to use instructional applications and the usual amount of instruction, it takes the user a lot of time to explain the machine what he/she is and what he/she wants and needs.

The tacit monitoring of the user method, however, has the benefit of encouraging the user to focus on the subject at hand and does not encourage him or her to ask multiple questions. A concern is that the system's assumptions may be inaccurate, leading to inadequate or even incomplete adaption without clear user input.

Thus, it is a good compromise between these three main approaches to analysis that can contribute to optimum strategies. Given that recent psychological and pedagogical work cannot fix this issue, it is very likely that realistic analyses of the application of educational software will offer answers and contribute not only to the advancement of study into educational software but also to reviews on the field of psychology and pedagogical science. They assume that optimum solutions entail integrating these approaches with a fine-tuning of the dynamic collection of priorities of user-friendliness, low overhead, and, finally, improved learning.

In comparison to isolated contexts, the results are as follows with the introduction with advanced ITS interface enhancement approaches in Web-based applications.

- Because of the architecture of database servers, large servers can hold material and models from tiny database computers, allowing the introduction of hardware that did not have a room for individual systems.
- However, the vast number of (current/potential) Internet users makes the use of normal behavior, grouping, etc. modelling and analysis more important. New app modelling approaches provide a grouping and adaptation directed at the country and area.
- Finally, the whole Internet is (potentially) filled with valuable educational content, so more than just the local data so services should be accessed by a new Educational network.

FUTURE FOR LEARNING WITH AI SYSTEM

Learning with the AI system's future relates to AI's future. With the rising use of AI technology, the number of people who are developing AI increases exponentially. Innovation and growth in general are at their highest rate. Innovation in AI in learning and Education will be a subject of interest for an increasing number of businesses, as it is already very common.

The impact of AI on education is only going to get bigger. Who knows where it's going to be in the future? Is the position of conventional education replaced by artificial intelligence? Will the computer screen or robot have information for future generations?

Considering some of the developments in education and learning from the edges of theory and reality, we believe AI to continue to evolve in education and learning, as well as some innovative technologies we hope to emerge. Others can appear faster than others and both should be viewed as both rewards and threats. That said, we see these trends favorably and have concentrated here on communicating AI for Education promising prospects for progress in education for everyone.

AI is widely recognized that so-called 21st-century skills are important to the working world of the present and future, with several organizations proposing a list of skills (short and long!) that individuals must have to engage completely in jobs and community.

Authoring tools: The purpose of authoring tools is to provide a (relatively) easy framework for development, thus allowing fewer developers to create educational applications. To accomplish this aim, two key solutions exist: (1) provide educators with a basic programming shell to build their classroom equipment; and (2) allow programmers to be more able to portray the environment and teaching techniques. Authoring devices falling under the first category provide a relatively narrow reach for the user's forms of educational experiences, whereas those in the second category have many more options for more complicated authors.

Modularity: The modularity of each device can be used to simplify ITS design. Although ITS breaks into the five previously discussed components, little effort has been made to reuse components from one system in developing another.

It does not mean that developers use their components alone, but that components should be exchanged between different designers.

This modularisation is hampered by various problems. First, tutors are written in different incompatible programming languages. Second, this perception of ITSs components is more of an expectation than reality. Developers also interconnect the components into a monolithic system. Besides, as the sector is new, specifications for components forms and their contents are not recognized. Finally, the coordination protocol between the various parts of an ITS is not in operation.

The time and cost required are one of the major problems in the design of intelligent tuition systems. To create one ITS, there is a big team, including computer programmers, field experts, and educational theorists. Building time estimates indicate that 100 hours of development are 1 hour of instruction. Techniques are needed to reduce these difficulties for educational development.

Collaboration involves students collaborating in groups to solve challenges. Collaborative study Such conditions are both cognitively and emotionally helpful. In these cases, the relationship between the teacher and the student does not normally centre, since students may teach one another without the instructor's guidance.

We will use the word "Collaborative Vocabulary" for this topic to mean students collaborating across the computer network with the help of an ITS.

Due to its presence with other classes, the nature of the ITS has to be simpler because the teaching is not to be flawless–when one student gets lost, a different student may support without having to focus on the ITS.

An important feature of teamwork settings is that not all individuals have the same ability in group contexts. This poses two problems. The first, the classic credit question, is how student templates are modified. Can the credit only be granted to the first person to respond correctly or will all community members provide a fair playing field? The second question is how to help the community move through the program. Should a student dictate the whole group's pace? Because if so, who's that?

While we described collaborative learning in its infancy, strides have been made in this direction. Belvedere, for instance, offers a set of resources for student groups to construct theories (e.g. evolution) and to then critique them (*Suthers et al., 1995*).

Adaptive instructional programs emphasize the distinction between learning processes. This unique instructional approach aims to incorporate a capacity to diagnosis each person's individual needs for the required learning to ensure that research materials and e-learning programs are tailor-made to inclusive learning. This approach aims to establish the correct learning pedagogy by providing the most relevant material to facilitate the experience of learning.

By simulation of the productive states, personality characteristics, competencies, rates, and level of knowledge of the various students it becomes vital to develop the correct student model and profile. To build an integrated learning environment, it is important to use acquired data effectively. Two forms can be used with learning learner styles. One is to educate the pedagogy of innovative curriculum program models and experts. The second goal is to provide the program with a complex learning capacity to build the correct pedagogy through the actions of the teachers and students and to change learning environments automatically.

CONCLUSION

The artificial intelligence technologies can be very useful, as in developing the learning environment they can improve and mimic the human reasoning and decision-making process. These learning skills are essential to providing a successful learning process for both the learner and the program. In chapter some emerging problems related to the use of integrated education frameworks of art intelligence techniques. Intelligent tutoring systems have shown themselves to be extremely effective in motivating and learning students. It is important to consider these structures composed of five components: the models for the students, the pedagogical module, the field experience, the communications module, and the model for the experts. It is a wide open-ended research issue to integrate many teaching techniques in the pedagogy section.

REFERENCES

Abou-Jaoude, S., & Frasson, C. (1998). An Agent for Selecting a Learning Strategy. NTICF 98, Rouen, France.

Brown, J. S., & Burton, R. R. (1978). Diagnostic Models for Procedural Bugs in Basic Mathematical Skills. *Cognitive Science*, *2*(2), 155–191. doi:10.120715516709cog0202_4

Chen, X., Barnett, D., & Stephens, C. (2013). Fad or future: The advantages and challenges of massive open online courses (MOOCs). Research-to-Practice Conference in Adult and Higher Education, 20–21.

Collis, B. (1999). *Design, Development and Implementation of a WWW-Based Course-Support System. ICCE99*. IOS Press.

Cristea, A., Okamoto, T., & Cristea, P. (2000). My English Teacher - An Evolutionary, Web-based, multi-Agent Environment for Academic English Teaching. Congress of Evolutionary Computation CEC 2000, San Diego, CA.

Daradoumis, T., Juan, A. A., Lera-Lpez, F., & Faulin, J. (2010). Using Collaboration Strategies to Support the Monitoring of Online Collaborative Learning Activity, in Technology Enhanced Learning. In Quality of Teaching and Educational Reform. Springer Berlin Heidelberg.

Daradoumis Haralabus, T., Fallin, J., Juan Prez, A., Martnez, F. J., Rodrguez-Ardura, I., & Xhafa, F. (2010). Customer Relationship Management applied to higher education: Developing an e-monitoring system to improve relationships in electronic learning environments. *International Journal of Services Technology and Management*, *14*(1), 103–125. doi:10.1504/IJSTM.2010.032887

Fauveland & Yu. (2016). *A Survey on Artiðcial Intelligence and Data Mining for MOOCs*. SciRate.

Fournier, H., Kop, R., & Sitlia, H. (2011). The Value of Learning Analytics to Networked Learningona Personal Learning Environment. *Proceedings of the 1st International Conference on Learning Analytics and Knowledge*, 104–109. 10.1145/2090116.2090131

Frasson, C., & Aimeur, E. (1996). A Comparison of Three Learning Strategies in Intelligent Tutoring Systems. *Journal of Educational Computing Research, 14*(4), 371–383. doi:10.2190/G6JP-3YPY-U7T1-CV8C

Gilmore, D., & Self, J. (1988). The application of machine learning to intelligent tutoring systems Teaching. In *Intl. Conference on the Learning Sciences*. AACE.

Grawemeyer, B., Mavrikis, M., Holmes, W., & Gutiérrez-Santos, S. (2015). Adapting feedback types according to students' affective states. In *Artificial Intelligence in Education 17th International Conference, AIEd. Madrid, Spain, June 22-26, 2015 Proceedings* (Vol. 9112). Madrid, Spain: Springer International Publishing.

Greer, J. (1996). Student modelling. Student Modelling workshop at the User Modelling Conference.

Haggard, S. (2013). *The maturing of the MOOC: Literature review of Massive Open Online Courses and other forms of Online Distance Learning* (BIS Research Paper Number 130). Department for Business, Innovation and Skills, londonuk, Research Papers Research paper number 130.

Hawking, S., Russell, S., Tegmark, M., & Wilczek, F. (2014). *Transcendence looks at the implications of artificial intelligence - but are we taking AI seriously enough?* Retrieved from http://www. independent.co.uk/news/science/stephen-hawkingtranscendence-looks-at-the-implications-ofartificial-intelligence--but-are-we-taking-ai-seriouslyenough-9313474.html

Inaba, A., & Okamoto, T. (1997). Negotiation Process Model for intelligent discussion coordinating system on CSCL environment. *AIED, 97*, 175–182.

Juan, A. A., Daradoumis, T., Faulin, J., & Xhafa, F. (2009). andF.Xhafa, A data analysis model based on control charts to monitor online learning processes. *Int.J.Bus. Intell. Data Min., 4*(2), 159–174. doi:10.1504/IJBIDM.2009.026906

Kaplan, H. (1998). Building your Web Course: The Case for Off-the-Shelf Component Software. *Cause/Effect Journal, 21*(4). https: //www.educause.edu/ir/library/html/ cem9849.html

Kasai, T., & Okamoto, T. (1999). *The Support for Collaborative Learning with Companion Agents, ICCE 99, IOS (Ohmsha)*. Press.

Kayama, M., Okamoto, T., & Cristea, A. (2000). Exploratory Activity Support based on a Semantic Feature Map. *Adaptive Hypermedia Conference (AH 2000)*, Trento, Italy. 10.1007/3-540-44595-1_44

Lin, L. C., & Prez, A. J. (2015). Educational Data Mining and Learning Analytics: Differences, similarities, and time evolution. *Rev. Univ. Soc. Conoc.*, *12*(3), 98–112. doi:10.7238/rusc.v12i3.2515

Marshall University's Center for Instructional Technology. (n.d.). *Comparison of Online Course Delivery Software Products*. http//multimedia.marshall.edu/cit/webct/compare/comparison.htm

Nkambou, R., IsaBelle, C., & Frasson, C. (1998). *Supporting some pedagogical issues in a Web-based distance learning environment.* NTICF'98, Conference Internationale sur les nouvelles technologies de la communication et de la formation, Rouen, France.

Nkambou, R., IsaBelle, C., & Frasson, C. (1998). *Supporting some pedagogical issues in a Web-based distance learning environment.* NTICF'98, Conference Internationale surles nouvelles technologies de la communication et de la formation, Rouen, France.

Okamoto, T., Cristea, A., Matsui, T., & Miwata, T. (2000). Development, and Evaluation of a Mental Model Forming Support ITS - the Qualitative Diagnosis Simulator for the SCS Operation Activity. OZCHI 2000, Sydney, Australia.

Onah, D., Sinclair, J., & Boyatt, R. (2014). Dropout rates of massive open online courses: behavioral patterns. *Proceedings of the 6th International Conference on Education and New Learning Technologies*, 5825–5834.

Paiva, A. (1996). Communicating with Learner Modelling Agents. *ITS 96 Workshop on Architectures and Methods for Designing Cost-Effective and Reusable ITSs.*

Pea-Ayala, A. (2014). Review: Educational Data Mining: A Survey and a Data Mining-based Analysis of Recent Works. *Expert Systems with Applications*, *41*(4), 1432–1462. doi:10.1016/j.eswa.2013.08.042

Prakash, Hanumanthappa, & Kavitha. (2014). Big Data in Educational Data Mining and Learning Analytics. *Int. J. Innov. Res. Comput. Commun. Eng*, *2*(12).

Romero, C., & Ventura, S. (2007). Educational data mining: A survey from 1995 to 2005. *Expert Systems with Applications*, *33*(1), 135–146. doi:10.1016/j.eswa.2006.04.005

Romero, C., & Ventura, S. (2010). Educational Data Mining: A Review of the State of the Art, IEEE Trans. Syst. Man Cybern. Part C Appl. *Rev.*, *40*(6), 601–618.

Romero, C., & Ventura, S. (2013). Data Mining in Education. *Wiley Int Rev Data Min Knowl Disc*, *3*(1), 12–27. doi:10.1002/widm.1075

Self, J. (1999). The Defining Characteristics of Intelligent Tutoring Systems Research: ITSs Care, Precisely. *International Journal of Artificial Intelligence in Education, 10*, 350–364.

Shneiderman, B. (n.d.). Educational Journeys on the Web frontier, Teaching your students where to go and how to get there. *Educom Review*. https://www.educause.edu/ir/library/html/erm9861.html

Shute, V. J., & Zapata-Rivera, D. (2012). Adaptive educational systems. In P. Durlach (Ed.), *Adaptive Technologies for Training and Education* (pp. 7–27). Cambridge University Press. doi:10.1017/CBO9781139049580.004

Siemens, G., & Baker, R. S. J. d. (2012). Learning Analytics, and Educational Data Mining: Towards Communication and Collaboration. *Proceedings of the 2nd International Conference on Learning Analytics and Knowledge*, 252–254.

Suthers, D., Weiner, A., Connelly, J., & Paolucci, M. (1995). Belvedere: Engaging Students in Critical Discussion of Science and Public Policy Issues. In J. Greer (Ed.), *Proceedings of Artificial Intelligence in Education* (pp. 266–273). AACE.

Synnes, K., Parnes, P., Widen, J., & Schefstroem, D. (1999). Net-based Learning for the Next Millennium. SCI/ISAS99.

Teletop. (n.d.). http://teletop.edte.utwente.nl/

Vanlehn, K., Lynch, C., Schulze, K., Shapiro, J. A., Shelby, R., Taylor, L., ... Wintersgill, M. (2005). The Andes Physics Tutoring System: Lessons Learned. *International Journal of Artificial Intelligence in Education, 15*(3), 147–204.

Vinge, V. (1993). *Vernor Vinge on the singularity*. Presented at the VISION-21 Symposium sponsored by NASA Lewis Research Center and the Ohio Aerospace Institute.

Woods, P. J., & Warren, J. (1996). Adapting Teaching Strategies in Intelligent Tutoring Systems. *ITS 96 Workshop on Architectures and Methods for Designing Cost-Effective and Reusable ITSs*.

Chapter 12
Impact and Role of AI Technologies in Teaching, Learning, and Research in Higher Education

Pradeep Tomar
Gautam Buddha University, India

Shivani Verma
Mayawati Government Girls Post Graduate College, India

ABSTRACT

The future of higher education is intrinsically linked with developments on new technologies and computing capacities of the new intelligent machines. In this field, advances in artificial intelligence open to new possibilities and challenges for teaching and learning in higher education with the potential to fundamentally change governance and the internal architecture of institutions of higher education. The role of technology in higher learning is to enhance human thinking and to augment the educational process, not to reduce it to a set of procedures for content delivery, control, and assessment. With the rise of AI solutions, it is increasingly important for educational institutions to stay alert and see if the power of control over hidden algorithms that run them is not monopolized by tech-lords. This chapter will cover all the positive and negative aspects of AI technologies on teaching, learning, and research in higher education.

DOI: 10.4018/978-1-7998-4763-2.ch012

1. INTRODUCTION

The future of advanced education is inherently connected with improvements on new advances and processing limits of the new machines. In this field, progresses in computerized reasoning open to additional opportunities and difficulties for instructing and learning in advanced education, with the possibility to on a very basic level change administration and the interior design of foundations of advanced education. With answers to the subject of 'what is man-made consciousness' molded by philosophical positions taken since Aristotle, there is little concession to an extreme definition. We are currently observing processing calculations affecting on the most commonplace parts of day by day life. Advanced education is put at the focal point of this significant change, which carries with it both uncommon chances and dangers by using supervised system. Supervised systems of learning may generate statistical estimates in whether a certain data pattern is a potential pre-given class. Therefore, supervised learning implies that we know what input patterns will mean for categories already. This is the most common model of learning in AI today since model classification is always appropriate for functional purposes in a series of predefined groups . For example, a car driver wants to know whether an object is a bike, truck, train, or child. Technically guided learning generates input models to be translated into a series of output groups. Their intelligence is also comparable to the most rising living beings and can balance the universe with learned behavior. The Pavlovian theory of reflexes and Skinnerian strengthening, for instance, are founded by these learning models in psychology. This type of learning, as Vygotsky emphasized in the 1920s, is the most complex learning paradigm and both pigeons and humans can do so.

The supervised learning models have a challenge: they can imagine the universe as a simulation of the past. Human beings have the appropriate definitions and performance metrics required for their preparation. Therefore, personal and cultural differences are an essential feature of supervised learning AI programs. The above three-tier model suggests that standards and values are often tacitly expressed in emotionally unarticulated reactions. Therefore, supervised learning structures are required to materialize and societal values are still not discussed. Supervised learning produces computers that can only interpret environments where individuals are positioned in predefined boxes in a very disturbing fashion. That is an ethical and pedagogical dilemma because it means that human beings are stripped of agency forces in encounters with these robots such that they can become fresh and take responsibility for their decisions.

Many neural learning models that have not been controlled or partly supervised, have been developed since the 1960s. Increased computer power also helps researchers to use simple networks which fit patterns in higher architectures as components.

For example, the Google Alpha Zero AI game uses 'enhanced learning' to simulate games and adapt the weights of networks to their games' successes. Enhanced learner enhanced behavior, inspired by Skinnerian behavioral conditioning theories, contributes to the positive results. An improvement is called generative opponent networks or GANs, where a network attempts to delude someone else into believing that the data it creates is derived from the collection of training data. This approach, for example, was used to create synthetic images of artworks and human faces that can not be distinguished by the system of image recognition from real images. It is also widely used in the textile industry, for example, for apparel design. A GAN version is called "Turing Learning," which is used to disseminate whether the data originate from a real environment or from a real computer. A computer system is dynamically connected to the universe.

2. IMPACT OF ARTIFICIAL INTELLIGENT

One important roles of modern education systems is the creation of skills that enable people to participate in life's economic sphere. Education systems history has an intimate relationship to the development of industrial society, and in industry societies and their daily lives, wage labour remains a central organization. Therefore, employment is also interpreted as a means of work in high-level political discussions. In this understanding, schooling is an important engine of economic development and competition, and in the sense of economic growth educational policies are framed. Therefore, it is important to understand how AI can change jobs and employment even in the sense of educational policies. The question of how automation and computerization raise unemployment was important to economists. Improved as computers. The future of general AI is rather agnostic for most current AI scientists.

Many AI studies have generally found Turing to be a test essential for AI, as it is consistent with the formal notion that all facts are statements that can at least be written on a TV keyboard.It does not seem relevant that the experimenter is not allowed to open the door and look inside to see if a human or a machine is present. From this point of view progress in the Turing test can also be seen not to mean that a machine has equal cognitive capabilities to humans. There is no logical discussion, in a limited set of Google Duplexes. More broadly, any final collection of simulations can not produce a precise biological system model (Rosen 1985; Louie 2009). It is possible to prove. However, this calls for the use of mathematical formalism called the theory of labor productivity, and the maintenance of production by fewer human workers. Because there is a reasonably strong demand for goods, unemployment would rise.

A simple model is too straightforward. When machines replace some jobs, people can move to other workplaces. In general, the automation of agricultural and industrial jobs and the movement of workers was what happened in the last century. This pattern has been verified by many influential studies.

Historical data show that more technology and increased labor productivity do not increase overall unemployment. In the other hand, one significant explanation why technology did not generate ongoing unemployment is the population growth, which has steadily raised demand for manufactured goods and services. In the 20th century, many other factors have been involved in the development of economy, such as education, globalization, increased intake of natural resources not renewable, as well as developments in science and health, which makes it hard to predict the future using historical models.

While some prominent surveys say automation has not created unemployment, the history of industrialization and its social implications should also also be recalled. Industrialization led to social upheavals and revolutions, often with brutal results, from Mexico, Prussia, Russia and worldwide countries.There have been thousands of deaths lost. People flocked into cities, and writers such as Jack London at the turn of the 20th century also detailed the oppressive lives of salaried workers at the docks of Oakland.The impact of the AI cannot be easily examined at national level, where useful economic information is usually provided,as the economic systems are now functioning globally. Whereas country-level data for cross-border comparisons can be aggregated, the global and networked knowledge economy is not merely an economically integrated collection of national economies. A broad view of social change is necessary to take account of AI's social, economic and human effects and their connection to policy on employment.

3. IMPACT ON LEARNING AND TEACHING

Educational implementations AI have primarily concentrated on the strategy dependent on information since the early 1980s and until recently. Intelligent tutoring systems or ITS were the most prominent research line. The structures use an architecture based on information. A regular ITS architecture has a defining domain model, the field of learning and a model student representing the existing information and learning state of the subject. The implementation of student learning materials the user interface is flexible and interactive.by a standardized framework or pedagogical model. Traditionally, the knowledge-based approach was adopted by these systems, now known as "gofai." (Ritter et al., 2007) Mainly in fairly small and simple fields, including mathematics and physics, they have been successful. Since the conduct and learning of students can also be monitored very closely in the ITS environment, smart tutoring environments are an important data source for learning research. (Porayska-Pomsta, Kaska. 2015) In addition, the challenge of developing ITSs in broad learning areas focused on the narrower issue of AI use and machine training in the creation of learning interfaces for student monitoring, training and diagnosis. This is often called Data Exploration Education (EDM). (Rose et al., 2018)

In many education systems, student testing plays an important role and many projects explore the use of IA to test and evaluate automatically. Much of this work aims to automate summative evaluation and to reduce the workload for teachers. One potential unintended outcome of this work is that high level assessment will be replaced sooner and faster by regular low-level formative evaluation, as the expense and commitment needed for evaluation reduces. Current AI systems are useful for integrating information from diverse and nuanced data sources and for real-time pattern recognition. For eg, a program of AIs with data both on individual student experience and answers can be readily reviewed and evaluated for students' homework. Consequently, accumulated formative evaluations could make high-stakes testing largely redundant. AI is also used to demagnetize student interest in computer-aided learning settings, e.g. for the creation and management of courses. The aim is to create effective groups for collective teaching activities and to find ways to deter students from dropping out.

Huge datasets are needed to train the systems to do this effectively. It is a significant technological bottleneck, as has been described above. In order to give feedback on learning, student behavior should also be monitored actively. Which poses technological demands to unobtrusively observe students with related legal and regulatory issues. For example, video encoding and distance eye monitoring. Ethically less problematic systems using less granular data to make recommendations. For example, students of UC Berkeley can now receive courses through a system based on new neural AI technologies, which were originally developed to process natural languages and machine translation. (Pardos et al, 2018)

Although many ITS systems are based on the cognitive tradition and on an educational approach, other pedagogical models are also often used. The belief that technology should be used for the advancement and development of learning as a skilled leader and accompanying person was influential for the first time. Work in this field has also been inspired by the associated work into social learning and construction and constructing awareness.

The emphasis has increased from teaching to more student-oriented approaches, including peer support learning as constructivist and constructionist models become more popular. It can be assumed to be one environment in which educational AI starters seek to build new business in the next future, when commercially viable natural language solutions like Google Duplex. (Scardamalia et al, 2006)

3.1 The Impact of AI on Learning

In formal training, AI can have both positive and bad effects on learning. Since AI is now a top priority on the political agenda, AI can tend to be used in the most educational environments. If a promising new technology emerges and the technology's limitations and challenges often are not fully understanding, it seems that technology offers radically new ways of solving older problems. In the early stages of the life sequence of universal electronics, this leads to the drive-in production. Visionary companies and politicians understand the promise of emerging technologies and how it can make a difference.

This passion is eased in the field of schooling as people understand that AI not only makes current education more successful but also shifts the context in which learning takes place and is socially important. Many emerging learning strategies meet the demands of a transforming urban society. Something that simply institutionalizes old habits can be easily automated. That also adds to dissatisfaction in a changing environment as the ideas have often become outdated before they are introduced.

Technology experts have very little knowledge at the technology push stage. This also overpower and surpass other sources of information as it is rare. This can become a challenge in the area of education and training, as technologists quickly transfer their own learning experiences and values into their projects. For example, learning is often interpreted in the field of machine learning as a basic combination of system inputs and outputs. An oxymoron can be a concept of machine learning to learning scientists. With technologies, learning may be revolutionized, but even concepts and activities that have nothing to do with learning may be streamlined and repeated.

The pledge of MOOCs, for example is well-known but still we know very little of their effects on "providing desired learning results." One of AI 's great promises is to conduct broad-based study of learning in such contexts, as a instructor may instruct multiple students, although with difficulties, in online environments. (Tuomi, Ilkka. 2013) It is also proposed, for instance, that AI should be used to measure student performance by evaluating test results without instructor bias objectively. Provided appropriate human-labeled data samples, based on test results, neural IA and computer education pupils can be easily identified. It is not obvious, however, whether the test findings are reliable markers of learning. Human intervention in growth can be more important than the general results of standardized tests in favor of learning. Neural AI does, however, support large and structured datasets of research. Present neural AI systems are adapted to the mind of students, with learning models. (Mislevy, Robert J. 2018, Gane et al, 2018)

If the acquisition of knowledge and abilities is known as learning, IA must be incorporated in various ways in learning processes. In the IBM Watson Classroom, for example, we are promising cognitive solutions which help educators gain insights into the styles, preferences, and skills of each student, "this would bring personal learning to a whole new level. The development of several cognitive skills that define advanced forms of thought, as Vygotsky pointed out long ago, depends on its social relevance and does not directly concern an individual learner. Mediated contact through written texts is, for example, abnormal to a child who can use speech beautifully early in life.

Without a dynamic system of collective values and behaviors, an adult learner does not have any significance in sophisticated intellectual structures such as mathematics. Therefore, also when large classes of scientific studies suggest that the idea of schooling is actually best described as a community legend, AI will have thrilling new chances for modifying content focused on experience by students and individuals.

Computer programs work well and poor pedagogical concepts will easily be created by AI. In general, AI can be used in three mainly different ways which can affect the development of human cognitive skills, both in children and adults. First, existing capabilities can be supported by AI. When abilities are known as variations of environments and interpersonal repertoires.

AI will that the need for people's awareness, skills and abilities and emphasize the value of behavioral arsenal. As a consequence, people don't really need to learn the realm of professional conduct, as was historically necessary. In addition, after the systemic transition of human brain now have big scientific testing bodies. Maguire et al. (2000; Woollett and Maguire 2011) are often cited studies in this field. The structural changes in the London Taxi hippocampus showed changes in space navigation in this area. For examples, musical training in childhood has been shown to contribute to an increased cortical auditory level representation only if the practice is initiated prior to 9 years of age (Pantev et al . 1998).

Although classical experiments have concentrated on the time during which normal development takes place, irregular feedback may also have a lasting deleterious effect after normal development has passed. The 'sensitive periods for damage' Lewis and Maurer (2005) called them and showed visual impairment to be a permanent visual acuity deficit of up to 10 years of age.

Hoekstra and Van Slujis (2003), for example, suggest this. Within the context of the three level model here presented, such a competence model seems to be too narrow and needs to be enriched by cultural and technical elements which enable and make relevant expressions of competence. For competency, transversal and domain-independent general competences may be fairly essential, domain-specific know how is becoming less relevant.

Secondly, AI can speed up cognitive development and develop cognitive capabilities which would not be possible without technology. Before science, mechanization or work of mankind made things impossible; cognitive mechanization often makes possible new tasks that were previously unlikely. That's something that has already happened, of course. Excluding comprehensive computer-assisted design software knowledge, the design of a modern microprocessor or a neural chip would be totally impossible.

Third, AI may decrease or render obsolete the importance of certain human cognitive abilities. For instance, because AI can convert language to text and vice versa, dyslexia may become less significant socially than in the past. However, even though there are major advantages for people in situations such as dyslexia and dyscalculia AI, it is not possible to determine the ultimate effect. Machines, for example, can help people add and subtract numbers. But, because they rely on machines, more complex mathematics abilities that include manual calculation and number skill can become more difficult to learn. It would be more effective from a pedagogical viewpoint to use AI to enable people to develop skills to solve read and count challenges rather than to use AI to build double skills supporting significant cognitive skills.

3.2 The Impact of AI in Teaching

If we assume that AI can be implemented more efficiently in the present learning environment, what was historically important can easily be condensed. The effect of an AI on future education and learning instead of on current education and learning structures is, thus, important to consider. The study of the effect of AI on education would also be related to potential learning activities.

However, certain teaching activities may have direct implications for AI. An evaluation in its various forms is one such task. A student's model which preserves knowledge on the learner's current state and attempts to infer a potential boot-blindness in the way of students understand the area they or they are studying is a central element in traditional intelligent tutoring systems.

In general, neural AI is perfect for diagnostic research. Particularly that the portrayal of student models is not evident in challenging fields or practical learning environments, the challenger of designing student models has to be faced by conventional knowledge-based intelligent learning systems. However, if there are enough data available, neural AI could generate student models. Words can also be seen in natural languages in a 300-dimensional world, with millions on the basis of thousands of examples, as described above. Machine learning can generate these dynamic representations functionally for all their intellectual and technological shortcomings. Machine learning will probably create student models with enough data that are good enough to be useful.

Neural IA can learn patterns of interaction and associate these with pedagogically relevant clusters so that a teacher can better understand how and how students are effectively guided. In order to focus on their analytical methods and future areas of improvement, the AI systems should also provide the student with diagnostic data. As a result, neural AI will have considerable potential for data mining, analysis and learning diagnosis.

New educational opportunities are also arising from rapid developments natural language and human-machine interfaces based on AI. In the context, for example, of increasing exposure to conversational robots and engaging partners, communicating by robotics reveals promise

Significant components of these networks are affective computation and emotional AI. In addition, translation in real time by machine opens up new opportunities in language learning and it allows AI systems to be used, for example to traduce texts written by students, in order to write texts more efficiently expressing students' expected communication.

Many exciting opportunities for IA in teaching can be imagined. However, without clear pedagogical principles, AI vendors are likely, rather than more basic social and economic issues, to offer goods and services that address the specific challenges faced by key decision makers Products and services that require changes in current education practices in the education sector to an AI start-up are difficult to provide.

The educational ACI is likely to be a solution for existing issues in a wider context of educational transformation and the future of education without clear visions and policies providing emerging technical opportunities. Thus, AI can mechanize, reinvent and complicate outdated practices of education, instead of renewing the System and focusing it on the needs of post-industrial economics and knowledge society.

It is also conceivable, by concurrently developing frameworks for schooling and teaching, that it may help to establish acceptable goals and policies. It is important to create concrete experiments with teachers and educational experts in an authentic context. Because AI is very top of the political agenda now, the argument that AI is the next technological breakthrough is much too relaxed to produce high-level images of the future. This is also crucial that teachers who already face practical challenges of everyday teacher instruction and innovative programs will not be electrified by this new technology. AI is often referred to as "the latest energy."

4. POLICY CHALLENGES ACCORDING TO AI

The continuing AI optimism leads to a technology drive, AI is used as a answer to a wide variety of issues in research and learning. The ability and difficulties of AI in education are possibly safe to say. It is not well understood. AI is a general purpose technology that can be interpreted and used in many respects. Although technological features can contribute to development in certain fields, technology can also be used in many ways, including in education, for many different reasons. Therefore, knowing whether and for what we need technology is perhaps more important for policy growth, than how it is used. In this perspective, the potential expectations of technology must be explained by voicing both the purpose and the core assumptions underlying the claimed incentive for use of the technology. This brings technology to a policy level, and we must ask ourselves what its purposes and aims are. We will only explain where we want to go and how technology will support us along the way if we have such a view of technical advances. They can also be critically evaluated when the assumptions and motives are made explicit.

A continuous dialog on the correct and transparent use of AI in education is therefore required.As technology and its applications shift, the "outsider" who are not reflective of existing stakeholder interests will make valuable contributions to the debate. The enabling and funding in this dialog of independent research such as political, ethical, social and economic implications of AI may be a practical way of providing helpful input.

Throughout the area of education policy, it is critical that educators and decision makers consider AI in the wider sense of the learning future. The discussion on AI now focuses on the ongoing globalization of information, digitalization and computer globalization. The latest forecasts of the impacts on the labor market of AI and other new technology show that demand for skills and qualifications is evolving rapidly, and that the education system must change, especially as training is aimed at the development of skills for the jobs.AI automates other important activities done by people in the past. As AI is being used to simplify manufacturing procedures, existing education institutions can need to be reinvented. For example, formal education may play a declining role in the creation of competences relevant to jobs. It could mean that education's future role in promoting human growth will be increasingly significant.

The new AI programs allow the student success to be measured almost continuously. Instead, the AI-supported assessment is used to help students develop skills and skills and keep students on effective learning paths rather than high-stakes testing that act as a social filter. High-stakes training can become inconsistent with other continuous evaluation, and greater data can be used to evaluate capabilities and competencies. This may be important for the evaluation of key cross-cutting competences now relatively difficult to evaluate. As informal learning is provided by AI and other information technology, it is also essential that we ask how formal and informal learning can divide work in the future.

In addition, the emphasis should then change from the basic position of education to its more evolved position. Perhaps, the connection between work and education in industrial age may be evolving. Today's educational establishments primarily serve the needs of an industrial society. Since the creation, use and learning of knowledge and data has now been carried out in ways previously impossible, it is important that AI is not only understood in the current education system as a solution to the problem.

In general, the profound changes now being made possible in society and the economy by AI and related technologies will create a world in which many social institutions change and people have to adapt. The social and human costs were high when the similar major transition took place almost two centuries ago. Although we today, in retrospect, often neglect the adverse consequences and stress the positive influence of technological change, it should be bored in mind that technology for general use may have an significant transformative impact on social life and human development. In 1848, the somewhat romantic assertion that "everything that is solid melts in the sun" was not merely a perception but a detailed scientific study of the day-to-day effects of industrialization.

A general policy issue, therefore, is to increase understanding of AI technologies and their future effects among educators and policy makers. One way to do so is to engage in processes that produce potential images, create principles that can be used to explain them, and design simulations and tests that will evaluate these imagined futures. Therefore, it is a rather simple policy proposal to explicitly initiate forward-looking processes that generate an understanding of current opportunities.

AI offers new learning research approaches, but also revisiting AI systems with proven learning experience is essential. All existing AI systems depend on associative and compartmental learning models. Neural AI's long history includes multiple efforts to move beyond such basic learning models. Apprenticeships could offer a lot in researching AI and this mutual interaction would allow us to better understand how to use AI both for apprenticeship and in education and in other fields of application.

Machine learning data are often very personal. Using AI, educational analytics and data mining, data security can become a key bottleneck if used to assess student performance. Because neural AI systems do not understand the data they are storing, data that tricks the decision process is therefore easy to counterfeit. AI security is a crucial concern, but it is also deterrent because neural AI systems typically employ complex, comprehensible or unlikely internal data representations. Therefore, there is significant interest in the development of "explainable AI." However, today's systems do not have all the necessary reflective and metacognitive capabilities to explain what they do. (Demiaux, 2017 and Luckin, 2018) Therefore, it's just as pointless, to rephrase Descartes, to ask a wall clock what hit it to 7 or 8, to question why it gave a specific class to a student with a deep learning AI program. Clocks are not designed to clarify their behavior and AI systems, have no explaining capabilities as we know them. At best they can better explain what happened and why to humans. Given that fundamental theoretical and functional shortcomings that exist in developing Systems of AI which can justify their actions and decisions must keep people in the decision-making process.

From a legal standpoint, ethical principles provide the basic framework on which to establish and explain new rules and laws. Developmental principles such as authority, accountability, personality, rights and intellectual potential endorse ethics and useful judgements. The machine needs to be presented with potential results of choice in supervised AI learning models before it begins to learn. This means that the environment has been defined in categories and interests. Furthermore, the divisions are based on previously collected data. Neural AI categorizes persons into clusters where evidence from other users is used to model human characteristics and conduct that are found identical on the machine.

That is highly problematic from a political and ethical point of view. Human action ensures we can make decisions and are accountable for future actions. While AI systems model our conduct using weighted historical data from a vast number of others, AI systems can not understand those who make real choices or break out of past conduct trends. So AI can also restrict the field of expression for people.

The recent performance of AI has been primarily based on the availability of vast volumes of data, as previously described. Only if sufficient data are available can products and services based on AI be generated within the educational field. Some of the existing datasets are natural monopolies at present and are often controlled by a couple of large corporations. An significant policy issue is how to make the vast data sets that are needed to build and use AI-based systems more readily accessible. The current general data protection legislation requires that the data subjects have a copy of the personal information in an electronically used form from data controllers. One solution is to broaden the current general data protection legislation. Technically, this will allow users to view their personal data locally, anonymize them and send them in a compatible format to sites used for AI learning and training purposes. Such functionality could be relatively easy to embed, for example in frequently used web browsers when data aggregation platforms are available.

5. CONCLUSION

In this field, advances in artificial intelligence open to new possibilities and challenges for teaching and learning in higher education, with the potential to fundamentally change governance and the internal architecture of institutions of higher education. The ascent of AI makes it difficult to overlook a genuine discussion about its future learning in advanced education and what sort of decisions colleges and universities will make as to this issue. The quick pace of innovation development and the related activity dislodging, recognized generally by specialists in the field (source), infers that instructing in advanced education requires a reexamination of instructors' job and instructional methods. We think about that there is a requirement for research on flow control on improvements of AI. We likewise accept that it is essential to concentrate further research on the new learning pathways for further extent understudies, with another arrangement of graduate characteristics, with an attention on creative mind, inventiveness, and advancement; the arrangement of capacities and abilities that can scarcely be ever reproduced by machines.

REFERENCES

Demiaux & Abdallah. (2017). *How Can Humans Keep the Upper Hand? The Ethical Matters Raised by Algorithms and Artificial Intelligence*. Report on the public debate led by the French Data Protection Authority (CNIL) as part of the ethical discussion assignment set by the Digital Republic Bill. Paris: CNIL.

Gane, B. D., Zaidi, S. Z., & Pellegrino, J. W. (2018). Measuring What Matters: Using Technology to Assess Multidimensional Learning. *European Journal of Education*, *53*(2), 176–187. doi:10.1111/ejed.12269

Hoekstra, H. A., & Van Slujis, E. (2003). *Managing Competences: Implementing Human Resource Management*. Koninklijke Van Gorcum.

Lewis, T. L., & Maurer, D. (2005). Multiple Sensitive Periods in Human Visual Development: Evidence from Visually Deprived Children. *Developmental Psychobiology*, *46*(3), 163–183. doi:10.1002/dev.20055 PMID:15772974

Louie, A. H. (2007). A Living System Must Have Noncomputable Models. *Artificial Life*, *13*(3), 293–297. doi:10.1162/artl.2007.13.3.293 PMID:17567248

Luckin, R. (2018). *Machine Learning and Human Intelligence: The Future of Education for the 21st Century*. UCL Institute of Education Press.

Maguire, E. A., Gadian, D. G., Johnsrude, I. S., Good, C. D., Ashburner, J., Frackowiak, R. S. J., & Frith, C. D. (2000). Navigation Related Structural Change in the Hippocampi of Taxi Drivers. *Proceedings of the National Academy of Sciences of the United States of America*, *97*(8), 4398–4403. doi:10.1073/pnas.070039597 PMID:10716738

Maguire, E. A., Gadian, D. G., Johnsrude, I. S., Good, C. D., Ashburner, J., Frackowiak, R. S. J., & Frith, C. D. (2000). NavigationRelated Structural Change in the Hippocampi of Taxi Drivers. *Proceedings of the National Academy of Sciences of the United States of America*, *97*(8), 4398–4403. doi:10.1073/pnas.070039597 PMID:10716738

Mislevy, R. J. (2018). *Sociocognitive Foundations of Educational Measurement*. Routledge. doi:10.4324/9781315871691

Pantev, C., Oostenveld, R., Engelien, A., Ross, B., Roberts, L. E., & Hoke, M. (1998). Increased Auditory Cortical Representation in Musicians. *Nature*, *392*(6678), 811–814. doi:10.1038/33918 PMID:9572139

Pardos, Z. A., Fan, Z., & Jiang, W. (2018). *Connectionist Recommendation in the Wild*. https://arxiv.org/abs/1803.09535

Porayska-Pomsta, K. (2015). AI in Education as a Methodology for Enabling Educational Evidence-Based Practice. *Seventeenth International Conference on Artificial Intelligence in Education (AIED 2015)*, 52–61.

Ritter, S., Anderson, J. R., Koedinger, K. R., & Corbett, A. (2007). Cognitive Tutor: Applied Research in Mathematics Education. *Psychonomic Bulletin & Review*, *14*(2), 249–255. doi:10.3758/BF03194060 PMID:17694909

Rosé, C. P., Martínez-Maldonado, R., Hoppe, U., Luckin, R., Mavrikis, M., Porayska-Pomsta, K., McLaren, B., & du Boulay, B. (Eds.). (2018). *Artificial Intelligence in Education: 19th International Conference, AIED 2018, London, UK, June 27–30, 2018, Proceedings, Part I. Lecture Notes in Artificial Intelligence*. Springer International Publishing.

Rosen, R. (1985). *Anticipatory Systems: Philosophical, Mathematical and Methodological Foundations*. Pergamon Press.

Scardamalia, M., & Bereiter, C. (2006). Knowledge Building: Theory, Pedagogy, and Technology. In *Cambridge Handbook of the Learning Sciences* (pp. 97–118). Cambridge University Press.

Tuomi, I. (2013). Open Educational Resources and the Transformation of Education. *European Journal of Education*, *48*(1), 58–78. doi:10.1111/ejed.12019

Vygotsky, L. (1986). *Thought and Language*. The MIT Press.

Chapter 13

Impact of Artificial and Natural Intelligence Technologies With Avatar-Based Teaching, Learning, and Research in Russian Modern Universities

Vardan Mkrttchian
https://orcid.org/0000-0003-4871-5956
HHH University, Australia

ABSTRACT

This chapter has presented the idea and use of artificial and natural intelligence technologies. A system of professional education, on the one hand, is one of the main institutions of human socialization, and the formation of a harmoniously developed, active, creative personality, on the other hand, ensures the reproduction and development of the personnel potential of the society. Realization of the goals of education is carried out in interaction with the socioeconomic environment, the dynamic change of which predetermines the conditions for the activity of educational institutions. An acceleration of scientific and technological progress in all areas of knowledge raises the task for ensuring the continuous growth of professional skills throughout the whole life. Structural and institutional replacing in professional education is reflected in various models of higher professional education. These alternative technology-mediated environments reflect the increasing need to serve a generation of learners who prefer to learn through experience or by interacting with learning tools.

DOI: 10.4018/978-1-7998-4763-2.ch013

INTRODUCTION

The model of teaching students in an environment enabled by the evolutions in modern virtual industry software tool is in need of a new paradigm for solving problems of human-computer interaction. This is especially so if Blockchain technology is to be adopted in order to implement human-computer interaction in the education sector in an economically viable way. The purpose of this chapter is not to consider existing literature on avatar-based models for the purpose of providing policy advice. Rather, the purpose is to attempt to evaluate the merits and problems of avatar-based Electronic/Ubiquitous/pervasive learning (E/U-learning 4.0) models as a solid basis for economic policy recommendations that are mainly based on performance The scope of performance covered in this chapter is the reflexive adaptability of the E/U learning software system. Now blockchain technology as a new effective way to manage avatar-based model used natural and artificial intellectual virtual knowledge for teaching, learning and research in modern Russian university. There is a need to change the way by which the conventional system avatar-based model used natural and artificial intellectual virtual knowledge works. We introduce using Blockchain technology as a new effective way to manage this system. It solves many problems associated with the conventional management system such as securing trade secrets and claiming copyrights. The current management system lacks efficiency, especially in terms of cost cutting, time saving, and legal procedures related to judicial disputes. Therefore, there is an urgent need to change the way by which the conventional intellectual property rights management system works. In doing so, we introduce using Blockchain technology as a new effective way to manage this system. This new technology has real potentials to disrupt the conventional management system. Deploying Blockchain technology within the current system will solve many problems associated with the conventional intellectual property rights management system such as securing trade secrets, claiming copyrights, proving prior use, confidentiality agreements, and technology licenses in modern Russian university for teaching, learning and research.

Blockchain technology was introduced in a systemic form by Satoshi Nakamoto in 2008, when he published his white paper about "Peer-to-Peer electronic cash system". This new system uses blockchain technology as tool to build a distributed network. The blockchain technology is "a distributed ledger representing a network consensus of every transaction that has ever occurred".

This new technology creates a network, where each participant has a copy of the ledger, where no one can change the information of transactions within this network. It can be said that this technology stores the information of all transactions on the network in an immutable way by using hash function.

Each participant represents a nod on the blockchain network and each one has two keys: public cryptographic key and private cryptographic key. These keys are used to conduct transactions among all participants without intervention from any third party.

Blockchain technology makes it very difficult to change the information within the network. There is only one possible way to change and control the blockchain network. It is when more 51% of the hashes are controlled by one nod or pool miners.

Blockchain is used in various forms, where each form serves a specific objective. Accordingly, blockchain is divided into four types. This division is associated with some feature such as writing and reading access, type of ownership, speed, and type of consensus:

- Public Permission less Blockchain: All participants can write on the network; all participants can read the transactions information on the network; there is no single owner of the network. Proof of work; Bit coin;
- Public Permissioned Blockchain: Only authorized participants are allowed to write on the network; All participants can read the transactions information on the network; There is a network owner; Faster than public permission less blockchain; Proof of work; Sovran;
- Consortium Blockchain: Only authorized participants are allowed to write on the network; Only authorized participants are allowed to read the transactions information on the network; There is a network owner; Faster than two previous blockchain networks; Proof of work and proof of stack; Hyper ledger;
- Private Blockchain: Only the network operator can write on it; Only authorized participants are allowed to read the transactions information on the network; There is a network owner; Faster than the first two blockchain networks; Proof of work and proof of stack; Multi Chain.

The present study aims to fill this gap by using of author's experience and professional position as an Editor in Chief of International Journal of Applied Research in Bioinformatics.

THE MODERN IGI GLOBAL PUBLISHER INITIATIVES OF INCREASING SUBMISSIONS USING PUBLISHED ENHANCEMENTS OF JOURNAL ARTICLE AND OF BOOK CHAPTER ADDRESSEE'S TO AUTHOR'S THIS STUDY

1. About Journal Articles

- Publish your work with IJICTHD

As a highly valued past contributor to the **International Journal of Information Communication Technologies and Human Development (IJICTHD)**, we (IGI Global) together with the editor-in-chief, are reaching out to you today with an invitation to submit your latest research work to the journal in the form of a new article manuscript. Due to the substantial value your previous contribution provided to the journal, we welcome a manuscript submission from you related to the content of your previously published work or a manuscript focused on an entirely new area relevant to the scope of the journal.

Since you last contributed, a lot has happened at IGI Global. For instance, all of IGI Global journals have been recognized by the Committee on Publication Ethics (COPE), as IGI Global is a full member of the organization. Being recognized by such a prestigious ethical organization is an honor, especially in an age when ethical publication practice is paramount in academia.

Result: International Journal of Information Communication Technology and Human Development JICTHD: Volume 11, Issue 4. **Avatar-Based Automated Tools and Testing Cloud System as a Gateway of Modern Feedback Control in Digital Era**

- Publish your work with IJARB

As a highly valued past contributor to the **International Journal of Knowledge Discovery in Bioinformatics (IJKDB)**, we (IGI Global) together with the editor-in-chief, are reaching out to you today with an invitation to submit your latest research work to the journal's new title, **International Journal of Applied Research in Bioinformatics (IJARB)**, in the form of a new article manuscript. Due to the substantial value your previous contribution provided to the journal, we welcome a manuscript submission from you related to the content of your previously published work or a manuscript focused on an entirely new area relevant to the scope of the journal.

Since you last contributed, a lot has happened at IGI Global. For instance, all of IGI Global's journals have been recognized by the Committee on Publication Ethics

(COPE), as IGI Global is a full member of the organization. Being recognized by such a prestigious ethical organization is an honor, especially in an age when ethical publication practice is paramount in academia.

Result: International Journal of Applied Research in Bioinformatics: Volume 10, Issue 1. **Levy Processes Simulation for Modeling in Bioinformatics**

- Publish your research with IJIDE

As a highly valued past contributor to the **International Journal of Innovation in the Digital Economy (IJIDE)**, we (IGI Global) together with the editors-in-chief, are reaching out to you today with an invitation to submit your latest research work to the journal in the form of a new article manuscript. Due to the substantial value your previous contribution provided to the journal, we welcome a manuscript submission from you related to the content of your previously published work or a manuscript focused on an entirely new area relevant to the scope of the journal.

Since you last contributed, a lot has happened at IGI Global. For instance, all of IGI Global's journals have been recognized by the Committee on Publication Ethics (COPE), as IGI Global is a full member of the organization. Being recognized by such a prestigious ethical organization is an honor, especially in an age when ethical publication practice is paramount in academia.

Result: International Journal of Innovation in the Digital Economy: Volume 11, Issue 3. **Sharing and Avatar-Based Innovation Tools on Digital Economy Perspectives Using Levy Processes Simulation: Modeling in the Globalization Era**

2. About Book Chapter

IGI Global publishes approximately 275 – 300+ book titles annually encompassing a wide range of topic areas. Recently, we have been affording chapter authors an additional opportunity for them to have their research benefit from increased exposure and further recognition in the research community, by extending to them an invitation to submit enhanced/updated/shortened (or lengthened) versions of their chapter as an article for consideration into a forthcoming issue of a journal. From those invitations, many will choose to submit an enhanced version of their chapter or even better, a brand new manuscript on their most recent research activities.

Result: This Chapter

BACKGROUND

Since 2008 there have been more than 5 760 patents filed and granted by more than 1 477 assignees/companies. While the number of published patents has shown strong growth over the past two years these published patents represent three groups:

- New inventions;
- Patents filed in other countries;
- Patents granted.

Currently, 41% of the patents have been filed in China and 32% in the United States, Korea and the UK account for 8% and 6% respectively. China shows that remains the most popular intellectual framework for major patent filers, USA ranks as a strong number two destination, ahead of the European Union and Japan. This is consistent with the strong activities in blockchain and crypto currencies shown by Chinese companies over the past three years, including a high concentration of Bit coin mining, Initial coin offering (ICOs) and blockchain-centric business models. About 10% of these patents are granted, with Korea and the United States holding 71% of these granted patents, the remaining patents are in China, Taiwan, Japan and Europe. Analyzing the patents highlights four patent groups; core technologies, applications, core/applications, and generic blockchain inventions.

According to the analysis of Blockchain patents, the most popular industries that have been witnessed the large patent applications numbers are:

- Payment systems;
- Secure communications;
- Financial Tech;
- E-commerce.

However, there is a future growing tendency of other industries such as: avatar-based model used natural and artificial intellectual virtual knowledge for teaching, learning and research in modern Russian university. Management system, avatar-based model used natural and artificial intellectual virtual knowledge for teaching, learning and research in modern Russian university. Protection of avatar-based model used natural and artificial intellectual virtual knowledge for teaching, learning and research in modern Russian university is considered a crucial issue at the national level influencing the intensity of innovation activities and plays an important role in creating motivation for entrepreneurs to innovate and invent as well.

The current avatar-based model used natural and artificial intellectual virtual knowledge for teaching, learning and research in modern Russian university. Lacks efficiency, especially in terms of cost cutting, time saving, and legal procedures related to legal disputes or litigations. Therefore, there is an urgent need to change the way by which the conventional avatar-based model used natural and artificial intellectual virtual knowledge for teaching, learning and research in modern Russian university works.

In doing so, we introduce using Blockchain technology as a new effective way to manage this system. This new technology has real potentials to disrupt the conventional avatar-based model used natural and artificial intellectual virtual knowledge for teaching, learning and research in modern Russian university. Deploying Blockchain technology within the current system will solve many problems associated with the conventional avatar-based model used natural and artificial intellectual virtual knowledge for teaching, learning and research in modern Russian university such as securing trade secrets, claiming copyrights, proving prior use, confidentiality agreements, and technology licenses.

Using such technology becomes a vital instrument enhancing the productivity and functionality of the avatar-based model used natural and artificial intellectual virtual knowledge for teaching, learning and research in modern Russian university management system. Using this technology to manage patent system, for example, will speed up patenting process that takes, in the current system, 3-5 years to fill patent application and examine the patentability of invention. Additionally, Blockchain-based avatar-based model used natural and artificial intellectual virtual knowledge for teaching, learning and research in modern Russian university platform also will cut the cost needed for legal procedures and litigations.

This technology will enable all stakeholders with entrepreneurial and unique ideas to convert them into inventions, or even individuals who have inventions and want to sell or exploit them commercially.

Regarding the workflow of this platform, it should be said that this platform links all stakeholders in the avatar-based model used natural and artificial intellectual virtual knowledge for teaching, learning and research in modern Russian university sphere, where they can interact (buy, sell, and transfer objects) through using the internal tokens of this platform. These tokens are considered an internal currency used to perform transactions within platform. They are exchangeable in the international crypto currencies market. Therefore, using tokens in this platform enables inventors commercializing their ideas and inventions. We also argued that using this new technology for managing the avatar-based model used natural and artificial intellectual virtual knowledge for teaching, learning and research in modern Russian university system should be done at the national level, where the government should be responsible for administrating this platform. We suggest creating a public permissioned blockchain platform in the first phase, where the government should be in charge. Taking into account that the government is the only actor in the market that can set the regulations, standards of the related transactions. Otherwise, there will be many private companies managing many platforms, which, in this situation will make it hard to dispute resolution and legal enforcement. In sum, we tried to propose a new holistic approach for studying Blockchain-based ecosystem by presenting the current problems of the conventional system, proposing a solution based on using blockchain technology, and drawing a map-road of this new management system.

MAIN FOCUS OF THE ARTICLE

Issues, Controversies, Problems

This chapter emphasizes the importance of mastering methodologies and modern means of designing information systems. The issues of designing a subsystem that includes the main features of CASE-modeling tools and an interactive learning environment for use in the educational process are considered. Case-tools with support for the modeling language UML are an effective tool for the design of information systems used in many organizations. Some developers and programmers refuse the stage of developing UML diagrams, referring to the fact that this stage takes a fairly long period of time, and when developing small information systems and programs, the design stage is not necessary at all. It should be noted that the documentation obtained at the design stage allows not only to eliminate defects in the future, but also to identify them immediately before the implementation stage. Correctly formed UML documentation allows you to look at the system being designed from different perspectives, and other developers to understand the essence of the task, methods and ways to solve it and make the system development process more efficient. Part of the strong rejection of the use of the UML language is a low level of language proficiency, and it should be the language of communication between developers. Therefore, it is so important to know the methodologies of designing systems and understanding graphic notations, which require significant costs from students.

Currently, there are a large number of CASE design tools that provide the construction of UML diagrams. Despite the fact that the process of constructing UML diagrams is strictly controlled by the CASE-tool, we can say that this is a check at the syntax level, and not the semantics of diagramming. High-level CASE systems perform diagram verification procedures; build diagrams and diagrams using design patterns. Unfortunately, the more affordable CASE tools used in the educational process do not have such capabilities. Therefore, an approach is interesting that allows one to teach theories and methods of UML design using design patterns in the process of constructing diagrams. The interactive learning process provides the best assimilation of the theoretical base along with practical application. For example, consider learning how to verify diagrams. CASE-tool step by step explains the principle of checking two diagrams for compliance, accurately describing the algorithm. The user, having understood this principle, will be able to avoid inaccuracies or inconsistencies when constructing diagrams in the future and not waste time correcting it. The situation is similar with design patterns, the use of which requires a certain amount of experience and knowledge. One way to understand the principle of the pattern is again a step-by-step execution of the algorithm for constructing a diagram according to the selected pattern. At each stage, a certain object of the pattern is built, with a description of its necessity and impact on the entire general structure of the pattern. At the same time, the question of choosing a pattern for specific tasks remains open. In addition to the officially published software products, we monitored repositories on the GitHub service. As a result, many projects were found devoted to the topic of teaching the UML language. However, almost all the solutions found are various variations of the electronic textbook and do not contain interactive learning elements. For example, the project "UML-Learning-App" contains theoretical information, which is conveniently divided into categories, and testing is provided to control the material read. At the same time, it is not possible to build any UML diagram. Another project, "JavaUML_Parser" explains the structure and purpose of the patterns, but the ability to create diagrams using any pattern, like other interactive elements, was not implemented.

PRACTICAL REALIZATION

Electronic Information and Educational Environment (EIOS) at Russian University

The problems of introducing the electronic educational environment of a university, unambiguous identification and organization of access, and ensuring a single end-to-end authorization are discussed. In the modern world, it is difficult to underestimate the role of information technology in all spheres of human and social life. One of the most important areas of the development of society - education of the population, also did not pass by the introduction of information and communication technologies. On the contrary, it is the modernization and informatization of the education process that will currently help both the development of the information technology industry and will have a significant impact in improving the quality of education received, because it is the quality of education and its assessment that are the most important problem both in Russia and abroad. The main goal of designing an electronic information and educational environment (EIOS) at Russian University is to create a holistic system, an information environment, which could serve as the main tool for organizing, managing and providing methodological support for educational programs of a university, as well as providing students with the maximum possible amount of information. EIOS can fully provide automation of the university's business processes, aggregation and accumulation of information that has not previously been accounted for, as well as information accumulated and often duplicated over many years in disparate automated control systems whose technical support is not provided to the proper extent or is completely absent . One of the main functions of the EEI is assistance in organizing the educational process: an electronic dean's office, a student's and teacher's personal account, a portfolio of achievements, monitoring the educational process, an electronic library, and a mobile application - all this together will ensure the work of the university's information and educational environment and will show to a qualitatively new level, training indicators. The database structure of the authorization system is shown in Fig. 1. The system has flexible user access rights to its modules. The basis for entering the system is a pair of "username" (login) and password. The User table stores basic information, full name, username and password, a sign of belonging to university co-workers or students. Also, a single table entry may contain group information. The user execution table sets the current status of the user: position or level of education, as well as communication with the university unit. Rights are defined by analogy with UNIX systems and can be of three types: read, use, write. Rights are set on the system as a whole or on a specific resource or module. Rights are set by user or group identifier from the User table. This ensures a plurality of access rights to each resource: many users and many groups can use one resource, but the mechanism for checking user or group rights is unified. As part of EIOS, along with other functional subsystems, the functioning of the main subsystem is implemented - a unified system of identification and authentication (ESIA). The subsystem provides a single pass-through authentication of EIOS users and allows you to access any information systems using ESIA tools during one session. When implementing this concept, re-identification and authentication of the user in the EIOS from other subsystems is not required, this corresponds to one of the basic principles of ACS development - the principle of the unity of the information base and input of information.

The process of end-to-end authorization is ensured by the operation of a standard programming language embedded in the browser and the language, the mechanism for the functioning of sessions (or sessions) and local cookies. Sessions and cookies are designed to store user information when navigating between multiple pages. When using sessions, authorization data is stored in temporary files on the server. Cookies are respectively stored on the user's computer, and are sent by the browser to the server upon request. The presence of an active session and cookies is checked when the EIOS user accesses from any subsystem when a file with a certain format

Figure 1. Database structure & avatar-based model used natural and artificial intellectual virtual knowledge

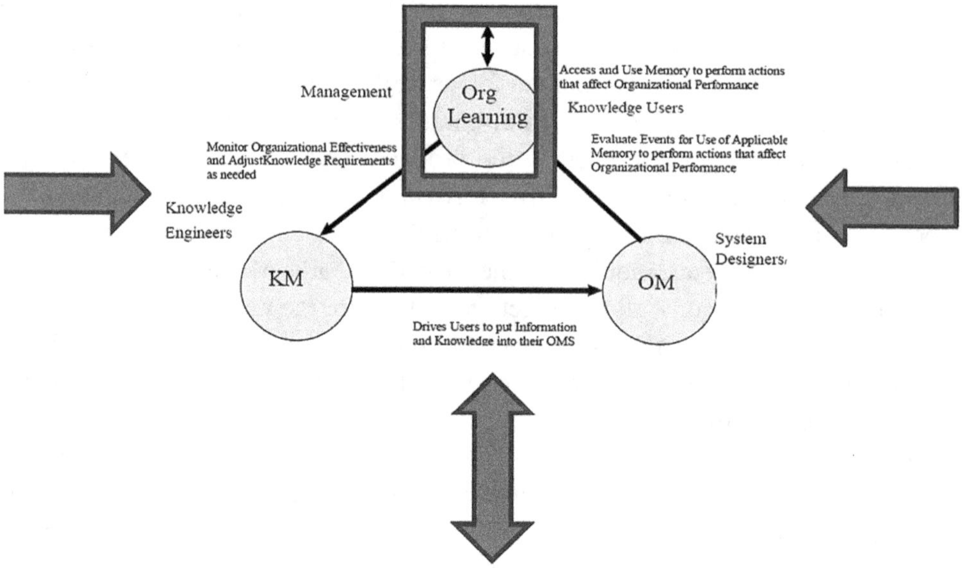

of the name and stored value and the active session is detected, the user is considered authorized in the EIOS. In this context, the question of the protection of authorization data becomes relevant, however, in case of failure to fulfill at least one condition, through authorization becomes impossible, and the information stored in cookies does not contain authorization data. n addition, control is carried out by the IP address from which authorization is carried out in the EIOS: after successful initial authorization, the client IP address is entered into the ESIA database. If the user logs in from another workstation, the IP address in the database is overwritten and authorization from the old login point is automatically canceled, despite the presence of an active session and cookies, since checking for the coincidence of the current IP address and the IP address entered in DB does not pass. In the case of a user forced termination of the authorization session, the IP address in the database is reset and the previous authorization is reset to the same place from another workstation, without having passed the check for the coincidence of the current IP address. ESIA also provides control over the authorization time in the system. After 3 hours of inactivity, the system will automatically delete cookies and interrupt the working session. Currently, more and more Russian universities support the concept of the rational creation of their own unified educational environment, and not just “for show” complies with the laws and recommendations of the Ministry of Education of the Russian Federation. Penza State University also adheres to this concept, having a number of implemented mechanisms, as well as a set of promising ideas for implementation. The implementation of the concept will ensure the implementation of the requirements of the current legislation, but it will actually provide students, faculty and staff of the university with a powerful and understandable tool for any internal university activity.

Development of a Controller to the World of Virtual Reality

The work is devoted to the development of a controller that will allow the transfer of movements to the world of virtual reality using leg and body movements in the real world and at the same time it will be inexpensive and compact. Various analogues of this project are considered. The text also provides a description, operating principles and analysis of a prototype of a peripheral device for modeling the movement of the human body in virtual reality. The controller monitors body tilts and leg movements to create a sense of walking in virtual space..

Purpose of work: creating a portable controller for simulating movement in a virtual space.

Tasks of work:

1. to study materials on the topic;
2. to think over the basic principles of the device;
3. design a controller;
4. develop software (software) for the controller;
5. check the controller for compatibility with equipment on the market;
6. Test and debug the controller.

Research Methods:

1. computer simulation;
2. mathematical modeling;
3. standard programming;
4. collection of statistics;
5. testing.

The main planned results of the project: to develop and construct a working prototype of the device, which will allow you to simulate movement in a virtual space using traceable movements of the legs and body.

Areas of possible use of the project results: the project is supposed to be used in the entertainment industry, as well as in the field of education.

Theoretical part. Nowadays, virtual reality technologies (Virtual Reality, VR) are rapidly developing and find their application in various fields. It has already become possible to create entire virtual worlds in high image quality, using a small amount of equipment, however, it is still problematic to implement movement in VR using human movements in the real world, i.e. by moving his legs and tilting the body.

Now on the market there are many controllers that the user controls with their fingers, which prevents full immersion in VR, or there are controllers with full transmission of movement, but they are very bulky and expensive. That is why it was decided to create your own controller, which will allow the transfer of movements to the VR world with the help of leg and body movements in the real world and at the same time be inexpensive and compact.

The first step was to explore the market for VR controllers. There are many analogues in the form of omnidirectional treadmills. All of them offer maximum immersion in the virtual world, but because of the design features they simply cannot be compact. Therefore, such devices are intended for use in specially equipped rooms and unsuitable for home use. In addition to treadmills, indirect competitors are conventional hand controllers that allow you to move around using analog controls. The advantage of this solution is that the controllers are usually bundled with VR glasses and do not need to be purchased. However, this type of movement is unnatural and greatly harms immersion in the virtual world.

The next step after studying analogues and materials on this topic was the design of the device. The main idea of the project was to transmit movement using walking on the spot, and the direction of movement was set by the body tilts in four directions. The Arduino platform, consisting of two Arduino UNO and Arduino Leonardo, was chosen as the basis, because of its accessibility and friendly interface. To determine the movement and inclinations, the GY-521 module was chosen, which contains an accelerometer and a gyroscope. A number of early controller prototypes were designed and a program was written for them in the Arduino IDE. The first versions were not reliable and served only for experimental purposes. The first version of the device was tested in the Serious Sam application using Google Cardboard. According to the test results revealed large delays that needed to be fixed.

In the future, it was decided to switch to the Arduino Nano platform, due to its compactness and ease of soldering to the board. In the course of subsequent work, it was possible to make the device wireless. For this, 433 MHz radio modules were used. It was decided to use four AAA batteries as a power source for the controller. At the moment, the first prototype of the device was designed, and the first tests were conducted in the following applications: Serious Sam Fusion, Subnautica, Minecraft Windows 10 Edition. Tests were also conducted to determine the delays of the controller. Since the device is wireless, two types of delay appear.

FUTURE WORK DIRECTION

Further work encountered difficulties associated with the features of the Arduino Nano software, so for the next prototype it was again decided to use Arduino Uno. As a result, a fully working controller was developed, which allows you to simulate movement in a virtual space using traceable movements of the legs and body. In the future, it is planned to work on compactness, stability, as well as the transition to more compact and professional microcontrollers

CONCLUSION

- Currently, more and more Russian universities support the concept of the rational creation of their own unified educational environment, and not just "for show" complies with the laws and recommendations of the Ministry of Education of the Russian Federation. Penza State University also adheres to this concept, having a number of implemented mechanisms, as well as a set of promising ideas for implementation. The implementation of the concept will ensure compliance with the requirements of the current legislation, but it will also provide students, faculty and staff of the university with a powerful and understandable tool for any internal university activity. At the moment, the first prototype of the device was designed and the first tests of work were carried out in the following Applications: Serious Sam Fusion, Subnautica, Minecraft Windows 10 Edition. Tests were also conducted to determine the delays of the controller. Since the device is wireless, two types of delay appear.
- In the course of work, the tasks were completed. A working prototype of the device was developed and constructed, which allows you to simulate movement in a virtual space using traceable movements of the legs and body.

REFERENCES

Ashrafi, R., & Murtaza, M. (2008). Use and impact of ICT on SMEs in Oman. *The Electronic Information Systems Evaluations*, *11*(3), 125–138.

Bachelier, L., Baresi, L., & Quinton, C. (2015). Dynamically Evolving the Structural Variability of Dynamic Software Product Lines. *Proceedings of the 10th International Symposium on Software Engineering for Adaptive and Self-Managing Systems*, 57–63. 10.1109/SEAMS.2015.24

Bershadsky, A. M., & Krevsky, I. G. (1996). The Organization of Distance Education in Penza Region of Russian Federation. *Proceedings of the Second International Conference on Distance Education in Russia: Open and Distance Learning as a Development Strategy*, 174-176.

Big Data in eLearning: The Future of eLearning Industry. (n.d.). Retrieved from https://elearningindustry.com/big-data-in-elearning-future-of-elearning-industry

Bjork, E., Ottosson, S., & Thorsteinsdottir, S. (2008). E-Learning for All. In E-Learning: 21st Century Issues and Challenges (pp. 49–69). Nova Science Publishers Inc.

Bransford, J., Brown, A., & Cocking, R. (2000). *How People Learn: Brain, Mind, Experience, and School.* National Academy Press.

Carr, P., Geman, H., Madan, D. B., & Yor, M. (2002). The Fine Structure of Asset Returns: An Empirical Investigation. *The Journal of Business*, *75*(2), 305–332. doi:10.1086/338705

Cont, R. (2004). *Financial modeling with jump processes.* Chapman and Hall CRC Press.

Cradler, J., & Bridgforth, E. (2002). *Recent Research on the Effects of Technology on Teaching and Learning.* http://www.oten.info/conferences/jukes/research.pdf

Czarnecki, K., & Helsen, S. (2006). Feature-based survey of model transformation approaches. *IBM Systems Journal, 45*(3), 621–646.

doi:10.4018/978-1-5225-2292-8

Goktas, Y., Yildirim, S., & Yildirim, Z. (2009). Main Barriers and Possible Enablers of ICTs Integration into Pre-service Teacher Education Programs. *Journal of Educational Technology & Society*, *12*(1), 193–204.

Hellerstein, J., Diao, Y., & Parekh, S. (2004). *Feedback control of computing systems.* Wiley Interscience. doi:10.1002/047166880X

Iglesia, D. G. (2014). *MAPE-K Formal Templates for Self-Adaptive Systems: Specifications and Descriptions. Smaland.* Linnaeus University.

Januszewski, A., & Molenda, M. (Eds.). (2008). *Educational technology: a definition with commentary*. Lawrence Erlbaum Associates.

Jennex, M. E. (2005). What is KM? *International Journal of Knowledge Management, 1*(4), i–iv.

Jennex, M. E., & Olfman, L. (2002). Organizational memory/knowledge effects on productivity, A lon-gitudinal study. In *Proceedings of the 35th Hawaii International Conference on System Sciences, HICSS35*. IEEE Computer Society. 10.1109/HICSS.2002.994053

Kendall, M.G. (1953). The analysis of economic time-series. *J. of the Royal Statistical Society, 96*, 11-25.

Keromytis, A. D. (2007). Characterizing Software Self-healing Systems. In *Computer Network Security* (pp. 22–33). Springer. doi:10.1007/978-3-540-73986-9_2

Kumunzhiev, K. V. (2003). *Teoriya sistem i sistemnyy analiz: ucheb*. Ulyanovsk: UlGU.

Kuzmina, A. V. (2010). Variance gamma process simulation and its parameters estimation. In *Computer data analysis and modeling: complex stochastic data and systems: Proc. of the ninth intern. conf.* Belorussian State University.

Lawrence, J. E. (2013). *A practical guide for developing research proposal in IS*. Lap Lambert Academic Publishing.

Lawrence, J. E., & Tar, U. A. (2013). The use of grounded theory technique as a practical tool for qualitative data collection and analysis. *Electronic Journal of Business Research Methods, 11*(1), 29.

Lawrence, J. E., & Tar, U. A. (2018). Factors that influence teachers' adoption and integration of ICT in teaching/learning process. *Educational Media International, 55*(1), 79–105. doi:10.1080/09523987.2018.1439712

Madan, D. B. (n.d.). *CGMY and Mexner subordinators are absolutely continuous with respect to one side stable subordinators*. https://arxiv.org/pdf/math/0601173v2.pdf

Mkrtchian, V., Bershadsky, A., Bozhday, A., & Fionova, L. (2015). Model in SM of DEE Based on Service-Oriented Interactions at Dynamic Software Product Lines. In *Identification, Evaluation, and Perceptions of Distance Education Experts* (pp. 231–248). IGI Global. doi:10.4018/978-1-4666-8119-4.ch014

Mkrttchian, V., & Aleshina, E. (2017). *Sliding Mode in Intellectual Control and Communication: Emerging Research and Opportunities*. IGI Global. doi:10.4018/978-1-5225-2292-8

Munster, W. W. U. OpenUSS. (n.d.). Retrieved from https://www.uni-muenster.de/studium/orga/openuss.html

Papazoglou, M. P., & Heuvel, W.-J. (2007). Service oriented architectures: Approaches, technologies and research issues. *The VLDB Journal, 16*(3), 389–415. doi:10.100700778-007-0044-3

Pelyushenko, A. V. (2006). Izvestiya Volgogradskogo gosudarstvennogo tekhnicheskogo uni-versiteta, University proceedings. Volga region. *Engineering and Science*, (8), 48–50.

Poirot, J. (2006). Monte Carlo option pricing for tempered stable (CGMY) processes. *Asia-Pacific Financial Market, 13*(4), 327.

Rosinski, J. (2002). Tempered stable and related processes. In *Miniproceedings of 2nd MaPhySto Conference on Levy processes: Theory and applications*. Aarhus University.

Schobbens, P. E., Heymans, P., & Trigaux, J. C. (2011). 14th IEEE International Requirements Engineering Conference (RE'06). *Computers & Society, 2011*, 139–148.

Schoutens, W. (2003). Levy processes in finance. John Wiley & Sons Ltd.

Smartsparrow. (n.d.). Retrieved from https://www.smartsparrow.com/

The Next Evolution of ERP. (n.d.). *Adaptive ERP // ERP the Right Way: Changing the game for ERP Cloud implementations.* Retrieved from https://gbeaubouef.wordpress.com/2012/09/05/adaptive-erp/

Tomei, L. A. (2005). *Taxonomy for the technology domain*. Information Science Publishing. doi:10.4018/978-1-59140-524-5

Villegas, N. M., Muller, H. A., Tamura, G., Duchien, L., & Casallas, R. A. (2011). Framework for evaluating quality- driven self-adaptive software systems. *Proceeding of the 6th International Symposium on Software Engineering for Adaptive and Self-Managing Systems*, 80-89. 10.1145/1988008.1988020

Volman, M., & Van Eck, E. (2001). Gender equity and information technology in education: The second decade. *Review of Educational Research, 71*(4), 613–634. doi:10.3102/00346543071004613

Voogt, J. (2003). Consequences of ICT for Aims, Contents, Processes and Environments of Learning. In J. van den Akker, W. Kuiper, & U. Hameyer (Eds.), Curriculum landscapes and trends (pp. 217–236). Academic Press.

WebC. T. (n.d.). Retrieved from http://www.cuhk.edu.hk/eLearning/c_systems/webct6/

Wodi, S. W. (2008). The concept of educational technology: problems and prospects of information and communication technology (ICT) in Nigeria. *International Journal of African Studies*, *1*, 4-10.

Younis, O., Ghoul, S., & Alomari, M. H. (2013). Systems Variability Modeling: A Textual Model Mixing Class and Feature Concepts. *International Journal of Computer Science & Information Technology*, *2013*(5), 127–139. doi:10.5121/ijcsit.2013.5509

Chapter 14
Artificial Intelligence and Its Implications in Education

Uttam Sharma
Gautam Buddha University, India

Pradeep Tomar
Gautam Buddha University, India

Harshit Bhardwaj
Gautam Buddha University, India

Aditi Sakalle
Gautam Buddha University, India

ABSTRACT

Computer equipment, software, and online service have succeeded in introducing improvements and enhancements to the classrooms and teaching methods in recent years. Yet, using artificial intelligence (AI), the real disruption of education has to come. Artificial intelligence has proven its position as a game-changing force in various fields, in the past causing unprecedented transformations. Using AI, expert systems can be programmed to communicate with the environment through technologies such as visual perception, speech recognition, and intellectual behavior, which we can find to be inherently human. This chapter aims to discuss the role of artificial intelligence in the education sector including its market size, the effect of AI in education, case studies of current AI presence in education (smart content, smart tutoring systems, virtual facilitators, and learning environments, etc.) to improve learning and life outcomes for all. Finally, chapter concludes with the issues and problems.

DOI: 10.4018/978-1-7998-4763-2.ch014

1.0 INTRODUCTION

Once you first hear of –Artificial Intelligence (AI), several movie images pop up in your mind like Star Wars and Robot where the robots in the movie gained the ability to think, feel and behave on their own like human beings. The definition of AI can be difficult to understand, especially when attempting I wonder how knowledge can be applied as well as to many other sectors of society. The Getting Smart AskAboutAI work started in December 2015 and over these two years, they have found more than 100 AI-to-life applications in areas such as recreation, transportation, education, health care, and gaming, to name just a few. The AI campaign focused on three priorities-jobs, ethics, and education. How does AI help various industries, what are some of the applications, what are the benefits and risks associated with it, and what are the possibilities for AI in education, of greater personal interest?

AI is a technology which aims to make computers like reasoning do human. That will accelerate the digital industrial transformation. Whether it's human beings, animals, plants, computers, tools, rocks, stones, lakes, buildings, or whatever one may think of, putting them together and making "good decisions" would make the planet an autonomous place. To make the world and its physical properties autonomous.

Machine Learning (ML) (R. S. Michalski, 2013)Emulating human thinking and analyzing data (DA)(H. Witten, 2016) module in the system. ML would create techniques for facilitating learning in various network components/devices to make them automatic and autonomous, while DA would evaluate/analyze all the data generated over time to determine past trends and be more efficient/effective in the future.This trend has increased, and efforts are now being made to incorporate ML and DA into the sensors of smart systems (L. Monostori, 2016) and embedded systems (E. A. Lee, 2016). The technology behind AI is truly fascinating, and what it can turn into forces us to reconsider the significance and intent of everything that we know about life and work. The pace at which ML and DA drive AI needs a strong need to tackle trends, challenges, and threats which will increase gradually.The Internet of Things (IoT) is one of the biggest ideas behind this move (Q. F. Hassan, 2017), This anticipates a world full of built-in intelligent devices, also known as "smart objects"(G. Fortino, 2014), Web links or other communication platforms, such as Bluetooth, Infrarot, etc. Such relationships will be mental, physical-human, and physical. The Internet of All (L. T. Yang, 2017) is also a similar idea to assume that any living, non-living, or virtual entity is linked employing some communication means. What we get when you introduce these ideas into the physical world is a Cyber Real System (CPS) (R. Baheti, 2011).

Machine learning is an approach to achieving artificial intelligence (J.Kaplan, 2016) based on the concept of giving machines Access to the information so that they can learn for themselves. Researchers have often talked about how Finally, as a certainty, we will create human-like AI. With expanding speed, we are certainly moving towards that goal. A significant portion of the progress we've seen over the past few years is all due to the fundamental changes in how we view AI working, mainly brought about by ML. Therefore, it would not be unfair to give ML the credit of instilling smartness in computers.

The notion behind AI is that machines can exhibit human intelligence according to Getting Smart's AskAboutAI article. Started in 1956, the idea of machine learning is When using algorithms to view data and take action or complete a function. AI, at its heart, is a computer code that shows some sort of intelligence, thinking, and problem-solving in what was called superintelligence. This is machine technology that can complete tasks that usually need human intelligence; however, it is learning by itself and continues to build on previous iterations. AI is getting smarter; awareness is growing and it is widening the realm of social possibilities.

Knowingly or unknowingly, we usually use certain AI software/resources in our everyday lives. Some of AI's-day today uses are:

- **Communication:** Spam filters, which are operated by AI, streamline the amount of spam in your inbox. When email senders (real or automated) are more diligent in choosing words that were not previously flagged, the filters need to adjust and continue to learn from words that the user often flags. There's an added aspect of machine learning in this, in that additional filters are then generated by the algorithms already in place by the email provider.
- **Travel:** You've seen Machine Learning if you've taken a ride using Uber, which is used to forecast rider demand and measure ETA (Estimated time of arrival). The aviation industry uses AI, as autopilot counts as AI, where it is calculated that just seven minutes of total flight duration is –human steered half flight time.
- **Social networking:** When we use Facebook to share images, artificial intelligence will detect faces in the picture and suggest a name for tagging the person. As part of its AI Program, Facebook has continued to incorporate new features, creating a more personalized and engaging user interface. Many social media platforms, such as Facebook, create accounts lists to be followed, chats to enter and fascinating news feeds based on user feedback and data analysis. Even Google can include a range of personal suggestions with its cards, based on your search history.
- **Online Shopping:** One that comes to mind easily is Amazon, as a result of your previous searches and order history, and how it recommends things you may be interested in. Systems are in place to protect customers from fraud, with warnings being sent almost immediately to an attempted transaction that

is not known as a normal purchase or that is located in a non-home base. All of this is done through AI, which is used to detect fraudulent transactions.

- **Education:** Teachers and students have a wide range of resources available, from Google Searches, where alternate search words are suggested Citing generators, plagiarism checkers, and even Siri instantly became a common search tool. Instantly produced an incredible amount of knowledge, Much more sophisticated than 30 years ago and dependent on society's card catalogs, calculators, and books.

Looking at these common applications of everyday life makes it easier to think about other aspects in which Artificial Intelligence can change classrooms. There are many developments in technology that change How we learn, and how we educate more available to educators with computers or mobile devices if they can't reach it to the college. Students are not the only ones benefiting as AI helpstoo, to simplify and speed up administrative processes, allowing organizations to reduce the amount of time spent on repetitive activities and optimize the amount of time spent on each student. In the next segment, we address the market size of AI in the education sector.

2.0 MARKET SIZE

The Global AI in the Education Market is expected to rise from USD 537.3 million in 2018 to USD 3,683.5 million by 2023, at a Compound Annual Growth Rate (CAGR) of 47 percent over the forecast period, according to the Research and Markets.com industry survey. The next segment shows the educational impacts of AI, with AI projected growth in education.

3.0 IMPLICATIONS OF AI IN EDUCATION

It is expected that the growing the adoption of IA technology for various applications in the education sector and the growing need for AI-integrated multilingual translators would drive AI growth in the education market.

Artificial Intelligence Is no longer solely used in science fiction films. This will be a part of our everyday lives and in our classrooms. When we use platforms like Siri and Alexa, we just starting to see the educational Artificial Intelligence possibilities. Mentioned below are only a few more impacts:

3.1 Administrative Tasks Automation

Artificial Intelligence has immense possible to simplify and accelerate admin activities for professors and organizations alike. This is where educators spend the most time assessing assignments, reviewing papers, and giving interest to the student responses. In multiple-choice exams, AI can already automate the grading process to allow educators to spend more time with one-on-one students, but more could be done by the technology soon. Software developers are creating new ways of classifying written answers and essays. This is also expected to benefit from the admission process with AI. Admission procedures can also be simplified and enhanced, thereby reducing workload for offices with high volume admissions. Automating the paperwork process and assisting students with common admission questions via chatbot and interactive web site materials will enhance the process for both administrators and prospective students.

3.2 Smart Content

The concept of smart content is a hot topic now that robots can create digital content with the same degree of grammatical sophistication as their human counterparts and this technology has finally reached the classroom. AI can help digitize textbooks or create immersive, customized learning experiences that are open to students of all ages and grades.One such tool, called Cram101, uses AI to condense textbook content with chapter summaries, practice tests, and flashcards into a more digestible study guide. Another platform called Netex Learning helps lecturers and professors to create a digital curriculum and content through a range of tools such as video, and an online assistant. Interactive content including immersive lectures and video conferencing is also a possibility now, thanks to AI.

3.3 Smart Tutors and Personalization

Artificial Intelligence will do more than condense a lecture into smart research guides and flashcards because this can even mentor a student on the problems with class content that they have. In the past, students had a short period in which teachers will see, suggesting time periods at the office or hoping they might replyto their emails. Intelligent tutoring programs like Carnegie Learning now exist that use individual data of students to send them performance and interact directly with them. Although this Artificial Intelligence technology is still in its early stages, and will soon be able to act as a full-fledged interactive teacher assisting students with their educational needs in just about any field of need. Additionally, these technologies will soon be able to adapt to a wide variety of learning styles to support both teachers and students.

3.4 Virtual Lectures and Learning Environment

Digital Lectures and Learn Even can be a replacement for a machine lecturer. Not completely, yet virtual human guides still exist, and facilitators capable of thinking, behaving, and reacting with humans naturally utilizing recognition of gesture technology, Answering both the verbal and the nonverbal signals. A more Learning world is now becoming an institutional reality like the Center for Creative Technology at the University of Southern California (USC) creating smart virtual worlds and platforms. The company creates actual virtual worlds and social interactions using AI, 3-D graphics, and computer animation. With the emergence of augmented and virtual reality and the advantages of getting these into the classroom for students to have a more immersive learning environment and seeing places and discovering things they may not otherwise have; AI can be a huge help to that. Tools may be immediately identified via AI based on student answers, or for the entire classroom to experience. These skills aren't something that would be constrained by classroom setting time and location. AI could show students they want to explore, find ways to immediately bring the content to life.

3.5 Teachers' Support

AI would also offer assistance to teachers in many areas in addition to assisting with the grading. AI will handle some of the daily work, as well as contact with the students. One college professor, for example, successfully used an AI Chatbot to interact with students every semester as a teaching assistant without students realizing they were not talking to a human being.

3.6 Students' Communication

Students and teachers would be able to interact with each other immediately as well as connect with other types of AI around the globe. Students immediately matched with peers, helping each student develop their learning networks, with customized and genuine interactions that will fulfill the desires and needs of the students at any given time. Think about the advantages of being able to speak to AI or a virtual mentor who has been focused on student needs evaluation and error analysis.

3.7 Catering to the Needs of Variety of Students

AI would also be able to support students with special needs by tailoring resources to guide them to success in addition to serving as a customized learning partner.

Research for example already shows promising outcomes for AI teaching social skills for ASD students.

3.8 Enable Teachers to Serve as Motivators for Learning

As AI takes on more of a teaching role by supplying the students with basic information, the task of the teachers in the classroom will change. Teachers join the position of facilitator in the classroom or learning motivator. Google Assistant, Apple Siri or Amazon Alexa and getting it to answer some of the questions that emerge in a lesson is going to be a relatively easy task for many computer teachers but to get them on the side, we need to think much more about the role of machine learning and much less about the advent of robots.

3.9 Provide Personalized Assistance

AI also should provide tailored tutoring for the students outside of the classroom. If students continue to develop skills or master concepts before an assessment, AI will be able to provide students with the additional tools they need for success. In the future, visual and immersive learning platforms outside the classroom will not only become more popular but will also be able to accommodate a range of learning styles, all while answering common questions and concerns students have that teachers, TA's, tutors, or parents cannot easily answer.

As AI becomes more common, the one-size-fits-all essence of compulsory education would almost certainly change. Students in Large Open Online Courses (MOOCs), online learning classes, and hybrid class experiences will be able to take advantage of personalized, individualized learning pathways in ways that were not possible until recently.

3.10 Dynamic Timeline and Statistical Data

By using predictive computation, AI can learn the students' habits and give them the most successful study timetable. It is an advantage for the customer service agent, medical professional, or anyone who performs repetitive or laborious tasks; a computer does not get tired, stressed, or need rest; and if the machine encounters a question or issue arising from its programming, a person will be called.

3.11 Voice Assistants

Those are voice services based on the cloud that serves as the personal top assist for the users to use. They perform different tasks in their immediate vicinity via other party applications and smart machines. They can answer questions, call cabs, make restaurant reservations, play music, turn on / off smart lights, and lots more user-based voice commands tasks. None of the famous speech supports are:

Just like Amazon Echo, Amazon Tap, and so on. Here is a broad collection of Alexa is Amazon's voice assistant, used in prods kills known as the Alexa Skills Kit (ASK), which can be changed and upgraded to modify or improve those abilities.

3.12 Reeling Robots

Recent developments in this area of robotics have led to the development of robots that have increased resemblance to humans and are able to communicate with humans while recognizing, reciprocating, and expressing certain human emotions. Robots are in themselves IoTs as they have many sensors and actuators along with AI that helps them learn and adapt over time.

4.0 CASE STUDIES OF AI IN EDUCATION

The interactive and complex existence of Artificial Intelligence Offers student engagement opportunities that cannot be found in often obsolete textbooks or the fixed environment of the conventional four-walled classroom.We also presented some case studies where AI is leading and being implemented in education. In terms of the long-term objectives envisaged, some of the implementations are still in a fairly primitive state. As one of the initial ideas for AI applications in education, intelligent tutoring systems appear could have made the most strides in the past 20 years. Both can help create a more individualized learning and sensitive teaching next generation.

4.1 Smart Content

The creation of intelligent content is being applied at all levels, from elementary to post-secondary to corporate environments, from digitized textbook guides to customized digital interfaces for learning.

fan Artificial Intelligence technology company specializing in business process automation and smart instruction design has developed a suite of smart secondary and beyond education learning services. Cram101 uses AI to help distribute and break down textbook content into digestible – a smart research guide that provides chapter summaries, true-false, multiple-choice practice tests, and flashcards. The fact has a similar but more streamlined feature, including highlighting and generating text.

Many companies are creating smart digital marketing platforms, complete with content delivery, practice events, and real-time feedback and assessments. Netex Education, allows teachers to create immersive instruction and content across apps, integrating rich media such as video and audio, as well as self- or online educator assessment. It also offers a new workplace interactive learning technology platform where workers can build customized learning experiences through software, gamification, and simulations.New workplace learning systems are designed to enable workers to develop new skills and gain continuous and automated input that can help boost performance that improves productivity when strategically used.

4.1.1 Smart Devices

There are smart objects/devices present in an IoT, excluding voice assist and robots that make the work easier for humans. AI-enabled smart objects use object detection technologies, face recognition, voice recognition, speech, and gesture analysis, DNN, learning transfer, the vision of computers.

An HD camera and food thermometer that will support Smart Oven by June automatically aims to cook food perfectly at all times. It has the food being cooked inside the oven monitoring and can switch cooking modes if necessary. Alexa can monitor this oven and can suggest and configure ana automatic cooking program.

4.1.2 Industrial IoT

In addition to being used in smart homes, IoT has an enormous use area in the various industrial sectors.Such solutions conduct business as a whole's statistical and financial analysis, and finally, make forecasts using certain algorithms for AI and machine learning.

4.2 Intelligent Tutoring Systems

Unlike the Intelligent tutoring programs of their early predecessors, they have made considerable strides. Mika Software for Carnegie Learning uses cognitive science and AI technology to provide customized tutoring and real-time feedback to post-secondary students, particularly beginners who would otherwise need remedial classes. Carnegie estimates the cost of such remedial learning as costing schools $6.7 billion a year, with a mere 33 percent progress rate for math courses. ITS provides students with the ability to work more effectively and continuously through flexible and more personalized learning modes.

Pearson, in collaboration with University College London Knowledge Lab, reports that today's model-based adaptive systems are becoming increasingly available, allowing educators to understand how a system has come to a next-step decision and making them more effective teaching tools in classrooms. The iTalk2Learn, a program developed and evaluated by Carnegie Mellon University to assess its impact on young people 's learning fractions, implemented a learner model that specifically included details about an individual's knowledge of mathematics, cognitive needs, emotional condition, as well as the input obtained and the people's responses in turn.

4.3 Environments Online Facilitators and Learning

While it seems obvious that no one in education is ready to come and replace virtual humans, an exciting area of progress is the idea of designing virtual human guides and facilitators for use in a variety of educational and therapeutic settings. In this area, though not yet a reality, the ultimate goal is to create virtual human-like characters that can naturally think, behave, react, and communicate, reacting to, and using both verbal and nonverbal communication.

The University of Southern California Institute for Creative Technologies is a leader in developing smart virtual worlds and applications which rely on AI, 3-D gaming, and computer animation to create authentic virtual characters and realistic social interactions. USC researchers have a number of ongoing projects in the room that suggest developments are to come over the next two decades.

Captivating Virtual Instruction for Training (CVIT) Is a digital learning method designed to integrate live classroom methods with best-fit interactive technologies — including interactive facilitators, augmented reality, smart tutors, and others — in remote learning and programming training. As AI advances in this field of education, more research continues to support the claim that both smart systems and humans are required to manage various aspects of students ' academic and social competencies. AI is unlikely to replace but can serve as an invaluable human expert extension, thus helping teachers meet the diverse needs of multiple students more efficiently at the same time.

From classroom facial recognition to computer-marking papers, China is completely integrating new technology into its education system. A recent study reported a high school in Eastern China is developing a new system of facial recognition designed to assess student interaction in a classroom, in real-time.

An advanced conduct control device in the classroom scans the space every thirty seconds logging the actions of the students and their facial expressions.By visually observing a student's face, the program can classify seven moods, including positive, sad, fearful, and furious. A camera at the front of the classroom, positioned on top of the blackboard, also monitors six forms of behavior: reading, writing, raising hands, stand up and listen to the teacher, then sit down at the desk.

A recent article verbatim from the South China Morning Post (SCMP) reported that one in four Chinese schools were experimenting with computer software for grade essays in an even more startling and wide-ranging Artificial Intelligence introduction into the education system. It is alleged that the machine-learning program has been in progress for almost a decade, using deep learning algorithms to continuously learn and enhance its ability to understand and analyze the work of a student. Currently, it is estimated that 60,000 schools are studying the technology and it will give up to 92 percent of the time the same grade as a human marker.

Automated labeling devices are not a revolutionary concept at all. Although computer-assisted marking software has been around for nearly as long as computers, computers have only begun to be used in the last decade or two to map out more abstract student work, such as writing argumentative essays. Such systems are introduced in China with degrees of a scale unseen anywhere else in the world.

Currently, China is training its neural network grading system on a central server storing the millions of works for the graduates. This program certainly provides a remarkable opportunity for the central government to track the progress of all students in the country, in real-time, as well as offering a possible way to take out the differences attributed to human subjectivity in marking.

And this appallingly extensive control of the education system will undoubtedly be aligned with the oncoming social credit program in the country due to complete activation by 2020. The proposed program would grant a social credit score to each individual that will decide a person's ability to travel abroad, receive a home loan, or even access the internet.

5.0 ISSUES AND CHALLENGES

Everyone knows, any technology has related pros and cons with it — and Artificial Intelligence is no exception to this law. A few of the problems and concerns are as follows:

- The production climate for IA projects is very different. Production is all about finding data sources and then collecting, cleaning, and data curating. What an approach needs different skills and mindsets, and different methodologies. Furthermore, AI-powered intellectual systems must be trained in a specific environment.
- The slow pace of digitization affects theadoption of Artificial Intelligence technology in developing economies as the introduction of AI-enabled technologies requires accurate reports from Information Technology

infrastructures. This factor may dampen the growth of AI in the education market.

- You need large and clean data sets with minimal biases to train machine learning algorithms.
- Data privacy issues should also be taken into consideration in respect to the processing of personal data, in particular in the light of the General Data Protection Act which will come into force in 2018.
- Gartner predicts that 20 percent of all company content will be generated by 2018. While there is evidence that AI is capable of creating certain types of content that are virtually indistinguishable from human content in terms of clarity and accuracy, the machine-manufactured content is substantially more boring and less readable in one study.
- It is easy – and exciting to imagine a diverse set of AI modules that work together to create fully automated, custom-made experiences! But this system is vulnerable to repeated failures as it meets conditions which it is not equipped to handle.
- ROI can be nearly impossible to predict.
- If additional costs are incurred for installation, maintenance, and repair, AI is expensive. Only well-funded schools are able to take advantage of AI.

6.0 CONCLUSION

Artificial intelligence is the most exciting development in the technology of our time. From designing sophisticated data-collection algorithms to offering comprehensive and personalized student input, AI shines like the most qualified AI can easily interpret the needs of a student and develop a suitable assessment. It can demonstrate mastery to the students, repeat lessons as required and develop a customized learning plan for each student quickly.AI may be offering a virtual teaching assistant to teachers. But it can be more than just teachers and students to assist parents by including them in the students ' learning experience and supplying them with the knowledge they need to help their children excel while they're not in the classroom. The future undoubtedly has plenty of promise for AI. This chapter addressed AI's possible impacts on education, several case studies around the world, related problems, and challenges.

REFERENCES

Baheti, R., & Gill, H. (2011). Cyber-Physical Systems. *The Impact of Control Technology*, *12*, 161–166.

Bayne, S. (2015). Teacherbot: Interventions in automated teaching. *Teaching in Higher Education*, *20*(4), 455–467. doi:10.1080/13562517.2015.1020783

Bostrom, N. (2006). AI set to exceed human brain power. *CNN Science &* Space. http://edition.cnn.com/2006/TECH/science/07/24/ai.bostrom/

Deakin University. (2014). *IBM Watson now powering Deakin. A new partnership that aims to exceed students' needs.* http://archive.li/kEnXm

Diss, K. (2015). *Driverless trucks move iron ore at automated Rio Tinto mines.* ABC. https://www.abc.net.au/news/2015-10-18/rio-tinto-opens-worlds-firstautomated-mine/6863814

Fortino, G., & Trunfio, P. (2014). *Internet of Things based on Smart Objects: Technology, Middleware and Applications.* Springer. doi:10.1007/978-3-319-00491-4

Gibney, E. (2017). Google secretly tested AI bot. *Nature*, *541*(7636), 142. doi:10.1038/nature.2017.21253 PMID:28079098

Hassan, Q. F., Khan, A. R., & Madani, S. A. (2017). Internet of Things: Challenges, Advances, and Applications. Chapman & Hall/CRC Computer and Information Science Series, CRC Press. doi:10.1007/978-3-319-55405-1

Kaplan, J. (2016). Artificial Intelligence: What Everyone Needs to Know. What Everyone Needs to Know. Oxford University Press.

Lee, E. A., & Seshia, S. A. (2016). *Introduction to Embedded Systems: A Cyber-Physical Systems Approach.* MIT Press.

Maderer, J. (2016). *Artificial intelligence course creates AI teaching assistant.* Georgia Tech News Center. http://www.news.gatech.edu/2016/05/09/artificialintelligence-course-creates-ai-teaching-assistant

Michalski, R. S., Carbonell, J. G., & Mitchell, T. M. (2013). *Machine Learning: An Artificial Intelligence Approach.* Springer Science & Business Media.

Monostori, L., Kádár, B., Bauernhansl, T., Kondoh, S., Kumara, S., Reinhart, G., Sauer, O., Schuh, G., Sihn, W., & Ueda, K. (2016). Cyber-Physical Systems in Manufacturing. *CIRP Annals*, *65*(2), 621–641. doi:10.1016/j.cirp.2016.06.005

Popenici, S. (2015). Deceptive promises: the meaning of MOOCs-hype for higher education. In E. McKay & J. Lenarcic (Eds.), *Macro-level learning through massive open online courses (MOOCs): strategies and predictions for the future*. IGI Global. doi:10.4018/978-1-4666-8324-2.ch009

Russell, S. J., & Norvig, P. (2010). *Artificial intelligence: a modern approach* (3rd ed.). Prentice-Hall.

Rutkin, A. (2015). Therapist in my pocket. *New Scientist*, *227*(3038), 20. doi:10.1016/S0262-4079(15)31169-6

Schleicher, A. (2015). *Schools for 21st-century learners: Strong leaders, confident teachers, innovative approaches, International summit on the teaching profession*. OECD Publishing. doi:10.1787/9789264231191-en

Witten, H., & Frank, E. (2016). *Data Mining: Practical Machine Learning Tools and Techniques*. Morgan Kaufmann.

Yang, L. T., Di Martino, B., & Zhang, Q. (2017). *Internet of Everything* (Vol. 2017). Mobile Information Systems.

Chapter 15
Learning With Artificial Intelligence Systems:
Application, Challenges, and Opportunities

Tarana Singh
Gautam Buddha University, India

Jyoti Mishra
Gautam Buddha University, India

ABSTRACT

Artificial intelligence (AI) is a part of our lives. Everything that we do on the internet is influenced to various extents by AI. It can automate various tasks in education as well as in other domains. Education domain is mainly benefited by AI, especially for the learning purpose. There may be the software to perform all activities which needs automation. This software can point out that course needs improvement. An AI software can give students and educators helpful feedback. Data, which is powered by AI, also helps schools, teachers, and supports students. There are lots of benefits of AI in education, which improves the learning experience of the students, for example personalization, teaching, grading, feedback on course quality, creating a global classroom, monitoring performance, and a lot more. When a new promising technology emerges and when the limitation of technology and the challenges of applying are often not perfectly understood, then the technology may seem to open radically new possibilities for solving old problems.

DOI: 10.4018/978-1-7998-4763-2.ch015

1. INTRODUCTION

Artificial intelligence (AI) is considered as the capacity and headway of information development-based PC systems or various machines to complete the assignments that regularly require individual data and cognitive thinking (Andrea et al., 2015). Notwithstanding the way that AI can improve the world a spot. Every single human activity depends on foreseen fates. We can't know the future since it doesn't exist yet, yet we can utilize our present information to envision fates and get them going. The better we comprehend the present and the history that has made it, the better we can understand the conceivable outcomes of things to come (Bayne, 2015). To value the chances and difficulties that computerized reasoning (AI) makes, we need both a decent comprehension of what AI is today and what the future may bring when AI is broadly utilized in the public eye. Simulated intelligence can empower better approaches for picking up, instructing, and training, and it might likewise change the network in manners that present new difficulties for instructive foundations (Bostrom, 2006). It might intensify ability contrasts and enrapture occupations, or it might even out open doors for learning. The utilization of AI in training may produce bits of knowledge on how learning occurs, and it can change how information is evaluated (Growing Science, n.d.). It might re-arrange study halls or make them old, it can expand the proficiency of educating, or it might constrain understudies to adjust to the prerequisites of innovation, denying people of the forces of office and opportunities for dependable activity. AI is presently a piece of our regular lives. This innovation encompasses us from a programmed stopping framework, keen sensors for taking terrific photographs, and individual help (Daisy Group, n.d.).

Also, AI in instruction is actuality handled, and the customary strategies remain evolving radically. The real world is turning out to be gradually valuable and modified on account of the numerous consumptions of AI for instruction; this has altered how people study meanwhile educational resources are receiving available to all finished shrewd gadgets and PCs (Frankish et al., 2011). AI is likewise permitting the computerization of authoritative errands, allowing organizations to confine the required to complete irksome assignments so the instructors can contribute more vitality with understudies (Botrel et al., 2015). An ongoing report from e-School news found that the utilization of AI in the instruction business would develop by 47% through 2021 as we move towards an increasingly associated world. The innovation's effect will exist somewhere in the range of kindergarten through advanced education, offering the chance to make versatile learning highlights with customized instruments to improve the understudy understanding (McGovern et al., 2011; Torrey, 2012). The innovation might have the option to hitter illuminate understudies what their activity possibilities may resemble dependent on their specific story also, helping them past their scholarly life. Work combination is helping associations with acute programmed stages that can improve the evaluating and documenting process in the homeroom (Kumar & Meeden, 1998; McGovern et al., 2011; Torrey et al., 2016).

Artificial Intelligence can raise platforms using which the paths required to expand. Educators might not by and large think about openings in their discussions and informative materials that can leave understudies jumbled about explicit thoughts (Barik et al., 2013; Li et al., 2014). Various understudies have diverse learning styles, capacities, premiums, and needs. One educator in a study hall of 30 understudies will infrequently have the option to take into account every one of those necessities (Albu, 2012; Dilger, 2005). Schoolwork and classes could be redone dependent on an understudy profile, and interests can be developed and improved by presenting understudies to various courses and substance. Human-made reasoning proposes a method to tackle problem. For example, Coursera, an online course provider, is as of now incorporating this (Fok & Ong, 1996; Heinze et al., 2010). At the point when an enormous number of replacements are originated to existing an inappropriate answer to a schoolwork task, the framework cautions the instructor. It provides coming replacements an altered communication that proposes insights to the correct reaction (Featherston et al., 2014; Shieber, 2004). This kind of strategy assists with filling in the holes in the clarification that can happen in courses and help with guaranteeing that all understudies are building the proportionate theoretical establishment. Instead of hearing over from the teacher, substitutes get fast information that grants them to grasp the thought and remember how to do it viably at whatever point around (Reyes et al., 2016).

2. RELATED WORK

Many existing strategies center around showing the idea of AI to undergrad and graduate understudies in colleges and schools (e.g., Torrey, 2012; McGovern et al., 2011; Kumar & Meeden, 1998; Torrey et al., 2016; Barik et al., 2013; Albu, 2012) or instructor preparing (e.g., Dilger, 2005). Instructs subjects chose by AI at school level, for example, Heinze (Heinze et al., 2010) or Fok and Ong (1996) either manage certain parts of AI (e.g., history, Turing's test (Shieber, 2004), chatbots, neural systems), or utilize just explicit ideas that clarify AI. Apparatus or stage (e.g., Featherston et al., 2014). Different techniques center around explicit AI-related programming ideal models, (for example, revelatory secondary school programming portrayed by Reyes et al., 2016) or explicit AI points (Layer et al., 2012). There are different approaches to advance training in STEM or STEM-C (science, innovation, building, arithmetic, software engineering, and so on.). For instance, Bojic and Arratia (2015) talk about a prologue to class understudies (Kindergarten to Grade 8) venture, STEM-C Field, Tsukamoto et al. (2015) examine how to train primary younger students to utilize a book language. Man-made reasoning wording in training (AIED; e.g., clever mentoring frameworks, intelligent learning environments [Sklar & Parsons, 2002]), there are numerous approaches to utilize AI as an instrument for learning (e.g., Pareto, 2016). Sklar and Parsons (Teach Thought, n.d.) portrayed how to utilize mechanical technology and apply autonomy rivalries (particularly RoboCupJunior) as an instrument to acquaint understudies with AI, apply autonomy and software engineering. He additionally disclosed how to utilize apply autonomy to show AI and software engineering in undergrad instruction.

3. APPLICATIONS OF ARTIFICIAL INTELLIGENCE IN LEARNING

Here are a few the manners by which those apparatuses and those that will tail them will shape and portray the enlightening experience of what might be on the horizon. These applications are as follows:

- **AI can mechanize central activities in guidance, for example, inspecting;** In school, evaluating schoolwork and tests for full talk courses can be tedious work, on any event. Certainly, even in junior assessments, educators from time to time find that keeping an eye on involves a lot of time, time that could be utilized to interface with understudies, get ready for class, or work on fit progress. While AI may not ever have the decision to override human evaluating amazingly, it's drawing near (Science Direct, n.d.). It's straightforwardly useful for educators to robotize demands for about a wide extent of different decision and fill free testing, and computerized researching of understudy making may not be a long way behind. Today, an article surveying composing PC programs is still in its beginning and not good. In any case, it can (and will) improve over the coming years, allowing instructors to focus more on in-class activities and understudy interface than assessing.
- **Learners can obtain anytime assistance from AI mentors;** While there are things that human partners can offer that machines can't, at any rate not yet, the future could see more understudies being coached by guides that specific exists in zeros and ones. Some arrangement programs reliant on human-made care starting at now live and can help understudies through head science, rewarding the earth, and various subjects. These activities can show understudies fundamentals, yet so far aren't ideal for helping understudies learn notoriety thinking and inventive mind, something that real teachers are so far required to help (Chen et al., 2015). Notwithstanding, that shouldn't prevent the opportunity of AI guides having the decision to do these things

later on. With the speedy pace of mechanical improvement that has suggested the past hardly any decades, advanced teaching structures may not be a senseless dream.

- **AI-driven tasks can substitute and teacher's cooperative analysis;** Artificial intelligence can't only assistance educators and substitutes to take courses that are changed to their necessities, yet it can in like way give a guarantee to both about the achievement of the class by and large. A few schools, especially those with online endowments, are using AI structures to screen understudy progress and to caution teachers when there might be an issue with understudy execution. Such AI systems grant understudies to get the assistance they with requiring and for educators to find territories where they can improve bearing for understudies who may fight with the point (De Lange, 2015). PC based understanding ventures at these schools aren't simply duty advance on solitary courses, regardless. Some are endeavoring to make systems that can help understudies with picking majors subject to locale where they succeed and fight. While understudies don't need to take the interest, it could check a challenging of-the-workmanship nearness of enormous school affirmation for future understudies.
- **AI could change the job of educators;** There will constantly be an occupation for educators in preparing, in any case what that activity is and what it fuses may move due to progress as shrewd figuring systems. As we've starting late discussed, AI can expect authority over assignments like assessing, can help substitutes with improving learning, and may even fill in for genuine preparing. Regardless, AI could be changed according to various bits of getting ready too. PC based understanding structures could be patched up to give health, filling in as a spot for understudies to present requests and find information or could even exchange instructors for basic course materials. A vital bit of the time, in any case, AI will move the activity of the teacher to that of the facilitator (Deakin University, 2014). Educators will redesign AI works out, help understudies who are doing fighting, and give human joint effort and hands-on experiences for understudies. From various perspectives, progress is starting at now driving an area of these adjustments in the evaluation gateway, especially in schools that are on the web or handle the flipped homeroom model.
- **Artificial Intelligence can make experimentation learning less unnerving;** Experimentation is a central piece of data, yet for solitary understudies, missing the mark, or even not knowing the sensible reaction, is covering. Some mainly couldn't consider being gotten out before their accomplices or authority figures like an instructor. A smart PC system, proposed to help understudies with learning, is an all things considered less overpowering

way to deal with oversee direct experimentation (DFKI, 2015). The human-made intellectual ability could offer understudies a method to test and learn in a reasonably without judgment condition, generally when AI mentors can respond to movement. Human-made data is the perfect plan for supporting such a learning, as AI structures themselves often learn by an experimentation framework.

- **AI may change where understudies recognize, who shows them, and how they secure the major aptitudes;** While basic changes may, in any case, be quite a few years, after the fact on, extremely human-caused thinking to can change in a general sense all that we mock about direction. Utilizing AI frameworks, programming, and backing, substitutes can get from any place on the planet at whatever point (Diss, 2015). With these sorts of exercises succeeding explicit kinds of study hall heading, AI may forever uproot instructors on specific occasions (regardless). Instructive activities fuelled by AI are beginning at now, helping substitutes to learn principal aptitudes. Taking everything into account, as these tasks create and as architects discover extra, they will most likely offer understudies a mostly progressively expansive extent of organizations.
- **The computerization of managerial undertakings;** AI has extraordinary potential in mechanizing and speeding up regulatory capacities for the two associations and teachers. Reviewing schoolwork, assessing papers, and offering an incentive to understudy reactions is the place teachers invest the most energy. Human-made intelligence would already be able to computerize the reviewing procedure in numerous decision tests to permit teachers to invest more energy with substitutes one-on-one. However, the innovation may, before long, have the option to accomplish more than this (Gallagher, 2015). Programming designers are making better approaches to review composed reactions and expositions too. The confirmation procedure is likewise set to profit as ai can mechanize the preparing and grouping of administrative work.
- **The expansion of keen substance;** The idea of unique content is a hotly debated issue now as robots can make an advanced substance with a similar level of linguistic ability as their human partners, and this innovation has, at last, arrived at the study hall. Artificial intelligence can help digitize reading material are made flexible learning advanced interfaces that apply to understudies of all age ranges and grades. One such framework called Cram101 utilizes Ai to consolidate the substance in course books into a progressively absorbable examination direct with section synopses, practice tests, and cheat sheets (Independent, n.d.). Another stage called netex learning permits speakers and teachers to plan a computerized educational program

and substance over an assortment of gadgets, including video, sound, and an online partner.

- **Smart Tutors and personalization;** AI can accomplish more than consolidating a talk into cheat sheets, and speedy investigation manages as it can likewise coach an understudy dependent on the troubles, they are having with class material. Previously, understudies had a restricted window of time where they could see their educators, which means available time or trusting they answer their messages. There are currently keen training agendas, for example, Carnegie discovering that use information from explicit substitutes to give them input and work with them directly (Gibney, 2017). While this AI application is still in its beginning periods, it will before long have the option to function as an undeniable computerized teacher that helps understudies with their instructive needs in pretty much any region of need.
- **A robot may before long supplant virtual teachers and Learning Environment;** Even your genuine speaker. Indeed, not so much, yet there are as of now virtual human aides and facilitators that can think, act, and respond with a human by straightforwardly utilizing motion acknowledgment innovation, reacting to both verbal and nonverbal prompts. A progressively computerized learning condition is additionally turning into a reality with foundations (Air CCSE, n.d.).
- **Global learning;** Instruction has no limitations, and AI can help with clearing out cut-off points. Development brings extraordinary advances by empowering the teaching of any course from wherever over the globe and at whatever point. Simulated Intelligence controlled guidance outfits substitutes with basic IT capacities. With more improvements, there will be a progressively broad extent of courses open on the web, and with the help of AI, replacements will pick up from wherever they are (Stottler Henke, n.d.).

4. CHALLENGES OF ARTIFICIAL INTELLIGENCE IN LEARNING

- In a training and learning condition, understudies' dynamic help with practices similarly as the use of learning approaches that help understudies review what they understand is central estimations. Practical learning approaches increase the idea of learning. Understudies learn best by doing and experiencing (González et al., 2015). To be amazing and gainful, science empowering tasks ought to be understudy focused and subject to research and assessment and should fuse exploratory activities. In an agreeable learning approach, understudies and educators are in a state of dynamic coordinated effort in the investigation corridor.

- **Each understudy' have an alternate learning capacity;** An understudy in one go can comprehend one case of a point clarified by an educator, or it will take more than a few instances of a similar issue to understand the subject. Some of the time, it may happen that the understudy was missing from the past class. Once in a while, the instructor can't give a fitting model, which is sufficiently simple to comprehend by each understudy in a study hall (Grove, 2015).
- **A persistent discourse on the proper and capable employments of AI in instruction is this way required;** As innovation and its applications change, fundamental commitments to this exchange may arise out of "pariahs" who don't speak to current partner interests. Empowering and subsidizing independent research on, for instance, the legislative issues, morals, social ramifications, and economy of AI might be a practical method to make helpful contributions to this discourse (Hillier et al., 2015).
- **In the space of instructive approach, instructors and policymakers need to comprehend AI in the more extensive set of things to come of learning;** to no small degree, the discussion about AI is presently about the progressing in formalization, digitalization, and PC intervened globalization. The present assessments of the effect of AI and other computerized advances on the work advertise feature the point that the interest for abilities and capabilities is evolving quickly, and the instructive framework needs to adjust, specifically when training plans to make for work (Kübler et al., 2015). Artificial intelligence empowers the mechanization of numerous profitable errands that, previously, have been finished by people.
- **As AI will be utilized to computerize creation forms, we may need to rehash current instructive foundations;** It is, for instance, conceivable that proper training will assume a lessening job in making work-related skills. This could imply that the next piece of encouraging will progressively be in supporting human improvement. For instance, the existing AI frameworks make a practically consistent appraisal of understudy progress conceivable (Lazarus et al., 2008). Rather than high-stakes testing that capacities as a social channel, AI-bolstered evaluation can be utilized to assist students with developing their aptitudes and abilities and keep understudies on dynamic learning ways. With such progressing appraisal.
- **A general approach challenge, along these lines, is to increment among instructors and policymakers familiarity with AI innovations and their latent capacity sway;** One method for doing this is to take an interest in forms that produce pictures of future, create ideas that can be utilized to depict them, and structure situations and investigations where such envisioned possibilities can be tried. A somewhat straightforward proposition for

arrangement improvement, along these lines, is to dispatch expressly future-situated procedures that produce a comprehension of the potential outcomes of the present (Luckin, 2017).

- **As there might be critical hypothetical and viable cutoff points in planning AI frameworks that can clarify their conduct and choices, it is fundamental to keep people in the dynamic circle;** As a few late reports have underscored, moral contemplations become exceptionally significant when AI is applied in the general public or instructive settings.89 From a strategy viewpoint (Maderer, 2016).
- **The morals of AI is a conventional test. However, it has explicit significance for instructive strategies;** From the administrative perspective, moral contemplations give the essential premise from which new guidelines and laws are made and supported. From a developmental perspective, morals, and worth decisions help basic ideas, for example, office, obligation, personality, opportunities, and human capacities. In directed AI learning models, the likely decision results should be given to the framework before it begins to learn. This implies the world gets depicted in shut terms, in light of predefined interests and classifications (Getting Smart, n.d.). Besides, the gatherings depend on the information that is gathered before. Neural AI orders individuals in groups where information from others, thought about like the framework, is utilized to anticipate unique qualities and conduct.
- **AI can, in this manner, additionally limit the space where people can communicate their organization;** As has been underscored over, the ongoing accomplishments in AI have, to a considerable degree, been founded on the accessibility of immense measures of information. Simulated intelligence-based items and administrations can be made in the instructive segment just if fitting details are accessible (IITM, n.d.). At present, a portion of the current datasets can be considered as regular syndications, and a couple of enormous enterprises frequently control them (Chen et al., 2016).
- **A critical approach challenge is how such massive datasets that are required for the improvement and utilization of AI-based frameworks could be made all the more broadly accessible;** One potential arrangement is to expand on the present General Data Protection Regulation which necessitates that information subjects can have a duplicate of their information from information controllers in a usually utilized electronic structure (Mitcham, 2005; Neven, 2013). This would make it workable for clients to get to their data, anonymize it locally, and submit it in a fitting configuration to stages that are utilized for AI learning and informative purposes. Such use may generally be handily implanted; for instance, it usually utilized internet

browsers, if steps for information accumulation would be accessible. One chance could be to pilot such collection stages on an appropriate scale and, if fruitful, gave at the EU level.

5. SOLUTIONS IN THE DOMAIN OF LEARNING WITH AI SYSTEM

There are many technical solutions in the education industry. Examples of AI such as Dream Box, Khan Academy, Achieve 3000. These platforms can analyze knowledge levels, provide upstream communication, and provide improvement plans.

- **Learning in the third area;** This system was created with the help of scholars at University College London, and actively took advantage of opportunities in artificial intelligence. The system may recommend ways to improve teaching skills (Neven, 2015). For example, the system sends a notification if the teacher speaks too fast or too slow.
- **Little Dragon;** A start-up company that uses artificial intelligence to create intelligent applications. Such applications can analyze user sentiment and adjust the user interface accordingly. The company also makes puzzle games for kids (Pasquale, 2015).
- **CTI;** AI is used to develop technology-based educational solutions. The main purpose is to create intelligent content. For example, Cram101 can analyze textbooks and other learning materials and select key information to create a textbook (Perez, 2016).
- **Carnegie Learning;** Systems tend to provide more personalized materials to make the learning process more comfortable. This solution provides school students with real-time education. The Carnegie Learning System analyzes user keys and allows tutors to visualize student progress (McKay et al., 2015).
- **Math Thinker;** This AI-enabled solution helps children learn math. There are different games and rewards for better participation. The app also offers personalized learning plans based on the child's knowledge (Popenici & Kerr, 2013).
- **Smart is a social network for student cooperation;** Learners can discuss homework issues and gain new knowledge from other students. The company uses machine learning to provide a better user experience. ML helps with spam and inappropriate content selection. In addition, it uses artificial intelligence to provide more personalized material.

6. OPPORTUNITIES IN THE DOMAIN OF LEARNING WITH AI SYSTEM

In the current day, there might be a decent number of chances in any area for innovative work. Here hardly any open doors in the area of instruction while utilizing AI have been examined. A few open doors in the learning space utilizing AI frameworks are as per the following:

- **Education whenever;** Young individuals invest a great deal of energy in the go. They incline toward doing regular errands utilizing their cell phones or tablets. AI-based applications give a chance to concentrate on the available time, going through ten or fifteen minutes. Also, the understudies can get input from guides in a continuous mode (Reuters/ABC, 2016).
- **Various choices because of the understudies' needs;** AI-based arrangements can adjust because of the understudies' degree of information, fascinating points, etc. The framework will, in general assistance, understudies with their powerless sides. It offers learning materials dependent on their shortcomings (ABC, n.d.). For instance, the understudy does the test before beginning to utilize the application; the application examines it and gives reasonable errands and courses.
- **Virtual coaches;** AI-based stages offer practical guides to follow the understudies' advancement. Just human instructors can comprehend the researchers' needs better. However, it's acceptable to get moment criticism from the virtual mentor.
- **Opportunity to see limitations;** Different instructional classes permit seeing the holes in understudies' information. For instance, the Coursera stage can advise the educator if numerous understudies picked off base responses to a specific inquiry. Thus, the guide has a chance to focus on the requested theme (Russell & Norvig, 2010).
- **Better commitment;** Modern advances like VR and gamification help include understudies in the training procedure, making it increasingly intelligent and customized. Different AI-empowered Algorithms can dissect the client's information and interests and give increasingly customized proposals and preparing programs.
- **Curriculum programmed making;** Teachers get an extraordinary profit by AI improvement. Nowadays, they don't have to make an educational plan without any preparation. Thus, guides invest less energy looking for vital instructive materials.
- **Opportunity to locate a decent educator;** Educational stages have a lot of instructors, so the understudy has a chance to speak with authorities

from different nations. The AI-empowered instructive stage offers suitable coaches, contingent upon the showing experience and delicate aptitudes (Rutkin, 2015).

- **Increase productivities and better understudy commitment;** Key drivers are to expand efficiencies and drive better understudy commitment with modernized learning and modernized study halls as top situations throughout the following coming months (Tsur et al., 2010).
- **Improving understudy results;** With the essential objectives of improving understudy results, empowering the workforce of things to come, and quickening development, advanced education foundations are bullish on the job AI will play in acknowledging achievement. The new IDC report shows that AI is relied upon to increment superior education intensity, subsidizing, and development twofold throughout the following three years (Wolpaw et al., 2012).

7. CONCLUSION

The capacity for data frameworks to give this degree of understanding spares time as well as can provide the degree of detail that may not be evident or workable for educators to perceive at face esteem. Homeroom AI apparatuses have capacities in breaking down numerous wellsprings of information and contrasting them with known examples. This can distinguish the main drivers for issues and drive towards progressively predictable results across various classes, paying little mind to the experience of instructing staff. Learning with the AI framework has different applications like AI that could change the job of instructors. Understudies could get extra help from AI coaches and some more. The rising of AI makes it hard to ignore a real conversation about its future occupation of teaching and learning in cutting edge instruction and what sort of choices universities will make concerning this issue. The snappy pace of development headway and the related action movement perceived extensively by pros in the field (source), derives that teaching in cutting edge training requires a reevaluation of instructors' activity and instructional techniques. The current usage of original game plans, for instance, 'learning the board structures' or IT answers for perceiving composed adulteration starting at now, raises the issue of who sets the arrangement for training and learning: corporate undertakings or establishments of cutting-edge instruction? The rising of tech rulers and the semi syndication of barely any tech beasts similarly go with questions concerning the centrality of security and the possibility of an inauspicious future. These issues merit phenomenal thought as schools should consolidate this game plan of risks while considering a potential future.

Additionally, various courses of action of tasks that are by and by a set at the focal point of training practice in cutting edge instruction will be replaced by AI programming subject to complex figuring's arranged by engineers that can transmit their inclinations or inspiration in working systems. A regular report and solicitation in proposed courses of action stay fundamental to guarantee that schools remain associations prepared to care for progress, advance, and make data and quickness. At this moment is a perfect open door for schools to rethink their ability and informational models and their future association with AI game plans and their owners. Also, associations of cutting-edge training find before the tremendous register of potential results and incite opened by the opportunity to get a handle on AI in teaching and learning. These courses of action present new openings for preparing for all while empowering profound established learning in an invigorated model that can secure the decency of crucial convictions and the inspiration driving propelled training. We imagine that there is a prerequisite for examining the ethical repercussions of the current control on headways of AI and the probability to wither the indulgence of personal data and perspectives with the limiting framework of barely any components. We in like manner acknowledge that it is principal to focus further research on the new openings of teachers on new learning pathways for higher endorsement understudies, with another plan of graduate properties, with consideration on the innovative brain, creative mind, and improvement; the strategy for limits and aptitudes that can scarcely be ever reproduced by machines.

REFERENCES

ABC. (n.d.). https://www.abc.net.au/news/2016-07-01/tesla-driver-killed-while-car-was-in-onautopilot/7560126

Air CCSE. (n.d.). http://airccse.org/journal/ijscai/papers/3114ijscai01. pdf

Albu, A. B. (2012). Learning Artificial Intelligence Clip by Clip. *IEEE Frontiers in Education Conference (FIE)*, 789–794.

Andrea, K., Holz, E. M., Sellers, E. W., & Vaughan, T. M. (2015). Toward independent home use of brain-computer interfaces: A decision algorithm for selection of potential end-users. *Archives of Physical Medicine and Rehabilitation*, *96*(3), S27–S32. doi:10.1016/j.apmr.2014.03.036 PMID:25721544

Barik, T., Everetty, M., Cardona-Rivera, R. E., Roberts, D. L., & Gehringer, E. F. (2013). A Community College Blended Learning Classroom Experience through Artificial Intelligence in Games. *IEEE Frontiers in Education Conference (FIE)*, 1525–1531.

Bayne, S. (2015). Teacherbot: Interventions in automated teaching. *Teaching in Higher Education*, *20*(4), 455–467. Advance online publication. doi:10.1080/13562517.2015.1020783

Bojic, I., & Arratia, J. (2015). Teaching K-12 students STEM-C related topics through playing and conducting research. *IEEE Frontiers in Education Conference (FIE)*, 548–555. 10.1109/FIE.2015.7344109

Bostrom, N. (2006). AI set to exceed human brain power. *CNN Science & Space*. http://edition.cnn.com/2006/TECH/ science/07/24/ai.bostrom/

Bostrom, N., & Yudkowsky, E. (2011). The ethics of artificial intelligence. In K. Frankish & W. M. Ransey (Eds.), *Cambridge handbook of artificial intelligence* (pp. 316–334). Cambridge University Press.

Botrel, L., Holz, E. M., & Kübler, A. (2015). Brain painting V2: Evaluation of P300-based brain-computer interface for creative expression by an end-user following the user-centered design. *Brain-Computer Interfaces*, *2*(2–3), 1–15. doi:10.1080/2326263X.2015.1100038

Chen, X., Wang, Y., Nakanishi, M., Gao, X., Jung, T. P., & Gao, S. (2015). High-speed spelling with a noninvasive brain– computer interface. *Proceedings of the National Academy of Sciences of the United States of America*, *112*(44), E6058–E6067. doi:10.1073/pnas.1508080112 PMID:26483479

Daisy Group. (n.d.). https://daisygroup.com/resource/how-artificialintelligence-will-improve-teaching-and-learning/

De Lange, C. (2015). Welcome to the bionic dawn. *New Scientist*, *227*(3032), 24–25. doi:10.1016/S0262-4079(15)30881-2

Deakin University. (2014). *IBM Watson now powering Deakin. A new partnership that aims to exceed students' needs*. http://archive.li/kEnXm

DFKI. (2015). *Intelligent Solutions for the Knowledge Society*. The German Research Center for Artificial Intelligence. https://www.dfki.de/web?set_language=en&cl=en

Dilger, W. (2005). *K¨unstliche Intelligenz in der Schule*. Technische Universit¨ at Chemnitz.

Diss, K. (2015). *Driverless trucks move iron ore at automated Rio Tinto mines*. ABC. http://www.abc.net.au/ news/2015-10-18/rio-tinto-opens-worlds-first-automated-mine/6863814

Featherston, E., Sridharan, M., Urban, S., & Urban, J. (2014). DOROTHY: Enhancing Bidirectional Communication between a 3D Programming Interface and Mobile Robots. *5th Symposium on Educational Advances in Artificial Intelligence.*

Fok, S., & Ong, E. (1996). A high school project on artificial intelligence in robotics. *Artificial Intelligence in Engineering*, *10*(1), 61–70. doi:10.1016/0954-1810(95)00016-X

Gallagher, P. (2015, Sept. 24). The University of Warwick launches new department to employ all temporary or fixed-term teaching staff. *The Independent.*

Getting Smart. (n.d.). https://gettingsmart.com/2015/11/8-ways-machinelearning-will-improve-education/

Gibney, E. (2017). Google secretly tested AI bot. *Nature*, *541*(7636), 142. doi:10.1038/nature.2017.21253 PMID:28079098

González, V. M., Robbes, R., Góngora, G., & Medina, S. (2015). Measuring concentration while programming with low-cost BCI devices: differences between debugging and creativity tasks. In *Foundations of augmented cognition* (pp. 605–615). Springer International Publishing. doi:10.1007/978-3-319-20816-9_58

Grove, J. (2015). TeachHigher 'disbanded' ahead of campus protest. *Times Higher Education.* https://www. timeshighereducation.com/news/teachhigher-disbanded-ahead-campus-protest

Growing Science. (n.d.). http://www.growingscience.com/ijiec/Vol7/IJIEC_2015_32.pdf

Heinze, C., Haase, J., & Higgins, H. (2010). An Action Research Reportfroma MultiYear Approach to Teaching Artificial Intelligence at the K6 Level. *1st Symposium on Educational Advances in Artificial Intelligence.*

Hillier, P., Wright, B., & Damen, P. (2015). *Readiness for self-driving vehicles in Australia.* http://advi.org.au/wp-content/ uploads/2016/04/Workshop-Report-Readiness-for-Self-Driving-Vehicles-in-Australia.pdf

IITM. (n.d.). http://www.cse.iitm.ac.in/~ravi/papers/Sarma_HOI T_07.pdf

Independent. (n.d.). https://www.independent.co.uk/news/education/educationnews/the-university-of-warwick-launches-new-department-to-employ-all-temporary-or-fixed-term-teaching10160384.html

Kübler, A., Holz, E. M., Sellers, E. W., & Vaughan, T. M. (2015). Toward independent home use of brain-computer interfaces: A decision algorithm for selection of potential end-users. *Archives of Physical Medicine and Rehabilitation, 96*(3), S27–S32. doi:10.1016/j.apmr.2014.03.036 PMID:25721544

Kumar, D., & Meeden, L. (1998). A Robot Laboratory for Teaching Artificial Intelligence. *29th Technical Symposium on Computer Science Education.*

Layer, R., Sherriff, M., & Tychonievich, L. (2012). Inform, Experience, Implement - Teaching an Intensive High School Summer Course. *IEEE Frontiers in Education Conference (FIE)*, 122–127.

Lazarus, S. S., Thurlow, M. L., Lail, K. E., & Christensen, L. (2008). A longitudinal analysis of state accommodations policies: Twelve years of change, 1993-2005. *The Journal of Special Education, 43*(2), 67–80. doi:10.1177/0022466907313524

Li, Z., O'Brien, L., Flint, S., & Sankaranarayana, R. (2014). Object-Oriented Sokoban Solver: A Serious Game Project for OOAD and AI Education. *IEEE Frontiers in Education Conference (FIE)*, 788–791. 10.1109/FIE.2014.7044115

Luckin, R. (2017). Towards artificial intelligence-based assessment systems. *Nature Human Behaviour, 1*(28). doi: 10. 1038/s41562-016-0028

Maderer, J. (2016). *Artificial intelligence course creates AI teaching assistant.* Georgia Tech News Center. http://www.news.gatech.edu/2016/05/09/artificial-intelligence-course-creates-ai-teaching-assistant

Mason, J., Khan, K., & Smith, S. (2016). Literate, numerate, discriminate—realigning 21st century skills. In W Chen (Ed.), *Proceedings of the 24th international conference on computers in education*, (pp. 609–614). Mumbai: Asia-Pacific Society for Computers in Education.

McGovern, A., Tidwell, Z., & Rushing, D. (2011). Teaching Introductory Artificial Intelligence through Java-Based Games. *2nd Symposium on Educational Advances in Artificial Intelligence.*

Mitcham, C. (2005). *Encyclopedia of science, technology, and ethics*. Macmillan Reference USA.

Neven, H. (2013). *Launching the quantum artificial intelligence lab.* Google Research Blog. http:// googleresearch.blogspot.com.au/2013/05/launching-quantum-artificial.html

Neven, H. (2015). *When can quantum annealing win?* Google Research Blog. http:// googleresearch. blogspot.com.au/2015/12/when-can-quantum-annealing-win.html

Pareto, L. (2016). A teachable agent game engaging primary school children to learn arithmetic concepts and reasoning. *International Journal of Artificial Intelligence in Education*, *26*(2), 582–599.

Pasquale, F. (2015). *The black box society. The secret algorithms that control money and information*. Harvard University Press. doi:10.4159/harvard.9780674736061

Perez, S. (2016). *Microsoft silences its new A.I. bot Tay, after Twitter users teach it racism*. TechCrunch. https://techcrunch.com/2016/03/24/microsoft-silences-its-new-a-i-bot-tay-after-twitter-users-teach-it-racism/

Popenici, S. (2015). Deceptive promises: the meaning of MOOCs-hype for higher education. In E. McKay & J. Lenarcic (Eds.), *Macro-level learning through massive open online courses (MOOCs): strategies and predictions for the future*. IGI Global. doi:10.4018/978-1-4666-8324-2.ch009

Popenici, S., & Kerr, S. (2013). *What undermines higher education, And how this impacts employment, economies and our democracies*. CreateSpace.

Reuters/ABC. (2016, July 2). Tesla crash: man who died in autopilot collision filmed previous near-miss, praised car's technology. *ABC News*.

Reyes, M., Perez, C., Upchurch, R., Yuen, T., & Zhang, Y. (2016). Using Declarative Programming in an Introductory Computer Science Course for High School Students. *6th Symposium on Educational Advances in Artificial Intelligence*.

Russell, S. J., & Norvig, P. (2010). *Artificial intelligence: a modern approach* (3rd ed.). Prentice-Hall.

Rutkin, A. (2015). *Therapist in my pocket. New Scientist, 227(3038)*.

Science Direct. (n.d.). https://www.sciencedirect.com/science/article/pii/0898122185900549

Shieber, S. M. (Ed.). (2004). *The Turing Test: Verbal Behavior as the Hallmark of Intelligence*. MIT Press. doi:10.7551/mitpress/6928.001.0001

Sklar, E., & Parsons, S. (2002). *RoboCupJunior: A Vehicle for Enhancing Technical Literacy*. AAAI Mobile Robot Competition 2002, Papers from the AAAI Workshop, Edmonton, Canada.

Stottler Henke. (n.d.). https://www.stottlerhenke.com/papers/ITS_using_AI_to_improve_training_performance_and_ROI.pdf

Teach Thought. (n.d.). https://www.teachthought.com/the-future-oflearning/10-roles-for-artificial-intelligence-ineducation/

Torrey, L. (2012). Teaching Problem-Solving in Algorithms and AI. *3rd Symposium on Educational Advances in Artificial Intelligence.*

Torrey, L., Johnson, K., Sondergard, S., Ponce, P., & Desmond, L. (2016). The Turing Test in the Classroom. *6th Symposium on Educational Advances in Artificial Intelligence.*

Tsukamoto, H., Takemura, Y., Nagumo, H., Ikeda, I., Monden, A., & Matsumoto, K. (2015). Programming education for primary school children using a textual programming language. *IEEE Frontiers in Education Conference (FIE)*, 1008–1014. 10.1109/FIE.2015.7344187

Tsur, O., Davidov, D., & Rappoport, A. (2010). Semi-supervised recognition of sarcastic sentences in Twitter and Amazon. In *Proceedings of the Fourteenth Conference on Computational Natural Language Learning*, (pp. 107-116). Uppsala: Association for Computational Linguistics.

Wolpaw, J. R., & Wolpaw, E. W. (2012). Brain-computer interfaces: something new under the sun. In W. Wolpaw (Ed.), *Brain-computer interfaces: principles and practice* (pp. 3–12). Oxford University Press. doi:10.1093/acprof:oso/9780195388855.003.0001

Compilation of References

ABC. (n.d.). https://www.abc.net.au/news/2016-07-01/tesla-driver-killed-while-car-was-in-onautopilot/7560126

Abou-Jaoude, S., & Frasson, C. (1998). An Agent for Selecting a Learning Strategy. NTICF 98, Rouen, France.

Agarwal, P. (2006). *Higher education in India: The need for change*. Working paper.

Ahuja, R., & Solanki, A. (2019). Movie Recommender System Using K-Means Clustering AND K-Nearest Neighbor. In *Confluence-2019:9th International Conference on Cloud Computing, Data Science & Engineering*. Amity Universty. DOI: 10.1109/CONFLUENCE.2019.8776969

Air CCSE. (n.d.). http://airccse.org/journal/ijscai/papers/3114ijscai01. pdf

Albu, A. B. (2012). Learning Artiðcial Intelligence Clip by Clip. *IEEE Frontiers in Education Conference (FIE)*, 789–794.

Alexander, P. M., Holmner, M., Lotriet, H. H., Matthee, M. C., Pieterse, H., Naidoo, S., & Jordaan, D. (2011). Factors affecting career choice: Comparison between students from computer and other disciplines. *Journal of Science Education and Technology*, *20*(3), 300–315. doi:10.100710956-010-9254-3

Al-Fedaghi, S. S. (2016). Knowledge representation in education: Diagramming Carroll's syllogisms. *Proceedings of the 2016 IEEE International Conference on Knowledge Engineering and Applications (ICKEA)*, 150-154. 10.1109/ICKEA.2016.7803009

Ali, A. M., & Gonzalez, A. J. (2017). Machine Learning from Conversation with Humans. *Proceedings of the Thirtieth International Florida Artificial Intelligence Research Society Conference*.

Alias, M., & Bakar, M. N. F. B. A. (2010). Factors Contributing to Programme Choice and Subsequent Career Selection among Engineering Students. *People*, *7*, 9.

Alimisis, D. (2013). Educational robotics: open questions and new challenges. *Themes in Science & Technology Education*, *6*(1), 63-71. Retrieved from https://files.eric.ed.gov/fulltext/EJ1130924.pdf

Allen, J. R. (2019). *Why we need to rethink education in the artificial intelligence age*. Retrieved from https://www.brookings.edu/research/why-we-need-to-rethink-education-in-the-artificial-intelligence-age/

Altinay, F., Karaatmaca, C., Altinay, Z., & Dagli, G. (2019). Developing at a great pace: Studies on artificial intelligence in higher education. *Bucharest, 2*, 330-337. Retrieved from https://search.proquest.com/openview/72ba8c770621633fdb11e1fbaad76430/1?pq-origsite=gscholar&cbl=1876338

Amazon AI Team. (2019). *Conversational AI: The Science Behind the Alexa Prize*. Author.

Andrea, K., Holz, E. M., Sellers, E. W., & Vaughan, T. M. (2015). Toward independent home use of brain-computer interfaces: A decision algorithm for selection of potential end-users. *Archives of Physical Medicine and Rehabilitation*, *96*(3), S27–S32. doi:10.1016/j.apmr.2014.03.036 PMID:25721544

Andriessen, J., & Sandberg, J. (1999). Where is education heading and how about AI? *International Journal of Artificial Intelligence in Education*, *10*, 130–150.

Anshu, K., Gaur, L., & Solanki, A. (2019). Impact of Chatbot in Transforming the Face of Retailing- An Empirical Model of Antecedents and Outcomes. *Recent Patents on Computer Science*, *12*. Advance online publication. doi:10.2174/2213275912666190809110804

Apple, M. W. (2013). *Educating the right way: Markets, standards, God, and inequality*. Routledge.

Arrieta, A. B., Díaz-Rodríguez, N., Del Ser, J., Bennetot, A., Tabik, S., Barbado, A., García, S., Gil-López, S., Molina, D., Benjamins, R., Chatila, R., & Herrera, F. (2020). Explainable Artificial Intelligence (XAI): Concepts, taxonomies, opportunities and challenges toward responsible AI. *Information Fusion*, *58*, 82–115. doi:10.1016/j.inffus.2019.12.012

Ary, D., Jacobs, L. C., Irvine, C. K. S., & Walker, D. (2018). *Introduction to research in education*. Cengage Learning.

Asci, F. H., Kosar, S. H., & Isler, A. K. (2001). The relationship of self-concept and perceived athletic competence to physical activity level and gender among Turkish early adolescent. *Adolescence*. Libra publications. *San Digego*, *36*(143), 499–507. PMID:11817631

Ashrafi, R., & Murtaza, M. (2008). Use and impact of ICT on SMEs in Oman. *The Electronic Information Systems Evaluations*, *11*(3), 125–138.

Asis, M. M. (2006). Living with migration: Experiences of left-behind children in the Philippines. *Asian Population Studies*, *2*(1), 45–67. doi:10.1080/17441730600700556

Aslam, M. Z., & Khan, A. R. (2011). *A proposed decision support system/expert system for guiding fresh students in selecting a faculty in Gomal university, Pakistan*. arXiv preprint arXiv:1104.1678

Bachelier, L., Baresi, L., & Quinton, C. (2015). Dynamically Evolving the Structural Variability of Dynamic Software Product Lines. *Proceedings of the 10th International Symposium on Software Engineering for Adaptive and Self-Managing Systems*, 57–63. 10.1109/SEAMS.2015.24

Baheti, R., & Gill, H. (2011). Cyber-Physical Systems. *The Impact of Control Technology, 12*, 161–166.

Ballantyne, D. (2004). Dialogue and its role in the development of relationship specific knowledge. *Journal of Business & Industrial Marketing, 9*(2), 114–123.

Barik, T., Everetty, M., Cardona-Rivera, R. E., Roberts, D. L., & Gehringer, E. F. (2013). A Community College Blended Learning Classroom Experience through Artiðcial Intelligence in Games. *IEEE Frontiers in Education Conference (FIE)*, 1525–1531.

Barson, J., Frommer, J., & Schwartz, M. (1993). Foreign language learning using e-mail in a task-oriented perspective: Interuniversity experiments in communication and collaboration. *Journal of Science Education and Technology, 2*(4), 565–584. doi:10.1007/BF00695325

Barta, B.-Z., Telam, M., & Gev, Y. (Eds.). (1995). *Information Technology in Educational Management*. Chapmann and Hall. doi:10.1007/978-0-387-34839-1

Bayne, S. (2015). Teacherbot: Interventions in automated teaching. *Teaching in Higher Education, 20*(4), 455–467. doi:10.1080/13562517.2015.1020783

Beaver & Freeman. (2020). *Towards Awareness of Human Relational Strategies in Virtual Agents*. Academic Press.

Beck, J., Stern, M., & Haugsjaa, E. (2005). *Applications of AI in education*. Retrieved from http://citeseerx.ist.psu.edu/viewdoc/download?doi=10.1.1.87.405&rep=rep1&type=pdf

Becker, B. E., & Luthar, S. S. (2002). Social-emotional factors affecting achievement outcomes among disadvantaged students: Closing the achievement gap. *Educational Psychologist, 37*(4), 197–214. doi:10.1207/S15326985EP3704_1 PMID:23255834

Bergmann, J., & Sams, A. (2012). *Flip your classroom: Reach every student in every class every day*. International Society for Technology in Education.

Bershadsky, A. M., & Krevsky, I. G. (1996). The Organization of Distance Education in Penza Region of Russian Federation. *Proceedings of the Second International Conference on Distance Education in Russia: Open and Distance Learning as a Development Strategy*, 174-176.

Berwick, R. (2003). *An Idiot's guide to Support vector machines (SVMs)*. Academic Press.

Best, J. W., & Kahn, J. V. (2016). *Research in education*. Pearson Education India.

Big Data in eLearning: The Future of eLearning Industry. (n.d.). Retrieved from https://elearningindustry.com/big-data-in-elearning-future-of-elearning-industry

Bill, F.(2017). *Intelligent Tutoring Systems: What happened?* Academic Press.

Bitter, G. G. (1989). *Micro Computers in Education Today*. Mitchel Publishing Inc.

Bjork, E., Ottosson, S., & Thorsteinsdottir, S. (2008). E-Learning for All. In E-Learning: 21st Century Issues and Challenges (pp. 49–69). Nova Science Publishers Inc.

Blumenfeld, P. C., Kempler, T. M., & Krajcik, J. S. (2006). *Motivation and cognitive engagement in learning environments*. Academic Press.

Bojic, I., & Arratia, J. (2015). Teaching K-12 students STEM-C related topics through playing and conducting research. *IEEE Frontiers in Education Conference (FIE)*, 548–555. 10.1109/FIE.2015.7344109

Borchert, M. (2002). *Career choice factors of high school students* (Unpublished Master of Science thesis). University of Wisconsin-Stout.

Bostrom, N. (2006). AI set to exceed human brain power. *CNN Science & Space*. http://edition.cnn.com/2006/TECH/ science/07/24/ai.bostrom/

Bostrom, N. (2006). AI set to exceed human brain power. *CNN Science &* Space. http://edition.cnn.com/2006/TECH/science/07/24/ai.bostrom/

Bostrom, N., & Yudkowsky, E. (2011). The ethics of artificial intelligence. In K. Frankish & W. M. Ransey (Eds.), *Cambridge handbook of artificial intelligence* (pp. 316–334). Cambridge University Press.

Botrel, L., Holz, E. M., & Kübler, A. (2015). Brain painting V2: Evaluation of P300-based brain-computer interface for creative expression by an end-user following the user-centered design. *Brain-Computer Interfaces, 2*(2–3), 1–15. doi:10.1080/2326263X.2015.1100038

Bourdieu, P., & Nice, R. (1977). *Outline of a Theory of Practice* (Vol. 16). Cambridge University Press.

Brachman, R. J., & Levesque, H. J. (2004). Knowledge Representation and Reasoning. Elsevier.

Bransford, J., Brown, A., & Cocking, R. (2000). *How People Learn: Brain, Mind, Experience, and School*. National Academy Press.

Breuker, J., & Muntjewerff, A. (1999). Ontological Modelling for Designing Educational Systems. *Proceedings of the AI & Education*, 101-122.

Brown, J. S., & Burton, R. R. (1978). Diagnostic Models for Procedural Bugs in Basic Mathematical Skills. *Cognitive Science, 2*(2), 155–191. doi:10.120715516709cog0202_4

Brown, R. (2000). Social identity theory: Past achievements, current problems and future challenges. *European Journal of Social Psychology, 30*(6), 745–778. doi:10.1002/1099-0992(200011/12)30:6<745::AID-EJSP24>3.0.CO;2-O

Bruner, J. (n.d.). *The Process of Education*. Cambridge, MA: Harvard University Press.

Bruner, J. S. (1996). *The culture of education*. Harvard University Press.

Brusilovsky, P. (1999). Adaptive and intelligent technologies for web-based eduction. *Ki, 13*(4), 19-25.

Brusilovsky, P., & Peylo, C. (2003). Adaptive and intelligent web-based educational systems. *International Journal of Artificial Intelligence in Education, 13*, 159–172.

Buchanan, B. G. (2005). A (very) brief history of artificial intelligence. *AI Magazine*, 26–53.

Burkart, N., Robert, S., & Huber, M. F. (2020). Are you sure? Prediction revision in automated decision making. *Expert Systems: International Journal of Knowledge Engineering and Neural Networks, 2020*, 1–19. doi:10.1111/exsy.12577

Burton, E., Goldsmith, J., Koenig, S., Kuipers, B., Mattei, N., & Walsh, T. (2017). Ethical considerations in Artificial Intelligence courses. *AI Magazine, 38*(2), 22–34. doi:10.1609/aimag.v38i2.2731

Burton, R. R., & Brown, J. S. (1979). An investigation of computer coaching for informal learning activities. *International Journal of Man-Machine Studies, 11*(1), 5–24. doi:10.1016/S0020-7373(79)80003-6

Callaghan, M. J. (2019). Voice Driven Virtual Assistant Tutor in Virtual Reality for Electronic Engineering Remote Laboratories. In M. Auer & R. Langmann (Eds.), *Smart Industry & Smart Education. Lecture Notes in Networks and Systems* (Vol. 47). Springer. doi:10.1007/978-3-319-95678-7_63

Carr, P., Geman, H., Madan, D. B., & Yor, M. (2002). The Fine Structure of Asset Returns: An Empirical Investigation. *The Journal of Business, 75*(2), 305–332. doi:10.1086/338705

Castelo, M. (2020). A 5-year vision for artificial intelligence in higher ed. *EdTech: Focus on Higher Education*. Retrieved from https://edtechmagazine.com/higher/article/2020/02/5-year-vision-artificial-intelligence-higher-ed

Chakarborty, R. C. (2010). *Knowledge Representation*. Retrieved from http://www.myreaders.info/03_Knowledge_Representations.pdf

Chen, X., Barnett, D., & Stephens, C. (2013). Fad or future: The advantages and challenges of massive open online courses (MOOCs). Research-to-Practice Conference in Adult and Higher Education, 20–21.

Chen, A. Y., Mashhadi, A., Ang, D., & Harkrider, N. (1999). Cultural issues in the design of technology-enhanced learning systems. *British Journal of Educational Technology, 30*(3), 217–230. doi:10.1111/1467-8535.00111

Cheney, G. R., Ruzzi, B. B., & Muralidharan, K. (2005). *A profile of the Indian education system*. Prepared for the New Commission on the Skills of the American Workforce.

Chen, X., Wang, Y., Nakanishi, M., Gao, X., Jung, T. P., & Gao, S. (2015). High-speed spelling with a noninvasive brain– computer interface. *Proceedings of the National Academy of Sciences of the United States of America, 112*(44), E6058–E6067. doi:10.1073/pnas.1508080112 PMID:26483479

Choi, E., Borkowski, M., Zakoian, J., Sagan, K., Scholla, K., Ponti, C., & Bielski, M. (2015). Utilizing content moderators to investigate critical factors for assessing the quality of answers on brainly, social learning Q&A platform for students: a pilot study. *Proceedings of the 78th ASIS&T Annual Meeting: Information Science with Impact: Research in and for the Community*. 10.1002/pra2.2015.145052010069

Choi, E., Munoz, R., Mukhlas, D., Balak, M., Farias, L., Jara, D., & Burkov, O. (2016). Understanding user motivations for asking and answering a question on brainly, online social learning network. *IConference 2016 Proceedings*.

Ciolacu, M., Tehrani, A. F., Binder, L., & Svasta, P. M. (2018). Education 4.0-Artificial Intelligence Assisted Higher Education: Early recognition System with Machine Learning to support Students' Success. *IEEE 24th Int. Symp. Des. Technol. Electron. Packag.*, 23-30.

Cole, S. A., & Shastry, G. K. (2009). *Smart money: The effect of education, cognitive ability, and financial literacy on financial market participation*. Harvard Business School Boston.

Collis, B. (1999). *Design, Development and Implementation of a WWW-Based Course-Support System. ICCE99*. IOS Press.

Conner & Miranda. (2002). The linkage among family structure, self-concept, effort and performance on mathematics achievement of American High School students by race. *American Secondary Education, 31*(1), 72-92.

Cont, R. (2004). *Financial modeling with jump processes*. Chapman and Hall CRC Press.

Cortese, A. D. (2003). The critical role of higher education in creating a sustainable future. *Planning for Higher Education, 31*(3), 15–22.

Cortez, P., & Silva, A. (2008). Using data mining to predict secondary school student performance. *Proceedings of 5th Annual Future Business Technology Conference*, 5-12.

Cradler, J., & Bridgforth, E. (2002). *Recent Research on the Effects of Technology on Teaching and Learning*. http://www.oten.info/conferences/jukes/research.pdf

Cristea, A., Okamoto, T., & Cristea, P. (2000). My English Teacher - An Evolutionary, Web-based, multi-Agent Environment for Academic English Teaching. Congress of Evolutionary Computation CEC 2000, San Diego, CA.

Criswell, E. L. (1989). *The Design of Computer-Based Instruction*. Macmillan Publishing Company.

Crowder, J., Carbone, J., & Friess, S. (2020). Abductive Artificial Intelligence Learning Models. In *Artificial Psychology* (pp. 51–63). Springer. doi:10.1007/978-3-030-17081-3_5

Crowe, S. (2018). *10 biggest challenges in robotics*. Retrieved from https://www.therobotreport.com/10-biggest-challenges-in-robotics/

Csorny, L. (2013). *Careers in the growing field of information technology services*. Academic Press.

Czarnecki, K., & Helsen, S. (2006). Feature-based survey of model transformation approaches. *IBM Systems Journal, 45*(3), 621–646.

Daisy Group. (n.d.). https://daisygroup.com/resource/how-artificialintelligence-will-improve-teaching-and-learning/

Daradoumis Haralabus, T., Fallin, J., Juan Prez, A., Martnez, F. J., Rodrguez-Ardura, I., & Xhafa, F. (2010). Customer Relationship Management applied to higher education: Developing an e-monitoring system to improve relationships in electronic learning environments. *International Journal of Services Technology and Management, 14*(1), 103–125. doi:10.1504/IJSTM.2010.032887

Daradoumis, T., Juan, A. A., Lera-Lpez, F., & Faulin, J. (2010). Using Collaboration Strategies to Support the Monitoring of Online Collaborative Learning Activity, in Technology Enhanced Learning. In Quality of Teaching and Educational Reform. Springer Berlin Heidelberg.

Davis, E., & Marcus, G. (2015). Commonsense Reasoning and Commonsense Knowledge in Artificial Intelligence. *Communications of the ACM, 58*(9), 92–103. doi:10.1145/2701413

De Lange, C. (2015). Welcome to the bionic dawn. *New Scientist, 227*(3032), 24–25. doi:10.1016/S0262-4079(15)30881-2

Deakin University. (2014). *IBM Watson now powering Deakin. A new partnership that aims to exceed students' needs.* http://archive.li/kEnXm

Delpit, L. (1988). The silenced dialogue: Power and pedagogy in educating other people's children. *Harvard Educational Review, 58*(3), 280–299. doi:10.17763/haer.58.3.c43481778r528qw4

Delpit, L. (2006). *Other people's children: Cultural conflict in the classroom.* The New Press.

Demiaux & Abdallah. (2017). *How Can Humans Keep the Upper Hand? The Ethical Matters Raised by Algorithms and Artificial Intelligence.* Report on the public debate led by the French Data Protection Authority (CNIL) as part of the ethical discussion assignment set by the Digital Republic Bill. Paris: CNIL.

Desai, G.H. (1979). A study of creativity in school teachers as measured by Mehdi's test in relation to their self-concept toward teaching, *M.U. Ind. Edu. Review, 22*(1).

Dewey, J. (2007). *Experience and education.* Simon and Schuster.

DFKI. (2015). *Intelligent Solutions for the Knowledge Society.* The German Research Center for Artificial Intelligence. https://www.dfki.de/web?set_language=en&cl=en

Dilger, W. (2005). *K¨unstliche Intelligenz in der Schule.* Technische Universit¨ at Chemnitz.

Diss, K. (2015). *Driverless trucks move iron ore at automated Rio Tinto mines.* ABC. http://www.abc.net.au/ news/2015-10-18/rio-tinto-opens-worlds-first-automated-mine/6863814

Diss, K. (2015). *Driverless trucks move iron ore at automated Rio Tinto mines.* ABC. https://www.abc.net.au/news/2015-10-18/rio-tinto-opens-worlds-firstautomated-mine/6863814

doi:10.4018/978-1-5225-2292-8

Doran, G. T. (1981). There'sa SMART way to write management's goals and objectives. *Management Review*, *70*(11), 35–36.

Drigas, A. S., & Ioannidou, R. (2012). Artificial Intelligence in special education: A decade review. *International Journal of Engineering Education*, *28*(6), 1366–1372.

Duque Méndez, N. D., Rodríguez Marín, P. A., & Ovalle Carranza, D. A. (2018). Intelligent Personal Assistant for Educational Material Recommendation Based on CBR. In A. Costa, V. Julian, & P. Novais (Eds.), *Personal Assistants: Emerging Computational Technologies. Intelligent Systems Reference Library* (Vol. 132). Springer. doi:10.1007/978-3-319-62530-0_7

Edwards, K., & Quinter, M. (2011). Factors influencing students career choices among secondary school students in Kisumu municipality, Kenya. *Journal of Emerging Trends in Educational Research and Policy Studies*, *2*(2), 81–87.

Eisenberg, M. B. (2010). Information literacy: Essential skills for the information age. *DESIDOC Journal of Library and Information Technology*, *28*(2), 39–47. doi:10.14429/djlit.28.2.166

Eisner, E. W. (2017). *The enlightened eye: Qualitative inquiry and the enhancement of educational practice*. Teachers College Press.

Elder, G. H. (2018). *Children of the great depression*. Routledge. doi:10.4324/9780429501739

Ercan, T. (2010). Effective use of cloud computing in educational institutions. *Procedia: Social and Behavioral Sciences*, *2*(2), 938–942. doi:10.1016/j.sbspro.2010.03.130

Erkolahti, R., Jonsson, J., Offer, D., & Steinhouser, H.C. (1992). Comparison of the self –mage of teenagers in Fineland, the united states and Germany. *Switzerland Journal of Adolescent Health*, *13*(5), 392–395. doi:10.1016/1054-139X(92)90036-B PMID:1390794

Etzioni, A., & Etzioni, O. (2017). Should Artificial Intelligence be regulated? *Issues in Science and Technology*, *33*(4), 32–36. https://papers.ssrn.com/sol3/papers.cfm?abstract_id=2993506

Etzioni, O., & Schoenick, C. (2018). Artificial Intelligence: What educators need to know. *Education Week*, *37*(16), 28–29. https://www.edweek.org/ew/articles/2018/01/10/artificial-intelligence-what-educators-need-to-know.html

Fägerlind, I., & Saha, L. J. (2016). *Education and national development: A comparative perspective*. Elsevier.

Faggella, D. (2017). *Examples of Artificial Intelligence in education*. Retrieved from https://www.techemergence.com/examples-of-artificial-intelligence-in-education/

Faure, E. (1972). *Learning to be: The world of education today and tomorrow*. Unesco.

Fauveland & Yu. (2016). *A Survey on Artiðcial Intelligence and Data Mining for MOOCs*. SciRate.

Featherston, E., Sridharan, M., Urban, S., & Urban, J. (2014). DOROTHY: Enhancing Bidirectional Communication between a 3D Programming Interface and Mobile Robots. *5th Symposium on Educational Advances in Artiðcial Intelligence*.

Fok, S., & Ong, E. (1996). A high school project on artiðcial intelligence in robotics. *Artificial Intelligence in Engineering*, *10*(1), 61–70. doi:10.1016/0954-1810(95)00016-X

Foltz, P. W. (2001). Semantic Processing: Statistical Approaches. In International Encyclopedia of the Social & Behavioral Sciences (pp. 13873-13878). Elsevier.

Fortino, G., & Trunfio, P. (2014). *Internet of Things based on Smart Objects: Technology, Middleware and Applications*. Springer. doi:10.1007/978-3-319-00491-4

Fournier, H., Kop, R., & Sitlia, H. (2011). The Value of Learning Analytics to Networked Learningona Personal Learning Environment. *Proceedings of the 1st International Conference on Learning Analytics and Knowledge*, 104–109. 10.1145/2090116.2090131

Frank, A., & Asuncion, A. (2010). *UCI machine learning repository*. University of California, School of Information and Computer Science, Irvine. http://archive.ics.uci.edu/ml

Frasson, C., & Aimeur, E. (1996). A Comparison of Three Learning Strategies in Intelligent Tutoring Systems. *Journal of Educational Computing Research*, *14*(4), 371–383. doi:10.2190/G6JP-3YPY-U7T1-CV8C

Friese, G. T., Pittman, J. T., & Hendee, J. C. (1995). *Studies of the use of wilderness for personal growth, therapy, education and leadership development: An annotation and evaluation*. University of Idaho, Wilderness Research Center.

Fry, E. (1960). Teaching Machine Dichotomy: Skinner vs. Pressey. *Psychological Reports*, (6), 11-14.

Gadanidis, G. (2017). Artificial Intelligence, computational thinking, and mathematics education. *The Information Journal of Information and Learning Technology*, *34*(2), 133–139. doi:10.1108/IJILT-09-2016-0048

Gallagher, P. (2015, Sept. 24). The University of Warwick launches new department to employ all temporary or fixed-term teaching staff. *The Independent*.

Gama, J. A. P., Caro, R., Hernan, C., Alvarado, D. B., Gomez, C. L. C., Gomez, G. H., & Mena, A. M. (2016). Work in progress—New education model based on competencies of higher education and iMIS with architectures. *IEEE Glob. Eng. Educ. Conf.*, 1065-70. 10.1109/EDUCON.2016.7474685

Gane, B. D., Zaidi, S. Z., & Pellegrino, J. W. (2018). Measuring What Matters: Using Technology to Assess Multidimensional Learning. *European Journal of Education*, *53*(2), 176–187. doi:10.1111/ejed.12269

Gartner, A., & Lipsky, D. K. (1987). Beyond special education: Toward a quality system for all students. *Harvard Educational Review*, *57*(4), 367–396. doi:10.17763/haer.57.4.kj517305m7761218

Gergen, K. J. (1994). Toward a post modern psychology. In S. Kavale (Ed.), *Psychlogy and Postmodernism*. Sage Publications.

Getting Smart. (n.d.). https://gettingsmart.com/2015/11/8-ways-machinelearning-will-improve-education/

Gibney, E. (2017). Google secretly tested AI bot. *Nature*, *541*(7636), 142. doi:10.1038/nature.2017.21253 PMID:28079098

Gilmore, D., & Self, J. (1988). The application of machine learning to intelligent tutoring systems Teaching. In *Intl. Conference on the Learning Sciences*. AACE.

Giordanella, K. B. (1996). *Self- concept in individual with learning disabilities: Influence of educational placement. (Ed.D.)*. Columbia University Teachers College.

Glaser, R. (1984). Education and thinking: The role of knowledge. *The American Psychologist*, *39*(2), 93–104. doi:10.1037/0003-066X.39.2.93

Goktas, Y., Yildirim, S., & Yildirim, Z. (2009). Main Barriers and Possible Enablers of ICTs Integration into Pre-service Teacher Education Programs. *Journal of Educational Technology & Society*, *12*(1), 193–204.

González, V. M., Robbes, R., Góngora, G., & Medina, S. (2015). Measuring concentration while programming with low-cost BCI devices: differences between debugging and creativity tasks. In *Foundations of augmented cognition* (pp. 605–615). Springer International Publishing. doi:10.1007/978-3-319-20816-9_58

Goodwin, G. P., & Johnson-Laird, P. N. (2005). Reasoning about relations. *Psychological Review*, *112*(2), 468–493. doi:10.1037/0033-295X.112.2.468 PMID:15783294

Gore, M. S. (1994). *Indian Education –Structure and Process*. Rawat Publication.

Gose, B. (2016). When the teaching assistant is a robot: Faculty members experiment with Artificial Intelligence in the classroom. *The Chronicle of Higher Education.* Retrieved from https://www.chronicle.com/article/When-the-Teaching-Assistant-Is/238114

Grawemeyer, B., Mavrikis, M., Holmes, W., & Gutiérrez-Santos, S. (2015). Adapting feedback types according to students' affective states. In *Artificial Intelligence in Education 17th International Conference, AIEd. Madrid, Spain, June 22-26, 2015 Proceedings* (Vol. 9112). Madrid, Spain: Springer International Publishing.

Greer, J. (1996). Student modelling. Student Modelling workshop at the User Modelling Conference.

Groffen, D. A., Koster, A., Bosma, H., van den Akker, M., Aspelund, T., Siggeirsdóttir, K., & Jónsson, P. V. (2013). Socioeconomic factors from midlife predict mobility limitation and depressed mood three decades later; Findings from the AGES-Reykjavik Study. *BMC Public Health*, *13*(1), 101. doi:10.1186/1471-2458-13-101 PMID:23379351

Grosan, C., & Abraham, A. (2011) Knowledge Representation and Reasoning. Intelligent Systems. Intelligent Systems Reference Library, 17. doi:10.1007/978-3-642-21004-4_6

Grove, J. (2015). TeachHigher 'disbanded' ahead of campus protest. *Times Higher Education*. https://www. timeshighereducation.com/news/teachhigher-disbanded-ahead-campus-protest

Growing Science. (n.d.). http://www.growingscience.com/ijiec/Vol7/IJIEC_2 015_32.pdf

Gustafson, S. M., & Gustafson, D. A. (2016). *Artificial Intelligence*. Retrieved from https://www. accessscience.com/content/artificial-intelligence/053300

Haggard, S. (2013). *The maturing of the MOOC: Literature review of Massive Open Online Courses and other forms of Online Distance Learning* (BIS Research Paper Number 130). Department for Business, Innovation and Skills, londonuk, Research Papers Research paper number 130.

Halford, G. S., Wilson, W. H., & Phillips, S. (1998). Processing capacity defined by relational complexity: Implications for comparative, developmental, and cognitive psychology. *Behavioral and Brain Sciences*, *21*(6), 803–831. doi:10.1017/S0140525X98001769 PMID:10191879

Hammond, L.D., Flook, L., Harvey, C. C., Barron, B., & Osher, D. (2019). *Implications for educational practice of the science of learning and development*. doi:10.1080/10888691.2018 .1537791

Hassan, Q. F., Khan, A. R., & Madani, S. A. (2017). Internet of Things: Challenges, Advances, and Applications. Chapman & Hall/CRC Computer and Information Science Series, CRC Press. doi:10.1007/978-3-319-55405-1

Hatzilygeroudis, I., & Prentzas, J. (2006). Knowledge Representation in Intelligent Educational Systems. In Web-based Intelligent E-learning Systems: Technologies and Applications (pp.175-192). IGI Global. Doi:10.4018/978-1-59140-729-4.ch009

Haugeland. (1985). *Artificial Intelligence: The Very Idea*. MIT Press.

Hawking, S., Russell, S., Tegmark, M., & Wilczek, F. (2014). *Transcendence looks at the implications of artificial intelligence - but are we taking AI seriously enough?* Retrieved from http://www. independent.co.uk/news/science/stephen-hawkingtranscendence-looks-at-the-implications-ofartificial-intelligence--but-are-we-taking-ai-seriouslyenough-9313474.html

Heath, N. L., & Brown, A. E. (1999). Self-concept differentiation and depressive symptomatology in children. *International Journal of Psychology*, *34*(2), 95–105. doi:10.1080/002075999399990

Heinze, C., Haase, J., & Higgins, H. (2010). An Action Research Reportfroma Multi Year Approach to Teaching Artificial Intelligence at the K6 Level. *1st Symposium on Educational Advances in Artiðcial Intelligence*.

Hellerstein, J., Diao, Y., & Parekh, S. (2004). *Feedback control of computing systems*. Wiley Interscience. doi:10.1002/047166880X

Heo, J., & Lee, J. (2019). CiSA: An Inclusive Chatbot Service for International Students and Academics. In C. Stephanidis (Ed.), Lecture Notes in Computer Science: Vol. 11786. *HCI International 2019 – Late Breaking Papers*. Springer. doi:10.1007/978-3-030-30033-3_12

Hillier, P., Wright, B., & Damen, P. (2015). *Readiness for self-driving vehicles in Australia.* http://advi.org.au/wp-content/ uploads/2016/04/Workshop-Report-Readiness-for-Self-Driving-Vehicles-in-Australia.pdf

Hoekstra, H. A., & Van Slujis, E. (2003). *Managing Competences: Implementing Human Resource Management*. Koninklijke Van Gorcum.

Hofstede, G. (1986). Cultural differences in teaching and learning. *International Journal of Intercultural Relations*, *10*(3), 301–320. doi:10.1016/0147-1767(86)90015-5

Holstein, K., McLaren, B. M., & Aleven, V. (2017). Intelligent tutors as teachers' aides. In *Proceedings of the Seventh International Learning Analytics & Knowledge Conference on -LAK 2017*. New York: ACM Press.

Hunter, J. D. (2008). *The death of character: Moral education in an age without good or evil.* Basic Books.

Iglesia, D. G. (2014). *MAPE-K Formal Templates for Self-Adaptive Systems: Specifications and Descriptions. Smaland.* Linnaeus University.

IITM. (n.d.). http://www.cse.iitm.ac.in/~ravi/papers/Sarma_HOI T_07.pdf

Inaba, A., & Okamoto, T. (1997). Negotiation Process Model for intelligent discussion coordinating system on CSCL environment. *AIED*, *97*, 175–182.

Independent. (n.d.). https://www.independent.co.uk/news/education/educationnews/the-university-of-warwick-launches-new-department-to-employ-all-temporary-or-fixed-term-teaching10160384.html

Intelligent Tutoring Systems. (2018). *Wikipedia*. Retrieved from https://en.wikipedia.org/wiki/ Intelligent_tutoring_system#Limitations

Irshat, K., Petr, R., & Irina, R. (2018). The Selecting of Artificial Intelligence Technology for Control of Mobile Robots. *Int. Multi-Conference Ind. Eng. Mod. Technol.*, 1-4.

Islam, J., & Zhang, Y. (2018). Brain MRI analysis for Alzheimer's disease diagnosis using an ensemble system of deep convolutional neural networks. *Brain Informatics*, *5*(2), 2. doi:10.118640708-018-0080-3 PMID:29881892

Jaiswal, S. (n.d.). *Knowledge represent.* Retrieved from https://www.javatpoint.com/knowledge-representation-in-ai

Januszewski, A., & Molenda, M. (Eds.). (2008). *Educational technology: a definition with commentary*. Lawrence Erlbaum Associates.

Jennex, M. E. (2005). What is KM? *International Journal of Knowledge Management*, *1*(4), i–iv.

Jennex, M. E., & Olfman, L. (2002). Organizational memory/knowledge effects on productivity, A lon-gitudinal study. In *Proceedings of the 35th Hawaii International Conference on System Sciences, HICSS35*. IEEE Computer Society. 10.1109/HICSS.2002.994053

Jing, F., & Shiying, K. (2010). Application of data mining for emotional intelligence based on cluster analysis. *IEEE Int. Conf. Artif. Intell. Educ.*, 512-15. 10.1109/ICAIE.2010.5640962

Johnstone, D. B., & Marcucci, P. N. (2007). *Worldwide trends in higher education finance: Cost-sharing, student loans, and the support of academic research.* Commissioned paper V. Lynn Meek and Dianne Davies, 81.

Jongbloed, B., Enders, J., & Salerno, C. (2008). Higher education and its communities: Interconnections, interdependencies and a research agenda. *Higher Education, 56*(3), 303–324. doi:10.100710734-008-9128-2

Jorgensen, M., & Shepperd, M. (2007). A Systematic Review of Software Development Cost Estimation Studies. *IEEE Transactions on Software Engineering, 33*(1), 33–53. doi:10.1109/TSE.2007.256943

Juan, A. A., Daradoumis, T., Faulin, J., & Xhafa, F. (2009). andF.Xhafa, A data analysis model based on control charts to monitor online learning processes. *Int.J.Bus.Intell. Data Min., 4*(2), 159–174. doi:10.1504/IJBIDM.2009.026906

Jury, L. E., Willower, D. J., & Delacy, W. J. (1976). Teacher self-concept and pupil control ecology. *The Alberta Journal of Educational Research, 21*(4), 295–300.

Kanchana, M. (2002). Self - concept and Career decision –marking self- efficacy of under graduate College students; Indian and American comparisons. *Journal of Psychological Researched, 46*(1), 17–26.

Kanda, T., Hirano, T., Eaton, D., & Ishiguro, H. (2004). Interactive robots as social partners and peer tutors for children: A field trial. *Human-Computer Interaction, 19*(1), 61–84. doi:10.120715327051hci1901&2_4

Kaplan, H. (1998). Building your Web Course: The Case for Off-the-Shelf Component Software. *Cause/Effect Journal, 21*(4). https: //www.educause.edu/ir/library/html/cem9849.html

Kaplan, J. (2016). Artificial Intelligence: What Everyone Needs to Know. What Everyone Needs to Know. Oxford University Press.

Kasai, T., & Okamoto, T. (1999). *The Support for Collaborative Learning with Companion Agents, ICCE 99, IOS (Ohmsha).* Press.

Kashtwari, D.M., & Wani, Z.A. (2019). *MOOCS: the Indian journey so far: Ubiquitous Inclusive Learning in a Digital Era.* Doi:10.4018/978-1-5225-6292-4.ch002

Katalnikova, S., Novickis, L., Prokofyeva, N., Uskov, V., & Heinemann, C. (2017). Intelligent Collaborative Educational Systems and Knowledge Representation. *Procedia Computer Science, 104*, 166–173. doi:10.1016/j.procs.2017.01.097

Kayama, M., Okamoto, T., & Cristea, A. (2000). Exploratory Activity Support based on a Semantic Feature Map. *Adaptive Hypermedia Conference (AH 2000)*, Trento, Italy. 10.1007/3-540-44595-1_44

Kendall, M.G. (1953). The analysis of economic time-series. *J. of the Royal Statistical Society, 96*, 11-25.

Keromytis, A. D. (2007). Characterizing Software Self-healing Systems. In *Computer Network Security* (pp. 22–33). Springer. doi:10.1007/978-3-540-73986-9_2

Kharb, L., Aggarwal, L., & Chahal, D. (2020). A Contingent Exploration on Big Data Tools. *Lecture Notes in Electrical Engineering, 637*. 10.1007/978-981-15-2612-1_71

Klein, Kim, Deng, Senellart, & Rush. (2107). *Opennmt: "Open-source toolkit for neural machine translation."* Academic Press.

Klix, F. (2001). Problem Solving: Deduction, Induction, and Analogical Reasoning. In International Encyclopedia of the Social & Behavioral Sciences (pp. 12123-12130). Elsevier.

Klutka, J., Ackerly, N., & Magda, A. J. (2018). *Artificial intelligence in higher education: Current uses and future applications*. Retrieved from https://49hk843qjpwu3gfmw73ngy1k-wpengine.netdna-ssl.com/wp-content/uploads/2018/11/201811-AI-in-Higher-Education-TLH.pdf

Knowledge representation techniques. AI lectures. (n.d.). Retrieved from http://www.hbcse.tifr.res.in/jrmcont/notespart1/node38.html

Kotsiantis, S. B. (2012). Use of machine learning techniques for educational proposes: A decision support system for forecasting students' grades. *Artificial Intelligence Review, 37*(4), 331–344. doi:10.100710462-011-9234-x

Kovarik. (2009). Cognitive Research: Knowledge Representation and Learning. Cognitive Radio Technology, 367-399. doi:10.1016/B978-0-12-374535-4.00012-6

Kruse, S. D., & Louis, K. S. (1993). *Developing Professional Community in New and Restructuring Urban Schools*. Academic Press.

Kumar, A. (2017). *10 roles for Artificial Intelligence in education*. Retrieved from https://www.linkedin.com/pulse/10-roles-artificial-intelligence-education-anil-kumar

Kumar, D., & Meeden, L. (1998). A Robot Laboratory for Teaching Artiðcial Intelligence. *29th Technical Symposium on Computer Science Education*.

Kumunzhiev, K. V. (2003). *Teoriya sistem i sistemnyy analiz: ucheb*. Ulyanovsk: UlGU.

Kuzmina, A. V. (2010). Variance gamma process simulation and its parameters estimation. In *Computer data analysis and modeling: complex stochastic data and systems: Proc. of the ninth intern. conf.* Belorussian State University.

Laanpere, M., Pata, K., Normak, P., & Põldoja, H. (2014). Pedagogy-driven Design of Digital Learning Ecosystems. *Computer Science and Information Systems*, *11*(1), 419–442. doi:10.2298/CSIS121204015L

Lambert, K. (2018). Could Artificial Intelligence replace our teachers? *Education World.* Retrieved from https://www.educationworld.com/could-artificial-intelligence-replace-our-teachers

Lantos, G. P. (2001). The boundaries of strategic corporate social responsibility. *Journal of Consumer Marketing*, *18*(7), 595–632. doi:10.1108/07363760110410281

Lardjane, S., & Anna Nuutinen, M. (2014). *Knowledge Representation for High Quality Learning. hal-01098521f.* Retrieved from https://hal.archives-ouvertes.fr/hal-01098521/document

Lasswell, H. D. (1948). The structure and function of communication in society. *The Communication of Ideas, 37*, 215-228.

Lawless, K. A., & Pellegrino, J. W. (2007). Professional development in integrating technology into teaching and learning: Knowns, unknowns, and ways to pursue better questions and answers. *Review of Educational Research*, *77*(4), 575–614. doi:10.3102/0034654307309921

Lawrence, J. E. (2013). *A practical guide for developing research proposal in IS*. Lap Lambert Academic Publishing.

Lawrence, J. E., & Tar, U. A. (2013). The use of grounded theory technique as a practical tool for qualitative data collection and analysis. *Electronic Journal of Business Research Methods*, *11*(1), 29.

Lawrence, J. E., & Tar, U. A. (2018). Factors that influence teachers' adoption and integration of ICT in teaching/learning process. *Educational Media International*, *55*(1), 79–105. doi:10.1080/09523987.2018.1439712

Layer, R., Sherriff, M., & Tychonievich, L. (2012). Inform, Experience, Implement - Teaching an Intensive High School Summer Course. *IEEE Frontiers in Education Conference (FIE)*, 122–127.

Lazarus, S. S., Thurlow, M. L., Lail, K. E., & Christensen, L. (2008). A longitudinal analysis of state accommodations policies: Twelve years of change, 1993-2005. *The Journal of Special Education*, *43*(2), 67–80. doi:10.1177/0022466907313524

Learner, R. A. (2006). teacher as researcher. *Teachers Engaged in Research: Inquiry Into Mathematics Classrooms. Grades, 3-5*, 129.

Lee, K. (2018). Tech companies should stop pretending AI won't destroy jobs. *MIT Technology Review.* Retrieved from https://www.technologyreview.com/s/610298/tech-companies-should-stop-pretending-ai-wont-destroy-jobs/

Lee, E. A., & Seshia, S. A. (2016). *Introduction to Embedded Systems: A Cyber-Physical Systems Approach.* MIT Press.

Lehtomäki, E., Moate, J., & Posti-Ahokas, H. (2016). Global connectedness in higher education: Student voices on the value of cross-cultural learning dialogue. *Studies in Higher Education*, *41*(11), 2011–2027. doi:10.1080/03075079.2015.1007943

Levinson, B. A. (1996). *The Cultural Production of the Educated Person. Critical Ethnographies of Schooling and Local Practice. SUNY Series, Power, Social Identity, and Education*. ERIC.

Levinson, B. U. (2001). *We are all equal: Student culture and identity at a Mexican secondary school, 1988–1998*. Duke University Press. doi:10.1215/9780822381075

Lewis, T. L., & Maurer, D. (2005). Multiple Sensitive Periods in Human Visual Development: Evidence from Visually Deprived Children. *Developmental Psychobiology*, *46*(3), 163–183. doi:10.1002/dev.20055 PMID:15772974

Li, Liu, Sun, & Yu. (2020). *Artificial intelligence based method and apparatus for generating information*. Google Patents.

Lickona, T. (1996). Eleven principles of effective character education. *Journal of Moral Education*, *25*(1), 93–100. doi:10.1080/0305724960250110

Lieto, A., & Radicioni, D. P. (2016). From human to artificial cognition and back, new perspectives on cognitively inspired AI systems. *Cognitive Systems Research*, *39*, 1–3. Advance online publication. doi:10.1016/j.cogsys.2016.02.002

Li, M., & Bray, M. (2007). Cross-border flows of students for higher education: Push–pull factors and motivations of mainland Chinese students in Hong Kong and Macau. *Higher Education*, *53*(6), 791–818. doi:10.100710734-005-5423-3

Lin, L. C., & Prez, A. J. (2015). Educational Data Mining and Learning Analytics: Differences, similarities, and time evolution. *Rev. Univ. Soc. Conoc.*, *12*(3), 98–112. doi:10.7238/rusc.v12i3.2515

Lin, X., Rivenson, Y., Yardimci, N. T., Veli, M., Luo, Y., Jarrahi, M., & Ozcan, A. (2018). All-optical machine learning using diffractive deep neural networks. *Science*, *361*(6406), 1004–1008. doi:10.1126cience.aat8084 PMID:30049787

Li, R., Li, Y., Meng, Z., Song, Y., & Jaing, G. (2020). Rumor Spreading Model Considering Individual Activity and Refutation Mechanism Simultaneously. *IEEE Access: Practical Innovations, Open Solutions*, *8*, 63065–63076. doi:10.1109/ACCESS.2020.2983249

Li, Z., O'Brien, L., Flint, S., & Sankaranarayana, R. (2014). Object-Oriented Sokoban Solver: A Serious Game Project for OOAD and AI Education. *IEEE Frontiers in Education Conference (FIE)*, 788–791. 10.1109/FIE.2014.7044115

Lockard, J., Peter, D. A., & Wesley, A. M. (1987). *Micro Computers for Educators*. Little Brown & Co.

Lodders, N., & Meijers, F. (2017). Collective learning, transformational leadership and new forms of careers guidance in universities. *British Journal of Guidance & Counselling*, *45*(5), 532–546. doi:10.1080/03069885.2016.1271864

Louie, A. H. (2007). A Living System Must Have Noncomputable Models. *Artificial Life, 13*(3), 293–297. doi:10.1162/artl.2007.13.3.293 PMID:17567248

Lu, J. J., & Harris, L. A. (2018). Artificial intelligence (AI) and education. *In Focus*. Retrieved from https://fas.org/sgp/crs/misc/IF10937.pdf

Lucas, S. (2017). *Artificial Intelligence (AI) in Architecture. What are the practical applications?* www.futurearchi.org

Luckin, R. (2017). Towards artificial intelligence-based assessment systems. *Nature Human Behaviour, 1*(28). doi: 10. 1038/s41562-016-0028

Luckin, R., Holmes, W., Griffiths, M., & Forcier, L. B. (2016). Intelligence unleashed: An argument for AI in education. London: Pearson. Retrieved from file:///C:/Users/Dr.%20S/Desktop/IGI%20(AI%20in%20education)/Intelligence-Unleashed-Publication%202016.pdf

Luckin, R. (2018). *Machine Learning and Human Intelligence: The Future of Education for the 21st Century*. UCL Institute of Education Press.

Luehrmann, A. W. (1972). Should the computer teach the student, or vice versa? *Proceedings of the Spring Joint Computer Conference*.

Lynch, M. (2018). *7 roles for artificial intelligence in education*. Retrieved from https://www.thetechedvocate.org/7-roles-for-artificial-intelligence-in-education/

Madan, D. B. (n.d.). *CGMY and Mexner subordinators are absolutely continuous with respect to one side stable subordinators*. https://arxiv.org/pdf/math/0601173v2.pdf

Madda, M. J. (2017). *Educators on Artificial Intelligence: Here's the one thing it can't do well*. Retrieved from https://www.edsurge.com/news/2017-11-20-educators-on-artificial-intelligence-here-s-the-one-thing-it-can-t-do-well

Maderer, J. (2016). *Artificial intelligence course creates AI teaching assistant*. Georgia Tech News Center. http://www.news.gatech.edu/2016/05/09/artificialintelligence-course-creates-ai-teaching-assistant

Maderer, J. (2016). *Artificial intelligence course creates AI teaching assistant*. Georgia Tech News Center. http://www.news.gatech.edu/2016/05/09/artificial-intelligence-course-creates-ai-teaching-assistant

Maguire, E. A., Gadian, D. G., Johnsrude, I. S., Good, C. D., Ashburner, J., Frackowiak, R. S. J., & Frith, C. D. (2000). Navigation Related Structural Change in the Hippocampi of Taxi Drivers. *Proceedings of the National Academy of Sciences of the United States of America, 97*(8), 4398–4403. doi:10.1073/pnas.070039597 PMID:10716738

Mahadevan, S. (2018). Imagination machines: a new challenge for artificial intelligence. *Thirty-Second AAAI Conf. Artif. Intell.*

Mahon, J., Bryant, B., Brown, B., & Kim, M. (2010). Using second life to enhance classroom management practice in teacher education. *Educational Media International*, *47*(2), 121–134. doi:10.1080/09523987.2010.492677

Mainzer, K. (2020). A Short History of the AI. In *Artificial intelligence - When do machines take over? Technik im Fokus*. Springer., doi:10.1007/978-3-662-59717-0_2

Mallawaarachchi, V. (2017). *Living with robots – the good, the bad and the ugly on humanity*. Retrieved from https://becominghuman.ai/living-with-robots-the-good-the-bad-and-the-ugly-on-humanity-1097f524f936

Mandela, N. (2014). Education is the most powerful weapon which you can use to change the world. *Computer, 8*.

Manju, A., & Nigam, M. J. (2014). Applications of quantum-inspired computational intelligence: A survey. *Artificial Intelligence Review*, *42*(1), 79–156. doi:10.100710462-012-9330-6

Mannino, A., Althaus, D., Erhardt, J., Gloor, L., Hutter, A., & Metzinger, T. (2015). *Artificial Intelligence: Opportunities and risks*. Retrieved from https://ea-foundation.org/files/ai-opportunities-and-risks.pdf

Marginson, S. (2006). Dynamics of national and global competition in higher education. *Higher Education*, *52*(1), 1–39. doi:10.100710734-004-7649-x

Marr, B. (2018). How Is AI Used In Education — Real World Examples Of Today And A Peek Into. *Future*.

Marshall University's Center for Instructional Technology. (n.d.). *Comparison of Online Course Delivery Software Products*. http//multimedia.marshall.edu/cit/webct/compare/comparison.htm

Martin, F. G. (2012). Will massive open online courses change how we teach? *Communications of the ACM*, *55*(8), 26–28. doi:10.1145/2240236.2240246

Mason, J., Khan, K., & Smith, S. (2016). Literate, numerate, discriminate—realigning 21st century skills. In W Chen (Ed.), *Proceedings of the 24th international conference on computers in education*, (pp. 609–614). Mumbai: Asia-Pacific Society for Computers in Education.

Masood, M., & Mokmin, N. A. (2017). Case-based Reasoning Intelligent Tutoring System: An Application of Big Data and IoT. *Proceedings of the 2017 International Conference on Big Data Research*, 28-32. 10.1145/3152723.3152735

McArthur, D., Lewis, M., & Bishay, M. (2005). The role of Artificial Intelligence in education: Current progress and future prospects. *I-manager's Journal of Educational Technology*, *1*(4), 42–80. doi:10.26634/jet.1.4.972

McCarthy, J. (2006). *The philosophy of AI and the AI of philosophy*. Retrieved from http://jmc.stanford.edu/articles/aiphil2.html

McCarthy, J. (2007). *What is Artificial Intelligence?* Retrieved from http://jmc.stanford.edu/artificial-intelligence/index.html

McCarthy, T., Rosenblum, P., Johnson, B. G., Dittel, J., & Kearns, D. M. (2016). An artificial intelligence tutor: A supplementary tool for teaching and practicing Braille. *Journal of Visual Impairment & Blindness.* Retrieved from https://files.eric.ed.gov/fulltext/EJ1114767.pdf

McCarthy, J., Minsky, M. L., Rochester, N., & Shannon, C. E. (2006). A proposal for the Dartmouth summer research project on Artificial Intelligence. *AI Magazine, 27*(4), 12–14. http://jmc.stanford.edu/articles/dartmouth.html

McClure, P. K. (2018). "You're fired," says the robot: The rise of automation in the workplace, technophobes, and fears of unemployment. *Social Science Computer Review, 36*(2), 139–156. doi:10.1177/0894439317698637

McEvoy, C. (2003). *Factors that Influence Parental Choice of School and Experiences in a Rural Education Market.* National University of Ireland Maynooth.

McGovern, A., Tidwell, Z., & Rushing, D. (2011). Teaching Introductory Artiðcial Intelligence through Java-Based Games. *2nd Symposium on Educational Advances in Artiðcial Intelligence.*

Mengash, H. A. (2020). Using Data Mining Techniques to Predict Student Performance to Support Decision Making in University Admission Systems. *IEEE Access: Practical Innovations, Open Solutions, 8*, 55462–55470. doi:10.1109/ACCESS.2020.2981905

Meredith, J. P. (2010). Combating cyberbullying: Emphasizing education over criminalization. *Fed. Comm. LJ, 63*, 311.

Michalski, R. S., Carbonell, J. G., & Mitchell, T. M. (2013). *Machine learning: An artificial intelligence approach.* Springer Science & Business Media.

Michalski, R. S., Carbonell, J. G., & Mitchell, T. M. (2013). *Machine Learning: An Artificial Intelligence Approach.* Springer Science & Business Media.

Mislevy, R. J. (2018). *Sociocognitive Foundations of Educational Measurement.* Routledge. doi:10.4324/9781315871691

Mitcham, C. (2005). *Encyclopedia of science, technology, and ethics.* Macmillan Reference USA.

Mkrtchian, V., Bershadsky, A., Bozhday, A., & Fionova, L. (2015). Model in SM of DEE Based on Service-Oriented Interactions at Dynamic Software Product Lines. In *Identification, Evaluation, and Perceptions of Distance Education Experts* (pp. 231–248). IGI Global. doi:10.4018/978-1-4666-8119-4.ch014

Monostori, L., Kádár, B., Bauernhansl, T., Kondoh, S., Kumara, S., Reinhart, G., Sauer, O., Schuh, G., Sihn, W., & Ueda, K. (2016). Cyber-Physical Systems in Manufacturing. *CIRP Annals, 65*(2), 621–641. doi:10.1016/j.cirp.2016.06.005

Morey, A. I. (2000). Changing higher education curricula for a global and multicultural world. *Higher Education in Europe*, *25*(1), 25–39. doi:10.1080/03797720050002170

Morey, A. I. (2004). Globalization and the emergence of for-profit higher education. *Higher Education*, *48*(1), 131–150. doi:10.1023/B:HIGH.0000033768.76084.a0

Morreale, S. P., & Pearson, J. C. (2008). Why communication education is important: The centrality of the discipline in the 21st century. *Communication Education*, *57*(2), 224–240. doi:10.1080/03634520701861713

Munster, W. W. U. OpenUSS. (n.d.). Retrieved from https://www.uni-muenster.de/ studium/orga/openuss.html

Murphy, R. F. (2019). *Artificial intelligence applications to support K-12 teachers and teaching: A review of promising applications, opportunities, and challenges*. Retrieved from https://www.rand.org/content/dam/rand/pubs/perspectives/PE300/PE315/RAND_PE315.pdf

Murphy, R., Murphy, R. R., & Arkin, R. C. (2000). *Introduction to AI robotics*. MIT Press.

Namayanja, J., & Janeja, V. P. (2012). An Assessment of Patient Behavior Over Time–Periods: A Case Study of Managing Type 2 Diabetes Through Blood Glucose Readings and Insulin Doses. *Journal of Medical Systems*, *36*(S1), 65–80. doi:10.100710916-012-9894-3 PMID:23104240

Nandi, A., & Mandernach, M. (2016). Hackathons as an informal learning platform. *Proceedings of the 47th ACM Technical Symposium on Computing Science Education*.

Nayor, P.R., Dave, P.N., & Arora, K. (1982). *The Teacher and Education in Emerging Indian Society*. NCERT.

Neven, H. (2013). *Launching the quantum artificial intelligence lab*. Google Research Blog. http:// googleresearch.blogspot.com.au/2013/05/launching-quantum-artificial.html

Neven, H. (2015). *When can quantum annealing win?* Google Research Blog. http://googleresearch.blogspot.com.au/2015/12/when-can-quantum-annealing-win.html

Ng, H.-W., Nguyen, V. D., Vonikakis, V., & Winkler, S. (2015). Deep learning for emotion recognition on small datasets using transfer learning. In *Proceedings of the 2015 ACM on international conference on multimodal interaction*, (pp. 443–449). ACM.- 2015. 10.1145/2818346.2830593

Nichols, J., & Goul, M. (2006). Synergizing the Artificial Intelligence and Decision Support Research Streams: Over a Decade of Progress with New Challenges on the Horizon. In *Intelligent Decision-making Support Systems. Decision Engineering*. Springer. doi:10.1007/1-84628-231-4_3

Nkambou, R., IsaBelle, C., & Frasson, C. (1998). *Supporting some pedagogical issues in a Web-based distance learning environment*. NTICF'98, Conference Internationale sur les nouvelles technologies de la communication et de la formation, Rouen, France.

Nkambou, R., IsaBelle, C., & Frasson, C. (1998). *Supporting some pedagogical issues in a Web-based distance learning environment.* NTICF'98, Conference Internationale surles nouvelles technologies de la communication et de la formation, Rouen, France.

Noddings, N. (2013). *Caring: A relational approach to ethics and moral education.* Univ of California Press.

Novak, E., Razzouk, R., & Johnson, T. E. (2012). The educational use of social annotation tools in higher education: A literature review. *The Internet and Higher Education, 15*(1), 39–49. doi:10.1016/j.iheduc.2011.09.002

Oblinger, D. G. (2018). Smart machines and human expertise: Challenges for higher education. *EDUCAUSE Review.* Retrieved from https://er.educause.edu/articles/2018/8/smart-machines-and-human-expertise-challenges-for-higher-education

Oddershede, L., & Petersen, K. D. (2015). Adjustment of foreign EQ-5D-3L utilities can increase their transferability. *Clin Outcomes Res, 7*, 629–639. doi:10.2147/CEOR.S93280 PMID:26719715

Ohler, J. (2011). Digital citizenship means character education for the digital age. *Kappa Delta Pi Record, 47*(sup1), 25-27.

Okamoto, T., Cristea, A., Matsui, T., & Miwata, T. (2000). Development, and Evaluation of a Mental Model Forming Support ITS - the Qualitative Diagnosis Simulator for the SCS Operation Activity. OZCHI 2000, Sydney, Australia.

Olamide, S. O., & Olawaiye, S. O. (2013). The factors determining the choice of career among secondary school students. *International Journal of Engineering Science, 2*(6), 33–44.

Onah, D., Sinclair, J., & Boyatt, R. (2014). Dropout rates of massive open online courses: behavioral patterns. *Proceedings of the 6th International Conference on Education and New Learning Technologies*, 5825–5834.

Ortiz, A. M., & Shaunna, S. (2015). The power of educational robotics as an integrated STEM learning experience in teacher preparation programs. *Journal of College Science Teaching, 44*(5), 42–47. doi:10.2505/4/jcst15_044_05_42

Owens, R. G. (1995). *Organizational behavior in education.* Academic Press.

Paiva, A. (1996). Communicating with Learner Modelling Agents. *ITS 96 Workshop on Architectures and Methods for Designing Cost-Effective and Reusable ITSs.*

Pandey, S., & Solanki, A. (2019). Music Instrument Recognition using Deep Convolutional Neural Networks. *International Journal of Information Technology.* doi:10.100741870-019-00285-y

Pantev, C., Oostenveld, R., Engelien, A., Ross, B., Roberts, L. E., & Hoke, M. (1998). Increased Auditory Cortical Representation in Musicians. *Nature, 392*(6678), 811–814. doi:10.1038/33918 PMID:9572139

Pan, Y. (2016). Heading toward Artificial Intelligence 2.0. *Engineering*, *2*(4), 409–413. doi:10.1016/J.ENG.2016.04.018

Pan, Z., Cheok, A. D., Yang, H., Zhu, J., & Shi, J. (2006). Virtual reality and mixed reality for virtual learning environments. *Computers & Graphics*, *30*(1), 20–28. doi:10.1016/j.cag.2005.10.004

Papazoglou, M. P., & Heuvel, W.-J. (2007). Service oriented architectures: Approaches, technologies and research issues. *The VLDB Journal, 16*(3), 389–415. doi:10.100700778-007-0044-3

Pardos, Z. A., Fan, Z., & Jiang, W. (2018). *Connectionist Recommendation in the Wild.* https://arxiv.org/abs/1803.09535

Pareto, L. (2016). A teachable agent game engaging primary school children to learn arithmetic concepts and reasoning. *International Journal of Artificial Intelligence in Education*, *26*(2), 582–599.

Pasquale, F. (2015). *The black box society. The secret algorithms that control money and information.* Harvard University Press. doi:10.4159/harvard.9780674736061

Patrizio, A. (2016). *Pros and cons of AI.* Retrieved from https://www.datamation.com/applications/pros-and-cons-of-artificial-intelligence.html

Pea-Ayala, A. (2014). Review: Educational Data Mining: A Survey and a Data Mining-based Analysis of Recent Works. *Expert Systems with Applications*, *41*(4), 1432–1462. doi:10.1016/j.eswa.2013.08.042

Pelyushenko, A. V. (2006). Izvestiya Volgogradskogo gosudarstvennogo tekhnicheskogo universiteta, University proceedings. Volga region. *Engineering and Science*, (8), 48–50.

Perez, S. (2016). *Microsoft silences its new A.I. bot Tay, after Twitter users teach it racism.* TechCrunch. https://techcrunch.com/2016/03/24/microsoft-silences-its-new-a-i-bot-tay-after-twitter-users-teach-it-racism/

Poirot, J. (2006). Monte Carlo option pricing for tempered stable (CGMY) processes. *Asia-Pacific Financial Market, 13*(4), 327.

Popenici, S. A. D., & Kerr, S. (2017). Exploring the impact of Artificial Intelligence on teaching and learning in higher education. *Research and Practice in Technology Enhanced Learning, 12*(22), 1-13. Retrieved from https://telrp.springeropen.com/articles/10.1186/s41039-017-0062-8

Popenici, S. (2015). Deceptive promises: the meaning of MOOCs-hype for higher education. In E. McKay & J. Lenarcic (Eds.), *Macro-level learning through massive open online courses (MOOCs): strategies and predictions for the future*. IGI Global. doi:10.4018/978-1-4666-8324-2.ch009

Popenici, S., & Kerr, S. (2013). *What undermines higher education, And how this impacts employment, economies and our democracies*. CreateSpace.

Porayska-Pomsta, K. (2015). AI in Education as a Methodology for Enabling Educational Evidence-Based Practice. *Seventeenth International Conference on Artificial Intelligence in Education (AIED 2015)*, 52–61.

Poth, R. D. (2018). *Artificial Intelligence: Implications for the future of education*. Retrieved from https://www.gettingsmart.com/2018/01/artificial-intelligence-implications-for-the-future-of-education/

Prakash, Hanumanthappa, & Kavitha. (2014). Big Data in Educational Data Mining and Learning Analytics. *Int. J. Innov. Res. Comput. Commun. Eng, 2*(12).

Priyadarshni, V., Nayyar, A., Solanki, A., & Anuragi, A. (2019). Human Age Classification System Using K-NN Classifier. In A. Luhach, D. Jat, K. Hawari, X. Z. Gao, & P. Lingras (Eds.), *Advanced Informatics for Computing Research. ICAICR 2019. Communications in Computer and Information Science* (Vol. 1075). Springer. doi:10.1007/978-981-15-0108-1_28

Rajaraman, V. (2014). John McCarthy – Father of Artificial Intelligence. *Resonance: Journal of Science Education.* Retrieved from https://www.ias.ac.in/article/fulltext/reso/019/03/0198-0207

Rajasingham, L. (2009). The impact of Artificial Intelligence systems on future university paradigms. *Journal of Online Learning and Teaching*, *5*(2), 386–394. https://jolt.merlot.org/vol5no2/rajasingham_0609.pdf

Rajput, R., & Solanki, A. (2016). Real Time Analysis of Tweets using Machine Learning and Semantic Analysis. In *International Conference on Communication and Computing Systems(ICCCS-2016)*. Taylor and Francis. 10.1201/9781315364094-123

Rameshwar, R., Solanki, A., Nayyar, A., & Mahapatra, B. (2020). *Green and Smart Buildings: A Key to Sustainable Global Solutions*. Green Building Management and Smart Automation with IGI Global USA. doi:10.4018/978-1-5225-9754-4.ch007

Ramirez, C., & Valdes, B. (n.d.). *A General Knowledge Representation Model of Concepts*. Retrieved from https://cdn.intechopen.com/pdfs/36656/InTech-A_general_knowledge_representation_model_of_concepts.pdf

Ramos, C., Augusto, J. C., & Shapiro, D. (2008). Ambient intelligence—The next step for artificial intelligence. *IEEE Intelligent Systems*, *23*(2), 15–18. doi:10.1109/MIS.2008.19

Rao, C., & Liu, H. (2009). Pricing Model of Higher Education Tuition Based on Multivariate Linear Regression. *IEEE Int. Conf. Artif. Intell. Comput. Intell.*, *4*, 228-31. 10.1109/AICI.2009.355

Ratho, T. N., & Prakash, R. (1995). *Emerging Trends in Teaching of Computer Science*. Kanishkha Publishers.

Raths, D. (2019). AI's impact on Ed Tech. *Campus Technology*. Retrieved from https://campustechnology.com/articles/2019/01/10/ais-impact-on-ed-tech.aspx

Renz, A., & Hilbig, R. (2020). Prerequisites for artificial intelligence in further education: Identification of drivers, barriers, and business models of educational technology companies. *International Journal of Educational Technology in Higher Education*, *17*(14), 1–21.

Reuters/ABC. (2016, July 2). Tesla crash: man who died in autopilot collision filmed previous near-miss, praised car's technology. *ABC News*.

Reyes, M., Perez, C., Upchurch, R., Yuen, T., & Zhang, Y. (2016). Using Declarative Programming in an Introductory Computer Science Course for High School Students. *6th Symposium on Educational Advances in Artiðcial Intelligence*.

Rieland, R. (2017). *Is Artificial Intelligence the key to personalized education?* Retrieved from https://www.smithsonianmag.com/innovation/artificial-intelligence-key-personalized-education-180963172/

Ritter, S., Anderson, J. R., Koedinger, K. R., & Corbett, A. (2007). Cognitive Tutor: Applied Research in Mathematics Education. *Psychonomic Bulletin & Review*, *14*(2), 249–255. doi:10.3758/BF03194060 PMID:17694909

Rizzotto, L. (2017). *The future of education: How A.I. and immersive tech will reshape learning forever: How immersive media and Artificial Intelligence can change education forever*. Retrieved from https://tfpodcast.io/2017/08/30/episode-36-the-future-of-education-how-a-i-and-immersive-tech-will-reshape-learning-forever/

Roblyer, M. D., & Doering, A. H. (2006). Integrating educational technology into teaching (Vol. 2). Pearson/Merrill Prentice Hall.

Roco, M. C., & Bainbridge, W. S. (2003). *Overview converging technologies for improving human performance Converging technologies for improving human performance*. Springer. doi:10.1007/978-94-017-0359-8

Rodriguez, M. (1994). Changes in academic self-concept self- confidence, and grade point average of migrant Mexican and Mexican American. Community College students who saved as mentors (Ed.D.). University of Southern California.

Roggers, C. R. (1994). *The facilitation of significant learning*. Speech, West Behaviour Science Institution.

Romero, C., & Ventura, S. (2007). Educational data mining: A survey from 1995 to 2005. *Expert Systems with Applications*, *33*(1), 135–146. doi:10.1016/j.eswa.2006.04.005

Romero, C., & Ventura, S. (2010). Educational Data Mining: A Review of the State of the Art, IEEE Trans. Syst. Man Cybern. Part C Appl. *Rev.*, *40*(6), 601–618.

Romero, C., & Ventura, S. (2013). Data Mining in Education. *Wiley Int Rev Data Min Knowl Disc*, *3*(1), 12–27. doi:10.1002/widm.1075

Rosé, C. P., Martínez-Maldonado, R., Hoppe, U., Luckin, R., Mavrikis, M., Porayska-Pomsta, K., McLaren, B., & du Boulay, B. (Eds.). (2018). *Artificial Intelligence in Education: 19th International Conference, AIED 2018, London, UK, June 27–30, 2018, Proceedings, Part I. Lecture Notes in Artificial Intelligence*. Springer International Publishing.

Rosen, R. (1985). *Anticipatory Systems: Philosophical, Mathematical and Methodological Foundations*. Pergamon Press.

Rosinski, J. (2002). Tempered stable and related processes. In *Miniproceedings of 2nd MaPhySto Conference on Levy processes: Theory and applications*. Aarhus University.

Russell, S. J., & Norvig, P. (2016). *Artificial intelligence: a modern approach*. Pearson Education Limited.

Rutkin, A. (2015). Therapist in my pocket. *New Scientist, 227*(3038), 20. doi:10.1016/S0262-4079(15)31169-6

Rutkin, A. (2015). *Therapist in my pocket. New Scientist, 227(3038).*

Sainz, M., & Eccles, J. (2011). Self-concept of computer and math ability: Gender implications across time and within ICT studies. *Journal of Vocational Behavior, 30*, 14.

Sakagasmi, Y., Watanabe, R., Aoyama, C., Matsunaga, S., Higaki, N., & Fujimura, K. (2002). The intelligent ASIMO: System overview and integration. In *Proceedings of the IEEE/RSJ International Conference on Intelligent Robots and Systems*. New York: IEEE. 10.1109/IRDS.2002.1041641

Sallis, E. (2014). *Total quality management in education*. Routledge. doi:10.4324/9780203417010

Sandu, N., & Gide, E. (2019). Adoption of AI-Chatbots to Enhance Student Learning Experience in Higher Education in India. *18th Int. Conf. Inf. Technol. Based High. Educ. Train.*, 1-5. 10.1109/ITHET46829.2019.8937382

Santa, C. M., & Santa, J. L. (1995). Teacher as researcher. *Journal of Reading Behavior, 27*(3), 439–451. doi:10.1080/10862969509547891

Saranya, D., & Phil, M. (2016). A study on Artificial Intelligence and its applications. *International Journal of Advanced Research in Computer and Communication Engineering*, *5*(4), 313–315.

Saravanan, K., Sreedevi, E., & Subhamathi, V. (2017). A review of Artificial Intelligence systems. *International Journal of Advanced Research in Computer Science*, *8*(9), 418–420. doi:10.26483/ijarcs.v8i9.5095

Saygin, A. P., Cicekli, I., & Akman, V. (2003). Turing Test: 50 Years Later. In J. H. Moor (Ed.), *The Turing Test. Studies in Cognitive Systems* (Vol. 30). Springer.

Scardamalia, M., & Bereiter, C. (2006). Knowledge Building: Theory, Pedagogy, and Technology. In *Cambridge Handbook of the Learning Sciences* (pp. 97–118). Cambridge University Press.

Schleicher, A. (2015). *Schools for 21st-century learners: Strong leaders, confident teachers, innovative approaches, International summit on the teaching profession*. OECD Publishing. doi:10.1787/9789264231191-en

Schmitz, H.V. (1972). Performance of self actualized college students in operant based methods of instruction, and of indices of study habits, extracurricular involvement and teaching vocational interest. *Dissertation Abstracts International, 33*(1), 198-A.

Schobbens, P. E., Heymans, P., & Trigaux, J. C. (2011). 14th IEEE International Requirements Engineering Conference (RE'06). *Computers & Society, 2011*, 139–148.

Schoutens, W. (2003). Levy processes in finance. John Wiley & Sons Ltd.

Schroer, A. (2019). *7 companies using AI in education to enhance the classroom*. Retrieved from https://builtin.com/artificial-intelligence/ai-in-education

Science Direct. (n.d.). https://www.sciencedirect.com/science/article/pii/0898122185900549

Scott, S. S., Mcguire, J. M., & Shaw, S. F. (2003). Universal design for instruction: A new paradigm for adult instruction in postsecondary education. *Remedial and Special Education, 24*(6), 369–379. doi:10.1177/07419325030240060801

Seidman, I. (2013). *Interviewing as qualitative research: A guide for researchers in education and the social sciences*. Teachers College Press.

Self, J. (1999). The Defining Characteristics of Intelligent Tutoring Systems Research: ITSs Care, Precisely. *International Journal of Artificial Intelligence in Education, 10*, 350–364.

Seligman, M. E., Ernst, R. M., Gillham, J., Reivich, K., & Linkins, M. (2009). Positive education: Positive psychology and classroom interventions. *Oxford Review of Education, 35*(3), 293–311. doi:10.1080/03054980902934563

Shabbir, J., & Anwer, T. (2015). Artificial Intelligence and its Role in Near Future. *Journal Of Latex Class Files. VOL, 14*(8).

Shafi, P. M., Jawalkar, G. S., Kadam, M. A., Ambawale, R. R., & Bankar, S. V. (2020). AI—Assisted Chatbot for E-Commerce to Address Selection of Products from Multiple Products. In N. Dey, P. Mahalle, P. Shafi, V. Kimabahune, & A. Hassanien (Eds.), *Internet of Things, Smart Computing and Technology: A Roadmap Ahead. Studies in Systems, Decision and Control* (Vol. 266). Springer. doi:10.1007/978-3-030-39047-1_3

Sharma, J., & Sidhu, R. (2011). Sources of stress among students preparing in coaching institutes for admission to professional courses. *The Journal of Psychology, 2*(1), 21–24. doi:10.1080/09764224.2011.11885458

Sharma, R. R. (1977). *Self concept, level of aspiration and mental health as factors in academic achievement (Ph.D. Psy)*. B.H.U.

Sharp, R., Green, A., & Lewis, J. (2017). *Education and social control: A study in progressive primary education*. Routledge. doi:10.4324/9781315210179

Shieber, S. M. (Ed.). (2004). *The Turing Test: Verbal Behavior as the Hallmark of Intelligence*. MIT Press. doi:10.7551/mitpress/6928.001.0001

Shneiderman, B. (n.d.). Educational Journeys on the Web frontier, Teaching your students where to go and how to get there. *Educom Review*. https://www.educause.edu/ir/library/html/erm9861.html

Shumba, A., & Naong, M. (2012). Factors influencing students' career choice and aspirations in South Africa. *J Soc Sci*, *33*(2), 169–178. doi:10.1080/09718923.2012.11893096

Shute, V. J., & Zapata-Rivera, D. (2012). Adaptive educational systems. In P. Durlach (Ed.), *Adaptive Technologies for Training and Education* (pp. 7–27). Cambridge University Press. doi:10.1017/CBO9781139049580.004

Siau, K. (2017). Impact of Artificial Intelligence, Robotics, and Automation on Higher Education. *Americas Conference on Information Systems (AMCIS 2017)*, Boston, MA.

Siau, K. (2018). Education in the age of Artificial Intelligence: How will technology shape Learning? *The Global Analyst*, *7*(3), 22–24.

Siemens, G., & Baker, R. S. J. d. (2012). Learning Analytics, and Educational Data Mining: Towards Communication and Collaboration. *Proceedings of the 2nd International Conference on Learning Analytics and Knowledge*, 252–254.

Singh, P., Chahal, D., & Kharb, L. (2020). Predictive Strength of Selected Classification Algorithms for Diagnosis of Liver Disease. *Lecture Notes in Electrical Engineering, 597*. 10.1007/978-3-030-29407-6_19

Singh, P., Barry, B., & Liu, H. (2004). Teaching Machines about Everyday Life. *BT Technology Journal*, *22*(4), 227–240. doi:10.1023/B:BTTJ.0000047601.53388.74

Sivakumar, S. C., Robertson, W., Artimy, M., & Aslam, N. (2005). A web-based remote interactive laboratory for Internetworking education. *IEEE Transactions on Education*, *48*(4), 586–598. doi:10.1109/TE.2005.858393

Skiba, D. J. (2017). Horizon report: Knowledge obsolescence, Artificial Intelligence, and rethinking the education role. *Nursing Education Perspectives*, *38*(3), 165–167. doi:10.1097/01.NEP.0000000000000154

Sklar, E., & Parsons, S. (2002). *RoboCupJunior: A Vehicle for Enhancing Technical Literacy*. AAAI Mobile Robot Competition 2002, Papers from the AAAI Workshop, Edmonton, Canada.

Skrtic, T. M. (1991). *Behind special education: A critical analysis of professional culture and school organization*. Love Publishing Company.

Smartsparrow. (n.d.). Retrieved from https://www.smartsparrow.com/

Smith, N. B. (2002). *American reading instruction*. International Reading Association.

Smith, S. C., & Piele, P. K. (2006). *School leadership: Handbook for excellence in student learning*. Corwin Press.

Solanki, A., & Nayyar, A. (2018). Green Internet of Things (G-IoT)- ICT Technologies, Principles, Applications, Projects, and Challenges: Green Internet of Things. In Handbook of Research on Big Data and the IoT. IGI Global. doi:10.4018/978-1-5225-7432-3.ch021

Stocker, M. (1979). Desiring the bad: An essay in moral psychology. *The Journal of Philosophy*, *76*(12), 738–753. doi:10.2307/2025856

Stottler Henke. (n.d.). https://www.stottlerhenke.com/papers/ITS_using_AI_to_improve_training_performance_and_ROI.pdf

Subrahmanyam, V. V., & Swathi, K. (2018). Artificial Intelligence and its Implications in Education. *International Conference on Improved Access to Distance Higher Education Focus on Underserved Communities and Uncovered Regions.*

Sugisaka, M., & Hazry, D. (2007). Development of a proportional control method for a mobile robot. *Applied Mathematics and Computation*, *186*(1), 74–82. doi:10.1016/j.amc.2006.05.214

Suthers, D., Weiner, A., Connelly, J., & Paolucci, M. (1995). Belvedere: Engaging Students in Critical Discussion of Science and Public Policy Issues. In J. Greer (Ed.), *Proceedings of Artificial Intelligence in Education* (pp. 266–273). AACE.

Synnes, K., Parnes, P., Widen, J., & Schefstroem, D. (1999). Net-based Learning for the Next Millennium. SCI/ISAS99.

Tan, S. C., Yeo, A. C. J., & Lim, W. Y. (2005). Changing epistemology of science learning through inquiry with computer-supported collaborative learning. *Journal of Computers in Mathematics and Science Teaching*, *24*(4), 367–386.

Tastimur, C., Karakose, M., & Akin, E. (2016). Improvement of relative accreditation methods based on data mining and artificial intelligence for higher education. *IEEE 15th Int. Conf. Inf. Technol. Based High. Educ. Train.*, 1-7. 10.1109/ITHET.2016.7760736

Tayal, A., Kose, U., Solanki, A., Nayyar, A., & Saucedo, J. A. M. (2019). *Efficiency analysis for stochastic dynamic facility layout problem using meta-heuristic, data envelopment analysis and machine learning. Computational Intelligence*. SCI Publication. Wiley Online Library., doi:10.1111/coin.12251

Teach Thought. (n.d.). https://www.teachthought.com/the-future-oflearning/10-roles-for-artificial-intelligence-ineducation/

Teletop. (n.d.). http://teletop.edte.utwente.nl/

The Next Evolution of ERP. (n.d.). *Adaptive ERP // ERP the Right Way: Changing the game for ERP Cloud implementations*. Retrieved from https://gbeaubouef. wordpress.com/2012/09/05/adaptive-erp/

Tomei, L. A. (2005). *Taxonomy for the technology domain*. Information Science Publishing. doi:10.4018/978-1-59140-524-5

Torrey, L. (2012). Teaching Problem-Solving in Algorithms and AI. *3rd Symposium on Educational Advances in Artiðcial Intelligence*.

Torrey, L., Johnson, K., Sondergard, S., Ponce, P., & Desmond, L. (2016). The Turing Test in the Classroom. *6th Symposium on Educational Advances in Artificial Intelligence*.

Trow, M. (2007). *Reflections on the transition from elite to mass to universal access: Forms and phases of higher education in modern societies since WWII. In International handbook of higher education*. Springer.

Tsukamoto, H., Takemura, Y., Nagumo, H., Ikeda, I., Monden, A., & Matsumoto, K. (2015). Programming education for primary school children using a textual programming language. *IEEE Frontiers in Education Conference (FIE)*, 1008–1014. 10.1109/FIE.2015.7344187

Tsur, O., Davidov, D., & Rappoport, A. (2010). Semi-supervised recognition of sarcastic sentences in Twitter and Amazon. In *Proceedings of the Fourteenth Conference on Computational Natural Language Learning*, (pp. 107-116). Uppsala: Association for Computational Linguistics.

Tuckman, B. W., & Harper, B. E. (2012). *Conducting educational research*. Rowman & Littlefield Publishers.

Tuomi, I. (2013). Open Educational Resources and the Transformation of Education. *European Journal of Education*, *48*(1), 58–78. doi:10.1111/ejed.12019

Umashankar, V., & Dutta, K. (2007). Balanced scorecards in managing higher education institutions: An Indian perspective. *International Journal of Educational Management*, *21*(1), 54–67. doi:10.1108/09513540710716821

Van Dalen, A. (2012). The algorithms behind the headlines: How machine-written news redefines the core skills of human journalists. *Journalism Practice*, *6*(5-6), 648–658. doi:10.1080/17512786.2012.667268

Vanlehn, K., Lynch, C., Schulze, K., Shapiro, J. A., Shelby, R., Taylor, L., ... Wintersgill, M. (2005). The Andes Physics Tutoring System: Lessons Learned. *International Journal of Artificial Intelligence in Education*, *15*(3), 147–204.

Vassileva, J. (2008). Social Learning Environments: New Challenges for AI in Education. In B. P. Woolf, E. Aïmeur, R. Nkambou, & S. Lajoie (Eds.), Lecture Notes in Computer Science: Vol. 5091. *Intelligent Tutoring Systems*. Springer. doi:10.1007/978-3-540-69132-7_5

Ventura, M. D. (2017). Creating inspiring learning environments by means of digital technologies: a case study of the effectiveness of whatsapp in music education. *EAI Endorsed Trans. e-Learn., 4,* 1–9. https://eudl.eu/pdf/10.4108/eai.26-7-2017.152906

Villegas, N. M., Muller, H. A., Tamura, G., Duchien, L., & Casallas, R. A. (2011). Framework for evaluating quality- driven self-adaptive software systems. *Proceeding of the 6th International Symposium on Software Engineering for Adaptive and Self- Managing Systems*, 80-89. 10.1145/1988008.1988020

Vinge, V. (1993). *Vernor Vinge on the singularity*. Presented at the VISION-21 Symposium sponsored by NASA Lewis Research Center and the Ohio Aerospace Institute.

Volman, M., & Van Eck, E. (2001). Gender equity and information technology in education: The second decade. *Review of Educational Research*, *71*(4), 613–634. doi:10.3102/00346543071004613

Von Glasersfeld, E. (1998). Cognition, construction of knowledge, and teaching. In *Constructivism in science education*. Springer.

Voogt, J. (2003). Consequences of ICT for Aims, Contents, Processes and Environments of Learning. In J. van den Akker, W. Kuiper, & U. Hameyer (Eds.), Curriculum landscapes and trends (pp. 217–236). Academic Press.

Vygotsky, L. (1986). *Thought and Language*. The MIT Press.

Wadhwa, D. (n.d.). *Using Artificial Intelligence Technologies For Personalized Learning And Responsive Teaching: A Survey*. Academic Press.

Wagner, K. (2018). *A blended environment: The future of AI and education*. Retrieved from https://www.gettingsmart.com/2018/01/a-blended-environment-the-future-of-ai-and-education/

Wals, A. E., & Jickling, B. (2002). "Sustainability" in higher education: From doublethink and newspeak to critical thinking and meaningful learning. *International Journal of Sustainability in Higher Education*, *3*(3), 221–232. doi:10.1108/14676370210434688

Wang, R., Wiesemes, R., & Gibbons, C. (2012). Developing digital fluency through ubiquitous mobile devices: Findings from a small-scale study. *Computers & Education*, *58*(1), 570–578. doi:10.1016/j.compedu.2011.04.013

Watson, G., McKeown, N., & Casado, M. (2006). *NetFPGA: A tool for network research and education*. Paper presented at the 2nd workshop on Architectural Research using FPGA Platforms (WARFP).

WebC. T. (n.d.). Retrieved from http://www.cuhk.edu.hk/eLearning/c_systems/ webct6/

Whitby, B. (2013). *Artificial Intelligence. Encyclopedia of philosophy and the social sciences*. SAGE Publications, Inc.

Wilson, H. J., Daugherty, P. R., & Morini-Bianzino, N. (2017). The jobs that Artificial Intelligence will create. *MIT Sloan Management Review*, *58*(4), 14–16. https://ilp.mit.edu/media/news_articles/smr/2017/58416.pdf

Winston, P. H., & Prendergast, K. A. (1984). *The AI business: commercial uses of artificial intelligence*. Massachusetts Institute of Technology.

Witten, H., & Frank, E. (2016). *Data Mining: Practical Machine Learning Tools and Techniques*. Morgan Kaufmann.

Wodi, S. W. (2008). The concept of educational technology: problems and prospects of information and communication technology (ICT) in Nigeria. *International Journal of African Studies, 1*, 4-10.

Wollowski, M., Neller, T., & Boerkoel, J. (2017). Artificial Intelligence education. Association for the Advancement of Artificial Intelligence. *AI Magazine*.

Wolpaw, J. R., & Wolpaw, E. W. (2012). Brain-computer interfaces: something new under the sun. In W. Wolpaw (Ed.), *Brain-computer interfaces: principles and practice* (pp. 3–12). Oxford University Press. doi:10.1093/acprof:oso/9780195388855.003.0001

Woods, P. J., & Warren, J. (1996). Adapting Teaching Strategies in Intelligent Tutoring Systems. *ITS 96 Workshop on Architectures and Methods for Designing Cost-Effective and Reusable ITSs*.

Woolf, B. P. (2015). AI and education: Celebrating 30 years of marriage. *AIED 2015 Workshop Proceedings, 4*, 38-47.

Woolf, B. P., Lane, H. C., Chaudhri, V. K., & Kolodner, J. I. (2013). AI grand challenges for education. *AI Magazine*. Retrieved from https://www.aaai.org/ojs/index.php/aimagazine/article/view/2490

Writers, S. (2012). *10 Ways Artificial Intelligence Can Reinvent Education*. Academic Press.

Xia, P. (2020). Application Scenario of Artificial Intelligence Technology in Higher Education. In *International Conference on Applications and Techniques in Cyber Intelligence ATCI 2019. ATCI 2019. Advances in Intelligent Systems and Computing*, (vol. 1017). Springer. 10.1007/978-3-030-25128-4_29

Yadav, A. (2016). Computational Thinking as an Emerging Competence Domain. In M. Mulder (Ed.), *Competence-Based Vocational and Professional Education: Bridging the Worlds of Work and Education* (pp. 1051–1067). Springer International Publishing AG.

Yang, G., Bellingham, J., Dupont, P. E., Fischer, P., Floridi, L., Full, R., . . . Wood, R. (2018). The gra.nd challenges of science robotics Science. *Robotics, 3*(14), 1-14 Retrieved from https://roboticssciencem.agorg/cont.ent/3/14/eaar7650

Yang, L. T., Di Martino, B., & Zhang, Q. (2017). *Internet of Everything* (Vol. 2017). Mobile Information Systems.

Younis, O., Ghoul, S., & Alomari, M. H. (2013). Systems Variability Modeling: A Textual Model Mixing Class and Feature Concepts. *International Journal of Computer Science & Information Technology, 2013*(5), 127–139. doi:10.5121/ijcsit.2013.5509

Zeide, E. (2019). Artificial Intelligence in Higher Education: Applications, Promise and Perils, and Ethical Questions. *Educause Review*.

Zhong, Y. (2006). A Cognitive Approach to Artificial Intelligence Research. *International Conference on Cognitive Informatics*. 10.1109/COGINF.2006.365682

Zhu, Z. T., Yu, M. H., & Riezebos, P. (2016). A research framework of smart education. *Smart Learning Environments, 3*(1), 4.

Zhu, F., Ip, H. H. S., Fok, A. W. P., & Cao, J. (2008). PeRES: A Personalized Recommendation Education System Based on Multi-agents & SCORM. In H. Leung, F. Li, R. Lau, & Q. Li (Eds.), Lecture Notes in Computer Science: Vol. 4823. *Advances in Web Based Learning – ICWL 2007. ICWL 2007*. Springer. doi:10.1007/978-3-540-78139-4_4

Zhu, W., Ma, C., Zhao, X., Wang, M., Heidari, A. A., Chen, H., & Li, C. (2020). Evaluation of Sino Foreign Cooperative Education Project Using Orthogonal Sine Cosine Optimized Kernel Extreme Learning Machine. *IEEE Access: Practical Innovations, Open Solutions, 8*, 61107–61123. doi:10.1109/ACCESS.2020.2981968

Zipes, J. (2013). *When dreams came true: classical fairy tales and their tradition*. Routledge. doi:10.4324/9780203949672

About the Contributors

Shivani Verma is working as Associate Professor in Department of Home Science, Km. Mayawati Govt. Girls Post Graduate College, Badalpur, Gautam Budh Nagar, U.P. Dr. Verma earned her Ph.D. from M. J. P. Rohilkhand University, Bareilly, and Master of Science (M.Sc.) in (Major- Human Development and Family Studies, Minor- Foods and nutrition) from G. B. Pant University of Agriculture and Technology, Pantnagar, Uttarakhand. Dr. Verma also earned degree of MBA. Dr. Verma has excellent teaching and research as well as vast administrative experience at collage level on various posts like HoD, Scholarship Incharge, Examination Coordinator, Time Table, Admission etc. She is also a member of Indian Science Congress Association, Society for Community Mobilization and Sustainable Development, Uttar Pradesh Govt. College Academic Society, Uttar Pradesh, INDIA, and Home Science Society of India. She is also qualified the National Eligibility Test (NET) for Lecturership. Dr. Verma was awarded India Development Education Award in World Children Summit, New Delhi and Women Empowerment and Livelyhood (WEAL) Award in World Women Summit, New Delhi. She delivered expert talks at FDP, workshops, national and international conferences. She has organized various conferences and seminar at national and international level. Apart from teaching, she has also been involved in research activities. She has contributed more than 50 papers/articles in national/international journals and conferences. She served as a member of the editorial board and reviewer for some Journals and national/international conferences.

Pradeep Tomar is working as Assistant Professor in the School of Information and Communication Technology, Gautam Buddha University, Greater Noida, U.P., India since 2009. Dr. Tomar earned his Ph.D. from MDU, Rohtak, Haryana, India. Before joining Gautam Buddha University, he worked as a Software Engineer in a multi-national company, Noida and lecturer in M. D. University, Rohtak, Haryana and Kurukshetra University, Kurukshetra, Haryana. Dr. Tomar has excellent teaching, research and software development experience as well as vast administrative experience at university level on various posts like HoD Computer Science and Engineering, Chairperson Admission, Vice Chairperson, Admissions, Research Coordinator, Examination Coordinator, University Coordinator, Admission, Time

Table Coordinator, Proctor and Hostel Warden. He is also a member of Computer Society of India (CSI), Indian Society for Technical Education (ISTE), Indian Science Congress Association (ISCA), International Association of Computer Science and Information Technology (IACSIT) and International Association of Engineers (IAENG). He qualified the National Eligibility Test (NET) for Lecturership in Computer Applications in 2003, Microsoft Certified Professional (MCP) in 2008, SUN Certified Java Programmer (SCJP) for the Java platform, standard edition 5.0 in 2008 and qualified the IBM Certified Database Associate - DB2 9 Fundamentals in 2010. Dr. Tomar was awarded Bharat Jyoti Award by India International Friendship Society in the field of Technology in 2012 and Bharat Vikas Award by Institute of Self Reliance in National Seminar on Diversity of Cultural and Social Environment at Bhubaneswar, Odisha, in 2017. He has been awarded for the Best Computer Faculty award by Govt. of Pondicherry and ASDF society. His biography is published in Who's Who Reference Asia, Volume II. Dr. Tomar has been awarded distinguished Research Award from Institute for Global Business Research for his work in "A Web-Based Stock Selection Decision Support System for Investment Portfolio Management in 2018. He delivered expert talks at FDP, workshops, national and international conferences. He has organized three conferences: one national conference with COMMUNE group and two international conferences, in which one international ICIAICT 2012 was organized by CSI, Noida Chapter and second international conference 2012 EPPICTM was organized in collaboration with MTMI, USA, University of Maryland Eastern Shore, USA and Frostburg State University, USA at School of Information and Communication Technology, Gautam Buddha University, Greater Noida, India. Apart from teaching, he is running a programming club for ICT students and he is guiding various research scholars in the areas of software engineering, reusability of code, soft computing technique, Big Data, and IoT. His major current research interest is in Component-Based Software Engineering. He is working as Co-investigator in a sponsored research project in High throughput design, synthesis and validation of TALENs for targeted Genome Engineering, funded by Department of Biotechnology, Ministry of Science and Technology Government of India. Two books "Teaching of Mathematics" and "Communication and Information Technology" at national levels, three books "Examining Cloud Computing Technologies through the Internet of Things (IoT)", "Handbook of Research on Big Data and the IoT", "Green and Smart Technologies for Smart Cities" at international level are authored and edited by Dr. Tomar. He has also contributed more than 100 papers/articles in national/international journals and conferences. He served as a member of the editorial board and reviewer for various Journals and national/international conferences.

* * *

Mani Arora is working as Assistant Professor Commerce in KMGGPG College Badalpur.The author is Ph.D, NET in the field of commerce with 8+ years of experience in Education Industry. As a researcher she has contributed 7 research papers in the various National/International Journals. Three Chapters in edited books is also into her credit. As an educationist she is mentoring and delievring lectures to the B.Com and M.B.A students. She has been into three different institutions during this tenure thereby performing various academic and administrative responsibilities to contribute in the field of higher Education.

Harshit Bhardwaj is B.Tech. (CSE), M.Tech. CSE and Presently pursuing a Ph.D. in Computer Science and Engineering from Gautam Buddha University, Greater Noida.

Shweta Chauhan has completed her PhD from Shoolini University Solan. She is working on different problems related to Science and Social science to make the world a better place to live.

Irene Chen received her Ed.D. in Instructional Technology. She is a professor of Educational Technology at the University of Houston-Downtown. In addition to teaching graduate and undergraduate courses in educational technology, Dr. Chen also served as the technology coordinator for the Department of Urban Education. Her research interest includes instructional technology, curriculum design, cybersecurity, and artificial intelligence.

Vandana Dhingra is working as Assistant Professor in Savitribai Phule Pune University, Pune. She is PhD, M.Tech (Information Technology),B.E. (Computer Science and Engineering) and is having experience of teaching to postgraduate and graduate engineering candidates for more than 20 Years . She was head of Department of Computer Science and Engineering in Apeejay College of Engineering, Sohna. She has published research papers in various reputed international and national journals and conferences. Her area of research include Semantic Web, Web Mining, Data Analytics, Ontologies.

Chander Diwaker is presently working as Assistant Professor in the Department of Computer Engineering, University Institute of Engineering & Technology, Kurukshetra University, Kurukshetra. He has nearly thirteen years of teaching experience. He obtained his M.Tech. degree from YMCA Institute of Engineering (Now J.C. Bose University of Science and Technology), Faridabad in 2004. He obtained his Ph.D. degree from School of ICT, Gautam Buddha University, Greater Noida in 2018. His current research interests mainly include Wireless Networks,

Software Engineering, Internet of Things (IoT), and Computer Engineering. He has published more than 50 research papers in Referred International Journals and International Conferences.

Anne Grey has taught at several levels from kindergarten to college and among diverse communities from Special Needs children in Abu-Dhabi to gifted African American undergraduates at Spelman College in Atlanta. She also served as a psychometric officer for Emirates Airlines and traveled to over 80 different countries recruiting cabin crew, pilots, and engineers. In addition to teaching, Anne has over ten years of experience as an instructional designer and curriculum developer working at Morehouse College, Emory University, and Concordia University, Portland. In 2017 she accepted the position of Faculty Chair Coordinator for the Ed.D. program at Concordia University. Besides developing curriculum, teaching graduate courses, and advising doctorate students. Anne also oversees the dissertation phase of the program working closely with Faculty Chairs and students.

Varun Jaiswal received his M.Tech degree in computational and system biology from Jawaharlal Nehru University (JNU), New Delhi and further pursued his PhD in Bio-Informatics from Jaypee University of Information Technology, Solan. He has computational expertise in data analysis of various fields and enjoys solving important issues primarily with computational means. He has applied machine learning methods in diverse fields which include biology, chemistry, medicine, computer science, and social science. He has authored dozens of paper in reputed top tier journals of diverse fields. He worked as an Assistant Professor in Shoolini University, Solan, India. Number of students have successfully completed their PhD and Master degree under his able guidance. Currently, he is working as an Assistant Director in National Center for Disease Control, Delhi, India. He prefers to work with new and emerging technology to answer different challenging problems of the nation and the world. He strongly believe that artificial intelligence powered with machine learning will change the global scenario in favor of humanity in almost all the fields.

Poonam Jatwani received the MCA and M.Phil (Computer Science) degrees from Maharshi Dayanand University and CDLU, Sirsa in 2005 and 2008 respectively. Presently she is working as Assistant Professor in Govt. College for Women, Faridabad. She had completed her PhD (Computer Science & Engineering) in May 2020 from GBU, Greater Noida and her interest spans the area in Semantic Web, Search Engine.

Latika Kharb has been working as a Professor in the Jagan Institute of Management Studies (JIMS), Delhi, INDIA since 2013. Dr. Kharb has been awarded the International Professional of the Year award by IBC, Britain in 2012. Several technical sessions in national and international conferences had been chaired by Dr. Kharb and she participated in various FDP, workshops, national and international conferences. Five international conferences have been organized by Dr. Kharb with Springer CCIS and CSI sponsorship. She has organized a fourteen-day FDP program sponsored and financed by AICTE. Apart from teaching, researches in the areas of software engineering, Artificial Intelligence, Cyber Laws, Bioinformatics, Mobile Computing, Data Analytics, Computer Forensic Science, Nanotechnology, Cyber Medicine & Dentistry, Machine Learning, and Data Analytics are being carried over by Dr. Kharb. She has contributed numerous Book chapters in renowned publishing houses like Elsevier, CRC, Taylor & Francis, IGI Global, Emerald, EAI-Springer and so on. She has published around one hundred forty papers with various International/National Editors like LNEE, LNCS, IEEE, CCIS, and AISC, etc.

Navita Malik is pursuing her Ph.D. from Gautam Buddha University, Greater Noida. She has done her MCA from MDU, Rohtak. She has completed her B.Ed., M.Ed, and M.Phill. from KUK, Haryana. Currently, She is working as an Assistant professor at Galgotia's University, Greater Noida from 2014.

Amit Mishra, Ph.D. in Computer Science Engg., is currently working in ST-DIT organization since more than 20 years, with more than 23 years of IT experience. Has authored and published 8 technical papers in journals and conferences. Also authored two book chapters published by CRC Press, Taylor and Francis group. Has special passion to work for industry and academia collaboration. Also working to trigger innovations with universities. Social work for children growth and environment on tree plantations and saving water . Authored several Nataks, Hindi Stories and Hindi Poetries. Already published book "KAB HANSE THE PICHHALI BAAR": on humorous poems. A book on collection of children poems under publishing.

Vardan Mkrttchian graduated from State Engineering University of Armenia, the Faculty of Cybernetics as an Electronics Engineer & received his Doctorate of Sciences (Engineering) in Control Systems from Lomonosov Moscow State University (former USSR). Dr. Vardan Mkrttchian taught for undergraduate and graduate student's courses of control system, information sciences and technology, at the Astrakhan State University (Russian Federation), where he was is the Professor of the Information Systems (www.aspu.ru) six years. Now he is full professor CAD&Economy departments of Penza State University (www.pnzgu.ru). He is currently chief executive of HHH University, Australia and team leader of the international academics (www.hhhuniversity.com). He also serves as executive director of the HHH Technology Incorporation. Professor Vardan Mkrttchian has authored over 400 refereed publications. He is the author of over twenty books published of IGI Global, included ten books indexed of SCOPUS in IT, Control System, Digital Economy, and Education Technology, and 41 works in SCOPUS and 17 in WoS. He also is Editor-in-Chief of International Journal of Applied Research in Bioinformatics (IJARB).

Aditi Sakalle is B.Tech (EE), M.Tech (Modelling and Simulation), and presently pursuing a Ph.D. in computer science and engineering from Gautam Buddha University.

Kapil Sethi was born in India and currently, he was perusing his Ph.D. in computer science under the Shoolini University, Himachal Pradesh, India. He has received a master's degree in three different courses i.e. MSc.IT, MCA and M.Tech from different universities of India. He is passionate about learning new things in Computer Science and apply these techniques in the field of Education. His research interests include Machine learning, Artificial intelligence, cybersecurity, K-12 education, higher education, and social science. He has published various papers and book chapters in reputed journals.

Atul Sharma is presently working as Assistant Professor in the Department of Computer Engineering, University Institute of Engineering & Technology, Kurukshetra University, Kurukshetra. He has nearly five years of teaching experience. He has been involved in the research related to Wireless Networks especially Delay Tolerance Networks (DTNs) for last 5 years. He received his Master's degree from Deenbandhu Chhotu Ram University of Science and Technology (DCRUST), Murthal, India. His current research interests mainly include Cloud Computing, Wireless Sensor Networks, Edge Computing. It will decrease the number of notifications from device to the owner and make life better and easier. He has published 35 research papers in Referred International Journals and International Conferences. He also has got the Editorial/Reviewer Board membership of more than 15 International Conferences till now.

Uttam Sharma is B.Tech (IT), M.Tech (Software Engineering) and presently pursuing a Ph.D. in Computer Science and Engineering from Gautam Buddha University, Greater Noida.

Libi Shen has a Ph.D. in Instruction and Learning from University of Pittsburgh, PA. She started her college teaching career in 1989 and has been teaching in numerous universities for many years. Libi is a contributing author for the following IGI books: (1) Educational, Behavioral, Psychological Considerations in Niche Online Communities; (2) Cases on Critical and Qualitative Perspectives in Online Higher Education; (3) Online Tutor 2.0: Methodologies and Case Studies for Successful Learning; (4) Emerging Priorities and Trends in Distance Education: Communication, Pedagogy, and Technology; (5) Identification, Evaluation, and Perceptions of Distance Education Experts; (6) Cybersecurity Breaches and Issues Surrounding Online Threat Protection; (7) Handbook of Research on Human Factors in Contemporary Workforce Development, (8) Psychological, Social, and Cultural Aspects of Internet Addiction, (9) Emerging Trends in Cyber Ethics and Education, (10) Emerging Economic Models for Global Sustainability and Social Development, (11) Diverse Learning Opportunities through Technology-Based Curriculum Design, and (12) Applied Psycholinguistics and Multilingual Cognition in Human Creativity. Her research interests include artificial intelligence, cybersecurity, education, curriculum design, online learning, and instructional technology.

Prateek Singh is a Final year student of Masters in Computer Science Program at Jagan Institute of Management Studies (JIMS), Delhi, India. He is currently working as an Intern in Freecharge Payment Technologies Pvt Ltd. He has a strong interest in the field of Data Science and Machine Learning and has written and presented two papers in International Conferences sponsored by Springer. He has written Book Chapters for Emerald, Springer, AAP and IGI Global (in press).

Arun Solanki is working as Assistant Professor in the Department of Computer Science and Engineering, Gautam Buddha University, Greater Noida, since 2009. He has worked as Time Table Coordinator, member Examination, Admission, Sports Council, Digital Information Cell, and other university teams from time to time. He has received M.Tech. Degree in Computer Engineering from YMCA University, Faridabad, Haryana, India. He has received his Ph.D. in Computer Science and Engineering from Gautam Buddha University in 2014. He has supervised more than 60 M.Tech. dissertations under his guidance. His research interests span Expert System, Machine Learning, IoT and Search Engines. He has published many research articles in SCI/ Scopus indexed International journals/conferences like IEEE, Elsevier, Springer, etc. He has participated in many international conferences. He has been a technical and advisory committee member of many conferences. He has organized several FDP, Conferences, Workshops, and Seminars. He has chaired many sessions at International Conferences. Arun Solanki is working as Associate Editor in International Journal of Web-Based Learning and Teaching Technologies (IJWLTT)" IGI publisher. He has been working as Guest Editor for special issues in Recent Patents on Computer Science, Bentham Science Publishers. Arun Solanki is the editor of many Books with a reputed publisher like IGI Global, CRC and AAP. He is working as the reviewer in Springer, IGI Global, Elsevier, and other reputed publisher journals.

Anchi Su has an MS and a BS in Electrical Engineering from University of California, Los Angeles. She is a systems engineer for Northrop Grumman Corporation. She is an IEEE member and Society of Women Engineers member. Her research interests include robotics design, embedded systems, wireless communication systems design, computer architecture, computer networking, VLSI design, and circuits and systems design.

Dimpal Tomar is pursing Ph.D from School of Information and Communication Technology, Gautam Buddha University, Greater Noida, U.P., India.with the specialization in Internet of Things. She also worked as a Asst. Professor in Dept of CSE, School of Engineering and Technology, Noida International University, Greater Noida, U.P., India since Sept 2014. She has earned his master's degree M.Tech. (Specialization in Software Engineering) from School of Information and Communication Technology, Gautam Buddha University, Greater Noida, U.P., India. Ms. Dimpal has good teaching experience as well as administrative experience at university level. Also she has worked as a guest faculty in School of School of Information and Communication Technology, Gautam Buddha University, Greater Noida, U.P., India. Ms. Dimpal has coordinated many workshops, seminars and quiz competitions. She has been member of organizing committee for international conference at university level. Ms. Dimpal has also contributed 07 papers & 03 book chapters in national/international journals and conferences. His areas of interest are IoT, Big Data, Data Structures, DBMS, Compiler, Analysis and Design of Algorithms.

Index

P

S

V

www.ingramcontent.com/pod-product-compliance
Lightning Source LLC
LaVergne TN
LVHW061544290926
849162LV00004B/897